W**O**RLD RELIGI**O**NS AND CULTS

Atheistic *and*
Humanistic Religions

Volume 3

General Editors

BODIE HODGE &
ROGER PATTERSON

First printing: November 2016
Fifth printing: August 2022

ISBN: 978-0-89051-970-7
ISBN: 978-1-61458-039-3 (digital)
Library of Congress Number: 2016917109

Cover by Left Coast Design, Portland, Oregon

Scripture taken from the NEW AMERICAN STANDARD BIBLE® (NASB), copyright © 1960, 1962, 1963, 1968, 1971, 1972, 1973, 1975, 1977, 1995 by The Lockman Foundation. Used by permission.

Scriptures taken from the Holy Bible, New International Version®, NIV®, copyright © 1973, 1978, 1984, 2011 by Biblica, Inc.™ Used by permission of Zondervan. All rights reserved worldwide.

Scripture taken from the New King James Version (NKJV), copyright © 1982 by Thomas Nelson, Inc. Used by permission. All rights reserved.

Scripture designated KJV is from the King James Version of the Bible.

Please consider requesting a copy of this volume be purchased by your local library system.

Printed in the United States of America

Please visit our website for other great titles: www.masterbooks.com

For information regarding promotional opportunities, please contact the publicity department at pr@nlpg.com.

Master
Books®
A Division of New Leaf Publishing Group
www.masterbooks.com

Acknowledgments

Our appreciation to the following for their contributions and help to bring this book to fruition:

Roger Patterson, Bodie Hodge, Troy Lacey, Ken Ham,
Dr. Terry Mortenson, Dr. Elizabeth Mitchell, Frost Smith,
Dr. Georgia Purdom, Avery Foley, Dan Zordel,
Shonda Snelbaker, Walt Stumper, Dan Lietha, Steve Ham,
Todd Friel, Pastor David Chakranaryan, Dr. Nathan Merrill,
Dr. Jerry Bergman, Dr. Carl Broggi, Bryan Osborne,
Eric Hovind, Dr. Stuart Burgess, and Jeremy Ham.

Contents

Introduction

Bodie Hodge

There are only two religions in the world. If there is only one thing to be remembered from reading this three-volume set (dealing with world religions, cults, and philosophical systems), it is that all religions outside of God's true religion are religions of man. They are simply variations of humanism (in its broadest sense).

It is the case of God's Word vs. man's word. In one fashion or another, man's ideas have been elevated to take people away from the truth of God's Word and deposit them in one version or another of a man-made religion. God vs. man is still the consistent theme with the final book in this series. This final volume focuses on religions that tend to oppose God by claiming He doesn't exist or reduces God to a strange concoction of illusion and irrelevancy.

These variations of humanistic/secular religions now dominate the state school systems, museums, media, universities, and so forth in our Western world. It has been causing a culture change from Christian to secular. Beginning about 200 years ago, there was a slow and gradual takeover — simply because few Christians have opposed this religion for so long.[1]

Interestingly, most of the secular religions in this volume usually have no problem calling themselves "humanistic." In fact, they are often proud of it. For example, they revel in the religion of man so much that secularists even have a "humanist of the year" award since 1953. Over the years, it

---

1. This is in part because many Christians began incorporating elements from secular religions into their doctrine. For example the most common way was to accept the secular origins account over the Bible's origins account. See chapter 11 on Christian syncretism in this volume for more on this subject.

included the likes of Sir Julian Huxley (agnostic), Dr. Carl Sagan (atheist), Dr. Richard Dawkins (atheist), and TV personality Bill Nye (agnostic)!

Notice how humanism can incorporate varied secular beliefs like agnosticism or atheism and so forth (materialists, naturalists, etc.). We see this clearly with the secular emblems frequently placed on cars that say "COEXIST." It is cleverly written out using each letter as a symbol of various religions like Islam's crescent moon and star for the "C" and the Yin Yang symbol of Taoism for the "S." And of course, they end with the "T" being the Christian cross symbol.

It is not unlike the cover of this book series where we have utilized certain letters from various world religions to be letters that are used in the title, *World Religions and Cults*. For example, the "A" in our *World Religions and Cults* title is the atheist "A," and the "C" in cults is the Muslim symbol of the crescent moon and star.

However, COEXIST has a much different purpose than this world religions book series. COEXIST is meant to impose or promote a religious belief (that all religions are acceptable except those that say they are the only way, like Christianity). In other words, the COEXIST worldview is that people, like Christians, should be tolerant and stop saying there is only way — through Jesus Christ. Make no mistake, COEXIST is a means to try to silence Christianity and any religion that would claim an exclusive answer to mankind's problems.

COEXIST is essentially a subtle statement that Christianity is false and those promoting COEXIST are right. Would those holding to a COEXIST philosophy, be tolerant of the Christian belief that Christ is the only way? Not at all. They cry for tolerance but are intolerant themselves. Notice how it is a self-refuting attack on Christianity.

Yet COEXIST appears on the bumpers of those holding to religions like atheism, agnosticism, and secular humanism. Interestingly, secularists like this are usually more than happy to allow for multiple lines of belief (this is *syncretism*, where more than one religion is mixed with another), as long as it is not biblical Christianity.

On several occasions, I have personally spoken to a number of humanists who have pushed for atheism, then switch to agnosticism, and then switch to argue positively for something else like angelology or Eastern religions. It sounds like religious schizophrenia — and it is! But this is more common than you might realize.

For example, the Darwinfish.com website (clearly secular) will sell you the COEXIST symbol, alien symbol, Yin Yang symbol of Taoism, satanic pentagram symbol and a Devil fish plaque, Egyptian mythology of Isis symbol, Namaste (Hindu greeting), evolutionary religious symbols, Buddha emblem, Jewish Gefilte fish, and an angelology emblem.

At the same time, Darwinfish.com has some items that mock Christianity like a no-preaching emblem, an evolution symbol raping a Christian Ichthus fish, a dinosaur eating the popular Christian fish emblem, and an emblem that mocks Jesus with "Jeebus."[2] Do you see how they are inconsistent with their profession of tolerance?

One might object and say that COEXIST simply means that we coexist alongside one another in a pluralistic society. But that would be like a bumper sticker that states the obvious like "Air Exists." It essentially becomes meaningless. Even if this were the case, we already coexist in a sin-cursed world *for now*.

The point is that in heaven only those who have repented and received Jesus Christ and His death, burial, and Resurrection will be saved. In hell, those who have not repented and did not believe will be punished for their sins for all eternity from an eternal and all-powerful God. There will be no rest from the wrath of God upon their sin.

This brings us to the final point of this introduction. As Christians, we want to see people repent and find salvation through Christ, who is the only way. But from a secular perspective, why actively promote a secular belief? There is no god commanding someone to proselytize a secular faith in that viewpoint. So pushing atheism, agnosticism, materialism, naturalism, and the like is a self-refuting position right from the word "go"!

It shows that in the heart of hearts of the unbeliever, they know God exists and they have no excuse so they actively try to suppress that knowledge of God. Romans 1:20–32 reveals this state of the heart and mind of those in willful rebellion. It explains why secularists entertain great acts of sinfulness and actively oppose the Christian God with their words and lifestyle. Their minds have become futile, debased, and are under judgment already. Romans 1 says:

> For since the creation of the world His invisible attributes are clearly seen, being understood by the things that are made, even His eternal power and Godhead, so that they are without excuse, because, although they knew God, they did not glorify Him as

2. www.darwinfish.com, accessed Monday July 11, 2016.

God, nor were thankful, but became futile in their thoughts, and their foolish hearts were darkened. Professing to be wise, they became fools, and changed the glory of the incorruptible God into an image made like corruptible man — and birds and four-footed animals and creeping things.

Therefore God also gave them up to uncleanness, in the lusts of their hearts, to dishonor their bodies among themselves, who exchanged the truth of God for the lie, and worshiped and served the creature rather than the Creator, who is blessed forever. Amen.

For this reason God gave them up to vile passions. For even their women exchanged the natural use for what is against nature. Likewise also the men, leaving the natural use of the woman, burned in their lust for one another, men with men committing what is shameful, and receiving in themselves the penalty of their error which was due.

And even as they did not like to retain God in their knowledge, God gave them over to a debased mind, to do those things which are not fitting; being filled with all unrighteousness, sexual immorality, wickedness, covetousness, maliciousness; full of envy, murder, strife, deceit, evil-mindedness; they are whisperers, backbiters, haters of God, violent, proud, boasters, inventors of evil things, disobedient to parents, undiscerning, untrustworthy, unloving, unforgiving, unmerciful; who, knowing the righteous judgment of God, that those who practice such things are deserving of death, not only do the same but also approve of those who practice them.

Even so, the souls of unbelievers are still not far from being rescued by the Holy Spirit unto salvation. We see secularists come to know the Lord all the time in sincere repentance. Just as Paul outlined the offenses of those who reject God in Romans 1, he also stated to the Corinthian church that they had formerly been in such a state (1 Corinthians 6:9–10), but now it could be said of them: But you were washed, but you were sanctified, but you were justified in the name of the Lord Jesus and by the Spirit of our God (1 Corinthians 6:11).

Our hope with this final volume is to help open the eyes of Christians and non-Christians to the futility and illogical positions of secular religions. Our prayer is for the Holy Spirit to use this for His Glory unto salvation of many through the gospel of Jesus Christ.

Chapter 1

Secular and Atheistic Religions: Overview

Bodie Hodge and Roger Patterson

Secular religions (e.g., atheism, agnosticism, secular humanism, natural-ism, etc.) possess a unique status in our Western world. Having a past that has typically been uneventful, the 1800s saw an explosion of these religious variants.

Fueled by the likes of Charles Lyell in the 1830s (geological evolution or "millions of years") and Charles Darwin beginning in 1859 (biological evolution from a common ancestor), the secular takeover of the West continued. We still see the fruit of these religious views in our day and age.

Secular religions now dominate areas like the media, education, law, museums, sexual expression, and, sadly, the minds of the next generation, according to recent statistics.[1] This makes sense since secular religious views flow freely in the education system due to secular laws imposed upon state schools. Young minds are molded into secular form, and few realize it until it is too late.

In the Western world (United States, United Kingdom, Germany, etc.), these secular religions are the biggest stumbling block for the next generation of Christians and Christian missionaries seeking to proclaim the gospel.

---

1. See Ken Ham, Britt Beemer with Todd Hillard, *Already Gone* (Green Forest, AR: Master Books, 2009); Ken Ham with Jeff Kinsley, *Ready to Return* (Green Forest, AR: Master Books, 2015).

The once great West, whose churches sent missionaries out to the whole world, is now crumbling at a foundational level due in part to the influence of secularism. Secular religious doctrines are even infiltrating the Church!

Essentially, the West needs missionaries to rise up and "rebuild the wall," so to speak, of the Church in the West. But to do so, we need to deal decisively with the religion of the day — the secularism that stands like Goliath in our culture. So how do we, as a Church, deal with it?

Immunizing the New Missionaries

Consider this hypothetical situation with which missionaries have to deal. Missionaries are sent to minister with the gospel to a place that has deadly diseases. The missionaries contract a disease and the missionaries die. You send more missionaries; they contract the same disease and die.

Now, if you were a sending church, what would you do? Do you simply send more missionaries to their potential doom? Or do you take the time to prepare your missionaries with the proper protection for what they are about to encounter — medicine or inoculation from the disease? Obviously, you want to protect your missionaries and give them what they need to be effective for the gospel work for which they are sent.

Now consider this same problem, but from a spiritual angle in our Western world. The United States and the United Kingdom were once nations greatly influenced by Christians, and churches could be found in abundance, particularly in cities. But now, churches have closed their doors *en masse* in many places in England. The same trend is happening to the United States, albeit at a delayed pace.

Today, cities have precious few churches, and those that are there are typically shallow with little doctrine (there are exceptions) and compromise the authority of God's Word. In other words, they are struggling and dying themselves. Many Christians recognize that there is a need for churches in cities. The cities like Cincinnati, New York, Salt Lake City, Los Angeles, Chicago, London, and Bristol are ripe for church plants.

Interestingly, few of these church plants are as effective as hoped. Some church plants grow slowly, others plateau, some merely take people from other churches, and others struggle and die. A lot of excuses are given — wrong church model, not enough funding, wrong music, too traditional, etc. But the main problem is that they were not dealing with the false religion that has entwined the people of the mission field.

When a missionary goes to Africa or the Amazon or Papua New Guinea, they train themselves to know what religions are in the area (e.g., Animism, Islam, Spiritism, etc.), and they learn how to refute those false beliefs so they can be an effective witness in presenting the truth of the Bible and the gospel. They don't go with the intent of just telling people to be moral and to add Jesus to what they believe.

How many church planters in cities in the UK and the USA have trained their missionaries to refute secular humanism, Darwinism, atheism, etc.? How many pastors in church plants in New York are trained to refute secular attacks on Christianity like radiometric dating, alleged missing links, big bang, and so on? The even bigger problem is that many of the church planters may have *agreed* with the secularists and believe the big bang is true, embrace millions of years, or even prefer evolution over the Bible's origins account. Imagine if we sent a missionary to Muslims who had bought into many tenets of Islam!

While we must certainly affirm that the message of the gospel is the power of God to salvation, apologetics is an important aspect of evangelism. While we proclaim the truth of Jesus as Lord and Savior, we must also help others see how their own religious views are insufficient to deal with their sin. We might also need to answer questions that explain the foundational elements of how sin entered the world and why they need a Savior.

If a missionary is not refuting the false religion prevalent in their mission field (i.e., secularism in much of the Western world), then why would we expect that missionary to be effective? Dealing with secularism and refuting it is a key to mission work in the "new" Western world. But refuting it is only part of the step. Secular refutations should not be divorced from the preaching of the gospel and teaching disciples to obey all Jesus commanded, embracing the authority of the Bible in all areas — starting in Genesis.

What Are Secular Religions?

There are a lot of forms of secularism. They are religions that are humanistic (i.e., man is the supreme authority). Here is a list of some of the forms or aspects of secular/humanistic religions:

- Atheism and New Atheism
- Agnosticism
- Existentialism

- Extraterrestrial Humanism
- "Nonreligious" Religious Humanism
- Naturalism
- Stoicism
- Materialism
- Relativism
- Nazism
- Hedonism (including perverted sexual expression)
- Communism
- Nature Worship
- Idealism/Dualism
- Satanism (Church of Satan)
- Epicureanism (Evolutionism)
- Modernism
- Scientism
- Post-modernism
- Secular Humanism

As you can see, there is a wide variety of secular/humanistic religious views. Those who profess a humanistic religion often blend these aspects in various ways. For example, a person might identify generally as an atheist and hold to a materialistic view of the universe and a relativistic understanding of morality. Professor Richard Dawkins is a new atheist but also believes in aliens/extraterrestrial life as a possible explanation for the origin of life on earth. Bill Nye professes to be an agnostic (he can't know for certain if God exists), but then proceeds to argue from an atheistic perspective (no God exists, cf., Psalm 14:1).

Sometimes these religions have great variations while sharing many commonalities. For example, Hedonism promotes sexual perversions like homosexuality (e.g., LGBT) and Nazism absolutely opposes them. Yet both share the same view that man is the supreme authority, and both share an evolutionary view of origins, opposing the Bible, looking to bring human prosperity, etc.

Some of these are philosophical aspects that are utilized by each variant — like naturalism, materialism, and relativism. Even *within* the various flavors of humanistic religions you can have variations. For example, within hedonism (cf., Ecclesiastes 9:7–10) there are two very different forms:

Quantitative Hedonism (get as much as you can for your enjoyment before you die)

Qualitative Hedonism (enjoy the highest quality of things in life before you die)

There are even variations within atheism. One view presents itself from *classical atheism* — says there is no God(s) but refrains from caring what others believe, also known as soft atheism. Then there is *new atheism,* which doesn't believe God(s) exists but tries to force this view on others, also known as hard atheism.

You may also notice that some of these religious flavors sometimes cross over with the moralistic religions described in *World Religions and Cults Volume 2.* Why such great variation and yet such similar commonalities based on the authority of man?

Consider what the Bible says:

In those days there was no king in Israel; everyone did what was right in his own eyes (Judges 17:6).

That we should no longer be children, tossed to and fro and carried about with every wind of doctrine, by the trickery of men, in the cunning craftiness of deceitful plotting (Ephesians 4:14).

It should not surprise us that a religious view that sets man as the authority has as many variations as there are people — since each person considers themselves the captain of their own soul. Man can invent all sorts of evil (Romans 1:30) and diversity of evil and deceptive doctrine (2 Timothy 3:12–13). These things should be tested against the absolute standard of God's Word (1 Thessalonians 5:21).

How Secular Religions Took Over the West — and the Failure of the Church to Properly Respond

About 200 years ago, the United States and England were strongly influenced by Christianity. England, at least in a legal sense, is a Protestant nation headed by a Protestant monarch. The queen or king is the supreme governor of the Anglican Church. They cannot take the throne without being of the Protestant faith — there is a long history to this establishment.

This influence extended to the British colonies and the nations that developed from those colonies.

But when we see the culture today, the USA, UK, and many other Western nations are highly secular. The ubiquity and brazen display of lies, immorality, murder, greed, hatred of Christians, child sacrifice, idolatry, the love of money, and many other evils are a daily reminder that our culture has changed. So how did it get this way?

One part of the answer is the failure of the Church to seriously engage these issues. And, *Deo volente* (God willing), they will be in a better position to address the trend. But the Church has failed in two areas:

1. Instead of combatting the slow secularization that began to unfold in the West in the early 1800s, many in the Church and their leaders embraced various aspects of secularization.
2. The Church gave most teaching of children over to a third party (that became secular), so subsequent generations within the Church were not equipped and fell to the secular onslaught.

In America in the 1800s, for example, Christians began giving their children over to state schools to educate them. At the time, it seemed like a good idea, as state schools used the Bible in the classroom. They used it to teach history, logic, philosophy, literature, science, and so forth.

So the Church, by and large, didn't have to focus on those subjects. Instead, they began concentrating on teaching the gospel, theology, and morality. As man's ideas about long ages, millions of years, astronomical evolution, and biological evolution began taking over school systems, most Christians either didn't notice or fell victim themselves.

By 1925, geological evolution (millions of years) and animal evolution were being taught in schools with full backing by the state. As human evolution began to be taught, the battle lines finally erupted with the famous Scopes Trial.

Even so, as the humanistic religion began to permeate the state schools under the influence of men like John Dewey, the Bible was removed, creation was taken out, prayer was silenced, the Ten Commandments banished, and so on. Now entire generations of kids have been raised up being taught the religion of secular humanism.

But what did the Church do to specifically counter this false religious teaching? By and large — nothing! Many churches still teach morality, the gospel, and theology (not that these are bad things), but then most parents (90 percent by the latest stats)[2] still send their children to state schools to be taught a different religion. So for about 40 hours a week, kids from Christian homes are taught the religious tenets of secular humanism, and the Church (who scarcely teaches the kids 2–3 hours per week) wonders why the kids are walking away from the faith and following after humanistic religions. Those that remain in the Church have often brought secular baggage with them. They often hold to evolution and millions of years, secular morality, secular views of sexuality, marriage, race, and so on.

What does this do to a local church? It causes it to be stagnant, impotent, or die as members are actually mixing secular religions with their Christianity. It is no different from the former godly Israelites in the Old Testament mixing true worship of God with worship of Baal. The mere difference is with *which religion* the modern Christians mix their Christianity — secularism rather than Baal.

With this in mind, we as Christians have to "pull the plank out of our own eye" in the Church before we "reach for the speck of sawdust" in the culture's eye. The Church needs to get back on the right track first. Thus, the Church has a big job to re-educate their congregations in the truth of the Bible in all areas like history, science, logic, and so forth.

"But We Don't Have a Religion!"

The secularists are the first to cry, "We are not part of a religion!" Why is this the case? There are a couple of reasons.

First, they don't want to be kicked out of the place of influence in the government school classrooms. Second, the secularist can more easily deceive kids into thinking that it is okay to believe what they teach and that it should have no conflicts with their respective religious beliefs.

Secular and humanistic religions like evolution, atheism, and agnosticism are part and parcel of the same pie. They have free reign under tax-supported dollars in the UK, USA, Australia, Germany, and so many other places. It is strange that Christianity was kicked out of the classroom and yet another religion is taught in its place.

---

2. Ken Ham, "Yes, We Are Losing the Millennials," Answers in Genesis, May 13, 2015, https://answersingenesis.org/christianity/church/yes-we-are-losing-millennials.

Tax dollars are spent on the secular religions through schools, state-funded museums, science journals, and so on. All the while, there is a false claim that "secularists aren't religious."

There is a simple way to test this claim. If something isn't religious, then it cannot oppose religious claims. Does the secular origins view (big bang, millions of years, and evolution) oppose the religious claim of special creation by God in six days and subsequently a young earth? Yes. Thus, secular views are religious. Anyone who claims that they are not religious and then makes judgments about religious topics (e.g., the deity of Christ, the existence of God, the morality of adultery, the truthfulness of the Bible, etc.) has made a religious statement. Though they may claim to be irreligious, they show that they are religious when they try to refute another religious view.

Does atheism, which says there is no God, oppose the religious claim that God exists (as found in the pages of the Bible)? Again, yes. Thus, atheism is religious. It is easy to prove that humanistic religions are religious.

Even many secularists openly admit to their faith. One instance is John Dunphy while writing for a secular magazine:

> I am convinced that the battle for humankind's future must be waged and won in the public school classroom by teachers who correctly perceive their role as the proselytizers of a new faith: a religion of humanity that recognizes and respects the spark of what theologians call divinity in every human being. These teachers must embody the same selfless dedication as the most rabid fundamentalist preachers, for they will be ministers of another sort, utilizing a classroom instead of a pulpit to convey humanist values in whatever subject they teach, regardless of the educational level — preschool day care or large state university. The classroom must and will become an arena of conflict between the old and the new — the rotting corpse of Christianity, together with all its adjacent evils and misery, and the new faith of humanism.[3]

The U.S. Supreme Court, in *Torcaso v. Watkins*, 81 S.Ct. 1681 (1961), stated the following: "Among religions in this country which do not teach what would generally be considered a belief in the existence of God, are

---

3. J. Dunphy, "A Religion for a New Age," *The Humanist*, Jan.–Feb. 1983, p. 23.

Buddhism, Taoism, Ethical Culture, Secular Humanism, and others." Additionally, these groups are eligible for the same tax benefits as other religious groups, and secular and atheist chaplains even function within the military. You can't have your cake and eat it too. Humanists are religious and they act in religious ways.

Is Science Secular?

Many people today insist that science can only be done by people who have a secular worldview — or at least by those who are willing to leave their religious views at the door as they enter the science lab. Several popular atheists and evolutionists have contended that people who reject the big bang and the evolution of living things are so backward that they cannot even be involved in developing new technologies.[4]

But is this really the case? Or are these opponents of a biblical worldview simply making assertions that cannot be supported with facts and substantial arguments, having an incorrect understanding of true science?

A friend of Answers in Genesis was challenged by the comment that science can only be done through a purely secular, evolutionary framework. Such statements are blatantly absurd and are a type of arbitrary fallacy called an "ignorant conjecture." In other words, these people simply do not know the past, nor are they familiar with what science really is.

Examples of Scientists Operating from a Christian Worldview

If science is a strictly secular endeavor without any need for a biblical worldview, then why were most fields of science developed by Bible-believing Christians? For example, consider Isaac Newton, Gregor Mendel, Louis Pasteur, Johannes Kepler, Galileo Galilei, Robert Boyle, Blaise Pascal, Michael Faraday, James Joule, Joseph Lister, and James Clerk Maxwell. Were these "greats" of science not doing science? Francis Bacon developed the scientific method, and he was a young-earth creationist and devout Christian.

Even in modern times, the inventor of the MRI scanning machine, Dr. Raymond Damadian, is a Christian working with Christian principles. The founder of catastrophic plate tectonics, Dr. John Baumgardner, is also a devout Christian. And those who recently founded the scientific field of

4. As an example of this dismissive attitude, Eugenie Scott (formerly) of the National Center for Science Education (NCSE), a leading religious humanist, says, "Like other pseudo-sciences, 'creation science' seeks support and adherents by claiming the mantle of science." http://ncse.com/rncse/23/1/my-favorite-pseudoscience.

baraminology are also Christians. Also, I (Bodie Hodge) developed a new method for production of submicron titanium diboride for the materials science and ceramics industry. Professor Stuart Burgess developed a new mechanism for the two-billion-dollar European (ESA) satellite *Envisat*. Dr. John Sanford developed the gene gun. And let's not forget Werner von Braun, the young-earth Christian who was the founder of rocket science and led the United States to the moon. These are but a few examples of people who held to a biblical worldview and were quite capable as scientists and inventors of new technologies.

The Foundation for Science Is Biblical Christianity

Furthermore, science comes out of a *Christian* worldview. Only the God described in the Bible can account for a logical and orderly universe. God upholds the universe in a particular way, such that we can study it by observational and repeatable experimentation (see Genesis 8:22). Because God upholds the universe in a consistent manner, we have a valid reason to expect that we can study the world we live in and describe the laws that God uses to sustain the universe (Colossians 1:17).

In the secular view, where all matter originated by chance from nothing, there is no ultimate cause or reason for anything that happens, and explanations are constantly changing, so there is no *basis* for science. Though many non-Christians do science, like inventing new technologies or improving medical science, they are doing it in a manner that is inconsistent with their professed worldview. On what basis should we expect a universe that came from nothing and for no reason to act in a predictable and consistent manner? When non-Christians do real science by observable and repeatable experimentation, they are actually assuming a biblical worldview, even if they do not realize it.

It makes sense why "science" in the United States is losing out to other nations since our science education system now limits science in the classroom exclusively to the religion of secular humanism (and its subtle variations).

It Is Not "Science vs. Religion"

So the debate is not "science versus religion." It is really "religion versus religion." Sadly, science is caught up in the middle.

The battle is between the religion of *secular humanism* (with its variant forms like agnosticism, atheism, and the like), which is usually called *secularism* or *humanism* for short, and *Christianity*. They both have religious documents (e.g., the Humanist Manifestos I, II, and III for humanists, and the Bible for Christians); both are recognized religions by the Supreme Court;[5] and both receive the same 501(c)(3) tax-exempt status. Both have different views of origins.

Humanism has astronomical evolution (big bang), geological evolution (millions of years of slow gradual changes), chemical evolution (life came from non-life), and biological evolution (original, single-celled life evolved into all life forms we have today over billions of years) in its view of origins. In other words, evolution (as a whole) is a tenet of the dogma of the religion of humanism in the same way as biblical creation (as a whole, with six-day creation, the Fall, global Flood, and the Tower of Babel) is a tenet of the dogma of Christianity. It is a battle between two different religions.

In recent times, the state and federal governments kicked Christianity out of the classroom, thinking they kicked religion out; but instead, they just replaced Christianity with a godless religion of humanism. This was done as an attack designed by humanists.

An Evolutionary Worldview Equals Science?

There is a misconception that this evolutionary subset of humanism *is* science. Science means knowledge and scientific methodology that is based on the scientific method (observable and repeatable experimentation). However, evolution (whether chemical, biological, astronomical, or geological) is far from scientific. Consider the following facts:

1. No one has been able to observe or repeat the making of life from non-life (matter giving rise to life or chemical evolution).
2. No one has been able to observe or repeat the changing of a single-celled life-form like an amoeba into a cow or goat over billions of years (biological evolution).
3. No one has been able to observe or repeat the big bang (astronomical evolution).
4. No one has observed millions of years of time progressing in geological layers (geological evolution).

5. U.S. Supreme Court, *Torcaso v. Watkins*.

The reason some people are confused about the religion of humanism — and specifically its subset of evolution — as being science is a bait-and-switch fallacy. Let me explain. One of the key components of humanism is naturalism. Basically, it assumes *a priori* there is nothing supernatural and no God. In other words, nature (i.e., matter) is all that exists in their religion (only the physical world).

As a clarifying note, Christians also believe in the natural realm; but unlike the naturalist or humanist, we believe in the supernatural realm, too (i.e., the spiritual, abstract, conceptual, and immaterial realm). Logic, truth, integrity, concepts, thought, God, etc., are not *material* and have no mass. So those holding to naturalism as a worldview *must* reject logic, truth, and all immaterial concepts if they wish to be consistent, since these are *not* material or physical parts of nature.

This is very important because naturalism or natural science has been added as one of the dictionary definitions of science. For example, it was not found in the 1828 Webster's dictionary, but it was added in one form in the 1913 edition. And, interestingly, they removed the definition that "the science of God must be perfect" in the 1913 edition.

So, although many appeal to observable and repeatable science through methodology to understand how the universe operates, another definition has been added to muddle this.[6] Science is now defined as "knowledge or a system of knowledge covering general truths or the operation of general laws especially as obtained and tested through scientific method."[7]

For example, evolutionists have continued to popularize Darwin's scientific observation of the changes in beaks of Galapagos finches as proof for the evolution of one animal kind into another. This is a great example of the bait-and-switch fallacy where scientists present real scientific evidence (the difference in finch beaks) but stretch the truth to say it gives validity to the mythology of microbes-to-man evolution (the "switch" part of the fallacy). This trick leads many to believe that evolution is real science. The only real science in this example is the observation of the difference in finch beaks.

People are baited with this good methodology of observational science (again developed by a Christian named Francis Bacon), and then they are

---

6. There is also the issue of operational science versus historical science. For more, see: http://www.answersingenesis.org/articles/ee/what-is-science.
7. Merriam-Webster Online, s.v. "science," accessed March 8, 2013, http://www.merriam-webster.com/dictionary/science.

told that evolution is science while subtly appealing to another added definition: that of "natural science" or "naturalism." This is like saying another definition of science is "Nazism." Then Nazis could say they are "scientists" and get into a classroom! This is what has happened with humanism. The religion of humanism (with its founding principle of naturalism) has been disguised as *science* by adding another definition to the word *science*. But it is not the good science we think of that makes computers, space shuttles, and cars. It is a religion. To call evolution science is a bait-and-switch tactic.

So, Is Science Strictly Secular?

No. In summary, science can never be strictly secular for these reasons:

1. Real science is observable and repeatable experimentation that only makes sense in a biblical worldview where God's power keeps the laws of nature consistent. In other words, science proceeds from a biblical worldview.
2. Secular humanism, with its subset of evolution, is in reality a religion and not science.
3. Many of the greatest scientists were Bible-believing Christians whose biblical worldview motivated their scientific studies, showing that a strictly secular view is not necessary for performing science.

Where Humanism Leads

Christians will continue to conduct scientific inquiry and invent things, processes, and science fields as we always have. If the United States and other places neglect our accomplishments and inventions and continue to push the religion of humanism on unsuspecting kids in the classroom (usually unbeknownst to most) by limiting its definition of science to the humanistic worldview, then my humble suggestion is that they will continue down the same road humanism leads. That is, people who are consistent in their naturalistic worldview shouldn't care about true science or the world, since nothing ultimately matters in that worldview.

Refutations

Secular worldviews like atheism (and the like) have serious problems. When refuting false worldviews, there are three ways that are typically used to prove them false. They are:

1. Arbitrariness
2. Inconsistency
3. Borrowing from the Bible (preconditions of intelligibility)

Arbitrariness includes things like mere opinions, relativism, conjectures (prejudicial), and unargued biases.

Inconsistencies include logical fallacies, "actions speak louder than words" in behavior and attitudes, presupposition issues that are irrational, and views that are *reduced to absurdity*, based on where the argument is heading.

Borrowing from the Bible is couched in philosophical terminology like preconditions of intelligibility. In brief, it is when a worldview cannot account for something that is foundational. For example, in a materialistic worldview, why would love exist? Love is not material. You don't drink some love to increase your daily dose of love.

So when a secular materialist claims they love something or someone, then it is highlighting a problem with their preconditions. In other words, the materialist in this case believes love exists, but his religious convictions say otherwise. Some of the problems with secular viewpoints will be analyzed using these criteria (arbitrariness, inconsistencies, etc.) without being exhaustive, of course.

Arbitrariness

In the case of God and His Word, they are not arbitrary. This is because there is no greater authority than God (cf. Hebrews 6:13). There is no greater authority that can be appealed to than God — and by extension His Word.

However, all secular views fail to appeal to God as their final authority, instead appealing to man. Man is a lesser authority and not absolute. Thus, any authority of man is a mere opinion to the absolute and supreme authority of God and His Word. All secular religions are based on the ideas of fallible man and thus arbitrary next to God.

The fact that many secular religions deviate from one another in their belief systems shows how relative they are regarding man's opinions. Thus, relativism reigns supreme among them. But relativism is fallacious, being arbitrary. So from two fronts, secular religions fail to pass the test.

In response, some secularists have touted that there is variation among Christians and the outworkings of the Bible, thus the Bible is arbitrary, too.

However, this misses the point — it is not about what Christians believe, but about what God says. Christian outworkings (e.g., denominations, church splits, doctrinal misinterpretations) are based on man's (less than perfect) understanding of the Scripture. But this has nothing to do with God being the absolute authority. Just because an authority is misinterpreted or misunderstood does not undermine its authority.

Inconsistent

Have you noticed that many secularists want to be good and want to do the moral thing? Herein lies the problem. If there is no God who sets what is right and wrong or defines good and bad, then why be moral and how can "good" be defined? It is utterly inconsistent to try to do good or be moral when your religion, *at its very base*, says there is no need or compulsion to do so.

We've seen atheists, agnostics, hedonists, and others get upset with brutality, people lying and deceiving, and terrorist activities, and yet they hold to positions that encourage abortion (murdering babies in the womb). Note the inconsistency.

Christians are commonly attacked for believing God's authority regarding the truth of the Bible, but they turn around and hold to a position based on trusting man's authority! Think of it like this:

> Secular claim: You Christians blindly take the Bible as an authority because the Bible tells you to.

> Christian response: By what authority do you reject God's Word?

> Secular response: I read a book (or heard someone) that told me to believe the Bible is wrong, and I trust them.

Again, note the inconsistency. The difference is that man's authority is meaningless when compared to the absolute authority that is God's Word. If God *is* God, then what authority would supersede God's? There is none. God must reveal Himself as the final and superior authority.

Another secular claim, particularly from empiricists, is that "seeing is believing." They argue that truth claims can only be known through the senses. But there is an inconsistency here. How does the secularist know that alleged truth claim is true? Their senses are not involved in that alleged truth claim (that all truth claims can only be known through the senses).

To further elaborate, they claim that all truth claims are known by senses, but how do they know that? Did they see or sense that truth? Sadly, they usually hold such a position because someone told them to — like a book or teacher.

Secular religions are largely materialistic and naturalistic. Matter (including energy and space-time) is all that exists — nature is all that exists . . . thus, the term *naturalism*. This stands in direct opposition to the Christian worldview based on the Bible where the supernatural also exists. God is God of both the natural and supernatural (i.e., spiritual realm). This is why Christians are not as limited as secularists on many issues.

But a materialistic/naturalistic worldview causes undeniable problems for secular views. If matter is all that exists, then nonmaterial (immaterial) things cannot exist. There are many things that cannot exist if materialism is correct. They include:

- Logic
- Truth
- Abstractions
- Propositions
- Concepts
- Rights
- Shame
- Reason
- Knowledge
- Dignity
- Honor
- Love
- Sadness

It would be inconsistent (i.e., a behavioral inconsistency) for a secularist to appeal to logic, reason, truth, etc., to argue for a secular worldview that says immaterial things cannot exist!

Another absurd inconsistency reveals itself during discussions of God's Word being the authority. Some secularists go so far as to proclaim that they don't believe the Bible, as though that settles the debate. But it doesn't. When a secularist (or anyone else) professes that they disagree with the Bible, then they are claiming to be God. To disagree with God is to view oneself as God. This is fallacious reasoning.

Allow me to explain this further. When one claims to disagree with God, then they are elevating their own thoughts to be greater than an omniscient, omnipotent, and omnipresent God. Therefore, one is (usually inadvertently) elevating themself to *be that* God! This is clearly absurd.

Borrow from Bible

Many secularists live their lives borrowing from God's Word, though they fail to realize it. If people are merely evolved animals and there is no God who sets right and wrong, then why wear clothes? Why get married? Why get an education? Squirrels don't set up universities to discuss philosophical methodology.

Why celebrate the popular Christian holidays called weekends, which is based on the Sabbath Day and the Lord's Day? Why have holidays anyway? A holiday is a holy day, yet there exists nothing holy in a secular worldview.

Why heal sick people (medicine) when survival of the fittest should take its course as it has in the past without our interference? Why have laws? God may set laws, but if we are our own authority, then law is meaningless.

Why waste time on science? In fact, how can the secularist know the laws of nature won't change tomorrow? (From a Christian perspective, God has promised to uphold nature as it is in the future.) From a secular viewpoint, they can't know the future will be uniform. If they argue that it has always been like that, then it begs the very question at hand! Thus it is a fallacious circular argument. Yes, even the possibility of observable and repeatable science is based on God's Word being true.

Conclusion

When it comes down to it, secular views fail on a number of aspects. Even more discussion and refutation is found in the various chapters in this volume. Sadly, many have been deceived into believing that secular worldviews are the truth, when in fact truth cannot exist if secular worldviews are correct (as truth is not material).

Our hope is that those caught up in secular religions, whether they knew it or not, will repent. Our hope is to see them realize the truth of the Scripture by the power of the Holy Spirit. Secular religions ultimately say things came from nothing, are going to nothing, and nothing matters. But with Christianity, there is the power of hope based on a truthful God who made a way to save us for all eternity. See chapter 15 in this volume for more on this precious subject.

Chapter 2

Atheism

Ken Ham and Bodie Hodge

> The fool has said in his heart, "There is no God." They are corrupt, and have done abominable iniquity; there is none who does good (Psalm 53:1).

The religion of atheism is nothing new. The godly have dealt with it since sin took a foothold in a fallen world (after Genesis 3).[1] King David dealt with it in the Old Testament; the Apostle Paul dealt with it in the New Testament when he argued against the atheistic Epicureans in Acts 17.

In our day and age, the atheistic religion is alive and thriving in the wake of declining Christianity in the Western world. Atheists make up about 3.1% of the U.S. population according to the Pew Research Center in 2014.[2] The UK has about 13% who profess the religion of atheism.[3]

These increases come as no surprise as the government schools in the West teach the religious tenets of atheism without restriction in many classes. One

---

1. Consider the very thoughts of the Pre-Flood world. Genesis 6:5 says, "Then the LORD saw that the wickedness of man was great in the earth, and that every intent of the thoughts of his heart was only evil continually."
2. "America's Changing Religious Landscape," Pew Research Center: Religion & Public Life, May 12, 2015, http://www.pewforum.org/2015/05/12/americas-changing-religious-landscape.
3. "Brits among the least religious in the world: UK comes 59th in poll of 65 countries after only 30% of population say they have a faith," DailyMail.com, April 12, 2015, http://www.dailymail.co.uk/news/article-3036133/Brits-religious-world-UK-comes-59th-poll-65-countries-30-population-say-faith.html.

of the founders of modern, atheistic evolutionary views, Charles Darwin, argued that man invented the idea of God.[4] Being from England, his views have been imposed on generations of people in the UK and beyond.

What Is Atheism?

Atheism is the king of the secular humanistic religious variations. It is the pinnacle of secular beliefs, taking the position to its extreme.

Atheism is the religious belief system that professes there is no God or gods. While agnostics claim it is not possible to know whether a god exists, atheists are absolute in their insistence that there are no gods. Many people who claim to be atheists will actually acknowledge they are agnostics when pressed.

Inherent to atheism is materialism — the concept that only material things exist. The atheist claims there is no immaterial realm (i.e., no spiritual realm), otherwise God could exist in that nonmaterial realm and thus atheism would be refuted. So there is an absolute commitment to the idea that every phenomenon can be explained as the result of matter interacting.

The term *theism* is based in belief in God (*theos* is "god" in Greek). Atheism means *without God* (*a-* without, *theos-* god). The term has been in use since the 1600s. Atheism is a fancy way of saying that they try to maintain a belief system without any notion of God. Some prefer the moniker *non-theist*. In reality, these are just different names of the same basic philosophy with slight variations in their outlook.

As with any religious worldview, there are variations in atheism:

- Classical Atheism (atheism without any flair)
- New Atheism (evangelistic and aggressive to impose the religion of atheism on people through schools, media, etc.)
- Non-theism (opposed to God but usually disinterested in discussions; also called soft atheism)

---

4. Charles Darwin, *The Descent of Man and Selection in Relation to Sex*, reprinted from the 2nd ed. (New York: A.L. Burt, 1919), p. 105–109. Some may object and suggest that Darwin was a theist because the name God does appear a few times in *On the Origin of Species*, the 6th and final edition. However, Darwin's fist edition had no mention of God. Due to his views being attacked for years by those who believed in God, Darwin's later editions added "God" as a possibility, though Darwin only ever described himself as an agnostic at best in his correspondence. His final book *Descent of Man* showed where his view of God truly was — that man invented the idea of God. For more, see Randall Hedtke, *Secrets of the Sixth Edition* (Green Forest, AR: Master Books, 2010).

- Anti-theist (opposes religions other than itself — outspoken and confrontational; also called hard atheism)
- Church of Satan (LaVeyan Satanism)
- Epicureanism (among the first atheistic evolutionists, a form of Greek philosophy)
- Ritual atheists (e.g., Atheist Church which models rituals after Christian elements but without God)

There are several religions that are atheistic in their outlook or act like atheism in practice. Without being exhaustive, two examples are agnosticism and Buddhism. Buddhism has elements of a "transcendental heavens" that lies outside the natural realm, but in practice it is atheistic in denying a being acknowledged as a god.

Though distinct from atheism but still a variation of Secular Humanism, agnosticism receives an honorable mention because many of its adherents act more like practical atheists. Agnostics (*a-* without; *gnosis-* knowledge) claim that it is not possible to know if a god or gods exist since they are not part of the natural realm. In his debate with Ken Ham, Bill Nye, a professing agnostic, used and argued for atheistic positions while not claiming to know with certainty whether God exists.

As a reminder, this book series is not arguing for a mere theistic position, but instead for *Christian* theism. We are unashamed about proclaiming and arguing for the God of the Bible.

Atheists — Seeing through the Facade

Professor Richard Dawkins, a well-known atheist and former professor at Oxford University in England, openly argues against gods — especially the Christian God — and claims that he doesn't believe in the God of the Bible. Nor does he believe in the Easter Bunny, Dionysus (an alleged Greek god), or the Tooth Fairy![5]

Interestingly enough, Dr. Dawkins doesn't spend his energy and effort arguing against the Easter Bunny, Dionysus, or the Tooth Fairy. Instead, he has spent much of his life writing books and articles and offering interviews and commentary arguing against the God of the Bible. Why the inconsistency?

Have you ever stopped to think about why Dr. Dawkins and other professing atheists spend so much of their waking hours arguing against God's

---

5. Although, Dawkins gets nervous about being critical of the Allah of the Koran.

existence? It is because in his heart of hearts (innermost part of his mind) Dr. Dawkins knows God exists and he is trying to suppress that knowledge and justify his denial of the obvious. It is an easy task to let go of the alleged existence of the Easter Bunny, Tooth Fairy, and so on. But the God of the Bible is not so easily cast aside. And there are good reasons.

Romans 1:18–25 says:

> For the wrath of God is revealed from heaven against all ungodliness and unrighteousness of men, who suppress the truth in unrighteousness, because what may be known of God is manifest in them, for God has shown it to them. For since the creation of the world His invisible attributes are clearly seen, being understood by the things that are made, even His eternal power and Godhead, so that they are without excuse, because, although they knew God, they did not glorify Him as God, nor were thankful, but became futile in their thoughts, and their foolish hearts were darkened. Professing to be wise, they became fools, and changed the glory of the incorruptible God into an image made like corruptible man — and birds and four-footed animals and creeping things. Therefore God also gave them up to uncleanness, in the lusts of their hearts, to dishonor their bodies among themselves, who exchanged the truth of God for the lie, and worshiped and served the creature rather than the Creator, who is blessed forever. Amen.

The Bible gives a consistent witness to the fact that God's existence as the eternal and divine Creator is obvious from the creation He has made, including man himself.

> He has made everything beautiful in its time. Also He has put eternity in their hearts, except that no one can find out the work that God does from beginning to end (Ecclesiastes 3:11).

> Who show the work of the law written in their hearts, their conscience also bearing witness, and between themselves their thoughts accusing or else excusing them (Romans 2:15).

> The heavens declare the glory of God; and the firmament shows His handiwork. Day unto day utters speech, and night

unto night reveals knowledge. There is no speech nor language where their voice is not heard. Their line has gone out through all the earth, and their words to the end of the world (Psalm 19:1–4).

Dr. Dawkins and others are trying to suppress their knowledge of God, which God has made evident to them. However, they cannot escape it, so they do what they can to hide from it, seeking to justify that God doesn't exist — with bold, yet bad, arguments no less. But there is no escaping that fact that God exists.

Why Is This Significant?

It means that atheism, though professed, doesn't really exist. In other words, there are no true atheists, just those who *claim* to be. If we agree with God we must disagree with atheists. An all-knowing and all-powerful God informs us that all people do have the knowledge of God's existence. Therefore, atheism is impossible. What you have are 3% of Americans who are openly suppressing that knowledge of God and lying, whether consciously or not, to say they are atheists.[6]

Here is an illustration to help understand the point. Imagine if someone professes that logic doesn't exist. Then they proceed to use logic to try to prove that logic doesn't work. Do you really believe them when they claim they don't believe in logic? No, they demonstrated that their claim was false the moment they used logic to disprove logic.

Furthermore, when atheists spend immense time trying to disprove God, it proves where the battle in their heart is. It is against the God they are trying to suppress.

Atheistic Origins: Big Bang, Millions of Years, and Evolution

Since materialism is one of the core tenets of atheism, naturalistic, evolutionary processes provide the foundation of the belief of origins. So the atheist must try to figure out where the universe came from naturalistically, *without* appealing to a Creator.

Big Bang

In the past, some atheists posited an eternal universe (which most now reject). The second law of thermodynamics destroys this position. If the

---

6. It is also possible that many of these professing atheists simply don't know what atheism is.

universe was eternal in the past, there should be no usable energy left whatsoever. So the fact that stars shine disproves this position.

Others have observed that the universe is expanding (which the Bible suggests was the case, e.g., Isaiah 40:22, 44:24; Zechariah 12:1; etc.). But those opposing God proposed that if the expansion of the heavens could be wound backward (in a general sense), there was a "creation point" or singularity (an almost infinitely hot and dense particle). Then this singularity blew apart (expanded outward in all directions rapidly) and this is where the space, matter, and energy came from to form the universe. But they say there was no God involved — pure naturalism.

This singularity could not have been eternal, as the second law of thermodynamics destroys that idea as well. It should have run down to a point where there is no more usable energy as eternity progressed. So the atheistic position is that there was nothing — no time, no space, no matter — and then this singularity just popped into existence from nothing and then expanded. This is essentially what the big-bang model promotes.

Based on modern observations of the expansion of the universe and measurements of distance between galaxies, scientists postulated that the expansion could be viewed in reverse. At some point, the universe must have been smaller, so the calculations attempted to determine when the universe began. This assumes that God had not created the universe in the recent past or with any initial size.

As time went on, the model was adjusted in light of new findings. But to rescue the model in the face of contrary evidence, ideas like cosmic inflation were added to make the numbers "fit" the model. There have been many changes to the initial concept and so many layers added that it barely resembles the original "cosmic egg" idea. Today, many scientists appeal to the unobserved idea of a multiverse to explain how something came from nothing — the origins fairy tale for the atheist.

The biblical creationist explains these modern observations as well, so the observations are not exclusive to the big-bang idea. Take note that this whole model is built on pure speculation! The big bang is not repeatable or observable at its very root, which means is it not observational or repeatable science. It is just fairy tale stories to fit with their preconceived religion of atheism and naturalism. As a loud and clear point, no God or gods are required in any big-bang model. It was always meant to explain the origin of the universe from a totally naturalistic, materialistic viewpoint. So for Christians who might consider the option that God could have *used* the big bang, then they are essentially adding God to a view that was formulated to explain the universe without God!

Millions of Years

Millions of years (in fact, billions of years) are a prerequisite for an atheistic worldview. We've never heard of a young earth atheistic evolutionist. For the earth to form as we know it through naturalistic processes, there must have been billions of years for its evolution, beginning with the big bang.

To the atheist, one must have *millions of years* for stars to form after the big bang, then *millions of years* for stars to supposedly make heavier elements, then *millions of years* for stars to explode, then *millions of years* for the heavier elements to coalesce into planets and asteroids and so forth. All of these naturalistic evolutionary processes are referred to as cosmological evolution.

Then the atheist needs *millions of years* for the molten planets to cool. Then one needs *millions of years* of naturalistic processes to finally arrive at sufficient water and a protective atmosphere for life to form. Then the atheist needs *millions of years* for the right planet to be at just the right size and just the right distance from a stable star. Then they need *millions of years* of chemical processes to occur so that maybe one of them accidentally produces the first life. As the earth continued to form, geological evolution supposedly produced the rock layers, seas, and landforms that we see today.

Keep in mind, we're just hitting the highlights. But see this for what it is: blind faith. This is just one arbitrary story layered upon another with no observable verification or witness.

Chemical and Biological Evolution

Chemical evolution or "abiogenesis" is how matter supposedly gave rise to life from non-living elements. The problem is that this has never been observed. Furthermore, one of the few laws in biology is the law of biogenesis that says life only comes from life. So to blindly believe in abiogenesis is not scientific, as it violates this verified law of science. Despite the evidence against it, atheists must believe it happened at least once in the past to be consistent in their materialistic worldview.

At any rate, once life supposedly formed, what did it eat? How did it excrete its waste? How did it protect itself from harsh chemicals all around it? How did it know to reproduce? Where did the coded information in its DNA come from? This complex initial life form apparently just happened by accident in the atheistic worldview — at least that is how the story goes.

Assuming life happened, this single-celled organism must evolve over billions of years, adding complex information to its genome like a circulatory system, a brain, a nerve system, ears, eyes, hair, immune system, and so forth. Of course, we do not observe these kinds of changes happening in nature today, nor have we been able to repeat this via naturalistic experiments. It is a story based on blind arbitrary assertions and opinions based on what we actually observe today.

From a big-picture perspective, atheism, based on its origins teaches that man (and the universe) is just an accidental mixture of chemicals doing what chemicals do. There is no purpose, no right, and no wrong — everything is ultimately meaningless.

Bahnsen-Stein Debate: When the World's Leading Atheist Met His Match

Along with Dr. Richard Dawkins, Dr. Gordon Stein (d. 1996) was another well-known champion of atheism. Dr. Stein was a brilliant man. He was an atheist and proud of it.[7]

Dr. Stein was well versed in the classical arguments for the existence of God (first cause, grand design, etc.) espoused by persons like Thomas Aquinas and Rene Descartes. Each of these arguments began with human reason and tried to derive a position that *a god* probably exists.

Starting from a possible god, the Christian would then argue that *that god* might be the God of the Bible. Each classical argument for the existence of God is *probabilistic*. In other words, the best you can argue is that a god probably exists and it might be the biblical God.

Dr. Stein knew this. He also figured out how to annihilate Christians in debate because of these faults, even writing a book on the subject. This should come as no surprise, since the arguments are flawed from the onset. These arguments rest on the premise that one should leave God out of the argument and stick strictly with human reason as the sole authority.

---

7. In the famous debate with Greg Bahnsen, Gordon Stein had a strange definition of atheism that was more akin to the definition of agnosticism (i.e., that an atheist just doesn't know if God exists). Perhaps this was a debate ploy, because atheism is rather easy to debunk.

Why would a Christian, who believes God is the absolute authority, argue on the basis that God *isn't* the absolute authority to develop a position based on the premise that man *is* the absolute authority? The moment that a Christian leaves God's absolute authority out of the debate, he has already lost the debate over God being the absolute authority!

Dr. Stein, with his string of victories, was set to debate philosopher and pastor Dr. Greg Bahnsen. Dr. Bahnsen didn't use the flawed classical arguments for the existence of God. Instead, he started with God and His Word as the absolute authority and didn't waiver.

Dr. Bahnsen argued that all other positions, including atheism, must borrow from God and His Word to make sense of anything — knowledge, logic, truth, morality, and so forth. This is called the Transcendental Argument for the Existence of God (TAG for short), although, it really isn't an argument as the name seems to imply, but rather a starting point for God being the absolute authority *in all arguments*.

In other words, Dr. Bahnsen stood on the authority of God's Word, which is what makes argumentation possible — even Dr. Stein was borrowing from God's authority and didn't realize it. This was devastating to Dr. Stein's case. Dr. Bahnsen pulled the rug out from underneath the atheistic position of Dr. Stein.

Dr. Bahnsen used the subject of logic (as well as absolute morality, and uniformity of nature) to destroy Dr. Stein's atheistic position. How did he do this? Dr. Stein was a professing atheist who had a materialistic worldview. Thus, when Dr. Stein argued that immaterial entities, like God, don't exist (based on his professed worldview), Dr. Bahnsen caught him in a trap.

Dr. Bahnsen kindly pointed out that logic, which is not material either, could not exist in Dr. Stein's atheistic view. Logic is not material. It is abstract, invariant, and universal. Truth, knowledge, information, absolute morality, etc. are not material either. Thus, Dr. Stein couldn't even make a logical case without presuming his professed religion of atheism was wrong in its materialistic foundations. Dr. Bahnsen pointed out that Dr. Stein must borrow from God's Word just to argue against it.

Dr. Stein kept trying to figure out how to answer and words came out of his mouth, but he left the debate in utter defeat. He and Dr. Bahnsen wrote letters back and forth until they died in 1995 and 1996. To his dying day,

Dr. Stein could not answer the devastating case made against his atheism. In subsequent debates, Dr. Bahnsen ultimately earned the name "The Man Most Feared by Atheists." Let's look more closely at specific refutations of the religion of atheism.

Arbitrariness

> Stop regarding man in whose nostrils is breath, for of what account is he? (Isaiah 2:22; ESV).

Would you believe something just because someone tells you to believe it? We should hope not! Next to God, the ideas of man are but a breath. God's ways are much higher than man's (Isaiah 55:9). This is logical, as God is all-knowing (Psalm 147:5) and man isn't.

When the opinions of man sit as the absolute authority on a subject, then they are arbitrary. Each person sits in the supposed position of authority, so no one is the authority. This is the case for atheism. There is no God or ultimate authority to appeal to in an atheistic mindset. In the absence of God, man is viewed as the final authority on all matters.

Appealing to man's opinions as the truth is a faulty appeal to authority. Thus, it is illogical. The entire philosophy of atheism is based on man being the ultimate authority on all matters — an arbitrary position that can never provide a source of truth.

Inconsistency and Borrowing from the Bible

Absolute Morality

If everything came from nothing and all things that happen are merely chemical reactions doing what chemicals do, then there is no such thing as right and wrong. In other words, if someone decides to kill all the atheists in the world, from an atheistic position that is okay since they cannot argue that killing atheists is wrong *within* their own worldview. If people are merely a sack of chemicals interacting, then there is no consistent reason to forbid killing others.

Don't get me wrong, many atheists want some sort of moral code (i.e., they don't want to get murdered or be lied to), but that doesn't come from *their* religion. Instead, it comes from God who has written the law on their hearts, and their consciences know it. Really, atheists must borrow morality from God's Word, whether they realize it or not.

Atheists might argue that they could borrow morality from other religions, but that fails too. First, all those other religions are also borrowing morality from the God of the Bible (they all have the law of God written on their hearts too). So the atheist is still ultimately borrowing it from God.

Second, if the atheist opts to borrow morality from other religions that have deviated from the Bible in their morality (like Islam or Eastern religions), it doesn't help them. Islam is generally fine with the extermination of the atheists (infidels).

Eastern thought says all things are illusions (doctrine of *maya*) — including people like atheists. If someone kills them it is no big deal since they don't really exist anyway. It merely changes their karma for the next life.

Absolute morality comes from God, as God is the ultimate and final lawgiver (Hebrews 6:13). Only God explains why morality exists in the universe that He created.

Laws of Logic

The atheist holds that all things consist of matter and energy (nature and matter only). They argue with the loudest voice that there is no immaterial, spiritual, or ideal realm. Their position relies on strict materialism.

If an atheist professes that he believes there are immaterial things that exist, then he is not an atheist. He would be a dualist. That is an entirely different religious framework.[8]

Atheists argue against the existence of an immaterial realm. If they left open the idea that the immaterial exists, then God, who is not material, could exist and atheism would be wrong. If this were the case, the atheist would be forced to move to a different religious system like dualism or agnosticism, conceding that atheism would be impossible.

This is why aspects like materialism and naturalism (everything can be explained by natural processes) must be held to unwaveringly in an atheistic religion. As a result, this also makes atheism one of the easiest religions to refute.

Consider things that are immaterial or abstract: truth, logic, knowledge, concepts, dignity, respect, love, care, conclusions, information, and so forth. The logically consistent position is that the atheist cannot believe these exist either. They are not material; they must not exist. To get around this issue they claim that love is an aspect of matter interacting, but they have no way

8. See chapter 10 in this volume on dualism.

to verify such a claim. They go on using the immaterial laws of logic while adhering to a materialistic worldview.

For example, what is the mass of logic or by what means would we measure it? It is an illogical question to ask what the mass is of something that has no mass because it is an abstract, immaterial concept. Yet logic, which is invariant and universal, exists, as the universe even obeys the laws of logic. For example, you cannot have the moon and not the moon at the same time in the same relationship (law of non-contradiction).

Many atheists appeal to reason and logic, but their worldview cannot account for either. So they must step out from under their atheism and borrow the Christian worldview that does make sense of logic. God created all things and He upholds things in a logical fashion. Logic is a tool we use to think God's thoughts after Him.

Consider truth, information, love, etc. These things cannot exist in a purely materialistic worldview. Even argumentations, reasons, conclusions, and so forth cannot exist in an atheistic worldview. The atheist cannot, based on his own professed worldview, make an argument for atheism without first giving up his atheism.

Uniformity of Nature

Doing scientific inquiry is predicated on the Bible being true. God upholds the world in a consistent fashion and has promised to do so (Genesis 8:22). So the Christian can do observable and repeatable science, knowing that the result will be the same day to day.

God, who knows all things past, present, and future, has promised the future will be like the past — not in the conditions of course, but in the way God upholds things. To clarify, the wind may not blow at the same speed each day, but the laws that govern the wind will be the same each day, allowing predictions about the future.

In an atheistic worldview, laws of nature changed in the past (i.e., the big bang defies the laws of physics; there were no laws, now there are laws). In the future they may change again. Since no one really knows the future in the atheistic framework, the laws of nature could change as early as tomorrow. Why do science if the laws of science might change tomorrow?

The atheist might argue that we know the future will be like the past, because in the past the future was like the past. But this is circular reasoning. It begs the very question we are asking.

Unless God reveals to us that the future will be like the past, science is impossible. It makes sense that leading scientists held a Christian worldview (Francis Bacon, Isaac Newton, Galileo Galilei, Johannes Kepler, Gregor Mendel, Michael Faraday, Robert Boyle, Raymond Damadian, etc.). Secular scientists are still resting on the shoulders of great Christians and their scientific works.

A Path to Absurdity

Let's assume for a moment the atheistic position could make sense of logic. To say there is no God would logically require someone to look everywhere in the entire universe at the exact same time *and* for all time, past and future, and find no God.

Furthermore, the atheist would have to be powerful enough to look in the immaterial, spiritual realm for all time too. They would also have to be powerful enough to supersede God to make sure God was not cloaking Himself from their search. In other words, for an atheist to say "there is no God" would require the atheist to be omnipresent and omnipotent. The atheist would essentially have to be all-knowing to say God doesn't exist (omniscience).

Thus, for an atheist to claim there is no God would require them to be God! Thus, it is an absurd and self-refuting worldview.

Regarding the Atheist

Do atheists get tired of all the evil associated with the philosophy of atheism — Stalin, Hitler, Pol Pot, and so on?[9] After all, most murderers, tyrants, and rapists are not biblical Christians, and most have rejected the God of the Bible. Even if they claim to believe in the God of the Bible, they are not really living like a true Christ follower (who strives to follow God's Word), are they?

Does an atheist feel conflicted about the fact that atheism has no basis in morality (i.e., no absolute right and wrong; no good, no bad)? If someone stabs an atheist in the back, treats them like nothing, steals from them, or lies to them, it doesn't ultimately matter in an atheistic worldview where everything and everyone are just chemical reactions doing what chemicals do. And further, knowing that a person is essentially no different from a

---

9. Bodie Hodge, "The Results of Evolution," Answers in Genesis, July 13, 2009, http://www.answersingenesis.org/articles/2009/07/13/results-evolution-bloodiest-religion-ever.

cockroach in an atheistic worldview (since people are just animals) must be disheartening.

Do atheists struggle with the fact that atheism has no basis for logic and reasoning?[10] Wouldn't it be tough to get up every day thinking that truth, which is immaterial, really doesn't exist? Would the atheist be bothered by the fact that atheism cannot account for uniformity in nature[11] (the basis by which we can do real science)? Why would everything expand from nothing and, by pure chance, form beautiful laws like $E=MC^2$ or $F=MA$?[12]

Perhaps the atheist would like a weekend to recoup and think about these things. Interestingly, the concept of a weekend is really meaningless in an atheistic worldview since animals, like bees, don't take a day of rest or have weekends. Why do atheists borrow a workweek and weekend that comes from the pages of Scriptures, which are despised by atheists? A consistent atheist should just work every day until they die.

Weeks and weekends come from God creating in six literal days and resting for a literal day; then the Lord Jesus resurrected on the first day of the week (Sunday). And why look forward to time off for a holiday (i.e., holy day), when nothing is holy in an atheistic worldview?

Does the atheist feel conflicted about proselytizing the faith of atheism, considering that if atheism were true then who cares about proselytizing? Let's face it, life seems tough enough as an atheist without having to deal with other minor concerns like not having a basis to wear clothes, or no basis for marriage, no consistent reason to be clean (snails don't wake up in the morning and clean themselves or follow other cleanliness guidelines based on Levitical laws), and no objective reason to believe in love.

In fact, why would an atheist care to live one moment longer in a broken universe where one is merely rearranged pond scum and all you have to look forward to is . . . death, which can be around any corner? And in 467 trillion years, no one will care one iota about what an atheist did or who they were or how and when they died — because death is the ultimate "hero" in an atheistic, evolutionary worldview.

---

10. Jason Lisle, "Atheism: An Irrational Worldview," Answers in Genesis, October 10, 2007, http://www.answersingenesis.org/articles/aid/v2/n1/atheism-irrational.

11. Jason Lisle, "Evolution: The Anti-science," Answers in Genesis, February 13, 2008, http://www.answersingenesis.org/articles/aid/v3/n1/evolution-anti-science.

12. Jason Lisle, "Don't Creationists Deny the Laws of Nature?" in Ken Ham, Gen. Ed., *The New Answers Book 1* (Green Forest AR: Master Books, 2006), p. 39–46, http://www.answersingenesis.org/articles/nab/creationists-deny-laws-of-nature.

The religion of atheism is a lie (Romans 1:25). As Christians, we understand that truth exists because God who is the Truth exists (John 14:6), and we are made in His image.[13] Unlike an atheist, whose worldview doesn't allow him to believe in truth or lies, the Bible-believer has a foundation that enables him to speak about truth and lies. This is because believers in God and His Word have an authority, the ultimate authority on the subject, to base their beliefs upon.

Atheists have no consistent reason to proselytize their faith, but Christians do have a reason — Jesus Christ, who is the Truth, commands us to (Matthew 28:19). We want to see people repent of their evil deeds and be saved from death to worship the God who created them (Acts 8:22, 17:30).

Where atheists have no basis for logic and reason (or even for truth, since truth is immaterial), Bible believers can understand that mankind is made in the image of a logical and reasoning God who is the truth. Hence, Christians can make sense of things because in Christ are "hidden all the treasures of wisdom and knowledge"(Colossians 2:3). Christians also have a basis to explain why people sometimes don't think logically due to the Fall of mankind in Genesis 3. The most logical response is to give up atheism and receive Jesus Christ as Lord and Savior to rescue you from sin and death (Romans 10:13). Instead of death, God promises believers eternal life (1 John 2:25; John 10:28) and in 467 trillion years, you will still have value in contrast to the secular view of nothingness.

Christians do have a basis to wear clothes (to cover shame due to sin; see Genesis 2:25, 3:7), a reason to uphold marriage (God made a man and a woman; see Genesis 1:27; Matthew 19:4–6), a reason to be clean (Leviticus contains many provisions to counter diseases in a sin-cursed world), and a source of real love (since God made us in His loving image; see 1 John 4:8). As Christians, we have a solid foundation for saying that things like back-stabbing, theft, and lies are wrong (see the Ten Commandments in Exodus 20).

The day is coming when we all will give an account before God for our actions and thoughts (Romans 14:12). For those who are atheistic and reading this, I invite you personally to become an ex-atheist, join the ranks of the saved through Jesus Christ, and become a new creation (2 Corinthians 5:17) as we continue to advance with the gospel in peace that only God can provide (Romans 5:1)

---

13. Keep in mind that Christians do fall short due to sin and the Curse, but God never fails.

Chapter 3

Agnosticism

Steve Ham, M.Div.

There is an old joke that has been going around for many years. Did you hear about the agnostic, dyslexic insomniac? He stayed awake all night wondering if there really is a *dog*. As silly (and funny) as that joke is, it actually captures the skeptical nature of an agnostic.

In this chapter, we will define agnosticism and look at its history. We will also answer the main concern for every agnostic. Agnostics are concerned with the concept of *knowing*. While agnostics swim in the sea of skepticism, Christians can confidently stand knowing that the God of the Bible exists and has powerfully revealed Himself. We don't just know *about* Him, but we also know Him.

Understanding the Dilemma

The Apostle Paul stood right in the midst of the Greek philosophers as they deliberated over the religious and civil life of Athens. One can only imagine Paul's spectacular view from the Areopagus (Mars Hill) as he looked over the city with its paths and buildings and statues to the various Greek gods. For Paul, the statues of these gods had not gone unnoticed. The inscription on one in particular had caught Paul's eye and gave him the theme for his famous Acts 17 sermon. Who is the *Agnosto Theo* — the "Unknown God"?

Most Greeks believed in many gods and, just in case they missed one, they built a statue to cover themselves. The Greeks wondered if these gods were all that there are. Are there more? Is there a god of the gods? Who is he, she, it? The questions are countless and lead people to the one huge question — *Is it possible to know if there really is a god at all?*

Derived from the same term as the inscription on the statue at Athens, agnosticism is basically about "not knowing." *Gnosis* means "knowledge" in Greek and *a-gnosis* would be "without knowledge." The fact that agnosticism has now been termed as an "-ism" means that for some people it has turned into a whole belief system.

There are varying degrees of agnosticism. When somebody uses this identifier, Christians should dig a little deeper to find out with what sort of agnostic they are conversing. There are agnostics who say that they *don't know* whether there is a god, and there are agnostics who say that *nobody can know* if there is a god. There are also different versions of these two positions.

Popular author and New Testament critic Bart Ehrman calls himself an Agnostic Atheist.[1] By this, he means that he believes that one cannot know if there is a god and therefore cannot believe that there is a god. The "not knowing" part makes him an agnostic, and the "not believing" part he claims makes him an atheist.[2]

On the other end of the agnostic scale are those who are much more pragmatic than Bart Ehrman. They are willing to say that they do not know whether a god exists, and may not even care since they believe that there is no real consequence either way. So the range of agnosticism is somewhere from "We cannot know and we cannot believe" to "I don't know and I don't care."

The Christian must, however, see the common denominator in all agnostic positions. Whether they lean in an atheistic or pragmatic position, the agnostic is always resting on his or her own autonomous judgment. This is an arbitrary position.

The agnostic has made a judgment, not just about "a god," but also about the God of the Bible who has specially revealed Himself to us in the

---

1. Bart D. Ehrman, "Am I an Atheist or an Agnostic," *The Bart Erhman Blog*, June 2, 2012, https://ehrmanblog.org/am-i-an-agnostic-or-an-atheist/.
2. Ehrman's argument is a leap in logic in which the conclusion does not follow. If one cannot know if God exists, then the conclusion that he doesn't is arbitrary and illogical. One can rightly profess the opposite by the same logic. Imagine if someone says one cannot know if God exists, therefore God exists. Besides, atheism is not about *believing* whether God might exist or not, but about the absolute denial of His existence, and atheists profess to "know" this. Ehrman's position is foolish (Psalm 14:1).

person of Jesus Christ and in His Word. Furthermore, as the Creator of all, He has positioned all mankind without excuse, having clearly revealed His power in creation (Psalm 19:1–4; Ecclesiastes 3:1; Romans 1:18–32).

In stark contrast to the agnostic position, the Christian can and does know God through the powerful gospel. Paul encouraged the Thessalonian church with this message when he told them, "knowing, beloved brethren, your election by God. For our gospel did not come to you in word only, but also in power, and in the Holy Spirit and in much assurance" (1 Thessalonians 1:4–5). The Thessalonians truly knew God in the one true saving sense, and this came through the proclamation of the gospel and the power of the Holy Spirit. First John 5:11–13 also reveals that Christians can *know* they are saved by God.

A Foundation for Agnosticism

In reality, a discussion of the history of agnosticism would require a survey of skepticism concerning the existence of deity well beyond the limits of this chapter. One can, however, trace a distinct line from some of the philosophies of the Enlightenment to the man who first used the term "agnostic" in a self-descriptive way. The period known as "the Enlightenment" ranges from the mid-17th century through to the 19th century. It is peppered with some of the names of the world's great philosophers such as Descartes, Spinoza, Locke, Hume, and Kant.

If there is one common word to describe this period, it is "rationalism." These philosophers placed confidence in the ability of unaided human reason to discover the truth in all areas of reality.

This is a significant factor for the Christian understanding of the basis of the agnostic worldview. The men of the Enlightenment, some of them theists, paved the way for a large-scale rejection of God's revelation as the authoritative basis for reason. It is important to have a short glimpse of how this happened and the wide-ranging effects of the impact.

Descartes (1596–1650) is best known for his statement, *"Cogito Ergo Sum," I think therefore, I am.* This statement is an example of what is known as deductive rationalism. Also evident in the works of the Greek philosopher Plato, deductive rationalism has its source of knowledge in human intuition, or innate ideas. In other words, man is seen as the absolute authority on the subject of reason, and God has been demoted or removed and subjected to man's judgment.

Descartes commenced with a journey of skepticism, doubting his very existence. He came to the conclusion that he could not doubt his existence unless there was a doubter, thus, "I think, therefore I am."[3] This statement triggered a generation of voices that says man is the authority over God. Unlike Descartes, God professes, I Am Who I Am (Exodus 3:14; John 8:58). God is the "I Am," and the existence of man and reason itself is predicated on God, not man. With Descartes, *God* was traded for *man* and this led many down a path of "man is the measure of all things" instead of God being the ultimate standard. Far too many were deceived in this movement, and we still feel the effects of it in today's culture.

In 1690, John Locke published his *Essay on Human Understanding* in which he denied the concept of innate ideas and posited that all ideas come from sense experience or reflection. His disagreement with Descartes' skeptical application of innate ideas was not subtle.

> If any one pretends to be so skeptical as to deny his own existence, (for really to doubt of it is manifestly impossible,) let him for me enjoy his beloved happiness of being nothing, until hunger of some other pain convince him of the contrary. This, then, I think I may take for a truth, which every one's certain knowledge assures him of, beyond the liberty of doubting, viz. that he is something that actually exists.[4]

Contrary to deductive rationalism, Locke opened the enlightenment period to *inductive* rationalism, also described as *Empiricism*.[5] More in line with the Greek philosopher Aristotle, empiricism only claims knowledge that comes through the senses — something must be observed through sense perception or testing to be known to be true. For Locke, if anyone were to claim intuitive knowledge, they were claiming something that was simply "self-evident," (an orange is not an apple).

Locke discussed different types of knowledge that could all be explained in terms of sense experience and reflection. He believed that demonstrative

3. Rene Descartes, *Discourse on the Method of Rightly Conducting the Reason and Seeking for Truth in the Sciences*, in Vol. 31 of *Great Books of the Western World*, edited by Robert Maynard Hutchins, et al. (Chicago, IL: Encyclopedia Britannica, Inc., 1952), p. 51.

4. John Locke, *Concerning Human Understanding*, in Vol. 35 of *Great Books of the Western World*, edited by Robert Maynard Hutchins et al. (Chicago, IL: Encyclopedia Britannica, 1952), p. 349.

5. See chapter 14 in this book for a full description of Empiricism.

knowledge derives from reason, sensitive knowledge from the senses, and, when considered together, one can make judgments based on probabilities.[6] In reasoning methodology, most modern agnostics would be examples of the school of inductive rationalism.

Neither Locke nor Descartes were agnostics. Both men believed in God, and Descartes was Roman Catholic. While Descartes reasoned that God must have placed innate ideas in the mind of man (the famous mind-body separation model),[7] Locke reasoned that beings cannot produce themselves and, therefore, something must have existed from eternity. Locke reasoned that God was the eternal, all-powerful, all-knowing being.[8]

Neither did Locke completely reject the idea of revelation. Revelation was acceptable only under the magisterial authority of reason (i.e., man determines which parts of revelation to accept).[9] In his discussion of revelation and reason, he states:

> In any truth that gets not possession of our minds by the irresistible light of self-evidence, or by the force of demonstration, the arguments that gain it assent are the vouchers and gage of its probability to us; and we can receive it for not other than such as they deliver it to our understandings. Whatsoever credit or authority we give to any proposition more than it receives from the principles and proofs it supports itself upon, is owing to our inclinations that way, and is so far a derogation from the love of truth as such: which, as it can receive no evidence from our passions or interests, so it should receive no tincture [tinge or infusion] from them.[10]

Five years after his *Essay on Human Understanding*, Locke published *The Reasonableness of Christianity*. While not accepting all the tenets of the Christian faith, Locke did note that Christianity was the most reasonable of all religions (by *his* fallible standard, no less). Church historian Justo L. Gonzalez summarizes his analysis of this work, stating that, "In the final

---

6. Locke, *Concerning Human Understanding*.
7. Justin Skirry, "René Descartes: The Mind-Body Distinction," Internet Encyclopedia of Philosophy, accessed 10/5/2016, http://www.iep.utm.edu/descmind/.
8. Locke, *Concerning Human Understanding*, p. 349–354.
9. Note Locke's fallacy here. He believed God was all-knowing, eternal, and all-powerful except when it comes to man's fallible and imperfect reason which must be elevated above God to make such a claim. This is self-contradictory.
10. Ibid., 384, definition added.

analysis, Christianity was little more than a very clear expression of truths and laws that others could have known by their natural faculties."[11]

Locke could be described as having a rational theism wherein the only revelation that was acceptable is that which could be naturally reasoned by the mind of man. This thinking had a wide and lasting effect. Locke's system of rationalism founded the philosophical basis for democracy, motivated some of the thinking behind the French Revolution, and even influenced the framing of key documents such as the United States Declaration of Independence.[12]

After Locke's work on rationalistic theism, deism became a popular alternative to Christian orthodoxy. Deism is a belief system that rejects any idea of particular revelation. In this way, deists took the demotion of revelation a step further than had Locke.

Deists believe that religion is universal and available through the natural instincts of all human beings. Basing his work on the foundation provided by John Locke, John Tolland, a British deist (1670–1722), wrote *Christianity Not Mysterious, A Treatise Showing That There Is Nothing in the Gospel Contrary to Reason nor Above It, and That No Christian Doctrine Can Be Properly Called a Mystery.*[13] This work (and others like it) was written in order to show that any real quality claimed in orthodoxy could be derived through natural reason apart from direct revelation.

It was also on the basis of Locke's work that philosopher David Hume brought a new type of skepticism, moving from Locke's ideas concerning rationality and revelation. David Hume's new empiricism was a great diving board from which to jump into agnosticism. Hume (1711–1776) held that logic was a mere habit of the mind and not demonstrable truth.

Like Locke, Hume did agree that all knowledge comes from the senses. He further argued, however, that no one has ever seen or experienced the principle of *cause and effect*. Cause and effect is not a result of experience but a result of our mental habits linking the phenomena we have experienced through our senses. Therefore, concepts such as cause and effect have no basis in Hume's empirical observation.

---

11. Justo L. Gonzalez, *The Story of Christianity, Vol. 2: The Reformation to the Present Day,* 2nd ed. (New York: HarperOne, 2010), p. 241.

12. Gregg L. Frazer, *The Religious Beliefs of America's Founders: Reason, Revelation, and Revolution* (Lawrence, KS: University Press of Kansas, 2014), p. 216–217.

13. John Toland, *Christianity Not Mysterious: Or, a Treatise Shewing, That There Is Nothing in the Gospel Contrary to Reason, nor Above It, and that No Christian Doctrine Can Be Properly Called a Mystery* (Gale ECCO, Print Editions, 2010).

Furthermore, supernatural phenomena such as miracles must also be denied unless individually experienced. Specifically, one cannot believe in a resurrection unless they themselves have risen from the dead. Declaring his inability to experience any part of it, Hume also rejected any consideration of a universal cause.

> It is confessed, that the utmost effort of human reason is to reduce the principles, productive of natural phenomena, to a greater simplicity, and to resolve the many particular effects into a few general causes, by means of reasonings from analogy, experience, and observation. But as to the causes of these general causes, we should in vain attempt their discovery; nor shall we ever be able to satisfy ourselves, by any particular explication of them. These ultimate springs and principles are totally shut up from human curiosity and enquiry.[14]

One would be hard pressed to find any more complete definition of agnosticism than this statement from Hume. Reading words such as this, we can understand why many have attempted to class Hume as an agnostic or even an atheist. And so it is, with the stage set and the curtain drawn, that we introduce the man as the first to name himself an agnostic, Thomas Huxley.

The Agnostic and the Anglican

It is reported that the term *agnostic* was first heard in public in 1869 at a party when spoken by the famous anatomist, Thomas Huxley (1825–1895). Huxley, today often referred to as Darwin's Bulldog, was negative toward organized religion. His term, *agnosticism*, gained immediate traction and was soon being debated, not only by Christian rivals, but also among those who shared Huxley's empiricism.

A strong opponent of agnosticism was a senior Anglican priest from St. Paul's Cathedral in London by the name of Henry Wace (1836–1924). Wace and Huxley, with others, commenced a series of papers and arguments against each other's positions.

The precise definition of agnosticism has remained debatable through to present times. Even so, the sole reliance upon human reason and/or empiricism for knowing truth, especially concerning deity, has remained a

---

14. David Hume, *Concerning Human Understanding*, p. 460.

common element. In 1888, Wace quoted the Oxford dictionary as already having a basic definition for the term.

> An agnostic is one who holds that the existence of anything beyond and behind natural phenomena is unknown, and (so far as can be judged) unknowable, and especially that a First Cause and an unseen world are subjects of which we know nothing.[15]

Apparently, Huxley, who did not want to be known as an atheist, coined the term referencing Paul's discussion of the *Agnosto Theo*, the "Unknown God," in Acts 17. Paul, of course, was not in any way advocating agnosticism by using the inscription on the statue in Athens. On the contrary, Paul referred to the "unknown God" to proclaim to the Greeks that the Creator had become the Savior and specially revealed Himself in the Lord Jesus Christ. Paul was seeking the Greeks to believe on the basis of this magnificent revelation. Wace, in a similar manner as Paul to the Greeks, was taking the position of revelation against Huxley's unknowable deity.

> But if this be so, for a man to urge as an escape from this article of belief that he has no means of a scientific knowledge of the unseen world, or of the future, is irrelevant. His difference from Christians lies not in the fact that he has no knowledge of these things, but that he does not believe the authority on which they are stated. He may prefer to call himself an agnostic; but his real name is an older one — he is an infidel; that is to say, an unbeliever.[16]

In a later argument, Wace also states in similar vein that,

> Prof. Huxley's learning is justified in being ignorant that it is not upon such knowledge, but upon supernatural revelation, that Christian belief rests. However, as he goes on to say, my view of "the real state of the case is that the agnostic does not believe the authority on which these things are stated, which authority is Jesus Christ."[17]

15. Henry Wace, "On Agnosticism," in *Christianity and Agnosticism: A Controversy*, 1889 (repr. London, England: Forgotten Books, 2013), p. 5.
16. Ibid, p. 8–9.
17. Henry Wace, "Agnosticism: A Reply to Professor Huxley," in *Christianity and Agnosticism: A Controversy*, 1889 (repr. London, England: Forgotten Books, 2013), p. 59.

Huxley's arguments for his agnosticism were many, but none of them were surprising. He denied miracles, Jesus' knowledge of the unseen world, and the basic biblical history of creation, the Fall, and the Flood. Since he saw these as the historical basis for Paul's theology, he rejected Paul's teachings.[18] Influenced by the textual critics of the Bible of his time, Huxley also denied the authenticity of the New Testament text itself. He questioned the credibility of the Gospels, particularly noting as a supposed contradiction the differing accounts of the same event in the Gospels.

Wace's argument was simple and profound. He did not agree with the textual critics who denied the credibility of the inspired text and the authorship of the Gospels; but he also noted that those same critics did believe that the Sermon on the Mount was the authentic sermon of Christ. In this sermon, however, Christ displays His authority, speaks of coming judgment and the Kingdom of heaven, and speaks often of God. The Lord's Prayer alone confirms all of these things. To say that no human has the ability to know that God exists, or to know anything about the unseen world, is to make a statement about the revelation of Jesus Christ. Wace writes:

> The position of an agnostic involves the conclusion that Jesus Christ was under an "illusion" in respect to the deepest beliefs of his life and teaching. The words of my paper are, "An agnosticism which knows nothing of the relation of man to God must not only refuse belief to our Lord's most undoubted teaching, but must deny the reality of the spiritual convictions in which he lived and died." The point is this that there can, at least, be no reasonable doubt that Jesus Christ lived, and taught, and died, in the belief of certain great principles respecting the existence of God, our relation to God, and his own relation to us, which an agnostic says are beyond the possibilities of human knowledge; and of course an agnostic regards Jesus Christ as a man. If so, he must necessarily regard Jesus Christ as mistaken, since the notion of his being untruthful is a supposition which I could not conceive being suggested. The question I have put is not, as Prof. Huxley represents, what is the most unpleasant alternative to belief in the primary truths of the Christian religion, but what

---

18. Thomas H. Huxley, "Agnosticism," in *Christianity and Agnosticism: A Controversy*, 1889 (repr. London, England: Forgotten Books, 2013), p. 22.

is the least unpleasant; and all I have maintained is that the least unpleasant alternative necessarily involved is, that Jesus Christ was under an illusion in his most vital convictions.[19]

Today we have heard this same argument put in a similar way by such people as C.S. Lewis and Josh McDowell. To deny the Lordship of Jesus Christ one must call Him either a lunatic or a liar. For Wace, as it should be for all Christians, we stand before agnostics concerned not so much for the limitations of their empiricist position, but for their denial of the authority of the revelation of Jesus Christ as Lord and Savior. They have made a choice about magisterial authority when it comes to human reason. They have chosen to submit to the fallibility of human autonomy rather than to the infallibility of the Word of God to inform reason.

It is no coincidence that the same man who coined the phrase "agnostic" and rejected biblical revelation also became the greatest cheerleader for Charles Darwin. Darwin, as a naturalist, also ignored revelation. He observed variation within animal kinds resultant from natural selection. This actual observation is something that perfectly corroborates the Genesis account of the reproduction of animals after their own kinds. Darwin's speculation about an evolutionary progression of kinds was in essence a rejection of God's Word. Huxley believed in this unobservable, untestable, non-repeatable idea of evolution, and became Darwin's bulldog.

Let's pause for a moment and reflect on the overall historical position of agnosticism. The position has been to reject God (no God allowed) but slyly take God's gift of reasoning and then falsely accredit it to autonomous man (who then messes it up due to sin). From there, agnostics (and their brothers) have used fallible man's reason as the absolute standard to reject God's revelation piece by piece.

Agnostics continued to judge God's revelation and demote it one piece at a time based on man's fallible and arbitrary opinions. And now they come to the idea of Jesus Christ and conclude, "He is false." Thus, no God is allowed.

What few realize is that the agnostic assumed the very thing for which he argues in the first place. He started with the premise, "no God allowed" and arrived at the conclusion "no God allowed." This is the fallacy of begging the question.

---

19. Henry Wace, "Agnosticism: A Reply to Professor Huxley," p. 60.

Modern Agnosticism

It would seem that Huxley's ideas of agnosticism are present, largely unchanged, in today's culture. Unbelief remains as unbelief. While there are some like Bart Ehrman who are prepared to call themselves agnostic atheists, others such as Ron Rosenbaum are careful to differentiate the terms in light of the "New Atheism" movement.

The new atheists, led in the vitriol of Richard Dawkins, the late Christopher Hitchens, and Sam Harris, are no longer content to simply not believe in God. They are zealous recruiters engaged in an anti-theistic battle as preachers of nothingness. The confidence of the new atheists has caused agnostics such as Ron Rosenbaum to call others to embrace an agnostic identity in a brotherhood of solidarity who have the "humility" to say they "just don't know." In an article for *Slate*, Rosenbaum wrote:

> Why has agnosticism fallen out of favor? New Atheism offers the glamour of fraudulent rebelliousness, while agnosticism has only the less eye-catching attractions of humility. The willingness to say "I don't know" is less attention-getting than "I know, I know. I know it all."[20]

"I Just Don't Know" is the T-shirt slogan Rosenbaum suggests. Perhaps a better slogan might be, "We're here, but it's just not clear!"

As much as some agnostics may wish to distance themselves from atheist terminology, there is a common ground when it comes to the practicality of living.[21] Both staunchly confident atheists and staunchly unconfident agnostics (oxymoronic statement intended) live without any accountability to the God that they don't, won't, or can't believe in. At the end of the day, they are both living under the autonomy of self-rule.

Australian agnostic blogger John Wilkins describes yet another group of agnostics that are not staunchly unconfident but only provisionally unconfident. For provisional agnostics, "a question is not *yet* — capable

---

20. Ron Rosenbaum, "An Agnostic Manifesto," *Slate*, June 28, 2010, http://www.slate.com/articles/life/the_spectator/2010/06/an_agnostic_manifesto.html.

21. Bill Nye, for example, claims to be an agnostic, but in the debate with Ken Ham he argued for the atheistic position repeatedly; see Ken Ham and Bodie Hodge, *Inside the Nye Ham Debate* (Green Forest AR: Master Books, AR, 2014).

of being answered, not that the evidence is equivocal or evenly balanced."[22] This still means that they are under self-rule until something better turns up. Either way, there is a practicality that brings all atheists and agnostics together.

Ron Rosenbaum uses the term "humility" to describe the agnostic position. One must also ask what sort of humility rejects any consideration of a special revelation of the world's history from the one revealing Himself as the Eternal Creator. Wouldn't humility require a serious consideration of looking at the world through these glasses before placing one's trust in human autonomy to seek knowledge? It is unlikely that any self-described agnostic can be found expending their energy in an attempt to find God rather than defending his or her own skeptical position. In Romans 3 (quoting Psalm 14)[23] there is a verse that points directly to the human condition in general, but also aptly describes the specific agnostic attitude: "None is righteous, no not one; no one understands; no one seeks for God" (Romans 3:10–11; ESV).

The Agnostic Problem

There are three basic problems that should be apparent from our introduction to agnosticism. There is a logic problem, a definition problem, and, most importantly, a spiritual problem.

A Matter of Logic

In a logical argument there are a series of premises (at least two) that lead to a conclusion. The validity and/or soundness of a conclusion will depend on the validity of both the premises and conclusion. As an example, a valid and sound logical argument might flow as follows:

    A. All mammals have kidneys
    B. All dogs are mammals
    C. Therefore, all dogs have kidneys

---

22. John Wilkins, "On the Suspension of Belief and Disbelief," *Evolving Thoughts*, accessed February 23, 2015, http://evolvingthoughts.net/2011/11/on-the-suspension-of-belief-and-disbelief/.
23. Psalm 14:1–3: The fool has said in his heart, "There is no God." They are corrupt, they have done abominable works, there is none who does good. The LORD looks down from heaven upon the children of men, to see if there are any who understand, who seek God. They have all turned aside; they have together become corrupt; there is none who does good, no, not one.

This argument is valid because it does not violate the laws of logic and the conclusion necessarily follows from the premises. It is sound because its premises are verifiably true.

The basic argument used by agnostics to support their position is often presented in the following way:

A. If we want to know that God exists, then we must be able to test His existence empirically

B. We cannot empirically test God's existence

C. Therefore, we cannot know if God exists

If you follow the reasoning of the premises leading to the conclusion, this argument is reasonable and logically valid. The conclusion follows necessarily from the premises. This is the valid logical form of *modus tollens*.[24]

The problem with this argument, however, is that it is not sound because there are other forms of testing that can be employed, so the premise is not verifiable. It makes a truth claim that is circular in nature — I believe things must be empirically testable to be true because all true things are empirically testable. This is the fallacy of begging the question — arguing in a vicious circle. Based on the faulty premise, the conclusion has become unsound. This objection holds true even if the argument is presented in a logically valid form.

The premise states that something must be empirically testable to know that it is true, but this assumes that empirically testing something is the only way to know truth. This premise in itself is not empirically testable, so how can anyone know that it is true? The basic empiricist argument, therefore, is unsound at its most foundational level — it is a self-refuting argument. Further, it is an arbitrary assertion that is not based on any ultimate authority. Why should empiricism be considered true? The agnostic can offer no ultimate reason.

A Matter of Definition

As one wades through the history of empiricism, a common word consistently mentioned is "science." The term "science" is most often recognized as the observable, testable, repeatable method of proving or falsifying hypotheses and forming theories. This is called *observational science*. It is this type of science where scientists who believe in God can work side by side with agnostic

---

24. Jason Lisle, *Discerning Truth* (Green Forest, AR: Master Books, 2010), p. 68.

or atheistic scientists doing the same experiments and coming up with the same conclusions. From this type of science we describe natural laws, cure diseases, and discover new technologies.

There is another form of science, however, that should be differentiated from observational science. *Historical science* is the discipline of assessing "evidence from past events based on a presupposed philosophical point of view."[25] Because the past is not observable or repeatable, we cannot test the past. We have evidence in the present that was left from past events that needs to be interpreted, and this is only possible within the worldview of the interpreter. In other words, our ideas about the past will determine the way we interpret the evidence in the present.

An agnostic and a Christian have very different assumptions about the past. The agnostic believes there must only be a natural explanation for past events (naturalism alone), whereas the Christian accepts God's revelation through biblical history that accounts for the major events in the history of the created world.[26]

Christians will often hear statements from both atheists and agnostics that they believe only in what can be determined through scientific study. This type of statement often suggests that Christians — and specifically biblical creationists — are religious while atheists and agnostics are scientific. This, too, is a logical fallacy called *equivocation*. Christians, atheists, and agnostics have the same observational science, but the definition of science used in conjunction with ideas such as evolution is a different type of science called historical science. The agnostic changes the definition of *science* to suit his argument. Once correct definitions are adopted, the Christian and the agnostic can discuss the interpretive worldview assumptions that each of them adopt before coming to the evidence.

A Matter of Spiritual Corruption

The most important problem that agnostics face is the same problem that every single human being faces from fertilization (formerly known as conception). There are many Scriptures that describe the corrupt nature of human beings as a result of our inherited sin nature from our original parents, Adam

---

25. Roger Patterson, "What Is Science?" Answers in Genesis, accessed February 23, 2015, https://answersingenesis.org/what-is-science/what-is-science.

26. The Christian is not limited to natural explanations alone, as the agnostic has imposed upon himself. Instead, the Christian holds to both supernatural and natural events in the past.

and Eve. Ever since humanity rebelled against our Creator in the Garden of Eden, we have been spiritually separated from God and from the knowledge of His divine glory. Through the biblical authors, God has described this position to us as "blindness" and "death."

> And you He made alive, who were dead in trespasses and sins, in which you once walked according to the course of this world, according to the prince of the power of the air, the spirit who now works in the sons of disobedience, among whom also we all once conducted ourselves in the lusts of our flesh, fulfilling the desires of the flesh and of the mind, and were by nature children of wrath, just as the others (Ephesians 2:1–3).

> But the natural man does not receive the things of the Spirit of God, for they are foolishness to him; nor can he know them, because they are spiritually discerned. (1 Corinthians 2:14).

> But even if our gospel is veiled, it is veiled to those who are perishing, whose minds the god of this age has blinded, who do not believe, lest the light of the gospel of the glory of Christ, who is the image of God, should shine on them (2 Corinthians 4:3–4).

> But He answered and said, "Every plant which My heavenly Father has not planted will be uprooted. Let them alone. They are blind leaders of the blind. And if the blind leads the blind, both will fall into a ditch" (Matthew 15:13–14).

The agnostic problem is not their problem alone. It is the same problem that every human being faces. Romans 3:23 places all humanity in the same position: "For all have sinned and fall short of the glory of God." All of humanity is conceived with the same sin problem and deserving of the same just, eternal condemnation. The good news is that this common problem that all humanity shares with agnostics has the same solution.

Can We Know God?

Modern agnostics, founded on the thinking of Locke, Hume, and Huxley, are primarily concerned with what they can know through sense experience. Christians, while not dismissing any degree of sense experience, understand that coming to the knowledge of God is not an autonomous exercise. "But as it is written: 'Eye has not seen, nor ear heard, nor have entered into the heart of man the things which God has prepared for those who love Him.' But God has revealed them to us through His Spirit. For the Spirit searches all things, yes, the deep things of God" (1 Corinthians 2:9–10).

Paul was referring to something that Christians know as illumination. Illumination happens through the work of the Holy Spirit drawing us through the power of his revealed Word, and specifically, the gospel of Jesus Christ. In short, we know God through the Spirit and the Word, and the two are never separated. Discussing this same passage, professor of apologetics John Frame, states, "The Spirit testifies to *words* that He has given to the apostles. The same is the case in 1 Thessalonians 1:5 and 2:13. Indeed I know of no passage in which the Spirit's witness has any object other than the Word."[27]

A wonderful explanation of this is seen in Ephesians 1. Paul talks of how the Ephesians have heard "the word of truth," the gospel of their salvation, and that they believed in Jesus Christ and were sealed with the promised Holy Spirit (verses 13–14). He has great joy that he has heard of their faith in Jesus Christ and their love for each other (verses 15–16) and further prays for this continued revelation and wisdom in them, "that the God of our Lord Jesus Christ, the Father of glory, may give to you the spirit of wisdom and revelation in the knowledge of Him, the *eyes of your understanding being enlightened; that you may know* what is the hope of His calling, what are the riches of the glory of His inheritance in the saints, and what is the exceeding greatness of His power toward us who believe . . ." (verses 17–19, emphasis added).

There is both an objective and subjective element working in coming to a true knowledge of God. The objective element is the objective propositional truth conveyed in God's revealed Word. Jude describes this as the faith "once for all delivered to the saints" (Jude 3).

God's Word is authoritative, infallible, and, therefore, trustworthy in totality. But how is the sin-corrupted human to open his or her eyes to this truth? Scripture makes it clear that their own thinking is futile and darkened and their hearts are blind due to the effects of original sin (Ephesians

27. John M. Frame, "a Presuppositionalist's Response," in *Five Views on Apologetics*, edited by Steven B. Cowan (Grand Rapids, MI: Zondervan Publishing Company, 2000), p. 74–75.

4:17–19). Further, the god of this world, Satan, has blinded their eyes to the truth of the gospel and they do not see the "glory of God in the face of Jesus Christ" (2 Corinthians 4:3–6). This requires the subjective enablement of the Holy Spirit (1 Corinthians 12:3).

Only in the union of these two factors — proclamation of the Word of God and the working of the Holy Spirit — is this illumination possible. This is why the Christian can have such confidence in the proclamation of the gospel. Christians are those who have heard the gospel proclamation and, in the power of the Spirit, come to repentance and faith in Jesus Christ, illuminated to the truth. The Apostle John writes, "But you have an anointing from the Holy One, and you know all things. I have not written to you because you do not know the truth, but because you know it, and that no lie is of the truth" (1 John 2:20–21).

When Saul was converted on the road to Damascus, it was through the revelation of Jesus Christ and the power of the Spirit (Acts 9:17–18). Perhaps this is why Paul later describes the gospel as the power of God unto Salvation (Romans 1:16).

Christians never need to fear discussions with agnostics, atheists, or anyone. Yes, we should attempt to answer the skeptical questions, and correct the logical fallacies. We should understand the definitions of observational and historical science, and do all we can to sanctify our hearts in the Word of God in preparation to give an answer for the hope we have within us (1 Peter 3:14–17).

Above all, however, we should use all these things to guide conversations toward the most powerful message that God uses to illumine the minds of His sheep and bring them into the knowledge of His truth, the gospel of Jesus Christ. Only by means of this message can the scales on the eyes of unknowing skeptics fall away, allowing the eyes of their hearts to be enlightened and causing them to find life in the Creator and Savior.

So, as prime importance, let us prioritize this one message to all we speak to. "For I delivered to you first of all that which I also received: that Christ died for our sins according to the Scriptures, and that He was buried, and that He rose again the third day according to the Scriptures" (1 Corinthians 15:3–4).

And let us seek all mankind everywhere, calling them to repent and believe the gospel.

In Conclusion

Agnostics are not just people who don't know. They are people who don't know what they don't know. They don't know the gospel of Jesus Christ, at least not in a saving way. Through this magnificent revelation of God, people can come to knowledge of God and they can come to actually know God.

We do not come to this knowledge through skeptical empiricism but through the Spirit and the Word. This truth should cause the Christian to rejoice in God's grace, and to gain a heart to reach out to agnostics everywhere with the message that is "the power of God unto Salvation."

Summary of Agnostic Beliefs

Doctrine	Teachings of Agnosticism
God	Deny the certainty of the existence of God, but in various forms. They would generally reject the idea of Divinity, the Trinity, and Jesus as the Son of God or Savior.
Authority/ Revelation	Mostly reliant on materialistic, empirical thinking with human reasoning coupled with sense perception being the ultimate standard of truth. Reject any form of supernatural revelation, including the Bible.
Man	Generally accept an evolutionary view of man. No concept of a sinful nature. Man is a mortal being and part of the animal kingdom, with no particularly special role in the universe.
Sin	Sin is not generally a part of agnostic thinking, though some would adopt certain cultural taboos. There is no view to judgment of sin since they reject knowledge of deity.
Salvation	There is no concept of salvation apart from some cultural ideas. Reject the need of Jesus as Savior.
Creation	Generally hold an evolutionary worldview, embracing cosmological, geological, and biological evolution. Reject the biblical creation and young-earth creation ideas.

Chapter 4

Secular Humanism

Todd Friel

Here are three recent headlines that will make your Christian head spin.

- 100,000 Atheists Are "Unbaptized"[1]
- California School Bans All Christian Books[2]
- InterVarsity "Derecognized" at California State University[3]

What is the cause of this contemporary outbreak of insanity? Two words: Secular Humanism.

Unfortunately, you will have more success naming the waves on the ocean than labeling secular humanists; atheists, agnostics, rationalists, empiricists, skeptics, and deists all fall under the banner of "Secular Humanism." What brings such a broad range of people together? God. Or more specifically, a lack of God's existence or involvement in the affairs of men.

Because secular humanism is arguably the fastest growing worldview in the Western world, Christians would do well to be acquainted with this very anti-Christ philosophy.

---

1. Jim Denison, "100,000 Atheists are 'Unbaptized,'" http://www.christianheadlines.com/columnists/denison-forum/100-000-atheists-are-unbaptized.html, accessed 5/20/2016.
2. Carey Lodge, "California School Bans All Christian Books," *Christianity Today*, http://www.christiantoday.com/article/california.school.bans.all.christian.books/41072.htm, accessed 5/20/2016.
3. Ed Stetzer, "InterVarsity 'Derecognized' at California State University's 23 Campuses: Some Analysis and Reflections," http://www.christianitytoday.com/edstetzer/2014/september/intervarsity-now-derecognized-in-california-state-universit.html, accessed 5/20/2016.

Identifying Secular Humanism

Humanism is a broad religious view that encompasses all religions that use human ideas rather than God and His Word as the foundation of truth. All religions outside of God's one and true religion are influenced by humanistic beliefs.

Secular Humanism is an umbrella that covers a vast number of sub-groups, all claiming to be free of religious dogmas.[4] These groups could be likened to different denominations within Secular Humanism. While they share some similarities, their distinctions are worth noting:

Rationalism — a belief that all human opinions and actions should be based on reason and knowledge as opposed to religious belief or emotional response.

Empiricism — the philosophical theory that all ideas are derived from some form of experience, be it internal or external. This theory posits that this is the sole foundation of true knowledge. It developed in the 17th and 18th centuries, expounded in particular by John Locke, Francis Bacon, and especially David Hume.[5]

Agnosticism — the view that the truth-values of metaphysical claims, such as the existence of a god, are either unknown or, in fact, unknowable.

Atheism — the view that rejects or disbelieves the existence of God or gods.

Nihilism — the rejection of all religious and moral principles.[6]

The History of Secular Humanism

In the broadest sense, anyone who denies the existence of God is a secular humanist. Anyone who believes that there may be a god who created the universe, but is not involved in the daily oversight of the universe (deism), is also influenced by secular humanistic thought. That means secular humanism's principles are as old as the rebellion of Adam and Eve in the Garden of Eden.

Throughout history, men have denied the existence of a supreme being. The Old Testament informs us that atheism was alive and well when the

---

4. While Secular Humanists claim to be irreligious, all worldviews are religious in that they seek to explain being and meaning and to act in accord with those beliefs. Secular Humanism is acknowledged as a nonprofit group for receiving tax benefits in the United States.

5. Walter A. Elwell, *Evangelical Dictionary of Theology*, 2nd ed. (Grand Rapids, MI: Baker Academics, 1984), p. 375–376.

6. The religion of nihilism is self-refuting. If they were consistent in rejecting all religious principles, then they should reject nihilism as well.

Psalmist wrote, "The fool has said in his heart, 'There is no God' " (Psalm 14:1). In ancient Greece, Socrates was executed, in part because of a charge that he was an atheist who rejected the Greek pantheon of deities.

History is replete with individuals who have either outright denied the existence of any god or lived in a way that demonstrated that conviction. However, the rise of secular humanism as a prominent worldview began to simmer in the 17th century, in part due to the Protestant Reformation. It came to a full boil in the 1700s and would change the course of history in the West.

A Foundation for Skepticism

During the 1500s, Luther, Calvin, Zwingli, Knox, and many others risked their necks to wage theological war against the Roman Catholic Church based on their deviations from biblical doctrine. While the Protestant Reformation was an overwhelming success in reclaiming the doctrine of justification (grace alone, through faith alone, in Jesus Christ alone), Protestant challenges to the predominant Christian authority (the Roman Catholic Church) unwittingly gave everyone permission to challenge the authority of the Church and Scripture. While it was certainly not the intention of the great Reformers to launch a secular humanist revolution, that was certainly a result of their godly efforts.

Seventeenth Century

The Enlightenment Era Philosophers of the 17th century took advantage of the "question authority" zeitgeist and began to argue against the Roman Catholic Church and even the very existence of God. Prominent names include:

> **Baruch Spinoza** (1632–1677) — "My opinion concerning *God* differs widely from that which is ordinarily defended by modern Christians. For I hold that God is of all things the cause immanent, as the phrase is, not transient."[7]

> **John Locke** (1632–1704) — "The end of a religious society, as I have already said, is the public worship of God, and from that the acquisition of eternal life."[8]

---

7. Baruch Spinoza, Benedict de Spinoza, *The Chief Works of Benedict de Spinoza, vol. 2, On Improvement of the Understanding, Ethics, Select Letters*, Letter 21 (73) to Henry Oldenburg, 1662; http://oll.libertyfund.org/titles/1711/144137, accessed 1/26/2015.
8. John Locke, *A Letter Concerning Toleration* (Ontario: Broadview Press, 1950), p. 54.

Voltaire (1694–1778) — "Every sensible man, every honorable man, must hold the Christian sect in horror."

David Hume (1711–1776) — "Survey most nations and most ages. Examine the religious principles, which have, in fact, prevailed in the world. You will scarcely be persuaded, that they are any thing but sick men's dreams: Or perhaps will regard them more as the playsome whimsies of monkeys in human shape, than the serious, positive, dogmatical asseverations of a being, who dignifies himself with the name of rational."[9]

Immanuel Kant (1724–1804) — "The wish to talk to God is absurd. We cannot talk to one we cannot comprehend — and we cannot comprehend God; we can only believe in Him. The uses of prayer are thus only subjective."[10]

Some scholars, such as Rene Descartes and Marin Marsenne, actually endeavored to prove the existence of God. Unfortunately, the way they attempted to do this was on the basis of pure reason (man's opinions alone). They sought to show that the existence of God could be demonstrated without the use of inspired Scripture. This proved to be a huge blunder.

In some regard, these men were geniuses; Descartes reinvented geometry, for instance. Yet their proofs for the existence of God were lacking. Not only did others begin dismantling many of their arguments, the Christian philosophers battled to promote their own pet views at the expense of other views. This ended up causing a framework of doubt on two fronts.

1. If the Bible is the inspired word of God, then why would the Christian set it aside to attempt to prove the existence of God?
2. Why are the Christian's arguments so inconsistent that they themselves cannot even come to an agreement on virtually any point?

9. David Hume, *Four Dissertations: I. The Natural History of Religion, II. Of the Passions, III. Of Tragedy, IV. Of the Standard of Taste* (London: Printed for A. Millar, 1757), p. 115.
10. H.L. Mencken, *A New Dictionary of Quotations on Historical Principles from Ancient and Modern Sources* (New York: AA Knopf, 1946), p. 955.

Godless Enlightenment philosophers saw these disagreements as proof that Christianity was demonstrably false. They concluded that the use of man's pure reason was the only way that humanity could reach its full potential.

Eighteenth Century

The 18th century successfully watered the secular humanist seeds planted in the previous century. However, it was one event that ultimately launched secular humanism into prominence — the French Revolution of 1789 and the subsequent advance of the Age of Enlightenment.

In 1788, there was a severe food crisis in France. In desperation, the king called a meeting of the estates to come up with a plan to deal with the problem on May 4, 1789. This council was made up of three estates: the aristocracy, the clergy, and the bourgeoisie (middle class). During the assembly, little attention was paid to the middle class, so the bourgeoisie broke away from the estate and formed a document called the "Declaration of the Rights of Man and of the Citizen." This declaration was aimed at bringing equality to all men under the law.

Article four in the document reads, "No corporate body, no individual may exercise any authority that does not expressly emanate from it. Liberty consists in being able to do anything that does not harm others: thus, the exercise of the natural rights of every man has no bounds other than those that ensure to the other members of society the enjoyment of these same rights. These bounds may be determined only by Law."

Notice that human rights actually come from other *humans*. Contrast that to the American Declaration of Independence, which acknowledges that our rights come from God: "We hold these truths to be self-evident, that all men are created equal, that they are endowed by their Creator with certain unalienable Rights, that among these are Life, Liberty and the pursuit of Happiness."

The French Declaration was a humanist manifesto that proved to be wildly popular and led to a massive uprising and ultimately the overthrow of the government. It also led the culture to a deep mistrust of not only the oppressive Catholic Church, but of religion in general.

While the French Revolution seemed to be the dawning of the age of the dominance of a secular humanist worldview, it was a short-lived victory. First came a time known as the Reign of Terror (1793–1794). Tens of thousands of people suspected of anti-revolutionary sentiment were sent to the guillotine. In 1799, Napoleon conquered France, and Catholicism was swiftly reinstated. Still, this period developed many ideas that would be expanded on more by future secular humanists. While this was a brief period, it left its mark on history as perhaps the first, and most certainly the largest, culture that operated free from God in Western history.

Nineteenth Century

One of the men who would further develop the godless worldview was none other than Karl Marx of Russia (1843–1881). Marx believed that the world consisted only of matter. He wrote that religion was an opiate; it was a way for the oppressed to deal with their plight. If oppression would end, then people's need for the opiate of religion would end, putting an end to religion itself.[11] These ideas would be used as the basis of communism,[12] and some of the most brutal governments in history would sprout from these seeds.

Enter Charles Darwin

Out of all the secular humanists that have ever lived, perhaps the most influential is Charles Darwin. Darwin doesn't easily fit into a category when it comes to his religious beliefs. Historian Frank Burch Brown, states it this way:

> His beliefs concerning the possible existence of some sort of God never entirely ceased to ebb and flow, nor did his evaluation of the merits of such beliefs.
>
> At low tide, so to speak, he was essentially an undogmatic atheist; at high tide he was a tentative theist; the rest of the time he was basically agnostic — in sympathy with theism but unable or unwilling to commit himself on such imponderable questions."[13]

Overall, his thought regarding theological matters could best be described as what he himself called a "muddle." In a letter he wrote to a theistic evolutionist, Asa Gray, he wrote that he couldn't completely affirm the idea of the world being designed, but it did not appear to have come into being purely by chance.

---

11. The primary religion in mind was Christianity, not Marx's religious humanism.
12. See chapter 7 on Communism in this volume.
13. Frank B. Brown, *The Evolution of Darwin's Religious Views* (Macon, GA: Mercer University Press, 1986), p. 27.

One thing is clear — Darwin was not a Christian. In his book *The Descent of Man*, Darwin went so far as to say man created the idea of God.[14] He loathed the idea of eternal punishment, referring to it as a "damnable doctrine."[15] It is impossible to understand Darwin rightly without being aware of this backdrop since his worldview colored his explanation of the past.

While on his journey aboard the *Beagle*, Darwin meticulously examined the flora and fauna of South America and its accompanying islands, as well as the geological features. Famously, he noted that the length and shape of finch beaks on the various Galapagos Islands differed. He assumed these variations happened according to the needs of the bird in obtaining food. Darwin posited that all the finches had a common ancestor from which they descended. Based on this and other observations, he concluded that small change was occurring within populations. Simply stated, the parents with the most advantageous characteristics would survive and pass those traits on to their progeny, who would then thrive and produce more of these organisms with the advantageous trait.

While this hypothesis is detectable and valid (even Christians like Ed Blyth described this process before Darwin), Darwin extrapolated it far beyond what is observable. He stated that these small changes could accumulate over millions of years to account for all life. He stated that all life on earth could be traced back to a single ancestor, and, over time, different advantageous mutations occurred and were passed on, while the organisms that lacked these advantages died off. This errant understanding of variation within a species gave a plausible hypothesis to those eager to explain life without God. Richard Dawkins famously stated, "Darwin made it possible to be an intellectually satisfied atheist."[16]

In line with the philosophy of modernism that was prevalent in the West, Darwin clearly saw man as just another animal: "My object in this chapter is to show that there is no fundamental difference between man

---

14. Charles Darwin, *The Descent of Man and Selection in Relation to Sex*, reprinted from the 2nd ed. (New York: A.L. Burt, 1919), p. 105–109.

15. For a person who opposed hell, which is what damning is, Darwin was not afraid to use the terminology. But notice that Darwin, whether he realized it or not, was holding religious convictions of humanism to take his own thoughts on a subject and then judge God and His Word based on his own fallible mind.

16. Richard Dawkins, *The Blind Watchmaker* (New York: Norton, 1986), p. 6.

and the higher mammals in their mental faculties."[17] Since man was just an animal, Darwin suggested that mankind would be better off if only the fit had children.

> With savages, the weak in body or mind are soon elimi-
> nated; and those that survive commonly exhibit a vigorous state
> of health. We civilised men, on the other hand, do our utmost
> to check the process of elimination; we build asylums for the
> imbecile, the maimed, and the sick; we institute poor-laws; and
> our medical men exert their utmost skill to save the life of every
> one to the last moment. There is reason to believe that vacci-
> nation has preserved thousands, who from a weak constitution
> would formerly have succumbed to small-pox. Thus the weak
> members of civilized societies propagate their kind. No one who
> has attended to the breeding of domestic animals will doubt that
> this must be highly injurious to the race of man. It is surprising
> how soon a want of care, or care wrongly directed, leads to the
> degeneration of a domestic race; but excepting in the case of
> man himself, hardly any one is so ignorant as to allow his worst
> animals to breed.[18]

Not only did Darwinian evolution become the skeptic's mechanism and cudgel for denying God's existence, social Darwinism justified much of the 20th century's eugenics atrocities. Unbelievers from Adolf Hitler to Margaret Sanger cited Charles Darwin as their source for justifying the murder of "inferior races" or unwanted children. The results of secular humanism have invariably led to licentiousness and death.

> Margaret Sanger — "As an advocate of birth control I wish
> . . . to point out that the unbalance between the birth rate of
> the 'unfit' and the 'fit,' admittedly the greatest present menace
> to civilization, can never be rectified by the inauguration of a
> cradle competition between these two classes. In this matter, the
> example of the inferior classes, the fertility of the feeble-minded,
> the mentally defective, the poverty-stricken classes, should not

---

17. Darwin, *The Descent of Man*, p. 74.
18. Ibid., p. 151–152.

be held up for emulation. . . . On the contrary, the most urgent problem today is how to limit and discourage the over-fertility of the mentally and physically defective."[19]

Adolf Hitler — "The law of selection justifies this incessant struggle, by allowing the survival of the fittest. Christianity is a rebellion against natural law, a protest against nature. Taken to its logical extreme, Christianity would mean the systematic cultivation of the human failure."[20]

Darwinian evolution gained entrance into American schools following the so-called "Scopes Monkey Trial" of 1925. The defendant in this case was John Scopes, a biology teacher accused of teaching human evolution. His defense attorney, Clarence Darrow, used many evolutionists to promote the scientific merits of evolutionary biology. Darrow put the prosecutor, William Jennings Bryan, on the stand to show he had little to no knowledge of what evolution was and to show his willingness to compromise the literal truth of the Bible. While Bryan won the battle and Scopes was fined $100, the war was lost; evolution had gained a level of popular acceptance and began moving into schools, replacing the creationist curriculums that were the norm. Secular humanism was on a roll.

Twentieth Century

The 20th century gave us Dr. Sigmund Freud, the father of modern-day psychoanalysis, who further expanded secular humanist ideas stating that God is merely an illusion: "Religion is an illusion and it derives its strength from the fact that it falls in with our instinctual desires."[21] He taught that the belief in God comes from a variety of different psychoses, such as the need for a father. To Freud, God was the imaginary figment of a delusional mind; a fictional father that some people needed in order to cope with reality, "At bottom God is nothing other than an exalted father."[22]

19. Margaret Sanger, *The Eugenic Value of Birth Control Propaganda* (1921), p. 5; http://www. nyu.edu/projects/sanger/webedition/app/documents/show.php?sangerDoc=238946.xml.
20. Adolf Hitler, *Hitler's Table Talk: 1941–1944*, trans. Norman Cameron and R.H. Stevens (New York: Enigma Books, 2000), p. 51.
21. Sigmund Freud, *New Introductory Lectures on Psycho-analysis*, trans. James Strachey (New York: W.W. Norton, 1965), p. 216.
22. Sigmund Freud, *Totem and Taboo; Some Points of Agreement between the Mental Lives of Savages and Neurotics*, trans. James Strachey (New York: W.W. Norton, 1950). p. 147.

In the meantime, a Christian movement attempted to combat liberalism in the early 20th century: Fundamentalism. This orthodox movement holds to a group of non-negotiable fundamentals of the Christian faith, such as the inerrancy of the Bible, the literal (plain/straightforward) nature of the Bible, the virgin birth of Christ, the bodily Resurrection and physical return of Christ, and the substitutionary atonement of Christ. These fundamentals came largely from 12 volumes of articles published in Chicago between 1910 and 1915.[23]

The articles were written polemically against liberalism and apologetically in defense of the sufficiency of the Bible. Unfortunately, this movement was soon overshadowed by the rising tide of liberalism, and fundamentalists were eventually on the outside looking in on many of the key areas of culture such as arts, entertainment, and academia.

The fundamentalist outlook fell out of favor with the "scientific community," and they were largely shunned.

> In science they [fundamentalists] were steadfastly committed to the principles of the seventeenth-century philosopher Francis Bacon: careful observation and classification of facts. These principles were wedded to a "common sense" philosophy that affirmed the ability to apprehend the facts clearly, whether the facts of nature or the more certain facts of scripture.[24]

The scientific landscape shifted, however, and the fundamentalists were now the outsiders. "These largely unspoken assumptions, as well as their faith in the Bible, separated the fundamentalists so entirely from the most of the rest of the twentieth century thought that their ideas appear simply anomalous. Thus in the fifty years following the 1870s, the philosophical outlook that had graced America's finest academic institutions came to be regarded as merely bizarre."[25]

Twentieth Century Postmodernism

The fall of the Berlin Wall in 1989 brought a crashing end to classic secular humanism and modernist thinking. Prior to the reuniting of East and West

23. Walter A. Elwell, *Evangelical Dictionary of Theology*, 2nd ed. (Grand Rapids, MI: Baker Academics, 1984), p. 475.
24. George M. Marsden, *Fundamentalism and American Culture* (Oxford: Oxford University Press, 1980), p. 7–8.
25. Ibid., p. 8.

Berlins, secular humanist modernists believed that human reason was superior and sufficient for determining morality. World Wars I and II undermined that notion. The bloodiest century in human history led philosophers and culture to conclude that man does not have the ability to make the world a better place.[26]

Unfortunately, the death of modernism gave birth to an even uglier stepchild — postmodernism.[27] It was clear to philosophers that neither God nor man had the solution for evil, so who does? Interestingly, the answer was "nobody and everybody."

Secular philosophers concluded that God doesn't exist and humans had made a mess of things, therefore, no single authority has the right or ability to declare universal truths for all men. Postmodernism insisted that truth could not be objectively known, therefore, each individual must determine what is true for himself. This philosophy is called moral relativism. Christians battle this form of relativistic humanism (postmodernism) today.

History Is Like a Baseball Game

Prior to the French Revolution, Western culture largely submitted to the Word of God — truth was determined by our Creator. Secular humanists insisted that God does not exist and only man has the answers to the problems that plague us. Unfortunately, the bloodiest wars in human history (World Wars I and II) left man with the sense that we don't know the answers.

Think of the history of the Western world like a baseball game where the umpire is determining the accuracy of the pitches, calling them as balls or strikes.

> **Premodern era:** Time of Christ until c. 1789. An umpire of a premodern baseball game would "call them as they are."
>
> **Modern era:** 1789 until c. 1989 (the fall of the Berlin Wall). An umpire of a modern baseball game would "call them as he sees them."
>
> **Postmodern era:** 1989 until today. An umpire of a postmodern game would "call them, and that is what they are."

---

26. Bodie Hodge, *The Results of Evolution*, Answers in Genesis, July 13, 2009, https://answersingenesis.org/sanctity-of-life/the-results-of-evolution.
27. See chapter 8 on Postmodernism in this volume.

Presently, we are living in a postmodern world where "all truth is valid truth" — at least that is what we are told. Nobody is wrong about anything. According to postmodernism, one man's truth is as valid as any other man's truth; even if the two "truths" are diametrically opposed to one another. Postmodernism's ultimate battle cry is, "All truth is valid truth."[28]

Twentieth-century French philosophers Jacques Derrida and Michael Foucault led the charge against modernism claiming that truth is not external but internal.

> Jacques Derrida — "I speak only one language, and it is not my own."[29]

> Michael Foucault — "Knowledge is not for knowing: knowl-edge is for cutting."[30]

What does postmodernism sound like today? "If being a Christian works for you, then it's true for you. But I don't believe Jesus Christ is God, and that is true for me. Which one of us is correct? Both of us." Logic is thrown out the window, which proves their postmodernism view is false.

While that sounds bonkers to your biblically trained mind, it makes perfect sense to godless secular humanists who exalt man to the position that only God should inhabit. The implications of this are considerable. Not only must a Christian wage war against an unbeliever's worldview, the Christian must battle against an entirely different way of thinking and perception. The Christian does not have the same starting point as the postmodern secular humanist. It is the Christian task to understand this if we are going to be effective witnesses for Jesus Christ.

Unfortunately, far too many Christians are adopting a postmodern mindset that allows for other religions to be equally as valid as Christianity. There are two deviant forms of Christianity that have embraced aspects of postmodernism:

1. Universalist Christians: while this term is an oxymoron (John 14:6), liberal denominations like the Unitarian Universalist[31]

---

28. Naturally, this position is illogical and self-refuting. The opposite claim, "all truth is not valid truth" would also be seen as true and valid to the postmodernist.

29. Jacques, Derrida, *Monolingualism of the Other: or, The Prosthesis of Origin* (Stanford, CA: Stanford University Press, 1998).

30. Michael Foucault, *The Foucault Reader* (New York: Pantheon, 1984).

31. See the chapter on Unitarianism in volume 2 of this book series.

    sect believe that ultimately everyone will go to heaven, regard-
less of their religious beliefs.

2. Anonymous Christian view: liberal theologians like Tony
   Campolo and even the Roman Catholic Church since Vati-
   can II believe that people who do not possess any knowledge
   of Jesus can still be saved by Jesus if they are striving to know
   God and be good.

Both of these views are grossly heretical. If people do not need to know Jesus
to receive salvation, then the Bible is very wrong:

- Go therefore and make disciples of all the nations, baptizing
  them in the name of the Father, and of the Son, and of the
  Holy Spirit, teaching them to observe all things that I have
  commanded you; and lo, I am with you always, even to the
  end of the age (Matthew 28:19–20).

- How then shall they call on Him in whom they have not
  believed? And how shall they believe in Him of whom they
  have not heard? And how shall they hear without a preacher?
  (Romans 10:14).

- So then faith comes from hearing, and hearing by the Word
  of God [Christ] (Romans 10:17).

Twenty-first Century: The New Atheists

In the early 21st century, a group of secular humanists emerged who became
popularly labeled as the "new atheists." The group sought to obliterate the
Christian religion (and a few others) by attacking it verbally and in written
form in an extremely abrasive manner. Some of the most notable members of
this group are the "Four Horsemen of the Non-Apocalypse": Sam Harris, the
late Christopher Hitchens, Daniel Dennet, and Professor Richard Dawkins.

    While the New Atheists were excellent at making headlines, their
scholarship was far less impressive. Their lack of philosophical prowess
was exposed quickly in debates with Christians like Frank Turek, Dinesh
D'Souza, William Lane Craig, and even Christopher Hitchens's brother
(and professing believer) Peter Hitchens. Nevertheless, books by the New
Atheists sold millions of copies to non-discerning secularists who continue
to parrot their flimsy arguments.

Thanks to their efforts, a 2012 Pew Forum on Religion and Public Life study concluded, "The number of Americans who do not identify with any religion continues to grow at a rapid pace. One-fifth of the U.S. public — and a third of adults under 30 — are religiously unaffiliated today, the highest percentages ever in Pew Research Center polling."[32]

Here is the bad news: America's non-religious, or "Nones," is growing at a faster rate than any other time in U.S. history. But just because they claim to have no formal religious affiliations does not mean that they are not religious. These individuals have a worldview that informs how they act and think about the world around them. Their religion is merely a secular religion that leads them to worship man as the supreme being, and they do so outside of the walls of a traditional church building.

Here is the good news — Secular Humanism is perhaps the easiest of all worldviews to undermine.

The Foundations of Secular Humanism

In order to engage with secular humanists, it is important that we rightly understand the foundations of their worldview. Since secular humanists claim that there is no higher power that has communicated his will, they are forced to base their worldview on one of two shaky foundations.

The first foundation is nature. According to some secular humanists, we are merely animals formed by evolutionary processes. Therefore, the most logical way to live and form our society is in a like manner. The problem with this? It is utterly impossible.

Animals live in a way that no secular humanist, if they were honest, would want to live. Animals are the epitome of selfishness; they kill each other so they can survive. Sometimes they care for their young, but some species frequently eat their young or their mates for nourishment or to promote the spread of their own genes. Certainly, no animal cares about the environment. Locusts don't worry about the damage they do to the planet when they eat everything they can in a swarm. The animal mentality is simple: Want. Take.

Ironically, evolution supports the "dog-eat-dog" lifestyle of animals, and yet no evolutionist would like to actually live in his own worldview. In other words, secular humanists believe one thing but live another (often borrowing from Christian morality).

---

32. " 'Nones' on the Rise," Pew Research Center, October 9, 2012, http://www.pewforum. org/2012/10/09/nones-on-the-rise, accessed May 24, 2016.

Furthermore, and despite Darwin's assertion, it is self-evident that man is different than every other creature. Observation reveals that we are superior in thinking, morality, creativity, wisdom, memory, emotions, and behavior. No matter how much the secular humanist may claim that he is just like every other animal, he betrays his own worldview by living in a house with heat, air conditioning, and running water.

The second secular humanist foundation is "common values." Secular humanists shun God's laws but find themselves in a conundrum that ultimately exposes the arbitrary nature and implausibility of their own worldview. Secular humanists recognize the need for morality in order to live in a safe and orderly society, so they must "create" values. Unfortunately, their worldview collides with their desire.

The secular humanist recognizes a need for laws, but their postmodern worldview demands there are no objective laws. So how does the secular humanist create laws?

1. By claiming that whatever doesn't cause someone harm is permissible.
2. By claiming that whatever promotes the greatest common good is best.
3. By getting amnesia. The secular humanist constantly creates laws that come from their God-informed conscience.

Unfortunately for the secular humanist, the argument for "common values" overlooks two glaring problems:

1. A secular humanist cannot explain where the concepts of right and wrong come from.
2. Common values cannot objectively condemn behavior. By pointing out that cannibalism is accepted in a few societies, the secular humanist is forced to admit that "common values" morality is not objectively wrong, only our temporary societal preferences.

Over the years, Secular Humanists have attempted to codify their beliefs while shunning any type of dogmatic formulations. In 1933, prominent humanists penned *A Humanist Manifesto* to lay out their beliefs. Among these are the self-existence of the universe, evolutionary processes, the rejection of supernaturally revealed morality, looking to human reason and natural cause to understand the world, and a rejection of old attitudes of worship and prayer.[33]

The second iteration came in 1973 with the addition of promoting the right to birth control, divorce, and abortion as well as speaking out against weapons of mass destruction and any notion of judgment or need for salvation. Among the most notable lines is the denial of any supernatural being:

> But we can discover no divine purpose or providence for the human species. While there is much that we do not know, humans are responsible for what we are or will become. No deity will save us; we must save ourselves.[34]

In 2003, a third and shorter version was created, still upholding the same godless, evolutionary views that make man the measure of all things, using seven guiding principles. If anyone doubts that Secular Humanism is a religion, you can direct them to this statement of faith to bolster your argument.

GOOD WITHOUT A GOD

The official logo of the American Humanist Association depicts the "happy human" who can be good without a god. Used with permission. (Source: Wikipedia)

Today, the International Humanist and Ethical Union is the umbrella group under which the secular humanist groups around the world sit. The American Humanist Association represents American humanism and publishes *The Humanist* magazine as well as maintains several websites and promoting humanism as a 501 (c)(3) charitable organization. The brights, freethinkers, skeptics, secularists, humanists, and other varieties all look to man as the standard of truth rather than God and His Word. They revere naturalistic science, rationalism, and human autonomy as their platform of beliefs. A reading of these humanist manifestos will help you see what the typical humanist affirms and allow you to have an informed conversation about why they believe what they believe.[35]

33. "Humanist Manifesto I," American Humanist Association, accessed May 24, 2016, http://americanhumanist.org/humanism/humanist_manifesto_i.
34. "Humanist Manifesto II," American Humanist Association, accessed May 24, 2016, http://americanhumanist.org/humanism/humanist_manifesto_ii.
35. Youi can read the entire manifesto here: "Humanist Manifesto III," American Humanist Association, http://americanhumanist.org/humanism/humanist_manifesto_iii.

Dismantling Secular Humanism

The Secular Humanist worldview is one of the easiest worldviews to demolish. It is as simple as a country road.

If a governing authority determines and announces that the speed limit on a country road is 35 mph, then you will receive a ticket if you exceed 35. If there are no signs posted by someone in authority demanding that your speed not surpass 35 miles per hour, then you are free to drive like the Dukes of Hazzard.

If the law does not determine which speed is right and which speed is wrong, then no speed is wrong and every speed is right. If the law does not determine what is lawful and what is not, then there are only speed preferences but no speeding laws. Without a posted sign, an old farmer on his porch can only yell at a speeding teenager, "I prefer you don't drive that fast."

That is the undoing of secular humanism. Without an objective standard of morality, the secular humanist is left in a world of preferences, but no absolute rights and wrongs. Without an objective, absolute lawgiver, the secular humanist cannot definitively claim, "That is evil."

- A secular humanist cannot state that murder is wrong, he can only claim that murder is not his preference, as it does not promote "human welfare."
- A secular humanist cannot find incest immoral, only not preferable.
- A secular humanist cannot call a rapist evil, he can only inform the rapist he does not prefer his raping behavior.
- A secular humanist cannot even claim with any certainty that Christianity is wrong because nothing can actually be wrong to a secular humanist.

If you would like to demonstrate the absurdity of the secular humanist worldview, simply grab the wallet or purse of a secular humanist and run away shouting, "You may not prefer this, but this is right for me! It promotes my happiness and helps me enjoy a good life."

If that is too bold for you, then ask the secular humanist who doesn't believe in moral absolutes if he can pay whatever he wants for a Quarter Pounder. The secular humanist adamantly denies the existence of God, yet he speaks and lives like a Christian. The secular humanist denies the existence of a moral lawgiver, but he lives and talks like a deist (at the least). Every time a secular humanist makes a moral judgment, he is admitting that God exists.

The plight and irrationality of secular humanism gets worse. The secular humanist should never do a laboratory experiment or try to solve a math equation. Without "laws of nature," lab work and math are a total waste of time, as no consistent outcome can be expected without "laws of nature." If we are accidents of time and chance, there is no rational grounding for physical laws of nature, and science and math should not exist.[36]

While it is quite easy to expose the incoherence of secular humanism, leaving a person with his crumbled worldview around his feet does not change his eternity.

How Not to Witness to a Secular Humanist

Many argue that the best way to reach this group is to dismantle their world-view by reasoning with them and exposing the inconsistency of their world-view apart from any use of the Bible. This approach cannot work because 1 Corinthians 1–3 informs us that an unregenerate man cannot and will not rightly reason his way to God (cf., 1 Corinthians 1:18–31, 2:14, 3:18–23).

> But the natural man does not receive the things of the Spirit
> of God, for they are foolishness to him; nor can he know them,
> because they are spiritually discerned (1 Corinthians 2:14).

To reason with someone who has no ability to reason about spiritual things is to try to teach algebra to a dog. An unregenerate man cannot see the folly of his worldview through reason and logic alone because he is entirely unreasonable and illogical when it comes to discerning spiritual matters. This is not to say that there is no value in showing someone the inconsistencies within their own worldview, but that cannot bring about conversion of the soul — a job only the gospel can accomplish.

Other approaches suggest we provide them with the overwhelming evidence for the Christian religion. When faced with this, they should be able to come to the conclusion that Christianity is true and bow the knee in repentance and faith. This approach attempts to bridge the vast differences between humanism and Christianity through man's intellect alone.

---

36. Jason Lisle, "Evolution: The Anti-science," Answers in Genesis, accessed May 24, 2016, https://answersingenesis.org/theory-of-evolution/evolution-the-anti-science.

This is what Rene Descartes did, and his method resulted in a colossal failure. This method is destined to fail every time it is used because it assumes some unbiblical points. It assumes that the natural man is simply ignorant of the existence of God and just needs to be shown that He exists. The natural man will meet the Christian on common ground, and if he is shown sufficient proof he will come around to a belief in God. This is simply not true.

Romans 1:18–32 instructs us that every person already knows God exists through the created world. Secular humanists *suppress* this truth, they refuse to give thanks to the real God, and they turn their praise back onto things created by God — namely nature or themselves. They aren't standing on common ground with an open mind. They stand on God's planet, knowing God created it, and shake their fist at Him.

> For the wrath of God is revealed from heaven against all ungodliness and unrighteousness of men, who suppress the truth in unrighteousness, because what may be known of God is manifest in them, for God has shown it to them. For since the creation of the world His invisible attributes are clearly seen, being understood by the things that are made, even His eternal power and Godhead, so that they are without excuse, because, although they knew God, they did not glorify Him as God, nor were thankful, but became futile in their thoughts, and their foolish hearts were darkened (Romans 1:18–21).

How to Witness to a Secular Humanist

If man's intellect, logic, or reason is not the connecting point, what is? To find this answer we need to consult our ultimate authority, the Bible. Genesis 1:27 tells us that God created man in His own image, meaning, unlike all the other creatures on earth, man has a moral aspect, absent from all other animals. Romans 2:14–15 states:

> For when Gentiles, who do not have the law, by nature do the things in the law, these, although not having the law, are a law to themselves, who show the work of the law written in their hearts, their conscience also bearing witness, and between themselves their thoughts accusing or else excusing them.

You have an ally in the conscience. A universal courtroom is hardwired into the brain of every human. Attack the conscience rather than merely the intellect (2 Corinthians 4:1–5). Use the laws of God to bring about the knowledge of sin (Romans 7:7). Let the law act as a schoolmaster to bring the secular humanist to the Cross (Galatians 3:24).

Every man bears the image of God and has the moral law of God written on his heart (Romans 2:15). This is "common ground" that acknowledges the sinfulness of each human being. The secular humanist needs to see their need for a Savior, not to be barraged with evidences and proofs. They need to see that they have broken the law that God has given them. They have sinned over and over by lying, stealing, blaspheming, and denying Jesus as Lord. They need to be confronted with the fact that they are criminals, and if they die in that state they will pay the eternal penalty for their rebellion against a perfectly holy God in a place called hell.

Then, once the humanist trembles before a just and holy law, give them the greatest news they can ever hear — "Jesus died for sinners!" (cf., Romans 5:6–8; 1 Corinthians 15:3). Jesus rose from the grave and defeated death so that secular humanists can be forgiven and reconciled to the Creator they know exists. Through the proclamation of the truth of God's Word, God the Holy Spirit will bring conviction of sin and open blinded eye and unstop deaf ears to the glorious gospel of Jesus Christ.

This is not to suggest that apologetics do not play an important role in evangelism. They do. Apologetics support the truth of the gospel, but apologetics can never save — only the proclamation of God's Word saves. "Faith comes from hearing and hearing from the word of God [Christ]" (Romans 10:17).

When, if ever, do we introduce apologetics? When the stony heart of the secular humanist heart is softened by the law and the gospel that utterly refutes their worldview, then you can reason with an unbeliever. Think of it like this:

You and a friend/spouse/sibling get into an argument and exchange angry words. After a period of separation, one of you makes a move toward reconciliation. There are two approaches one of you can make:

1. "So, are you still going to be an idiot or what?"
2. "I hate it when we fight; can we please sit down and work through our differences so we can get along?"

Which approach works and which approach leads to more fighting? The answer is obvious. If you are witnessing to an argumentative, belligerent, aggressive secular humanist, apologetics without the law will not silence their mouth. Only the law can do that:

> Now we know that whatever the law says, it says to those who are under the law, that every mouth may be stopped, and all the world may become guilty before God. Therefore by the deeds of the law no flesh will be justified in His sight, for by the law is the knowledge of sin (Romans 3:19–20).

If a secular humanist sincerely seeks to understand the answers to the questions that have plagued him, then answer him apologetically. Should the humble humanist ask questions of genuine concern (the age of the earth, why evil exists, supposed contradictions in the Bible, etc.), then bring out your apologetics to wipe away their confusion, never neglecting to share the hope of the gospel.

Be Encouraged

Witnessing to a secular humanist is not hard — you have every advantage. You have the power of a "two-edged sword" (Hebrews 4:12). Take it out and use it. You are engaging in a spiritual battle (Ephesians 6); use the spiritual weapon that God has provided you. Use the Word.

Sadly, all you have to do is leave your home to find a secular humanist. Unfortunately, they are everywhere. But fortunately, God loves secular humanists so much that He died to save them.

So find a secular humanist, and share the law and the gospel, trusting that God will work through you to bring many to worship Him around His throne.

Summary of Secular Humanist Beliefs

Doctrine	Teachings of Secular Humanism
God	Deny the existence of God or any divine being; or they acknowledge a god may exist, but he is not involved in the affairs of man. Believe nature is self-existing. Reject Jesus as Savior or God.
Authority/ Revelation	Man is the measure of all things. Naturalism, materialism, and rationalism are key concepts in determining truth. Scientific inquiry is the highest pursuit of truth.
Man	All men are the result of "unguided evolutionary change" and have no existence beyond this earthly life. The goal of man is to maximize his own pleasure without harming others. Man is a social animal.
Sin	Sin is denied as any type of moral absolute. "Ethical values" are based in "human welfare" and change with new experience and knowledge.
Salvation	There is no belief in an afterlife and no need to consider salvation since death is the end.
Creation	The universe is self-existent and its physical structure originated at the big bang. Naturalistic evolutionary processes explain all of existence.

Chapter 5

Nazism: A Variant of Secular Humanism

Jerry Bergman, PhD

The main religious influence on the Nazi movement can best be described as Secular Humanism, the belief that human reason, not Christianity or any theistic religion, is the solution to human social and psychological problems. Especially important to the Nazi variation of Secular Humanism is secular science and the use of the scientific method, both tools that the Nazis applied with abandon. Claims that they relied on the occult or some other religious influence were found to be without foundation. Their religion was totally secular and materialistic.

The Occult Claim

Determining the occult aspects of Nazism is fraught with misinformation, especially as to the putative influence of the occult on its major leaders. As indicated by the number of books, films, and articles about the topic, much fascination with the occult exists in both America and Europe, both in the early 20th century and today.

One reason for the popularity of the occult explanation is that in attempting to explain the horrific atrocities committed by Nazi leaders, some writers have made various claims about the alleged involvement of Hitler and his close associates in various occult movements and practices. This involvement, the supporters of this view claim, is important in understanding Nazi behavior. Most of these claims, though, have proven to have little solid substantiation. It is well documented that Hitler and most of the leading Nazis had disdain for the occult in all its forms, but rather relied on the science of eugenics for their conclusions.[1] Some writers have focused on the occult in an effort to divert attention from the major influence of Darwinism and eugenics on the Nazi atrocities.

The two highest-ranking Nazi officials who had occult interests were Heinrich Himmler and Rudolf Hess. Many others, including Hitler, Goebbels, and Heydrich, were openly opposed to involvement in the occult. Hitler's opposition is illustrated by an incident when Hess flew on his own to Scotland to, he claimed, obtain a peace agreement to end the war. Hitler blamed the escapade on Hess's occult interests and ordered a roundup of astrologers, fortune-tellers, and other occult prognosticators. Goebbels recorded in his diary that none of the occult prognosticators foresaw their arrests coming, which occurred in May of 1941, sarcastically remarking that this was "not a good professional sign" of their ability to predict the future. Himmler's own police forces and the SS were responsible for these arrests. However, Himmler rescued Wilhelm Wulff, one of the astrologers, from the concentration camp to work as his personal astrologer.[2]

The use of astrology was a desperate attempt toward the end of the war to respond to the critical problem that the German military position had progressively worsened, forcing Himmler to rely more and more on Wulff's astrological predictions, which obviously failed. Wulff himself concluded that the Nazis had little regard for astrology except as a propaganda tool. Likewise, the British also exploited astrology for its propaganda value by publishing phony astrological forecasts to boost British morale and dire astrological predictions for the Third Reich that were smuggled into Germany in an effort to undermine German morale.

Rejection of Christianity

One thing can be said with certainty — most of the leading Nazis rejected Christianity, and many leading Nazis sometimes aggressively opposed Christianity.[3] Another truism is that the 12 years of Nazi dictatorship occurred in the heart of Europe in one of the most educated, civilized, and industrially

---

1. Ken Anderson, *Hitler and the Occult* (Amherst, NY: Prometheus Books, 1995).
2. Wilhelm Wulff, *Zodiac and Swastika: How Astrology Guided Hitler's Germany* (New York: Coward, McCann & Geoghegan, 1973).
3. Richard Weikart, *Hitler's Ethic: The Nazi Pursuit of Evolutionary Progress* (NY: Palgrave MacMillan, 2009).

advanced countries in the world. This movement was in vivid contrast to the moral and religious values that existed in the Christian world at that time. How could this have happened?

One factor that helps to explain the Nazi movement is the fact that the main religious influence on the Nazi leaders was a form of Secular Humanism, the belief that mankind can create a better society by applying reason and science to society apart from any theological influence or revelation. A major conclusion of the first part of the 20th century was Darwinism, especially eugenics. The Nazis garnered strong support from most secularists, especially those in academia, mostly the biologists and the medical establishment.[4] The involvement of academia was so strong that a separate trial was held for them at the end of the war called the doctors' trial.

"Inferior Races"

The Nazis claimed that it is difficult to snuff out the lives of many millions of persons, but the Nazi genocide program would, in the end, produce both a superior race and society. An example is that Hitler and some of his leading Nazis compared their genocide goals to a surgeon that removes a cancer, causing much suffering to the patient, but in the end saving the patient's life. So too, what they had to do was difficult now, but would be a boon to humanity. To produce a superior society requires a superior race that must not be allowed to be polluted by breeding with "inferior races," namely Jews, Gypsies, and Slavic peoples, especially Poles and Russians.

To create this perfect people and perfect society, or at least a society as close to this ideal as possible, the "Aryan race" (mostly Germans and Scandinavians) must reproduce faster and the non-Aryans must reproduce slower, or, ideally, not at all. And the Nazis believed that Aryans breeding with the inferior races always brings down the superior race, causing race degeneration.[5] Thus, only two years after the Nazis' takeover of Germany, Nazi Germany passed laws forbidding marriage and sexual intercourse with Jews and other inferior races. These racist laws were called the Nuremberg Laws because they were formally introduced to the faithful Nazis at the annual Nazi Party Nuremberg Rally of 1936.

---

4. Heather Pringle, "Confronting Anatomy's Nazi Past," *Science* 329:274–275. July 16, 2010; Dieter Kuntz. *Deadly Medicine: Creating the Master Race* (Washington, DC: United States Holocaust Memorial Museum, 2004).

5. Regardless of the Nazi's beliefs, there is only one race, the human race, descended from Adam and Eve.

The Nuremberg Laws classified people with four Germanic grandparents as German or "kindred blood"; those persons that descended from three or four Jewish grandparents were classified as pure Jews. A person with one or two Jewish grandparents was a *Mischling*, a crossbreed or a person of "mixed blood." These laws were later extended to people described as "Gypsies, Negroes or their bastard offspring." These laws deprived Jews and other non-Aryans of German citizenship and prohibited mixed sexual relations and marriages between Germans and other non-Aryans.[6] These rules proved difficult to implement for several reasons and were consequently modified or even ignored at times, especially in cases where an esteemed German general or other Nazi military man was classified as Jewish according to these rules.[7] In these cases, certain Nazi leaders are claimed to have famously proclaimed, "I will determine who is a Jew."

Hitler realized that his end-goal of a world populated only by Aryans would take a long time to implement, and he worked slowly at first toward this goal. As time went on, he accelerated this goal, even using troops and trains to murder non-Aryans instead of using these resources to support the war effort in the Eastern front. This clearly showed his priorities — elimination of putative "inferior races" was more important than winning the war.[8]

Hitler's Main Opposition Was Christianity

Hitler and his leading Nazis realized very early that the main opposition to their eugenic goals was Christianity.[9] The Nazi Darwinists deduced that under Christianity the natural struggle for existence, which in the long run allows only the strongest and healthiest to survive, would be replaced by the mistaken Christian anti-evolutionary desire to aid the weakest and sickest. Naturally, this would interfere with the Nazi goal of the stronger race eventually replacing the weaker. Hitler reasoned the result of what he regarded as this misguided approach would be that the progeny of the strong who breed

---

6. Eric Ehrenreich, *The Nazi Ancestral Proof: Genealogy, Racial Science, and the Final Solution* (Bloomington, IN: Indiana University Press, 2007), p. 9–10.
7. Bryan Mark Rigg, *Hitler's Jewish Soldiers: The Untold Story of Nazi Racial Laws and Men of Jewish Descent in the German Military* (Lawrence, KS: University Press of Kansas, 2002), p. 82.
8. Ron Rosenbaum, *Explaining Hitler: The Search for the Origins of His Evil*, 2nd edition (Boston, MA: Da Capo Press, 2014), p. 398–399.
9. Joseph Keysor, *Hitler, The Holocaust, and the Bible* (Greenwood, WI: Athanatos Publishers, 2010).

with the weak would be inferior to the strong, resulting in the degeneration of the race.

It was for this reason that the Darwinian drive for survival would decimate what Hitler described as germs, bacilli, and weak "so-called humaneness of individuals." In other words, the inferior "races" must be destroyed to make room for the superior "races." What Hitler believed was that misplaced Christian humaneness would only interfere with this goal.[10]

Hitler also knew that the vast majority of the German population was at least nominally Christian; thus, he realized he must move slowly against the churches. One illustration of this is the belt buckles and cigarette lighters issued to Nazi soldiers with Christian phrases, such as *Gott Mit Uns* (God with Us). The first step was to endeavor to get the churches' cooperation, a goal in which Hitler was largely successful.[11] Then smaller steps

Propaganda tools like Christian slogans on belt buckles have led to confusion about the religious beliefs of the Nazi regime.
(Source: Daderot, own work, Creativecommons)

were implemented, such as the Nazi Bible (Third Reich Bible or Hitler's Bible) — a rewriting of the Bible to promote Nazi views instead of pure Christianity. Even the 10 Commandments were rewritten into Hitler's 12 commandments. Then finally, after the war was supposed to have been won by Germany, his plan was to work toward Christianity's total eradication. Like the Secular Humanists in the modern West, so too the Nazi Secular Humanists were at war against Christianity.[12]

An example is Martin Bormann, Hitler's right-hand man and the second most powerful man in the Third Reich. Although the Nazis were forced to tolerate Christianity until after the war, Bormann let his colleagues know that a clear conflict existed between Nazism and Christianity, stating that

10. Jerry Bergman, *Hitler and the Nazis Darwinian Worldview: How the Nazis Eugenic Crusade for a Superior Race Caused the Greatest Holocaust in World History* (Kitchener, Ontario, Canada: Joshua Press, 2012).
11. Erwin Lutzer, *Hitler's Cross* (Chicago, IL: Moody Press, 1995).
12. Bruce Walker, *The Swastika against the Cross* (Denver, CO: Outskirts Press, 2008).

"National Socialism and Christianity are irreconcilable."[13] Hitler supported this view openly by proclaiming that "one day we want to be in a position where only complete idiots stand in the pulpit and preach to old women."[14] To replace the old religion, the Nazis offered the German people a new religion openly based on Secular Humanism and secularized science. The fact is "the Nazis were no different here to earlier revolutionaries who tried to offer the people a brave new secular world. It was no surprise that racial supremacy played a large part in the new 'religion.' "[15]

Bormann made his absolute disdain for Christians and his open hostility and support of breaking them absolutely clear as rapidly as possible.[16] He was one of many high-level Nazis who "intended eventually to destroy Christianity" for the reason that "National Socialism and Christianity are irreconcilable," because in his mind, Nazism was based on science, and science had superseded the Christian church, which he regarded as anti-science.[17] He added that "National Socialism and Christian concepts are incompatible" because the Christian Churches were all built on

> the ignorance of men and strive to keep large portions of the people in ignorance because only in this way can the Christian Churches maintain their power. On the other hand, National Socialism is based on scientific foundations. Christianity's immutable principles, which were laid down almost two thousand years ago, have increasingly stiffened into life-alien dogmas. National Socialism, however, if it wants to fulfill its task further, must always guide itself according to the newest data of scientific researchers.[18]

Bormann added that the "Christian Churches have long been aware that exact scientific knowledge poses a threat to their existence" and instead have relied on pseudo-science such as theology. Furthermore, Bormann concluded the church takes "great pains to suppress or falsify scientific research.

13. Ibid.
14. Ibid.
15. Matthew Hughes and Chris Mann, *Inside Hitler's Germany: Life Under the Third Reich* (New York: MJF Books, 2000), p. 80.
16. Keysor, *Hitler, the Holocaust, and the Bible*, p. 180–181.
17. William Shirer, *The Rise and Fall of the Third Reich* (New York: Simon and Schuster, 1960), p. 240.
18. Bormann, 1942, reprinted in George L. Mosse, *Nazi Culture; Intellectual, Cultural, and Social Life in the Third Reich* (New York: Schocken Books, 1966) , p. 244.

Our National Socialist worldview stands on a much higher level than the concepts of Christianity." This rhetoric is very similar to that offered by Western Secular Humanists today.[19]

Support of the Scientific and Academic Establishment

As is true of Secular Humanism today, a major source of supporters of Hitler was the German scientific establishment. During the 20th century, Germany was more scientifically advanced than any other nation in the world at the time. Cambridge University historian John Cornwell wrote that during the first three decades of the last century Germany held the premier position for scientific achievement compared to all other nations of the world. German scientists were then among the most accomplished and honored in most fields, as demonstrated by the fact that they were then awarded the lion's share of Nobel prizes.[20]

One professional group that did not become active supporters of Hitler, at least after the persecution against them began, were Jewish professors. Professor Kater concluded that by expelling Jews "Germany may have lost as many as 40 percent of its medical faculty to racist fanaticism; the harm to science and education [in Germany] was unfathomable."[21]

The well-documented fact is that the leading German "scientists played a significant role in the formulation of Nazi racial ideology."[22] German academics provided the scholarship, the putative scientific support, and the "techniques that led to and justified . . . unparalleled slaughter" of Jews, Catholic Poles, and other groups that the Nazis deemed biologically inferior, a conclusion well supported by numerous scholars such as Weinreich.[23]

Both "Nazi medicine and science . . . were integral" to the Holocaust and "the monstrous crimes committed in occupied Europe out of hatred for . . . so-called inferior races and groups."[24] The fact is, "biomedical scientists played an active, even leading role in the initiation, administration, and execution

19. Michael D. LeMay, *The Suicide of American Christianity: Drinking the "Cool"-Aid of Secular Humanism* (Bloomington, IN: WestBowPress, 2012).
20. John Cornwell, *Hitler's Scientists: Science, War and the Devil's Pact* (New York: Viking, 2003).
21. Michael Kater, *Doctors Under Hitler* (Chapel Hill, NC: The University of North Carolina Press, 1989), p. 142.
22. Aaron Gillette, *Racial Theories in Fascist Italy* (New York: Routledge, 2002), p. 185.
23. Max Weinreich, *Hitler's Professors* (New Haven, CT: Yale University Press, 1999), p. 6.
24. Elie Wiesel, "Without Conscience" foreword to Vivien Spitz 2005, *Doctors from Hell.* (Boulder, CO: Sentient Publications, 2005).

of Nazi racial programs . . . scientists actively designed and administered central aspects of National Socialist [Nazi] racial policy."[25] Professor Caplan opines that a major reason for the "innocuous rise of eugenics in Weimar Germany" was because the Germans saw eugenics as

> an adjunct to efforts at public health reform. Germans eager for a rebirth after the disaster of the First World War eagerly seized on the hope extended by physicians, geneticists, psychiatrists, and anthropologists that using social Darwinism to guide public health was the vehicle for German regeneration.[26]

The level of support by doctors in Nazi Germany was so strong that "there were so many doctors and scientists involved in the Nazi crimes that to weed them all out would have left post-war Germany with hardly any at all, an intolerable situation in a nation reeling from starvation and decimation."[27] Medawar and Pyke documented the major loss of scientists that ended Germany's 50-year record of world supremacy in science.[28] The many scientists deemed to be members of an inferior race who managed to escape from Germany, mostly Jewish, turned out to be Hitler's gift to America.

Recognizing their central role in the Holocaust, "professors Astel, de Crinis, Hirt, Kranz and Dr. Gross committed suicide, and so, later, did Professors Clauberg, Heyde and Schneider, when charges [of genocide] were brought against them" by the victorious Allies.[29]

The importance of Darwin and his disciples' writings in causing the Holocaust was illustrated by Viktor Frankl, a Jewish physician who survived the horrors of Auschwitz. Dr. Frankl astutely evaluated the influence of modern scientists and academics in helping to prepare the way for the Nazi atrocities by concluding:

> The gas chambers of Auschwitz were the ultimate consequence of the theory that man is nothing but the product of

---

25. Robert Proctor, *Racial Hygiene: Medicine Under the Nazis* (London: Harvard University Press, 1998), p. 6.

26. Arthur Caplan, "Deadly Medicine: Creating the Master Race," *The Lancet*, 363:1741–1742, May 22, 2004, p. 1742.

27. Ibid.

28. Jean Medawar and David Pyke, *Hitler's Gift: The True Story of the Scientists Expelled by the Nazi Regime* (New York: Arcade Publishing, 2001).

29. Benno Müller-Hill, *Murderous Science: Elimination by Scientific Selection of Jews, Gypsies, and Others in Germany, 1933–1945* (New York: Oxford University Press, 1988).

heredity and environment — or — as the Nazis liked to say, of "Blood and Soil." I am absolutely convinced that the gas chambers of Auschwitz, Treblinka, and Maidanek were ultimately prepared not in some Ministry . . . in Berlin, but rather at the desks and in the lecture halls of nihilistic scientists and philosophers.[30]

Dr. Frankl accurately summarized the case for academia and the scientists in Germany causing, or at least making a major contribution to, the Holocaust and the horrors of World War II and the loss of 55 million lives.[31]

Dr. Josef Mengele: Darwin's Angel of Death

Dr. Josef Mengele best personifies the Secular Humanists of Nazi Germany. Today, he symbolizes the worst of the Nazi Germany criminals for his grossly barbaric and often lethal medical experiments on prisoners. He is a prime example of where the logical implications of Darwinism can lead. Mengele was awarded a PhD for a thesis completed in 1935 "proving" that a person's "race" could be determined by examining their jawbone. Mengele's chosen fields of anthropology and genetics were especially influenced by the racist theories of Nazi dogma. His strong

> interest in genetics and evolution happened to coincide with the developing concept that some human beings afflicted by disorders were unfit to reproduce, even to live. Perhaps the real catalyst in this lethal brew was that Mengele, first at Munich and later at Frankfurt, studied under the leading exponents of this "unworthy life" theory. His consummate ambition was to succeed in this fashionable new field of evolutionary research.[32]

Unfortunately, he succeeded all too well, but in ways that the world now regards as one of the worst tragedies in human history. The evolutionary ideas that Mengele so enthusiastically absorbed at his university "were precisely the ones that would propel him down the road to Auschwitz. His apprenticeship as a mass murderer formally began not on the selection

---

30. Victor Frankl, *The Doctor and the Soul; From Psychotherapy to Logotherapy*, third ed. (New York: Vintage Books, 1986), p. xxxii.
31. Richard Weikart, *Socialist Darwinism: Evolution in German Socialist Thought from Marx to Bernstein* (Lantham, MD: International Publications, 1998).
32. Gerald L Posner. and John Ware, *Mengele: The Complete Story* (McGraw-Hill Books Company, 1986), p. 9.

lines of the concentration camp but in the classrooms of the University of Munich."[33]

Jewish historian Robert Lifton, in his extensive study of Nazi doctors, wrote that he (Lifton) "began and ended" his study of Nazi crimes with Mengele.[34] Indeed, few men are as closely associated with the horrors of the Holocaust in the public's mind as Professor Josef Mengele, MD, PhD.

Conclusions

The dominant religion in the Nazi German hierarchy and government policy was that which is today called Secular Humanism. Nazism would properly be considered a variant or subset of Secular Humanism. Although differences exist and most Secular Humanists today rightly condemn some aspects of Nazi Germany, numerous major parallels exist. Some of these include both Nazism and Secular Humanism's endorsement of anti-Christian policies, and the long-term goal of both groups is to replace Christianity with a highly secular society. Another parallel is that both the Nazis and the modern Secular Humanists strongly support secular science (e.g., geological evolution, "millions of years," and astronomical evolution) and especially Darwinism (biological evolution).

Both movements are totalitarian and use the government to suppress Christianity, first in state-supported entities, such as government institutions and government-controlled schools and colleges, then later in the private sphere, such as requiring denominational schools to teach evolution or risk loss of state funds and accreditation, as occurred in Nazi Germany[35] and is now beginning to occur in the West and particularly in America.[36]

33. Lucette M. Lagnado and Sheila Cohn Dekel, *Children of the Flames: Dr. Josef and the Untold Story of the Twins of Auschwitz* (New York: William Morrow, 1991), p. 42.
34. Robert Jay Lifton, *The Nazi Doctors: Medical Killing and the Psychology of Genocide* (New York: Basic Books, 1986).
35. Anonymous, *The Persecution of the Catholic Church in the Third Reich Translated from the German* (Fort Collins, CO: McCaffrey Publishing, 2007). Originally published in 1941.
36. Jerry Bergman, *Slaughter of the Dissidents: The Shocking Truth About Killing the Careers of Darwin Doubters* (Southworth, WA: Leafcutter Press, 2012); and Jerry Bergman, *Silencing the Darwin Dissidents* (Southworth, WA: Leafcutter Press, 2016).

Chapter 6

Scientology (Thetanism/Church of Scientology/Hubbardism)

Pastor David Chakranarayan

The Church of Scientology spent millions of dollars to air a Super Bowl XLIX ad in light of ongoing controversy over a documentary centered on the religion.[1] The ad features a voiceover accompanied by quick clips of footage including a person hiking, a DNA strand, and a close-up of an eye. The announcer in the ad says:

> We live in an age of searching: to find solutions, to find ourselves, to find the truth. Now imagine an age in which the predictability of science and the wisdom of religion combined. Welcome to the age of answers.

The commercial is filled with real-life experiences and the latest innovations in science meant to portray a union capable of giving human beings the answers to life. This is not the first time the church has paid to air an ad during the pricey platform. Scientology ads aired during the Super Bowl in 2013 and 2014 as well, promoting their message to the largest audience in the United States during the most popular sporting event.

The ad followed the 2015 release of the documentary *Going Clear: Scientology and the Prison of Belief* debuting at the Sundance Film Festival. The

---

1. "Scientology Super Bowl Commercial 2015, 'Age of Answers,'" YouTube video, 0:32, Scientology, February 1, 2015, https://www.youtube.com/watch?v=jXf3pWVJOkA.

church launched a Twitter account to discredit the film, which focuses on Hollywood's connection to the faith.

The Church of Scientology has many famous followers such as actors Tom Cruise and John Travolta, actress Kirstie Allie (who claims the church helped her overcome cocaine addiction), singer Beck Hansen, TV personality Greta Van Susteren (who says she is a "strong advocate of their ethics"), and EarthLink founder Sky Dayton. Dayton notes on his website that "communication is the solvent for all things" — the words of none other than L. Ron Hubbard, the founder of the Church of Scientology.[2]

The Origin of Scientology

It is no secret that the religion was inaugurated by Hubbard in the 1950s. Hubbard was a science fiction author who struggled financially. His book *Dianetics: The Modern Science of Mental Health* eventually became a bestseller and was the foundation for his emerging religious philosophy. Dianetics began as Hubbard's explanation of the connection between the mind and the body and the urge to survive. While he promoted Dianetics as a scientific idea, its rejection by the scientific community led him to adapt his thinking into a self-help religious philosophy. He had this idea that religion, particularly a cult, is where the money was. Hubbard said:

> You don't get rich writing science fiction. If you want to get rich, you start a religion.[3]

> I'd like to start a religion. That's where the money is![4]

So start one he did — the Church of Scientology, or what might rightly be called Hubbardism (as it is purely the invention of Hubbard). It was an interesting mixture between modern secular humanism, self-help psychology, and Eastern thought with a little science fiction thrown in. And the money came in for him. Was Hubbard worried about his venture? Not at all. He openly wrote, "The only way you can control people is to lie to them.

2. Aly Weisman, Kirsten Acuna, and Ashley Lutz, "21 Famous Church of Scientology Members," *Business Insider*, November 26, 2014, http://www.businessinsider.com/famous-scientology-church-members-2014-11.
3. Sam Moskowitz, Affidavit, regarding the Eastern Science Fiction Association meeting of November 11, 1948, that Hubbard made this statement, April 14, 1993.
4. L. Ron Hubbard to Lloyd Eshbach, in 1949; quoted by Eshbach in *Over my Shoulder: Reflections on a Science Fiction Era* (Hampton Falls, NH: Donald M. Grant Publisher, 1983).

You can write that down in your book in great big letters. The only way you can control anybody is to lie to them."[5]

The religion was meant as a money maker, and it succeeded with its ups and downs throughout Scientology's early years. This chapter is a Christian response to Scientology, as Christians have seen it as a challenge to Christianity and want to have a response. Hubbard taught "that all men have inalienable rights to their own religious practices and their performance."[6]

Christians are commanded to demolish arguments and every pretension that goes against the knowledge of God (2 Corinthians 10:4–5). According to Hubbard, we have the inalienable right to practice our religion, which means responding to Hubbard's challenges of Christianity.

What Is Scientology?

Scientology is a 20th-century religion invented by a man as a variation of religious humanism that might rightly be called Hubbardism. Unlike other humanistic religions in this volume, Scientology tends to meld self-help psychology with Eastern religions and even borrows some Christian ideas.

From the Scientology website we read how they view the name scientology:

> Scientology: *Scio* (Latin) "knowing, in the fullest sense of the word," *logos* (Greek) "study of." Thus Scientology means "knowing how to know." Developed by L. Ron Hubbard, Scientology is a religion that offers a precise path leading to a complete and certain understanding of one's true spiritual nature and one's relationship to self, family, groups, Mankind, all life forms, the material universe, the spiritual universe and the Supreme Being.
>
> Scientology addresses the spirit — not the body or mind — and believes that Man is far more than a product of his environment, or his genes.
>
> Scientology comprises a body of knowledge which extends from certain fundamental truths. Prime among these are:
>
> - Man is an immortal spiritual being.
> - His experience extends well beyond a single lifetime.

5. L. Ron Hubbard, "Off the Time Track," lecture of June 1952, excerpted in *Journal of Scientology* issue 18-G, reprinted in *Technical Volumes of Dianetics & Scientology*, vol. 1, p. 418.

6. "The Creed of the Church of Scientology," February 18, 1954, http://www.scientology.org/what-is-scientology/the-scientology-creeds-and-codes/the-creed-of-the-church.html.

- His capabilities are unlimited, even if not presently realized.[7]

As with any religion, Scientology seeks to help humanity understand what is broken in the world and how to fix it. By understanding the Eight Dynamics (more on this in a moment) and how man relates to both the physical and spiritual realms, each individual can achieve a spiritual awareness that will lead to ultimate fulfillment and longevity. Focusing on improving relationships and communication, counselors offer "auditing" to help individuals recognize the things from their past that are blocking the expression of their potential.

Church of Scientology

The Church of Scientology International is the mother church under which individual Church of Scientology groups are organized. With its headquarters in Los Angeles, the 11,000 local churches or groups exist in over 160 nations.[8]

Scientology's Scriptures

It is important to understand that the Church of Scientology regards the teachings of Hubbard as authoritative. These materials are essentially the "Bible" for scientologists where Hubbard is seen as the only "prophet." In order to properly contrast the beliefs of scientology with those of Christianity, there must be an emphasis on the writings and teachings of Hubbard.

On the Church of Scientology's website under the question "Does Scientology have a Scripture?" we read:

> Yes. The written and recorded spoken words of L. Ron Hubbard on the subject of Scientology collectively constitute the scripture of the religion. He set forth the Scientology theology and technologies in tens of millions of words, including hundreds of books, scores of films and more than 3,000 recorded lectures.[9]

Although Scientology sees Hubbard's writing as authoritative, they claim to be tolerant of other religious views.

Scientology, like many of the dominant religions such as Islam, Buddhism, and Mormonism, has a single author as the revealer of truth. The

---

7. "What Is Scientology?" Scientology.org, accessed July 18, 2016, http://www.scientology.org/scientology.html.
8. "Scientology Religion Facts," Scientology.org, accessed July 18, 2016, http://www.scientologynews.org/quick-facts/scientology.html.
9. "Does Scientology have a Scripture?" Scientology.org, accessed July 18, 2016, http://www.scientology.org/faq/background-and-basic-principles/does-scientology-have-a-scripture.html.

authors of these religions have all attested to some sort of "private" interpretation or revelation, and they alone have the authority in its message.

The Bible is different to the scriptures revered by other religions. There is ultimately only one author for Scripture — God the Holy Spirit who moved through human authors to communicate His perfect and eternal message.

> Knowing this first, that no prophecy of Scripture is of any private interpretation, for prophecy never came by the will of man, but holy men of God spoke as they were moved by the Holy Spirit (2 Peter 1:20–21).

> All Scripture is given by inspiration of God, and is profitable for doctrine, for reproof, for correction, for instruction in righteousness, that the man of God may be complete, thoroughly equipped for every good work (2 Timothy 3:16–17).

Not only is the Holy Spirit the author of Scripture, He is also the one who opens our eyes to receive the truth that God gives to us.

> Revelation is God's making his truth known to humankind. Inspiration guarantees that what the Bible says is just what God would say if he were to speak directly. One other element is needed in this chain, however. For the Bible to function as if it is God speaking to us, the Bible reader needs to understand the meaning of Scriptures, and to be convinced of their divine origin and authorship. This is accomplished by an internal working of the Holy Spirit, illuminating the understanding of the hearer or reader of the Bible, bringing about comprehension of its meaning, and creating a certainty of its truth and divine origin.[10]

Wayne Grudem further illustrates this point.

> It is one thing to affirm that the Bible claims to be the words of God. It is another thing to be convinced that those claims are true. Our ultimate conviction that the words of the Bible are God's word comes only when the Holy Spirit speaks in and through the words of the Bible to our heart and gives us an inner assurance that these are the words of our Creator speaking to us. Apart from

---

10. Millard J. Erickson and L. Arnold Hustad, "The Power of God's Word: Authority," *Introducing Christian Doctrine*, 2nd ed. (Grand Rapids, MI: Baker Academic, 2001), p. 77.

the work of the Spirit of God, a person will not receive or accept the truth that the words of Scripture are in fact the words of God.[11]

There is also complete harmony in Scripture when compared to the disharmony of holy books of other world religions. Even though the Scriptures were written by men from different times, lands, professions, and ways of life, they all consistently attest to the glory of God and the revelation of the Messiah who would redeem people from their sin. Consider the argument from Living Waters:

> If just 10 people today were picked who were from the same place, born around the same time, spoke the same language, and made about the same amount of money, and were asked to write on just one controversial subject, they would have trouble agreeing with each other. But the Bible stands alone. It was written over a period of 1,600 years by more than 40 writers from all walks of life. Some were fishermen; some were politicians. Others were generals or kings, shepherds or historians. They were from three different continents, and wrote in three different languages. They wrote on hundreds of controversial subjects yet they wrote with agreement and harmony. They wrote in dungeons, in temples, on beaches, and on hillsides, during peacetime and during war. Yet their words sound like they came from the same source. So even though 10 people today couldn't write on one controversial subject and agree, God picked 40 different people to write the Bible — and it stands the test of time."[12]

View of God

The theology of Scientology will sound somewhat familiar to Christians, but the words have very different meanings. While they speak of a Supreme Being or God, it is not the Creator God of the Bible.

> In Scientology, the concept of God is expressed as the Eighth Dynamic — the urge toward existence as infinity. This is also identified as the Supreme Being. As the Eighth Dynamic, the

11. Wayne Grudem and Jeff Purswell, "The Authority and Inerrancy of the Bible." In *Bible Doctrine: Essential Teachings of the Christian Faith* (Grand Rapids, MI: Zondervan, 1999), p. 36.
12. "The Bible Stands Alone," Living Waters, accessed July 18, 2016, http://www.livingwaters.com/witnessingtool/Biblestandsalone.shtml.

Scientology concept of God rests at the very apex of universal survival. As L. Ron Hubbard wrote in *Science of Survival*:

> No culture in the history of the world, save the thoroughly depraved and expiring ones, has failed to affirm the existence of a Supreme Being. It is an empirical observation that men without a strong and lasting faith in a Supreme Being are less capable, less ethical and less valuable to themselves and society. . . . A man without an abiding faith is, by observation alone, more of a thing than a man.[13]

Based on his observation, Hubbard asserts that faith is an important element of humanity, but he does so in an arbitrary way. He points not to any real authority, but to personal experience. He also asserts that an atheist is of less benefit to society than a person who believes in a Supreme Being of some sort, but does not provide any justification for his claims. The explanation continues:

> Unlike religions with Judeo-Christian origins, the Church of Scientology has no set dogma concerning God that it imposes on its members. As with all its tenets, Scientology does not ask individuals to accept anything on faith alone. Rather, as one's level of spiritual awareness increases through participation in Scientology *auditing* and *training*, one attains his own certainty of every dynamic. Accordingly, only when the Seventh Dynamic (spiritual) is reached in its entirety will one discover and come to a full understanding of the Eighth Dynamic (infinity) and one's relationship to the Supreme Being.[14]

From the quote, it is worth noting that even though the Church of Scientology used the words "Supreme Being," it clearly rejects the teachings of the biblical God and absolutely rejects the Trinity. As will be discussed later on in this chapter, the Church of Scientology has been heavily influenced by Eastern thought, like Hinduism.

Their book (*A World Religion*) on world religions leaves little doubt that the Hindu Brahma is closely paralleled with Scientology's

13. "Does Scientology Have a Concept of God?" Scientology.org, accessed July 18, 2016, http://www.scientology.org/faq/scientology-beliefs/what-is-the-concept-of-god-in-scientology.html.
14. Ibid.

understanding of the Supreme Being. Here God is spoken in terms of Hinduism. Though Hubbard provides no strict definition of the Supreme Being, his descriptive characteristics are enough for the Christian reader to see its unbiblical nature. Hubbard rejects the Christian doctrine of the trinity. His *Phoenix Lectures* state "The Christian god is actually much better characterized in Hinduism than in any subsequent publication, including the Old Testament." Again, he said, "The god the Christians worshiped is certainly not the Hebrew god. He looks much more like the one talked about in the Veda (Hindu scripture). What he mistakenly assumed is that the Hindu "triad" is the basis for the Christian "Trinity.""[15]

The Bible rejects the idea of multiple gods and affirms that there is one true God (Deuteronomy 4:39; Isaiah 43:10; 1 Timothy 2:5). The Bible always provides a clear distinction between God and man. Unlike other religions that mix the two and even attribute deity to human beings (not to be confused with being made in the image of God), the Bible clearly shows the difference between God and man, depicting God's incommunicable attributes as something beyond man's grasp (Numbers 23:19).

In scientology, this view of a Supreme Being is more like Eastern Mysticism's transcendental heavens, though it differs in that it holds that *infinity* is that Supreme Being. So the concept of a God like the God of the Bible is absent in scientology. This means it operates like an atheistic or dualistic religion. As a religion, it is essentially a cross between atheism and Eastern Mysticism (e.g., Taoism, Hinduism, Jainism, New Age, etc.) where each individual forms their own view of the god of the Eighth Dynamic.

View of Christ

It isn't a surprise that Hubbard has no reverence for Christ and sees him as just another moral teacher among many. In his Phoenix Lectures from 1968, Hubbard believes Jesus was "the Christ legend as an implant in preclears a

---

15. Walter Martin, "Jehovah's Witnesses and the Watchtower Bible and Tract Society," in *The Kingdom of the Cults*, 3. Rev. and Expanded ed. (Minneapolis, MN: Bethany House Publishers, 1985), p. 83. "Christianity does not believe that the Trinity was incarnate in Christ and that they were 'three-in-one' as such during Christ's ministry. Christ voluntarily limited himself in His earthly body, but heaven was always open to Him and He never ceased being God, Second Person of the Trinity. Even in the Incarnation itself (Luke 1:35) the Trinity appears (see also John 14:16 and 15:26). Of course it is not possible to fathom this great revelation completely, but this we do know: There is a unity of substance, not three gods, and that unity is One in every sense, which no reasonable person can doubt after surveying the evidence."

million years ago." In these lectures, he also casts doubts upon the authenticity of Jesus as Messiah. He states:

> Now the Hebrew definition of messiah is one who brings wisdom, a teacher, in other words. Messiah is from messenger. But he is somebody with information. And Moses was such a one. And then Christ became such a one. He was a bringer of information. He never announced his sources. . . . Now here we have a great teacher in Moses. We have other messiahs, and we then arrive with Christ. And the words of Christ were a lesson in compassion, and they set a very fine example to the western world, compared to what the western world was doing at that moment.[16]

Hubbard makes a mistake here in reference to the meaning of Christ. The name "Christ" means "anointed" and is a proper name or title of "the Anointed One" to translate the Hebrew word "Messiah."[17] This is further explained by the apologists at Got Questions, when they write:

> To the surprise of some, "Christ" is not Jesus' last name (surname). "Christ" comes from the Greek word *Christos*, meaning "anointed one" or "chosen one." This is the Greek equivalent of the Hebrew word *Mashiach*, or "Messiah." "Jesus" is the Lord's human name given to Mary by the angel Gabriel (Luke 1:31). "Christ" is His title, signifying Jesus was sent from God to be a King and Deliverer (see Daniel 9:25; Isaiah 32:1). "Jesus Christ" means "Jesus the Messiah" or "Jesus the Anointed One."
>
> When someone was given a position of authority in ancient Israel, oil was poured on his head to signify his being set apart for God's service (e.g., 1 Samuel 10:1). Kings, priests, and prophets were anointed in such fashion. Anointing was a symbolic act to indicate God's choosing (e.g., 1 Samuel 24:6). Although the literal meaning of *anointed* refers to the application of oil, it can also refer to one's consecration by God, even if literal oil is not used (Hebrews 1:9).[18]

16. L. Ron Hubbard, "General Background Part III," (lecture, Phoenix, Arizona, July 19, 1954), The Phoenix Lectures, p. 19, accessed at http://www.stss.nl/stss-materials/English%20Tapes/EN_BW_CR_Phoenix_Lectures.pdf.

17. A.T. Robertson, *Word Pictures in the New Testament: Matthew* (Grand Rapids, MI: Christian Classics Ethereal Library, 1985), p. 3.

18. http://www.gotquestions.org/what-does-Christ-mean.html#ixzz3U2Tn7BTR.

Not only is Jesus Christ the true Messiah promised in the Old Testament by the prophets, He is also fully God and fully man, a view that would be rejected by the Church of Scientology.

Among the many passages that attest to the deity of Christ,[19] three passages specifically stand out. The first is:

> In the beginning was the Word, and the Word was with God, and the Word was God. He was in the beginning with God. All things were made through Him, and without Him nothing was made that was made (John 1:1–3).

In verse one, John uses "was" to illustrate Jesus' pre-existence and eternal personhood as part of the Trinity. John further illustrates that Jesus was eternal by saying that the "Word was with God and the Word was God." Christ was in an intimate fellowship with God the Father before time existed. John's thoughts flow from Christ leaving the glories of heaven and putting on humanity.

In verse 14 of John 1, John says, "And the Word became flesh and dwelt among us, and we beheld His glory, the glory as of the only begotten of the Father, full of grace and truth." John MacArthur in his commentary on John states:

> While Christ as God was uncreated and eternal . . . the word "became" emphasizes Christ's taking on humanity (cf., Heb. 1:1–3, 2:14–18). This reality is surely the most profound ever because it indicated that the infinite became finite; the Eternal was conformed to time; the invisible became visible; the supernatural One reduced Himself to the natural. In the incarnation, however, the Word did not cease to be God but became God in human flesh, i.e., undiminished deity in human form as a man (1 Tim. 3:16).[20]

In referencing the word "begotten," skeptics suggest Jesus was a created being instead of eternal. Again, MacArthur speaks to this very issue.

> The term "only begotten" is a mistranslation of the Greek word. The word does not come from the term meaning "beget"

---

19. Bodie Hodge, "God Is Triune," Answers in Genesis, February 20, 2008, https://answers-ingenesis.org/who-is-god/the-trinity/god-is-triune.

20. John MacArthur, *The MacArthur Study Bible, NKJV,* John 1:14 (Nashville, TN: Word Publishing, 1997), p. 1574.

but instead has the idea of "the only beloved one." It, therefore, has the idea of singular uniqueness, of being beloved like no other. By this word, John emphasizes the exclusive character of the relationship between the Father and the Son in the Godhead (cf., 3:16, 18; 1 John 4:9). It does not connote origin but rather unique prominence.[21]

The Apostle John had no doubt that Jesus was the eternal Son of God with full deity in His nature.

A second passage which refutes the view of the Church of Scientology in regard to the person of Christ is:

> He has delivered us from the power of darkness and con-veyed us into the kingdom of the Son of His love, in whom we have redemption through His blood, the forgiveness of sins. He is the image of the invisible God, the firstborn over all creation. For by Him all things were created that are in heaven and that are on earth, visible and invisible, whether thrones or dominions or principalities or powers. All things were created through Him and for Him. And He is before all things, and in Him all things consist (Colossians 1:13–17).

In this passage, Paul's letter to the church at Colossae highlights the fact that not only is Christ eternal but He is also Creator of all things. According to Greek scholar A.T. Robertson, "all things were created" has the idea of "stand created" or "remain created." Robertson adds, "The permanence of the universe rests, then, on Christ far more than on gravity. It is a Christ-centric universe."[22]

A third passage that clearly refutes Scientology's view of Jesus is found in the opening of Hebrews.

> God, who at various times and in various ways spoke in time past to the fathers by the prophets, has in these last days spoken to us by His Son, whom He has appointed heir of all things, through whom also He made the worlds; who being the brightness of His glory and the express image of His person, and

---

21. Ibid.
22. David Guzik Commentary, http://www.studylight.org/commentaries/guz/view.cgi?-book=col&chapter=001.

> upholding all things by the word of His power, when He had by Himself purged our sins, sat down at the right hand of the Majesty on high having become so much better than the angels, as He has by inheritance obtained a more excellent name than they (Hebrews 1:1–4).

God spoke through the prophets by means of parables, poetry, historical narrative, psalms, proverbs, and prophetic confrontation. God chose to pronounce His message through a time span of 1,600 years and 40 different authors reflecting different locations, times, cultures, and situations. What was the message? Even in the midst of the failure of Israel, God would redeem them through a perfect Savior.

From the very Fall of mankind, God had promised to send a Savior to restore the corruption that entered through sin. God would preserve the seed promised in Genesis 3:15: "And I will put enmity between you and the woman, and between your seed and her Seed; He shall bruise your head, and you shall bruise His heel." Throughout the narrative of the Old Testament, God promises once and for all through His Son's death and Resurrection to deliver His people from sin.

The Jews understood the "last days" to mean the time when the Messiah would come. Although it can be said that Jesus had a message from the Father, even truer is the statement that HE IS the message from the Father. The author of Hebrews also says Jesus has been "appointed heir of all things," showing that Jesus has been given the authority to save and to judge.

The author of Hebrews further states that Jesus Christ is the Creator of all things. He made the worlds. This statement is damaging to the view that Christ is not fully God since Scripture states He is "the brightness of His glory and express image of His person." The Greek denotes the radiance shining forth from a source of light. The idea of exact likeness as made by a stamp is reference to Christ being of the same substance as God. Both of these expressions point clearly to the deity of Christ.

When we read that Jesus is "upholding all things by the word of His power," we see that He is maintaining or actively sustaining the universe. We see this manifested in the ministry of Jesus Christ, as He is able to heal, forgive sins, cast out demons, and calm nature's fury.

Another comparison is that of Christ vs. all other religious leaders. All of them, including L. Ron Hubbard, Joseph Smith, Charles Taze Russell,

Muhammad, Buddha, and so forth, died. Jesus did too, but unlike these others, Jesus resurrected. Jesus, being God, had the power to lay down His life and take it up again.

> Therefore My Father loves Me, because I lay down My life that I may take it again. No one takes it from Me, but I lay it down of Myself. I have power to lay it down, and I have power to take it again. This command I have received from My Father (John 10:17–18).

Only Christ has power over death as proved by His Resurrection. Only He is in a position to inform us what happens after death.

For all of Hubbard's teachings that through one's self they can solve their problems, everyone still dies — even Scientologists. Those in scientology, even its founder, could not conquer death. Ron Hubbard finally died of a stroke. According to the Bible, death is a punishment for sin as far back as the first sin with Adam and Eve in Genesis 3 (see also Genesis 2:17 and Romans 5:12).

View of Man and Sin

Scientologists believe that "man is basically good."

> A fundamental tenet of Scientology is that Man is basically good; that he is seeking to survive; and that his survival depends upon himself and upon his fellows and his attainment of brotherhood with the universe. However, his experiences in the physical universe, through many lifetimes, have led him into evil, where he has committed harmful acts or sins, causing him to become *aberrated* (departing from rational thought or behavior). These harmful acts further reduce Man's awareness and innate goodness as a spiritual being.
>
> Through Scientology, one confronts these acts, erases the ignorance and aberration which surrounds them, and comes to know and experience truth again.
>
> All religions seek truth. Freedom of the spirit is only to be found on the road to truth. Sin is composed, according to Scientology, of lies and hidden actions and is therefore untruth.[23]

---

23. "Does Scientology Believe Man Is Sinful?" Scientology.org, accessed August 23, 2016, http://www.scientology.org/faq/scientology-beliefs/does-scientology-believe-man-is-sinful.html.

This raises the question of who defines "good." By what standard is something good or bad in this religion? Scientologists consider things that are constructive and enhance survival as good and things that are destructive as evil. The exact outworking of one's actions in light of the Eight Dynamics is determined by the individual, so there is no absolute view of right and wrong.

Scientology, like Eastern religions, also holds to a form of reincarnation, though it is slightly different. They have a varied understanding of the soul (which they call a *thetan*) that endured countless lifetimes. They also hold to a multitude of races of mankind.

Each person is seen as a spirit or thetan (what makes you, you) that has a mind (the expression of thoughts and emotions) and inhabits a body (a temporary physical expression of the self). Hubbard described the odd account of the origin of man in *Scientology: A History of Man*. The book has gone through several editions, but the history of the thetans and their origin on alien planets and subsequent evolution is described in detail. The engrams of trauma in these previous lives hinders survivability and must be removed through auditing. These ideas are solely the product of Hubbard's imagination and have no foundation in any facts. As such, his teaching has been ridiculed by many people.

Contrary to the teachings of the Church of Scientology, Scripture paints a completely different narrative regarding man's origin and nature and the nature of sin. Man was made by a perfect God in original perfection (Genesis 1:26–27, 31; Deuteronomy 32:4). We were made in the image of the God who created us. Man's original perfection was marred when Adam and Eve, the first two people and our direct ancestors, sinned (Genesis 3). Thus, we die and are in need of a Savior. Morally, mentally, and socially, man fell into sin and had to deal with a Curse upon the ground for man's sake (Genesis 3:17). This culminates in death (Romans 5:12), which results in the second death (e.g., Revelation 21:8) if we do not get saved from death and sin through Jesus Christ, who is the ultimate substitutionary atonement for our sin (1 Peter 2:24).

In Genesis 3, man goes from a having a perfect relationship with God and a perfect nature, to a relationship which is severed and a nature that is sinful. Genesis 3 describes this historical account of the Fall. Genesis 3:6–7 states:

> So when the woman saw that the tree was good for food,
> that it was pleasant to the eyes, and a tree desirable to make one

wise, she took of its fruit and ate. She also gave to her husband with her, and he ate. Then the eyes of both of them were opened, and they knew that they were naked; and they sewed fig leaves together and made themselves coverings.

In Romans chapter 5, Paul ties this account into his reasoning on the topic of justification by faith through grace, which is found in Christ.

Therefore, just as through one man sin entered the world, and death through sin, and thus death spread to all men, because all sinned — (For until the law sin was in the world, but sin is not imputed when there is no law. Nevertheless death reigned from Adam to Moses, even over those who had not sinned according to the likeness of the transgression of Adam, who is a type of Him who was to come. But the free gift is not like the offense. For if by the one man's offense many died, much more the grace of God and the gift by the grace of the one Man, Jesus Christ, abounded to many. And the gift is not like that which came through the one who sinned. For the judgment which came from one offense resulted in condemnation, but the free gift which came from many offenses resulted in justification. For if by the one man's offense death reigned through the one, much more those who receive abundance of grace and of the gift of righteousness will reign in life through the One, Jesus Christ.) Therefore, as through one man's offense judgment came to all men, resulting in condemnation, even so through one Man's righteous act the free gift came to all men, resulting in justification of life. For as by one man's disobedience many were made sinners, so also by one Man's obedience many will be made righteous. Moreover the law entered that the offense might abound. But where sin abounded, grace abounded much more, so that as sin reigned in death, even so grace might reign through righteousness to eternal life through Jesus Christ our Lord (Romans 5:12–21).

In a moment, Adam's disposition changed from absolute worship of God to whatever his sinful heart desired. Throughout the Old and New Testament, the authors of Scripture paint a narrative not only of the sinful condition of man but his actions, which show that he has a fallen nature. In the Old

Testament, God implemented a sacrificial system to remind us of the need for a sacrifice and to point to the One who would redeem mankind from their sin. In the New Testament, we have the ultimate and final sacrifice in the crucifixion of Christ on a Cross to show the need for God's wrath to be satisfied. Christ, being God, was an acceptable sacrifice to endure the punishment from God the Father. Jesus said:

> Therefore My Father loves Me, because I lay down My life that I may take it again. No one takes it from Me, but I lay it down of Myself. I have power to lay it down, and I have power to take it again. This command I have received from My Father (John 10:17–18).

Upon death, God will judge man based on His Word. Those who die without receiving Christ, who covers all our sin with His death, burial, and Resurrection, will die an eternal death in hell (described as eternal fire). There will be no rest from this punishment.

God reveals to us, out of His infinite knowledge, that man's heart is deceitful and wicked (Genesis 8:21; Jeremiah 17:9). Since sin came into the world, our hearts and minds have been corrupted and can only be set free through the Lord Jesus Christ.

Yet the entirety of Scientology comes from the mind and actions of one man, L. Ron Hubbard. The authority of God has been replaced with authority in a man. Thus, in the simplest sense, it is merely a variant form of humanism. But man is not the authority. Even God writes of man:

> Stop regarding man in whose nostrils is breath, for of what account is he? (Isaiah 2:22; ESV).

View of Creation

As with any religion, Scientology has an explanation for the origin of the physical universe.

> In Scientology, this view flows from the theory of theta (the life force, or spirit) creating MEST (a coined word for the physical universe, Matter, Energy, Space and Time). In fact, it could be said that the creation of the universe is an inseparable part of that theory. The origins of theta and the creation of the

physical universe set forth in Scientology are described in *The Factors*, written by L. Ron Hubbard in 1953.[24]

Theta is expressed as an impersonal force or spirit manifested in individual thetans which created the physical universe. The thetan is the impersonal creator or god for Scientology (hence the name Thetanism is sometimes used).

Scientologists recognize that a god exists and this god is mentioned twice in the Creed of the Church of Scientology.[25] *The Thetan* (original) is claimed to be the creator, but this is not to be confused with the *Operating Thetan*, which is a level a person can supposedly achieve and then is able to study the advanced materials of Hubbard. Even so, it is tricky to understand as *one is a thetan* and doesn't *have a thetan*, somewhat equivalent to the soul or spirit of a man. Even so, when "God" is mentioned in scientology, it is referring to one moving "toward existence as infinity."[26]

The age of the earth is not addressed by the Church of Scientology specifically on their website. However, tidbits on their website reveal they believe in an older earth, as opposed to the biblical age of the earth. For example, they write, "Based upon the tradition of fifty thousand years of thinking men, Scientology beliefs are built upon the fundamental truths of life."[27]

Couple this with their view of nearly infinite past lives for individuals makes for a very old existence. So the concept of millions and billions of years is a common factor among scientologists. Hubbard dates some of the early events in his creation myth to a quadrillion years in the past. So naturally you can see the friction between Scientology's origins account and six-day creation as described in the Bible. Curiously, Hubbard once wrote, "Dianetics is a science; as such, it has no opinion about religion, for sciences are based on natural laws, not on opinions."[28]

---

24. "What Are Scientology Religious Beliefs about the Creation of the Universe?" Scientology.org, accessed July 18, 2016, http://www.scientology.org/faq/scientology-beliefs/what-are-scientology-religious-beliefs-about-creation-of-the-universe.html.

25. "The Creed of the Church of Scientology," Scientology.org, accessed July 18, 2016, http://www.scientology.org/what-is-scientology/the-scientology-creeds-and-codes/the-creed-of-the-church.html.

26. "Does Scientology Have a Concept of God?" Scientology.org, accessed July 18, 2016, http://www.scientology.org/faq/scientology-beliefs/what-is-the-concept-of-god-in-scientology.html.

27. "Scientology Beliefs," Scientology.org, accessed July 18, 2016, http://www.scientology.org/faq/scientology-beliefs.html.

28. L. Ron Hubbard, "Dianetic Auditor's Bulletin," October issue, 1950; see also https://sites.google.com/site/scientologyschafftunsab/scientology-is-not-a-religion.

In the Internet age, however, many details have come to light about Hubbard's origins account. It is clearly in conflict with the Bible's account of material creation.

Salvation

There are many erroneous beliefs built into the Church of Scientology regarding salvation. The first issue is the problem of reincarnation.

> The orthodox Hindu idea of reincarnation teaches that when you die, your soul does not go to heaven or hell. Instead, you soul goes into some other kind of body here on earth. This body can be an insect, fish, animal or human body. [29]

Scientologists prefer to use rebirth instead of reincarnation to describe their means for salvation even though reincarnation is included in many of their teachings. Hubbard believed that the way to salvation is to end the continuous cycle of birth and rebirth — a distinctive of Eastern religions. The key to the Scientologist view of salvation is the idea of "auditing."

> One of the fundamental principles of scientology is that a person can improve his condition only if he is allowed to find his own truth about himself. In Scientology, this is accomplished through auditing. Auditing is the process of asking specifically worded questions designed to help and find areas of distress. This is done with an auditor, meaning one who listens. An auditor does not offer solutions or advice. They are trained to listen and help you locate experiences that need to be addressed. But some experiences are so deeply buried in the mind, they are not easily recalled. The auditor helps you pinpoint these with an aid of an "e" meter. If you think of something that has upset or has stress connected to it, this shows up on the meter. Your attention can now be directed to that thought. Through auditing, one is able to look at their own existence and discover the past experiences that are holding them back against their will. [30]

29. Kirk Cameron and Ray Comfort, "Reincarnation," in *The School of Biblical Evangelism: 101 Lessons: How to Share Your Faith Simply, Effectively, Biblically — the Way Jesus Did*, 1st ed. Vol. 1 (Alachua, FL: Bridge-Logos Publishers, 2004), p. 511.
30. "What Is Auditing?" Scientology.org, accessed July 18, 2016, http://www.scientology.org/faq/scientology-and-dianetics-auditing/what-is-auditing.html.

Many cultists realized a system that teaches that people can be reincarnated into animal or insect would not appeal to Western thought, so they decided to change the concept.

> Using the Western concepts of evolution and progress, they taught that through reincarnation the soul always progressively evolves up the scale of being. Thus you cannot regress back into an insect or animal body once you have reached the human stage. You are either born into another human body or you are absorbed back into oneness depending on your karma.[31]

Karma is the teaching that your present condition in life is a result of your actions from a previous life. Scripture answers the question of reincarnation with two important passages found in the Gospel of John. In chapter 3 which is a familiar account among people who are saved and not saved, a Pharisee named Nicodemus wants to have a meeting with Jesus. He was an influential and educated leader within the Sanhedrin. He comes to Jesus by night and begins the conversation with a startling statement for a Pharisee. He says "Rabbi, we know that You are a teacher come from God; for no one can do these signs that You do unless God is with him" (John 3:2).

Multiple times throughout His ministry, Jesus's miracles were discredited by the Pharisees and even attributed as works of Satan. Following this confession, Jesus makes an even greater statement that confused Nicodemus. Jesus said, "Most assuredly, I say to you, unless one is born again, he cannot see the kingdom of God" (John 3:3).

Nicodemus's confusion is further illustrated when he asked Jesus in verse 4, "How can a man be born when he is old? Can he enter a second time into his mother's womb and be born?" Jesus was not referring to a physical rebirth or reincarnation. He was referring to a state of regeneration. The word translated "born again" literally means "to be born from above." Jesus was telling this man Nicodemus that the only way to achieve salvation was to have a change of heart through faith in God.

Another passage in Scripture which attacks the idea of reincarnation and karma is found in John chapter 9 where Jesus heals a blind man. As Jesus passes the blind man with his disciples, they ask, "Rabbi, who sinned, this man or his parents, that he was born blind?" (v. 1).

---

31. Cameron and Comfort, "Reincarnation," in *The School of Biblical Evangelism*, p. 511.

In our Western culture, we might think this to be an insensitive remark, however, it was a common belief among the Jews that physical illness resulted from sin. It isn't necessarily the same definition of karma, but the implications are the same. Jesus corrected His disciples and told them this was done for God's glory. The reason this man was blind was not due to a personal sin, his parent's sin, or any other circumstance. He was experiencing the results of the Fall, and Jesus was going to give the man a new nature beginning with the healing of his blindness.

The second problem in their view of salvation is the idea that there can be multiple lifetimes to correct past behavior. In the process of auditing, a person is mentored as they look into their "history" to discern the conditions that have put them in their current condition. This is done through the help of an E-meter that pinpoints areas that are causing stress in their lives. As an individual processes these events and frees themselves of the influence of implants or engrams experienced in previous lives or the present life, they advance toward a state of "clear." To be clear is to free one's "reactive mind" from any engrams that cause anxiety as well as toxins that impair the physical body.

Much like a pastor would guide a Christian in dealing with indwelling sin, an auditor assists in understanding the principles of affinity, reality, and communication (represented as an ARC triangle) to become clear. At this point, the secretive teachings of the Operative Thetan levels are studied to advance in understanding toward the Eighth Dynamic and spiritual freedom. There is no concept of a future state of heaven or hell, only spiritual freedom in a future that is built through right actions and thinking in the present.

The Bible paints a completely different narrative in regard to past lifetimes. There is only mention of the current life and the brevity of it. Hebrews 9:27 states, "And as it is appointed for men to die once, but after this the judgment." Another passage is found in Luke chapter 16 in the Parable of the Rich Man and Lazarus. While the rich man enjoyed the luxuries of life, Lazarus was confined to the gate where he would beg for the crumbs that fell from the rich man's table.

On the other side of eternity, the rich man makes a request of Abraham. The dialogue goes:

> "I beg you therefore, father, that you would send him to my father's house, for I have five brothers, that he may testify

to them, lest they also come to this place of torment." Abraham said to him, "They have Moses and the prophets; let them hear them." And he said, "No, father Abraham; but if one goes to them from the dead, they will repent." But he said to him, "If they do not hear Moses and the prophets, neither will they be persuaded though one rise from the dead" (Luke 16:27–31).

Both these passages affirm the teaching of the Bible that an individual only has their current life to trust through saving faith in Christ. Our existence today is the only one we have known and the only one we will ever live. After our time on earth has been completed, we will stand in judgment before God to give an account of our lives.

Conclusion

The Church of Scientology shares the same worldview as all the false religions of the world. They share in a rejection of the deity of Christ and His offer of salvation as being the only acceptable way of being right with God, the Bible as the only word of God, eternal judgment, and absolute authority. Scientologists have a pluralistic belief system that allows the individual to embrace whatever lifestyle they choose in order to make them happy.

> The goal of Scientology is making the individual capable of living a better life in his own estimation and with his fellows. Although such a statement may seem simple and modest, the ramifications are immense and embody the dream of every religion; the attainment of complete and total rehabilitation of man's native, but long obscured abilities — abilities that place him at knowing cause over matter, energy, space, time, form, thought and life. Yet even well before one reaches this state, the changes Scientology can bring are profound. Personal relationships can be repaired or revitalized. Personal goals can be realized and happiness restored. Where once there were doubts and inhibitions, there can be certainty and self-confidence. Where once there had been unhappiness and confusion, there can be joy and clarity.[32]

In contrast, the Bible tells us that "There is a way that seems right to a man, but its end is the way of death" (Proverbs 14:12), and it calls us to repentance

---

32. "The Bridge to a Better Life," In *What Is Scientology?: The Comprehensive Reference on the World's Fastest Growing Religion* (Los Angeles, CA: Bridge Publications, 1992). p. 173.

and faith in Christ, because we have sinned against a holy God. We are called to be reconciled to God (2 Corinthians 5:20–21) through Christ, and we would call all those in the Church of Scientology to do the same.

Summary of Scientology Beliefs[33]

Doctrine	Teachings of Scientology
God	Deny the existence of the biblical God, but believe in a supreme force (*theta*) and manifestations of that force (*thetan*). The Eighth Dynamic is the infinite expression of the Supreme Being. Reject Jesus as anything more than a good man.
Authority/ Revelation	The writings of L. Ron Hubbard, especially *Dianetics*.
Man	All men are basically good. The self is a *thetan* that has a mind and inhabits a body.
Sin	Sin is anything that leads to destruction or inhibits survivability, though each person must determine what constitutes wrong actions and truth for themselves.
Salvation	The *thetan* is impaired by engrams that must be removed through auditing so that the *thetan* can achieve spiritual freedom. There is no concept of heaven or hell.
Creation	MEST (matter, energy, space, and time) was created by *thetans* at some point beyond a quadrillion years ago. The creation of worlds and humans reads like a science fiction novel including alien life and other planets.

---

33. *One God, Many Gods: Bible Studies for Postmodern Times,* Student/Stdy Gd edition (St. Louis, MO: Concordia Publishing House, 1998), p. 72.

Chapter 7

Communism: The Failed Social Experiment

Dr. Nathan Merrill

"The control of the production of wealth is the control of
human life itself." — Hilaire Belloc

As the summer heat faded in 1989, the Autumn Revolutions of Eastern
Europe began to dismantle the most bellicose socialist economic system
to ever govern human civilization. Citizens of the West sat transfixed to their
television sets, watching as the Germans tore down the Berlin Wall, the
Romanians executed their dictator, and the USSR dissolved into the Com-
monwealth of Independent States. Undoubtedly, communism had failed.

The Communist utopia — a society of equality and abundance for all
— was never realized; there was only equal poverty for the greater populace and lavish abundance for the privileged few. The chief reason for this
epic failure was communism's mistaken worldview. The errors are plentiful
because the philosophical foundation of communism misunderstands the
true nature of man and denies the supernatural. Thus, it is manifestly different than Christianity, which acknowledges the existence of the supernatural
and correctly apprehends man's true nature. The philosophical incongru-
ences are numerous, the chief of which will be highlighted in this chapter.

Communism, as many Enlightenment Age ideas are, is rooted in philosophical humanism. Humanism teaches that man alone can bring about an earthly utopia if only inequality and oppression are abolished. Karl Marx, the father of communism, springboards off this notion to formulate the Communist ideology. He postulated an economic system that would abolish the economic divide between the rich and poor. Society would be forced to distribute its wealth equally among all its people. Each person would receive a comparable wage (no matter the amount of time or effort labored), possess a similar size house, receive equal amounts of food, have equivalent amenities, etc. Thus, there would be no more rich or poor.

The above pictures, taken by this author in his hometown of Sibiu, Romania, depict the vast economic inequality between the greater populace (left picture) and the Communist leaders (right picture). The building on the left is where a normal citizen of the Communist state would reside. The state gave each family a small, unremarkable apartment within one of these buildings. All the apartments were basically the same size and layout. The large house on the right is where a Communist official in Sibiu, Romania, once lived. The Communist leaders generally lived in lavish residences in this most desirable part of the city.

Communism's Metaphysical Incongruencies with Christianity

Atheism Is Incongruent with Christianity

Though Marx posited an egalitarian society, he ended up creating an economic system of equal poverty for the greater populace and lavish abundance for the privileged few. This is because he presupposed the erroneous worldview of philosophical materialism. Materialism posits that matter is the elemental building block of reality; all processes and phenomenon, including feelings, thought, will, etc., are ultimately the result of material agencies.[1] There is no Supreme Being or supernatural realm. Man was created via natural processes without purpose or cause. He lives life merely to fulfill his animal instincts and to ensure the propagation of his species. Atheism and evolution are core doctrines of communism. Thus, communism is fundamentally contrary to Christianity. Christians believe man was created by a personal God for God's glory (Isaiah 43:7). Moreover, no Christian can deny God and the supernatural realm since these are the central tenets of its teaching.

Furthermore, the atheism of communism is not of the benign philosophical type (traditional atheism). It is a militant atheism which persecutes religious followers (new atheism). Communist regimes have razed thousands of religious buildings, banned religious gatherings, censored religious books, and imprisoned and murdered religious leaders. Vladimir Lenin, the father of Soviet communism, wrote:

> We must combat religion — that is the ABC of *all* materialism, and consequently of Marxism. But Marxism is not a materialism which has stopped at the ABC. Marxism goes further. It says: We must *know how* to combat religion, and in order to do so we must explain the source of faith and religion among the masses *in a materialist way*. The combating of religion cannot be confined to abstract ideological preaching, and it must not be reduced to such preaching. It must be linked up with the concrete practice of the class movement, which aims at eliminating the social roots of religion. . . . And so: "Down with religion and long live atheism; the dissemination of atheist views is our chief task!"[2]

Communism, being a totalitarian system, views religion as a threat (all religious views but its own, of course). It calls for undivided allegiance from its subjects. There can be no higher cause above the Communist state. Since religions teach a higher allegiance than the state, in the Communist mind

1. Merriam-Webster Online, s.v. "Materialism," accessed December 1, 2014, http://www.merriam-webster.com/dictionary/materialism.
2. Vladimir Ilyich Lenin, *The Attitude of the Workers' Party to Religion*, Marxist Internet Archive, accessed December 1, 2014, http://www.marxists.org/archive/lenin/works/1909/may/13.htm.

they usurp the authority of the state. Religion for the Communist is like an "opiate" by which the bourgeois control the masses in order to protect their interest.[3] Thus, religion is seen as an obstacle, since the Communist regime alone must wield the power to ensure a classless society. The regime must either utterly control a said religion or eradicate it.

Communism Denies the Depravity of Man

Communism, deeply entrenched in humanistic ideology, envisages a future earthly utopia. Unlike Christianity, however, this utopian dream is not brought about by a sovereign God. It is the result of a group of exceptionally benevolent, elite human planners who supposedly can foresee and understand all the contingencies involved in effectuating a human paradise.[4] This conception of an earthly utopia occasioned by munificent social organizers (the governing body of a Communist State) presupposes the essential goodness of the human nature. It is a direct contrast to Christianity, which teaches the depravity of mankind due to sin. For example, the prophet Micah states:

> The faithful man has perished from the earth, and there is no one upright among men. They all lie in wait for blood; every man hunts his brother with a net. That they may successfully do evil with both hands — the prince asks for gifts, the judge seeks a bribe, and the great man utters his evil desire; so they scheme together. The best of them is like a brier; the most upright is sharper than a thorn hedge; the day of your watchman and your punishment comes; now shall be their perplexity (Micah 7:2–4).[5]

Thus, men — as magnanimous as they may be — will only usher in pain and destruction; God alone can establish an earthly utopia as will be done with a new heavens and a new earth (Revelation 21:1) where the Curse has been removed (Genesis 3:14–17; Revelation 22:3).

Communism Denies the Dignity of Man

Though communism holds a few human beings to be exceptional (elite), in reality it denies the dignity of man. It believes man is nothing more than a

---

3. Karl Marx, *Deutsch-Französische Jahrbücher*, Marxist Internet Archive, accessed December 1, 2014, https://www.marxists.org/archive/marx/works/1843/critique-hpr/intro.htm.
4. Ronald H. Nash, *Poverty and Wealth: Why Socialism Doesn't Work* (Richardson, TX.: Probe Books, 1986), p. 68.
5. Consider also Genesis 8:21 and Jeremiah 17:9.

This highlights how *un-utopian* communism really is. The common citizens wait in long lines to get food for their families (left picture). Moreover, they are only rationed a certain amount of food per week (right picture: a ration card from communist-era Romania). Food outside the common staples, luxury items, and other non-essential commodities are scarce and hardly ever obtained by the common citizen. (Wikimedia; left photo: Scott Edelman)

cog in a machine to be shaped and discarded at will by the "all-wise" state.[6] Men have value only as part of the collective whole. They have no individual liberty, will, or self-worth. Once they cease to be useful for the collective cause they are no longer of any consequence. Thus, according to the arbitrary assertions of Communist theory, there is no room for individuality or personal liberty. Trofimov stated:

> In the Soviet Union under the guidance of the Ail-Union Communist Party (B.) a new type of man is being shaped — the man of Communist society. . . . He is not an individualist sealing himself up in a shell, and therefore he is not poor and empty spiritually. Soviet man has been fused with the whole people and the socialist fatherland.[7]

Hence, a man's value is merged with that of the Communist state. There is consequently marked ambivalence toward improving the individual's standard of living. For example, within Communist countries, housing is often

6. Mary E. Ali, *Through Three Miracles . . . Pulling the Sail in Together and Resetting "the Middle of the Political Spectrum"* (Pittsburgh, PA: Dorrance Publishing, 2013), p. 24.
7. P. Trofimov. "Edinstvo Eticheskikh i Estetichekikh Printzipov v Sovietskom Iskusstvo" ("Unity of Ethical and Aesthetical Principles in Soviet Art"), Bolshevik, No, 18 (1950): 34. as cited from Dr. Kazys Gečys, "Communist Ethics," accessed December 1, 2014, http://www.lituanus.org/1955/55_23_03Gecys.htm.

inadequate, personal possessions are few, and wages are meager. No solution is ever proposed to alleviate the long food lines. There is no such thing as workplace safety. Roads, houses, and other structures are ill designed. Services are poorly rendered and goods are shoddily manufactured. There is little time for entertainment or self-advancement because it is spent in advancing the goals of the Communist Party.[8]

This materialist view of man is utterly amiss. The Bible proclaims that human life is sacred. Individuals are not mere pawns of the state to be used and disposed of at will. They have individual freedom and self-worth. Their value is not determined by their role within the collective. Human dignity is innate; it is endowed by God because man is created in His image with special care and forethought (Genesis 1:26–27). The Psalmist writes:

> For You formed my inward parts; You covered me in my mother's womb. I will praise You, for I am fearfully and wonderfully made; marvelous are Your works, and that my soul knows very well. My frame was not hidden from You, when I was made in secret, and skillfully wrought in the lowest parts of the earth. Your eyes saw my substance, being yet unformed. And in Your book they all were written, the days fashioned for me, when as yet there were none of them (Psalm. 139:13–16).

Thus, humans, created in God's image, are to be served by the state, not exploited by it as a means to achieve the Communist utopia.

Communism Denies Private Property

In connection with denying the dignity of man, communism dictates the abolition of private property. Marx regarded private property as a great detriment to society. He believed it spawned the pernicious class struggle between the rich and poor; hence, the first mandate of his *Communist Manifesto* stipulated the "abolition of property in land and application of all rents of land to public purposes."[9] The second mandate appealed to the "abolition of all right of inheritance."[10] Acknowledgement of private property and

8. David A. Law, *Russian Civilization* (New York: MSS Information Corp., 1975), p. 138–39.
9. Karl Marx and Friedrich Engels, *Communist Manifesto*, Marxist Internet Archive, accessed December 2, 2014, https://www.marxists.org/archive/marx/works/1848/communist-manifesto/ch02.htm.
10. Ibid.

inheritance laws are fundamental to the biblical ethic. The confiscation of private property by state is a blatant violation of the biblical commands "you shall not steal" and "you shall not covet" (Exodus 20:15, 17). Moreover, these commandments become irrelevant without private ownership.

Christianity's influence on a society safeguards private ownership for institutions, families, and individuals. It reinforces inheritance practices (Numbers 27:6–11), exhorts individuals toward good stewardship, and makes laws against robbery and covetousness. By abolishing private property, communism disavows God's pre-ordained structure for society. Furthermore, the domination of all property rights in a sense equates the state with God himself; God is the sovereign owner of creation not the state. If God endows men with property and safeguards it via biblical mandates (Deuteronomy 27:17; Ezekiel 46:18), who is the state to alter this divine establishment?

Communism's Ethical Incongruencies with Christianity

In addition to being at variance with Christianity regarding the views of God and the nature of man, communism also differs ethically. It adheres to a form of ethical relativism which teaches right and wrong are determined by that which is most expedient for effecting a classless society. Lenin explained to a group of Communist youth:

> Communist morality is based on the struggle for the consolidation and completion of communism. . . . [It] is what serves to destroy the old exploiting society and to unite all the working people around the proletariat, which is building up a new, communist society.[11]

For the Communist, the end justifies the means. Hence, it is admissible in their ethical system to use any means necessary to achieve the Communist utopia. For example, Lenin declared one "must be ready to employ trickery, deceit, law-breaking, withholding and concealing truth. There are no morals in politics. There is only expedience.[12]

For the Communist there are no moral absolutes. Something is deemed moral by the party leaders if it promotes their agenda and immoral if it hinders it.

---

11. Vladimir Lenin, *On Culture and Cultural Revolution* (Rockville, MD: Wildside Press LLC, 2008), p. 137,139.
12. Oleg Kalugin, *Spymaster* (New York: Basic Books, 2009), p. 297.

Christianity, on the other hand, espouses moral absolutism. It argues that right and wrong are such because God's immutable nature makes them so. "All His precepts are sure. They stand fast forever and ever" (Psalm 111:7–8). Thus, Christianity posits an ethical system of moral absolutes. It does not propound that the end justifies the means as does communism. Something is moral or immoral because God makes it such (if it agrees or disagrees with His nature and subsequent law), not because it is expedient for a given cause.

The disparity between the ethical systems of communism and Christianity is clearly illustrated in how they operate practically within society. For example, communism promotes hatred, violence, coercion, and deceit to accomplish its objective, i.e., the classless society.[13] One must trample on the enemy to attain victory and retain power. Lenin explains, "The revolutionary dictatorship of the proletariat is rule won, and maintained, by the use of violence, by the proletariat, against the bourgeoisie, rule that is unrestricted by any laws."[14] Furthermore, "if you exploiters attempt to offer resistance to our proletarian revolution we shall ruthlessly suppress you; we shall deprive you of all rights; more than that, we shall not give you any bread, for in our proletarian republic the exploiters will have no rights, they will be deprived of fire and water, for we are socialists in real earnest, and not in the Scheidemann or Kautsky fashion."[15] So communism declares one must be hard and merciless when it comes to defeating the enemy.

Christianity, on the contrary, advocates love for one's enemies. Christ urges his followers to love their enemies and "do good to those who hate you" (Luke 6:27). Likewise, the Apostle Paul exhorts the Church to "be kind to one another, tenderhearted, forgiving one another, even as God in Christ forgave you (Ephesians 4:32). Thus, the ethical difference between communism and Christianity is clear. Communism adopts whatever means necessary — even hatred and ruthless violence — to achieve its ends. Christianity charges its followers to abide by peace and love no matter the cause.

Despite the obvious ethical differences between Christianity and communism, some still regard Christianity and communism to be morally

---

13. Nash, *Poverty and Wealth: Why Socialism Doesn't Work*, p. 64.
14. Vladimir Lenin, "How Kautsky Turned Marx Into a Common Liberal," in *The Proletarian Revolution and the Renegade Kautsky*, Marxist Internet Archive, accessed December 2, 2014, http://www.marxists.org/archive/lenin/works/1918/prrk/.
15. Ibid., "The Soviet Constitution."

compatible since they both share a concern for humanity. Communism claims to be the defender of the common man, but it has demonstrated otherwise. Indeed, there has been no other political system in human history that has caused so much human misery and bloodshed.[16] It has been variously estimated that communism killed between 85–100 million people in less than 70 years.[17] This unheard of level of violence and destruction is the result of an ethical system that maintains the end justifies the means — even the harshest means.

Some Christians have tried to draw support for communism by referencing the actions of early Christians in Jerusalem. Acts 2:44–45 states:

> Now all who believed were together, and had all things in common, and sold their possessions and goods, and divided them among all, as anyone had need.

However, this was a specific group in a specific area that knew what was going to happen to Jerusalem. It was foretold by Christ of the desolation that would come upon Jerusalem (e.g., Luke 21:20, 13:34–35). So it was wise to sell what you had there and not make life in that place. Better to sell and give to those in need. Plus, the words of the Apostle Peter to Ananias in Acts 5:4 make plain that this was not a mandatory giving up of goods and possessions, but was wholly voluntary by the individual. Soon after this, these Christians were scattered to various places anyway (Acts 8:1–4). So any use of this specified example in the Book of Acts to support a communistic mindset is not the best.

Conclusion

Communism is not merely an economic ideology — it is a religion in that it explains the cause, purpose, and nature of life. The economic aspects are merely an outworking of its inherent humanistic and atheistic religious system. Furthermore, it espouses an ethical code, gives hope for a better tomorrow, and seeks undivided devotion – all hallmarks of religion. Unlike Christianity, which values the individual and preaches love, communism is a somber religion. It devalues the individual and preaches envy, hatred, and violence to achieve its utopian polity. This earthly utopia, how-

---

16. Stéphane Courtois, *The Black Book of Communism: Crimes, Terror, Repression* (Cambridge, MA: Harvard University Press, 1999), p. ix–xx.
17. Ibid., p. 15.

ever, was never realized. In fact, most Communist regimes were toppled in fewer than 90 years after they began because they failed to offer the paradise they had promised. Instead, they brought about equal poverty for the greater populace and lavish abundance for a privileged few. These negative economic results stem from communism's erroneous worldview. Any economic system that begins with a mistaken worldview cannot work practically; it will have severe economic and social ramifications, as seen among Communist states.

Given that communism is a religious system that still affects a major portion of the world's population (China, Cuba, Laos, North Korea, and Vietnam), Christians should be very much interested in understanding it. Its negative implications for God's Kingdom are far-reaching since it denies God and endeavors to completely dominate or eradicate any semblance of organized religion. Christian believers must stand strong against such a system that promotes militant atheism, debases human value, and attempts to spread its materialistic message through hatred and violence.

Summary of Communist Beliefs

Doctrine	Teachings of Communism
God	Deny the existence of God. Man is viewed as the supreme being.
Authority/ Revelation	The writings of various authors are appealed to, though there is no notion of an authoritative revelation.
Man	Man is the measure of all things and basically good. Certain individuals are intended to lead others, but there is broad equality in humanity.
Sin	Sin is not a prominent concept. Right and wrong are relative to achieving the goals of the state.
Salvation	The goal of humanity is to achieve equality. There is no view to an afterlife.
Creation	Most would accept evolutionary views.

Chapter 8

Postmodernism

Dr. Carl J. Broggi

I was recently on an airplane where, as God sometimes allows to happen, the subject of conversation was turned to religion and Christianity. The individual sitting next to me was a pediatrician from Thailand. I asked her if she had ever considered the claims of Jesus Christ upon her life. She said, "There is no need to. All religions are the same." Then she added, "No one can claim that one religion is right and another is wrong. One can believe whatever they wish, as long as they believe it sincerely. All religions can be equally true."

This woman, who said she was a Buddhist, told me that this is what Buddhists have believed for centuries. Her statement reminded me of what God said through King Solomon, "There is nothing new under the sun" (Ecclesiastes 1:9). This perspective, that all religions are equally valid, and that no one can dogmatically say that one religion is more valid than another is known as postmodernism.

This notion, held by this Buddhist physician, is a perspective that many Americans are now embracing.

Postmodernism Defined

Defining postmodernism is a difficult process because the term can be used differently between disciplines. To understand the word, it might be helpful to break it down. Historically, when the word "modern" was used in a philosophical context, it referred to a worldview based on the principles of the Enlightenment. During the 17th and 18th centuries, the Enlightenment emphasized the autonomy of the individual, trust in the power of reason, conviction that human reason is objective, and that truth can be discovered by the rational human mind.[1] The "modern" mindset valued scientific investigation, absolute truth, logical and pragmatic organizations, and orderly surroundings.[2]

For this reason, long-established institutions that were deeply rooted in society, such as religion and the government, began to be questioned. There was a new and greater emphasis being placed on man's ability to reform the world by his own thought, by scientific investigation, and skepticism.[3]

Someone might think, "Well, what is wrong with that? What is wrong with using your mind and using science to determine what is true or false?" Please understand, the Bible is not necessarily against using our minds — it simply recognizes the limitations of human thought. God Himself says, " 'Come now, and let us reason together,' says the Lord" (Isaiah 1:18). Even the casual reader of Scripture is familiar with the Apostle Paul, who when evangelizing the lost people would "reason from the Scriptures" the truths concerning Jesus Christ (Acts 17:2, 18:4). God made us with minds, and in the commandment that the Lord referred to as the greatest of all the commandments He said, "You shall love the Lord your God with all your heart, with all your soul, and with all your mind" (Matthew 22:37).

But the Scriptures also recognize that man's mind is fallen. God tells us that the natural man, someone without a spiritual birth, "does not receive the things of the Spirit of God, for they are foolishness to him; nor can he know them, because they are spiritually discerned" (1 Corinthians 2:14). For the same reason, the Apostle Paul can declare, "For the wisdom of this world is foolishness with God" (1 Corinthians 3:19). This is why he warns us, "Beware lest anyone cheat you through philosophy and empty deceit, according to the tradition of men, according to the basic principles of the world, and not according to Christ" (Colossians 2:8). For this reason, once we receive Christ as our Savior and are given this second birth, making us

---

1. B.E. Benson, "Postmodernism" in *Evangelical Dictionary of Theology*, 2nd ed., ed. Walter A. Elwell (Grand Rapids, MI: Baker Academic, 2001), p. 939–945.
2. Gene Edward Veith Jr., *Postmodern Times: A Christian Guide to Contemporary Thought and Culture* (Wheaton, IL: Crossway Books, 1994), p. 42.
3. Skepticism is the process of applying reason and critical thinking to determine whether something is valid.

new persons inside (2 Corinthians 5:17), we are then commanded to let God renew our minds through the truth of the Scripture (Romans 12:2). The fact that the Bible tells us that our minds need to be renewed informs us that from God's perspective they have been damaged by the Fall.

Logically, most people can understand the principle that all human reasoning is not necessarily good. Hitler, with his reason, believed the Jewish people were an inferior race that needed to be exterminated. While the modernism of the Enlightenment period encouraged people to look to reason and science as a source of authority, if man's mind is fallen, if man's mind is by nature rebellious as the Bible reveals (Romans 3:10–12), then the conclusions one may make from science and reason alone will at times be faulty.

Scientific thought has been proven wrong on many occasions. There was a time when a minority of the scientific world was convinced that the world was flat. In hindsight, it did not matter how confidently they believed and taught it to be true — their position was still erroneous.[4] Modern secular science goes against a literal six-day creation despite the fact that God clearly reveals this truth.[5]

So when we speak of *modernism*, we are referring to a term that goes back to the time of the Enlightenment where man's autonomous reason was considered sovereign.[6] The problem with modernism is that it did not recognize that man's reason must be brought under the authority of the Bible (hence, "autonomous"). Therefore, it is not surprising that today in theological realms, *liberalism*, the rejection of the Bible as the absolute and final authority, was once called *modernism*.[7]

Bible-believing evangelicals recognize that "reason" is valuable in that God has called us to use our minds, but only to the degree that our reasoning process is tempered and corrected by Scripture. Those of us who

---

4. Had they only tempered their scientific discoveries with passages like Isaiah 40:21–22 or Proverbs 8:27 they would have discovered that their scientific conclusions were false.

5. For a good discussion on this subject, see "Could God Have Created Everything in Six Days?" in *The New Answers Book* by Ken Ham, ed., (Green Forest, AR: 2006), p. 88–112; available online at https://answersingenesis.org/days-of-creation/could-god-really-have-created-everything-in-six-days.

6. Essentially, man's ideas were elevated to a position of absolute authority by leaving the Bible out of it. It is a religion where man is basically seen as replacing God.

7. Today, when a person departs from theological orthodoxy, we say that he has embraced theological *liberalism*. Interestingly, during the late 19th century and during the first part of the 20th century, theologians who departed from orthodoxy were said to be guilty of *modernism*. Such people, who have departed from biblical Christianity, place their mind and reason above the authority of the Bible.

believe the Bible to be the inspired, inerrant, and infallible word of God tend to emphasize biblical thinking formed by logical analysis, propositional teaching, and a historical, grammatical interpretation of Bible passages. We embrace theological and moral absolutes as forming the foundation of our faith and typically are unafraid to challenge those who do not fully agree with this perspective.

But while we would say that we have "reasoned our way" to this position, we would also acknowledge that this "reasoning" was not done without the help of the Holy Spirit and apart from submitting any conclusions we have made to the litmus test of Scripture. In other words, we would say that our use of logic and reasoning are still predicated on the ultimate authority of God and His Word. Christ promised this helping ministry of the Spirit when He said, "when He, the Spirit of truth, has come, He will guide you into all truth" (John 16:13). The Holy Spirit's guidance never contradicts the Bible that He Himself inspired. For this reason, the Apostle Paul taught us that conclusions about life and God and the world around us that are contrary to what has been revealed in Scripture, are to be rejected.[8] So while the "modern" of the Enlightenment used his mind, he rejected the Bible as the final authority to guide it. In his thinking, if reason and science dictated the Bible was wrong, then it must be wrong.

So what do we mean by postmodernism and how can we best define the term? As previously stated, it can be difficult to define, and definitions tend to differ. Earl Creps posits that due to its absence of a central, unifying trait, trying to define postmodernism "is like nailing Jell-O to the wall."[9] Students of the social sciences generally agree that there was a shift that began to take place in the way some people began to think as early as the 1930s.[10] While some date postmodernism to the 1930s, most agree that it did not begin to take root in the West and in the United States until the 1960s and '70s, progressing ever since.[11]

Initially, the term "postmodernism" gained popularity as a term used to describe a period of architecture and art that began to emerge especially

---

8. Romans 16:17; 2 Thessalonians 3:14; 1 Timothy 6:3–4.
9. Earl G. Creps, "Moving Target: Reframing Discipleship for Postmoderns," *Enrichment Journal* (Winter 2008), p. 68.
10. For a discussion of this shift, see Stanley J. Grenz, *A Primer on Postmodernism* (Grand Rapids, MI: Eerdmans, 1996), p. 173; see also Heath White, *Postmodernism 101: A First Course for the Curious Christian* (Grand Rapids, MI: Brazos Press, 2006), p. 12–17.
11. Grenz, *A Primer on Postmodernism*, p. 17.

during the 1970s. Many found modern art and modern architecture to be confusing because it seemed to lack a sense of order, rhyme, and reason. By previous standards, this new expression of art and architecture seemed so bizarre, because it had abandoned traditional standards for new ideals. These new "postmodern" standards rejected a previous way of thinking about life based on objectivity and reason.

The Fruit of Modernism

Modernism began to deviate into a man-centered reality (as opposed to a God-centered reality) — postmodernism is like the fruit of this man-centered religion. It goes one more step toward relativism. Where modernism still retained certain aspects of Christianity (such as absolute conclusions) within its parameters, postmodernism tried doing away with any semblance of Christian influence (no absolutes).

Postmodern art and architecture had abandoned all previously held conventional standards in these fields. As a young man, when I would see this new kind of art and architecture, my first reaction was typically, "This is rather odd and confusing to me." The rejection of absolutes — the rejection of being able to rationally define something as acceptable or unacceptable — eventually made its way into the realm of theology.

Postmodernism is a philosophy that says absolute truth, solid concrete values, does not necessarily even exist. Since the postmodernist thinks there is no real valid way to measure truth from error, acceptable from unacceptable, or right from wrong, all beliefs and perspectives are determined to be equally valid. This way of thinking is determinatively different from the way Americans and Westerners have thought in the past.

A survey of research and literature indicates that Americans under the age of 35 have been raised in a postmodern culture, with many having distinctly different values and preferences from those in earlier generations.[12] At least with the person raised under the influence of the Enlightenment, through the process of reason, someone would come to a conclusion. Sometimes, a proper conclusion is made, consistent with the revelation of God in Scripture, and sometimes an improper conclusion. But in either case, a decision could be formulated, such that they would view an opposing decision as wrong.

---

12. Webber, *The Younger Evangelicals*, p. 41.

However, in postmodernism it is argued that each decision is equally valid and that two opposing decisions can be true at the same time.[13] Postmodernism embraces relativism to the highest degree. Relativism is the idea that truth and moral values are not absolute but are relative to the persons or groups holding them.

This means that what is right for one person, may not necessarily be right for another person. Therefore, truth is not really knowable. Truth is whatever you want it to be. This makes truth a moving target. What one believes, what one considers to be right or wrong, is really left up to the individual. I'm OK; you're OK — the famous saying brought to us by the psychology of the past — is an effective mantra for this viewpoint. What is true for you might not be true for me. In the thinking of the postmodernist, no one is really wrong except for those who hold to absolute truth.

But how can they know that those who hold to absolute truth are wrong? Are they absolutely sure? In their religion, there were no absolutes! By their own admission, they can't know the most basic tenant of their own religion! So they are inconsistent and self-refuting at their most basic level. More on this as we progress in the chapter.

The Postmodernist and Tolerance

Today, those who embrace postmodernism ridicule Christianity as intolerant, egotistical, and arrogant because of its exclusive claims about God and morality. To say that there is only one way to heaven through Christ[14] is viewed as intolerant by those who say there are many paths to heaven. To embrace a strict moral code that condemns sexual perversion like homosexuality[15] or sexual permissiveness like fornication or adultery[16] is to be restrictive, judgmental, and lacking sophistication. The battle cry of the postmodernist is a redefined understanding of "tolerance."

Because truth cannot absolutely be known in their religion, the highest virtue for the postmodern man is tolerance, but not as the word has traditionally been defined. In the past, when Americans used the term *tolerance*, it was understood to mean that everyone has a right to have their viewpoint respected. When brought over into the realm of religious belief, while you

13. For a discussion of this shift in thought, see Heath White, *Postmodernism 101: A First Course for the Curious Christian*, p. 12–17.
14. Clearly, this is what the Bible teaches in John 14:6 and Acts 4:12.
15. Leviticus 18:22; Romans 1:26–27; 1 Corinthians 6:9–11; 1 Timothy 1:8–10.
16. Exodus 20:14; Matthew 5:27–28; Galatians 5:19; Ephesians 5:3–5; Hebrews 13:4.

might reject someone else's religious system because you believed it was inferior or just wrong, you still allowed that person the right to embrace it. You might even try to convince someone that you believe his or her beliefs are wrong.

Nonetheless, because everyone is made in the image of God and are free moral agents, you recognize they are free to choose and tolerate their choice. However, in the postmodern worldview, no one has a right to say that his or her viewpoint is better or more correct than someone else's point of view (except, of course, the postmodernist who is imposing this belief system on others). "Tolerance" for the postmodernist is to be extended only to those who embrace a relativistic worldview. In practice, since postmodernism cannot possibly coexist with a worldview that embraces absolute truth, they are intolerant of those who do not agree, particularly Christians.

Postmodernism and Biblical Christianity

Some postmodernists argue that evangelical Christians are intolerant, not allowing other positions to exist or express their viewpoints. However, to paint this picture of Bible-believing Christians is utterly incorrect. It is true that in the history of the Church there have been some people who, in the name of Christianity, have not allowed other people to embrace or present their viewpoints. In this sense, such people were truly intolerant. However, what they did was contrary to Scripture, for the Lord Jesus said, "If anyone wills to do His will, he shall know concerning the doctrine, whether it is from God or whether I speak on My own authority" (John 7:17). This statement that Christ made to those who questioned His authority, implies the opportunity to decide for oneself.

Christianity is not intolerant in prohibiting people from considering certain options. But when postmodernists accuse Christians of intolerance, what they really mean is that because Bible-believers insist their point of view concerning moral absolutes and salvation in Jesus Christ is correct and other views are aberrant, they should be defined as intolerant.

Such a premise is a misunderstanding of tolerance. There is a difference between tolerating a belief and refuting it (showing it to be false). It is impossible for two viewpoints that contradict each other to be true.[17] They might

---

17. In formal logic this is known as the law of non-contradiction. Those who adopt a postmodern mindset seem to be comfortable with logical inconsistencies like this one in many situations.

both be false, but they cannot both be true at the same time. Therefore, just because Christ claimed to be the only way to God, and because Christianity maintains that there are moral absolutes, does not by definition make it intolerant. It would only be intolerant if it did not allow people the freedom to believe their viewpoints. The postmodern man will allow the conservative evangelical to have a place at the table for discussion, only if we quit being conservative evangelicals. We must leave Jesus' unique claims, the truth of the gospel, fiat creationism,[18] moral absolutes, and the offensive teaching about hell on the back shelf. In postmodern thought, exclusive claims about Jesus and His work violate the highest virtue of their understanding of tolerance, and so they want it silenced in the name of their religion.

Unfortunately, this kind of thinking has now permeated the university campuses of America. To spend any time in a meaningful discussion with the average college student, you soon discover that this way of thinking is widespread. Today, if you are a Christian on the secular university campus, you will be told that since all viewpoints are equally valid, what is right for one group is not necessarily right or true for someone else.

The most obvious example is sexual morality. For instance, Christianity teaches that marriage is defined as a union between a man and a woman because God created a man and woman. Therefore, by definition homosexual behavior and homosexual "marriage" are wrong.[19] Yet, more and more young Americans who have adopted a postmodern point of view would simply claim that such a position might pertain to some Christians but not to other Christians or to those who do not follow Christ at all. Following this line of thought to its logical conclusion, postmodernism argues that the Judeo-Christian ethic on which our legal system was built, is now antiquated.

---

18. Millard Erickson, in his systematic theology, defines succinctly the biblical revelation of fiat creationism: "This is the idea that God, by a direct act, brought into being virtually instantaneously everything that is. Note two features of this view. One is the brevity of time involved, and hence the relative recency of what occurred at creation. . . . Another tenet of this view is the idea of direct divine working. God produced the world and everything in it, not by the use of any indirect means or biological mechanisms, but by direct action and contact." Millard Erickson, *Christian Theology* (Grand Rapids, MI: Baker, 1988), p. 479–480).

19. Many who support same-sex "marriage" and the promotion of privileges for gays argue that, since Jesus never mentioned homosexuality, He did not consider it to be sinful. While it is technically true that Jesus did not specifically address homosexuality by name in the Gospel accounts, He did speak clearly about sexuality in general as well as in the rest of His Word (the Bible). In Matthew 19:4–6 Jesus clearly referred to Adam and Eve and affirmed God's intended design for marriage and sexuality.

So it is now maintained that while homosexual behavior was once considered against the law, such statutes should now be considered archaic. There was a time in the recent past when most Americans viewed homosexual behavior as objectionable. Prior to 1962, sodomy was a felony in every state, punished by a lengthy term of imprisonment and/or hard labor.[20]

There was a time in our nation's history when the average American would have had little or no problem with the Apostle Paul's instruction to Timothy, his young pastor protégé in the faith:

> But we know that the law is good if one uses it lawfully, knowing this: that the law is not made for a righteous person, but for the lawless and insubordinate, for the ungodly and for sinners, for the unholy and profane, for murderers of fathers and murderers of mothers, for manslayers, for fornicators, for sodomites, for kidnappers, for liars, for perjurers, and if there is any other thing that is contrary to sound doctrine (1 Timothy 1:8–10).

In this passage, God plainly tells us that laws are to be written not to condone this kind of behavior, but to curb it. However, if you believe that truth is different for each person, which is at the core of postmodernism, then you will favor laws endorsing any lifestyle the individual chooses. History demonstrates, and God's Word illustrates, that when the sin of homosexuality is left unchecked it will destroy a nation and invite the judgment of God.[21] Of course, to group the lifestyle of a homosexual with those that God refers to as *lawless, insubordinate,* and *ungodly* — not to mention *murderers of fathers and murderers of mothers* along with *kidnappers* and *perjurers* — informs us that this behavior is not some genetic predisposition. Just as murder and perjuring oneself and kidnapping are moral issues, so also is homosexuality.

Yet, while God's Word, the Bible, tells us that laws are to be written against this deviant lifestyle, our politicians, who have been influenced by

---

20. For a helpful discussion tracing the sodomy laws in American history and the changes that began to slowly take place after 1962, see Margot Canaday, "We Colonials: Sodomy Laws in America," *The Nation,* September 3, 2008.

21. If someone really wants to understand how God feels about the sin of sodomy, all they need to do is read Genesis chapter 19. In fact, in the New Testament, God uses the judgment that fell on Sodom and Gomorrah as an example of the wrath that is yet to come on all those who reject God's Son (Jude 7).

postmodern thought, have written laws in favor of this behavior. The same could be said concerning the use and legalization of marijuana. Postmodernism is turning our legal system upside-down because those things that were once consider wrong are now being embraced as right.

What Is Truth?

Hours before the Crucifixion, Jesus Christ stood before Pontius Pilate, and, as the Apostle John records:

> Pilate therefore said to Him, "Are You a king then?" Jesus answered, "You say rightly that I am a king. For this cause I was born, and for this cause I have come into the world, that I should bear witness to the truth. Everyone who is of the truth hears My voice." Pilate said to Him, "What is truth?" (John 18:37–38).

Pilate's question, "What is truth?" has reverberated down through history. It does not appear that Pilate was looking to find the answer, but rather was giving a cynical, indifferent, even irritated reply to Jesus' answer. However, if the postmodern man were to attempt to answer Pilate, he would say, "Truth cannot be known definitively — truth is whatever you want it to be." A profound response to that would be, "How do you know that is true?"

Of course, in our day Americans have differing definitions of what truth is, due to the influence of postmodernism. Some would say that truth is whatever works. The pragmatic outlook embraces that the end justifies the means. It is easy to see the fallacy in this line of thinking. For instance, one could lie and accomplish the objective they were trying to achieve, all the while doing it in a non-truthful way. Still, some would argue that truth is whatever makes you feel good. Many people build their morality on this proposition. However, if truth is what makes you feel good, what will the postmodernist do with bad news that one knows to be true but makes them feel miserable?

Others would say that truth is what the majority of people think is correct. Upon a recent visit to Yad Vashem, the World Center for Holocaust Research in Jerusalem, I was reminded again that during World War II, the Jewish people fled to nation after nation, including America, only to be turned away, with no place to go but back to Germany. While the majority of nations embraced the thought that the Jewish people should not be received into their countries, clearly the majority was wrong in light of the peril they faced in Germany.

Postmodernism has also influenced the popular position that truth is based on sincerity. It is reasoned that if you sincerely embrace something, then it is must be true. But if you pause and think about it, you will meet people who are sincere, but sincerely wrong. A person who is wrong but sincere is deceived, like so many in the various cults. Being sincere is not enough. The physician I sat next to in the airplane said, "It doesn't matter what you believe, just as long as you are sincere." Of course, people who say this typically only apply this fallacy to morality and religion, but never to other disciplines like mathematics or mechanics or medicine. They fragment their worldview and apply it selectively. I reminded her of some absolutes that she embraced as a practicing physician, for which she had no argument. I mean, who would want to have a heart surgeon operate on you who thought it did not matter what you believed concerning the function of the heart? Who would want a pediatrician to unnecessarily prescribe an antibiotic for a virus like the common cold because he believed it was best for your child? It doesn't matter how much one sincerely believes a wrong key will fit a door, if it is not the right key, the lock cannot be opened. Truth is unaffected by sincerity.

Someone who picks up a bottle of poison and sincerely believes it is lemonade will still suffer the unfortunate effects of the poison. My pediatrician friend from the airplane was quick to concur that believing two plus two equals five is foolish no matter how sincere you may be. Yet, what is sometimes so mind-boggling is that when it comes to spiritual truth, the one area of life that determines your spiritual destiny, people will tell you to believe whatever you want. Encounters like this serve as constant reminders that we are in a spiritual battle.[22] Indeed, the question Pilate asked, "What is truth?" is a very important question.

I find it interesting that in the Bible the Hebrew word for truth is *emeth* — which literally can be translated as "firmness," "constancy," or as "duration."[23] In other words, truth is something that is rock-solid and unchanging. In the original language of the New Testament, the Greek word for "truth" is *aletheia*, which literally means to "un-hide" or "to reveal."[24] It

---

22. 2 Corinthians 4:4; Ephesians 6:12.
23. See *Strong's Exhaustive Concordance*, #571.
24. For a good discussion on truth versus postmodernism, see B.E. Benson, "Postmodernism," in *Evangelical Dictionary of Theology*, 2nd ed., edited by Walter A. Elwell (Grand Rapids, MI: Baker Academic, 2001), p. 939–945.

conveys the thought that truth is always there, always open and available for all to see, with nothing being hidden or obscured. Unlike the postmodernist's perception of truth, God reveals that truth is knowable and available for those who desire to find it.[25] Truth is simply telling it like it is because truth reflects a sure and certain reality that exists and is unchanging. Truth comes from an unchanging God who is the truth.

Evangelizing the Postmodernist

Remember, the focus of this entire volume is to better equip those reading to become sharper tools in God's hand for breaking through the inaccuracies of our day. We are studying subjects like postmodernism not simply for our own edification, but rather to "always be ready to give a defense to everyone who asks you a reason for the hope that is in you, with meekness and fear" (1 Peter 3:15).

So precisely how do we reach so many who have embraced this faulty way of thinking? Please note, I did not say a *new* way of thinking because there really is nothing new under the sun. This premise of questioning truth, questioning what God has clearly revealed, is as old as the Garden of Eden.[26]

Critical to evangelizing those who are lost is to ask, "Why have they believed postmodernism to begin with?" Generally speaking, people embrace any error about God and morality for one of two reasons. Some are just deceived. In describing Satan, the Lord Jesus said to the Pharisees, "He was a murderer from the beginning, and does not stand in the truth, because there is no truth in him. When he speaks a lie, he speaks from his own resources, for he is a liar and the father of it" (John 8:44). Satan has a very simple strategy, and it is to sow error, that people might believe falsehood and be captured in his kingdom forever.[27] Some embrace postmodernism because the first to reach them deceived them. Unfortunately, many of God's people are not as faithful and fervent in sharing the truth as some of Satan's ambassadors are in sharing error.[28] It is essential that as Christians we are obedient to the Great Commission that Christ has entrusted to us. In many ways, postmodernism appears to be winning because so many of God's people are silent when it comes to sharing the gospel. So first, some

---

25. John 7:17.
26. Genesis 3:1–7.
27. Matthew 13:37–42.
28. 2 Corinthians 11:13–15.

embrace postmodernism simply because they are deceived. And the reason they are deceived is because they have not yet heard the truth, only error.

Still, others embrace postmodernism because they have heard the truth, but have chosen to reject the truth, driven by a love for sin.[29] Somebody once said that first God made us in His image, and ever since we have been returning the compliment. As rebellious sinners, we often like to make God in our image — as we would like Him to be.

The truth of Christianity is inevitably a threat to some because it immediately raises the question, "Who is going to be God in your life?" Some are not willing to admit that as created people, we have no right to tell the Creator what to do.[30] Some are not willing to admit that our hearts are desperately wicked and rebellious and that we need salvation from the coming wrath of God.[31] However, if one believes that they should be the center of their own universe, until their attitude changes, they are not going to consider the claims that Jesus Christ makes on their lives. Some people embrace postmodernism because while they may have understood something about God's truth, they have chosen to suppress that truth, and as a result have believed a lie.[32]

The Apostle Paul describes in the first chapter of Romans the downward progression into error that people take when they refuse to believe what they know in their hearts and minds to be true.[33] In their rebellion against God they "exchanged the truth of God for a lie" and as a result God gives them over, "to uncleanness" and, "to vile passions" and, ultimately, "to a debased mind."[34] The Greek word for "debased" is translated in many languages of the world as, "an upside-down mind."[35] In other words, a rejection of the truth results in a warping of values, where one calls right to be wrong and wrong to be right.[36] People who sin against God's revelation because of a love for sin can easily embrace falsehood.

For such people, postmodernism becomes a coping mechanism of sorts by which they can justify their guilty consciences and their sinful behavior.

---

29. John 3:19–20.
30. Romans 9:19–20.
31. Jeremiah 17:9; Luke 19:12–27.
32. John 12:35–41; 2 Thessalonians 2:8–12.
33. Romans 1:18–32.
34. Romans 1:24, 26, 28.
35. All of the Slavic languages of the world translate the Greek word in this fashion.
36. Our generation would do well to heed the warning of Isaiah 5:20.

The old adage is true, that a man's theology is often dictated by his morality. Nonetheless, people who are caught up in postmodernism are by no means unreachable for Christ. Even after the Apostle Paul gives a long list of sins describing depraved idolatrous behavior, he can still say of such people, "who, knowing the righteous judgment of God, that those who practice such things are deserving of death, not only do the same but also approve of those who practice them" (Romans 1:32).

When evangelizing the lost, we must never forget that even when a person is in the depths of sinful choices, they still do not totally lose the reality that they are sinning against clear absolute standards set by a holy God. We should be encouraged by the fact that even those who have been deceived into thinking that truth is not knowable and morality is relative still know better.

When describing those individuals who had never even read a Bible, God can say of them in Romans chapter 2, "For when Gentiles, who do not have the law, by nature do the things in the law, these, although not having the law, are a law to themselves, who show the work of the law written in their hearts, their conscience also bearing witness, and between themselves their thoughts accusing or else excusing them" (Romans 2:14–15). Gentiles who do not have the written Law or Scripture, nevertheless by nature, "do the things" required by "the Law."

You may be thinking, "How can we explain this paradox that although they do not have the Law, they appear to know it?" Paul's answer is that they "are a law to themselves." Not in the sense that they can frame or make up their own laws, as in postmodernism, such that truth can be whatever one wants it to be. But they, "are a law to themselves" in the sense that their own human person is their "law" because God created them as people with consciences.

Although the Gentiles being described in Romans chapter 2 do not have the Bible "in their hands," they do have some of the requirements of the Bible "in their hearts" because God wrote it there. This is the reason that people innately have a sense of what is right and wrong, what is just and unjust, what is fair and unfair. They understand principles of morality and justice because God wrote His moral dictates into our persons. It is important that we understand this as we attempt to evangelize the postmodern man. I asked the pediatrician on the airplane if she thought it was ok if I broke into her home, murdered her husband and children, and stole all her valuables. She saw my point. All truth is not relative. All truth is not whatever we want it to be. There are some absolutes.

Some Questions to Ask the Postmodernist

When I was in campus ministry working with many a skeptical college student, some who were trying to justify their immoral lifestyle, I was trained to ask three questions about statements students would make that clearly contradicted biblical truth.

First, "How do you know that is true?" Second, "Where do you get your information?" Third, "What if you are wrong?"

How Do You Know That Is True?

In asking this question, you want someone to examine the foundation of why they believe what they believe. For the postmodernist, you are asking them to explain why it is that they think their belief that "truth is not absolute" is correct. Of course, if they give the standard answer that truth cannot be definitively known, you can ask them, "Are you absolutely sure?" If they respond positively, they have revealed the absurdity of their position.

When the postmodernist states that there is no such thing as absolute truth, he is either stating that as an absolute or not. Obviously, if they are stating it as an absolute, then there is absolute truth. Whether his answer is in absolute terms or with a degree of uncertainty, we can still reason with him on the basis of the moral code written in his heart. In addition, we have the promise of the Holy Spirit's help working behind our witness.[37] If they are open to investigating the nature of truth, then you will have the opportunity to present the evidence for why you believe what you believe.[38] The Christian's faith is an issue of fact — God really did enter into human history, and there is either evidence for this or there is not. This is what contrasts Christianity with all the other religions in the world. Virtually all the other religions of the world are based upon an inner faith experience. They are not based on any objective, factual foundation. Knowing, as the Bible teaches, that God has written a sense of eternity into our hearts,[39] I find it helpful to remind people that eternity

---

37. John 16:8.
38. 1 Peter 3:15.
39. Ecclesiastes 3:11.

is for a long, long time. I am trying to help them see that it is at least worth their consideration to examine the objective evidence Christians claim to have.

Where Do You Get Your Information?

A second question I often ask the postmodernist is, "Where do you get your information?" Remember, everything you believe, and everything I believe, is based on something. You either made it up in your mind, someone told you, or possibly you read it in a book somewhere. There is always some basis, some source for an individual embracing the belief system he or she embraces. This becomes a good lead-in to remind them that everything the Christian believes is based on the Bible.

That opens the door for them to ask, "Why should I believe the Bible?" Of course, our argument is that the Bible is the only book on planet Earth that God ever inspired. Think about it, since God actually is the author behind the human authors of Scripture, and since the Bible is the only book God inspired, then it stands to reason that humanity has a reliable standard of absolute truth. Based on this premise, anyone can take any belief they have and look into the mirror of Scripture to see if it is true. If you need help in defending the unique authority of the Bible, you might find helpful the chapter that I authored in the book, *How Do We Know the Bible Is True.*[40]

What If You Are Wrong?

A third question I sometimes ask is, "What if you are wrong?" I finished my time with the physician on my long airplane ride with a challenge. I reminded her that her perspective on God and the afterlife was so broad that, according to her belief system, we could both believe what we believe and we would be just fine when we die. But then I reminded her that my viewpoint, really the Bible's viewpoint, is so narrow that both cannot be true. Jesus did not claim to be a good way to God, or even the best way to God, but the *only* way to God.[41] Unlike in postmodern thought, all roads do not lead to God. If one takes the position that all roads lead to God

---

40. "Why is the Bible Unique?" Dr. Carl J. Broggi, found in *How Do We Know the Bible Is True, Volume 2*, edited by Ken Ham & Bodie Hodge (Green Forest, AR: Master Books, 2012), p. 53.
41. John 14:6.

because all roads can be equally true, then that person is going against the clear teaching of the Bible.

Again, since the Bible is absolutely true, then they are embracing human opinion when they take a position that opposes the Bible. They are basing their eternal outcome on assertions others (mere people) have made, who have no authority to make them, because unlike Jesus Christ, they have not risen from the dead. It is much wiser to put one's faith in the objective evidence of the Resurrection, which demonstrated Christ's deity,[42] and proved His assertion that He is the only way to heaven. Facts are facts, and facts cannot be disputed. For some, their problem is that they are afraid to examine the evidence. However, a wise person will be willing to examine the objective evidence that the Christian faith is built on. Eternity is for a long time, and the Bible reminds us that, someday, "every tongue should confess that Jesus Christ is Lord."[43]

The issue is not whether one will do this, but when one is going to do this. People will either do it now, when it will bring them salvation, or they will do it when it is too late and they are eternally separated from God.[44] This is why the Apostle Peter boldly proclaimed, "Nor is there salvation in any other, for there is no other name under heaven given among men by which we must be saved" (Acts 4:12).

I reminded my physician friend that I was going back to my home in South Carolina and she was headed back to her home in Thailand. She could certainly continue to believe what she believed and never give it another thought. So I challenged her with the question, "What if you are wrong?" You see, if she is right and I am wrong, it really does not matter because, according to her postmodern position, we will both be just fine in the end. According to her belief system, my narrowness will someday be broadened to her perspective, but in either case we both would be just fine. If she is right and I am wrong, it really does not matter.

However, I reminded her, if I am right and she is wrong, then nothing else really matters. I gently reminded her that if the Bible is true, that means she is spiritually bankrupt and without salvation.[45] It is one thing to claim a belief, but it is quite another to stake your life and eternity on it.

---

42. Romans 1:4.
43. Philippians 2:11.
44. Matthew 7:23, 25:46.
45. 2 Thessalonians 1:8; Revelation 20:14–15.

Conclusion

As we think about evangelizing the postmodernist, as Christians we are to be involved in both apologetics and evangelism. Evangelism is the presentation of the gospel. The gospel is defined in 1 Corinthians 15 in the following words: "that Christ died for our sins according to the Scriptures, and that He was buried, and that He rose again the third day according to the Scriptures" (1 Corinthians 15:3–4). The death, burial, and Resurrection took place just as the Old Testament Scriptures prophesied centuries before would happen. Evangelism presents the essence of Christianity — that God came to earth in Christ and by His death and Resurrection provided a means by which we could be forgiven. We must never forget that evangelism is our primary responsibility and apologetics is our secondary responsibility.

Apologetics comes into play just as soon as people have objections. If a person raises an objection like Christ never lived, or the Bible is not true, or all truth is relative, then we should attempt to address these issues. As Christians, we need to be prepared to show the unbeliever that they cannot rationally justify unbelief. This means that as ambassadors for Christ we cannot remain intellectually lazy but must study to be able to respond to their objections. If someone remains a non-Christian, if someone embraces postmodernism, they will do so in the face of the evidence, but not because there is a case for unbelief.

In this day, many of God's people are distracted by the entertainments of the world, and so they have lost their edge in being used of God to win people to the Savior. Just before his death, the Apostle Paul reminds Timothy in his *last will and testament* to, "Be diligent to present yourself approved to God, a worker who does not need to be ashamed, rightly dividing the word of truth" (2 Timothy 2:15). This verse reminds us that not all Christians can be usable in God's hand, because not all are "approved."

Certainly, the Bible is clear that all who have been saved are equally loved and accepted by the Father.[46] But as Paul reminds Timothy, while all may be equally loved, not all are equally approved. Clearly, some are more usable than others because of their willingness to *study* the Scriptures and their readiness to *share* the Scriptures. If the instrument that the Holy Spirit uses to bring about conversion is the word of God,[47] then we would be wise

---

46. John 17:23; Romans 8:38–39; 2 Corinthians 5:21.
47. Romans 10:17; James 1:18; 1 Peter 1:23.

to study it and be ready to defend it. May God help us to be faithful to this high and holy call.

Summary of Postmodern Beliefs

Doctrine	Teachings of Postmodernism
God	Deny the exclusivity of the God of the Bible. Various positions exist, but all would deny the exclusivity of Jesus as Savior.
Authority/ Revelation	Holds a humanistic view of truth, looking to man as the source of truth.
Man	All men are able to determine truth on their own. Various positions exist on the nature of man, but most would view man as basically good.
Sin	Sin is a relative concept and generally denied. The Bible cannot be seen as the absolute authority on what is sinful.
Salvation	Most would hold the position that if there is an afterlife, there are many different paths to get there.
Creation	Most would hold to evolutionary views, though positions vary.

Chapter 9

Epicureanism and Evolutionary Religions

Bodie Hodge with Troy Lacey

What Is Evolution?

Evolution is a fundamental tenet in many religious philosophies. It is believed and held with fervor by its adherents as the religious origins model in most secular religions.

Most people in the Western world are familiar with evolution, since this religious view is openly taught in state-funded schools. It is inherent to many textbooks, secular media, secular museums, and even kids programming and books.

When most hear the word "evolution," they think of the "*general theory of evolution (GTE)*," or in laymen's terms "molecules-to-man," "electron-to-engineer," or "goo-to-you" evolution. But there are really four types of evolution that make up the broad view of evolution:

- *Cosmological/Astronomical Evolution:* The big bang (everything came from nothing) created the universe and gradually formed into elements, stars, galaxies, and planetary systems

- *Geological Evolution:* Millions of years of slow, gradual accumulations of rock layers, including fossils

> ***Chemical Evolution:*** Life came from non-living matter, otherwise called abiogenesis

> ***Biological Evolution:*** A single, simple life form gave rise to all other life forms down through the ages

These four aspects make up pure evolution, or an essentially evolutionary worldview. This is materialistic/naturalistic evolution, not to be confused with theistic evolution where God is mixed in with the evolutionary origins account and chemical evolution is optional (more on this in chapter 11 on syncretism in this volume).

There is a widespread belief that evolution originated with Charles Darwin, but this is not true. Darwin described a modern form of biological evolution, but even it has changed since Darwin's day. Darwin built his biological understanding of evolution on Charles Lyell's understating of geological evolution. What makes these modern forms of evolutionary religion so disruptive is how it has been devastating the Church. Many within the Church, particularly the youth, have been indoctrinated to believe this religious view . . . or at least aspects of it.

Many Christians have little training in the defense of the Bible and Christian doctrine. At the same time, many of these same people are being taught by the state school system and secular media. Many Christians then yield (knowingly or unknowingly) and mix these two religions. See the chapter on syncretism in this volume to see how modern Christians try to mix these very different religions and the problems therein.

Regardless, this causes a problem within the Church because some members have walked away from doctrine that was set forth in the Bible and moved from biblical positions to beliefs that incorporate evolution. Some Christians even criticize those biblical Christians who say that you should not mix these religions! This brings us to an interesting question. What would Paul say about this?

If Paul Were Around Today, Would He Argue against Evolutionists?

We don't have to wonder if Paul would have argued against evolutionists, because he did — the Epicureans!

If we go back to Paul in the Book of Acts and consider his missionary journeys, sermons, and epistles, he saw a great number of people and surely encountered a great number of beliefs. Taking a closer look at the Scriptures, consider:

> Then certain Epicurean and Stoic philosophers encountered him. And some said, "What does this babbler want to say?" Others said, "He seems to be a proclaimer of foreign gods," because he preached to them Jesus and the resurrection (Acts 17:18).

In the greater context, we find Paul forced into a debate with Epicureans and Stoics. Because they disagreed with Paul, they take him to Mars Hill (the Areopagus) to defend his views in front of the whole assembly of philosophers. Paul masterfully begins his defense with God as Creator, which has gone on to become the basis for creation evangelism.[1]

Epicureans

Most readers skim past the Epicureans with the basic understanding that this group of people was obviously not Christian and held to some other views. Though this is true, it is only the half of it. The Epicureans were the evolutionists of the day. They typically held a belief derived from Epicurus that there were no gods that intervened in the world. They did not believe in the typical Greek gods. The Epicureans viewed the alleged Greek gods as mere material that sat on shelves in the homes of many Greeks.

The Epicureans further believed that over long ages, atoms, the basic component of all matter, gave rise to life. Then that life gave rise to higher life such as mankind. But there was no God or gods involved.

Sound familiar? It should; because in its basic form the Epicurean beliefs mimic the evolutionary worldview of today. Of course, there are some differences from the modern views of evolution (Lamarckian, Traditional Darwinian, Neo-Darwinian — more on this in a moment), but this is likely the first time an evolutionary worldview held any prominence with a group of people (from around 300 B.C.).

The Famous Epicurean Mantra

The materialistic Epicureans were known for their argument against God (and alleged gods) using the problem of evil:

---

1. For more on the method of creation evangelism, see Ken Ham, *Why Won't They Listen?* (Green Forest, AR: Master Books, 2002).

God either wants to eliminate bad things and cannot, or can but does not want to, or neither wishes to nor can, or both wants to and can. If he wants to and cannot, then he is weak — and this does not apply to god. If he can but does not want to, then he is spiteful — which is equally foreign to god's nature. If he neither wants to nor can, he is both weak and spiteful, and so not a god. If he wants to and can, which is the only thing fitting for a god, where then do bad things come from? Or why does he not eliminate them?[2]

Even today, evolutionists try to use this claim without realizing that Christ Himself addressed it:

> Another parable He put forth to them, saying: "The kingdom of heaven is like a man who sowed good seed in his field; but while men slept, his enemy came and sowed tares among the wheat and went his way. But when the grain had sprouted and produced a crop, then the tares also appeared. So the servants of the owner came and said to him, 'Sir, did you not sow good seed in your field? How then does it have tares?' He said to them, 'An enemy has done this.' The servants said to him, 'Do you want us then to go and gather them up?' But he said, 'No, lest while you gather up the tares you also uproot the wheat with them. Let both grow together until the harvest, and at the time of harvest I will say to the reapers, "First gather together the tares and bind them in bundles to burn them, but gather the wheat into my barn" ' " (Matthew 13:24–30).

The existence of evil is no surprise to Christians, and God explains this in the Bible. In Genesis 3, God explains the origin of evil — and its final demise at the end of Revelation 20. God will destroy evil just as He has said in numerous places, but it will happen at the time appointed by God (harvest), not on the timing or desires of humanity — as the Epicureans tried to force upon God (i.e., if God doesn't do it *now*, then He can't exist).[3] God is not subject to man, but man to God.

---

2. As stated by Lactantius, an early Christian who responded to this claim; Lactantius, *De Ira Deorum*, 13.19.
3. Imagine if some used this argument for the existence of the president of the United States. They could say, "If the president doesn't take care of this economic problem *now*, then he doesn't exist." It would be a ludicrous argument!

In the same manner, God could have created everything in one second, but selected six days for the benefit and pattern of our workweek (Exodus 20:11). So God has an appointed time for the elimination of evil for the benefit of man.[4]

But consider how the Epicureans would answer the question, "On what basis, in your Epicurean worldview, does evil exist?" They must borrow from the biblical concept of evil to argue against the God of the Bible! So, they refute themselves by posing the very thing they believe refutes the existence of God!

Paul's Response to the Epicureans

You can see why the Epicureans opposed Paul! They didn't want God to exist, and they did not want Him to be the Creator (recall they view a god or gods as being material idols simply made from matter). Rather, they believed that people ultimately came from matter — a view where ultimately nothing *matters*.

Paul responded to these claims. In Acts 17:24, Paul defines God as the "God, who made the world and everything in it since He is Lord of heaven and earth." He refutes the Epicurean ideas that a relational, Creator God does not exist and that there is a spiritual realm, refuting their materialistic thinking.

Then Paul says that God "does not dwell in temples made with hands. Nor is He worshiped with men's hands, as though He needed anything" (v. 24–25). He refutes the belief that God is limited to materials (idols), and this is proper, since God is spirit (John 4:24). Greek culture often made images of their gods, and the Epicureans realized these idols were made of materials, which is why they argued against them. So, Paul is distancing the God of the Bible from what the Epicureans were used to arguing against.

Next, Paul says God "gives to all life, breath, and all things" (v. 25). Paul explains the true origin of life and refutes that atoms came together to form life of their own accord. But notice how Paul actually goes further in a presuppositional argument here. If the Epicureans start with matter, where did the matter come from? Paul reveals that God created it ("all things"). Paul, through the beginning of verse 29, continues to explain that all people come from one person ("one blood") and that person came about as a result

---

4. "For the earnest expectation of the creation eagerly waits for the revealing of the sons of God" (Romans 8:19). The harvest is taking place.

of God supernaturally creating him. This explanation refuted their views of evolution and established God as the special Creator of mankind.

In the rest of verse 29 and into 30, Paul reiterates his devastating critique of their materialistic understanding of God. Paul also points out that mankind is really acting as the ultimate authority by worshipping man-made gods when he says, "We ought not to think that the Divine Nature is like gold or silver or stone, something shaped by art and man's devising. Truly, these times of ignorance God overlooked." Then Paul gives the call to repent and presents the gospel.

Lastly, Paul mentioned that God confirmed this to all by the Resurrection of Jesus. It was at this point that Scripture says "some mocked" (Acts 17:32). This would have been the Epicureans, who did not believe in a bodily resurrection. They believed that once the body died, there was nothing else. In fact, a common Epicurean epitaph found on many Greek and Roman graves of the time was the phrase: "I was not; I was; I am not; I do not care."[5]

How Should Christians Deal with Evolutionism?

Paul did not compromise his stand on Genesis (alluding to Genesis 1–11), which he used as the foundation for understanding the gospel when he spoke at Mars Hill in front of the Epicureans, Stoics, and others. He did not encourage them to mix some of the evolutionary ideas the Epicureans were espousing with the Bible, but told them to repent and acknowledge God as Creator and Savior.

So, if Paul were around today, would he argue against the evolutionists? Well, he *did!*

Other Early Evolutionists

Epicurus was not the "inventor" of the belief in the materialistic origin of everything. It appears that the atomist school of thought went back almost a hundred years before to the Greek philosophers Leucippus (fifth century B.C.) and Democritus (c. 460–c. 370 B.C.). Little is known about Leucippus, but Democritus' beliefs have been preserved through the writings of Aristotle (384–322 B.C.) and Diogenes Laertius (early third century A.D). Democritus believed that all matter was made up of indivisible particles called atoms (the

---

5. Eric Gerlach, "Epicurus and Epicureanism," accessed August 2, 2016, https://ericgerlach. com/greekphilosophy14.

Greek meaning is "no parts," an indivisible particle). To Democritus, every atom was eternal and could neither be created nor destroyed.[6]

His idea of the universe was entirely materialistic, with no guiding order, intelligence, or purpose, and no god or gods who controlled the destiny of humanity.[7] Democritus even proposed that the human soul was nothing more than a collection of atoms. Since no intelligence produced atoms, nor organized them, then according to Democritus, atoms must be self-organizing. But knowing that organization takes time, Democritus postulated an infinite number of atoms and an eternal and infinite universe, moving in an infinite void; and even more so, he postulated infinite other universes.[8] In the view of Democritus, infinite possibilities exist in an infinite universe, and so inevitably lead to life.

It is against this backdrop that Epicurus refined the teachings of Democritus (he rejected the concept of an infinite number of atoms, for example[9]) and expanded the materialistic atomist philosophy into an argument for practical atheism. If nothing created atoms, and everything is made up of self-organized atoms, then any discussion of a god or gods becomes meaningless. In the view of Democritus, and later the Epicureans, the gods were merely a collection of atoms as well. Likewise, all matter and all life is merely a collection of self-organizing atoms. This abiogenesis hypothesis, as well as the concept of an unlimited past (later refined to finite, but deep time of billions of years) would be grasped as fundamental principles by later evolutionary proponents.

When discussing Epicureanism, it is difficult to ignore the lifestyle of many Epicureans — based on the religious aspect of hedonism. Epicurus, along with Cārvāka, Artippus, and the Cyrenaics are all counted as formulating early Hedonism in India and Greece (600–300 B.C.). Here is a quick evaluation of hedonism.

Hedonism

In simplicity, hedonism is a belief that individual pleasure is the ultimate goal in life. However, even Solomon, whose wisdom was unsurpassed in

---

6. Robert C. Solomon and Kathleen M. Higgins, *A Short History of Philosophy* (New York: Oxford University Press), 1996, p. 37.
7. Ibid., p. 38.
8. David Sedley, *Creationism and Its Critics in Antiquity* (Berkeley and Los Angeles: University of California Press), 2007, p. 136.
9. Ibid., p. 161.

judging the people of Israel (e.g., 1 Kings 3:7–12), tried to find pleasure in a great many things such as women, money, and labor (e.g., Ecclesiastes 2:10).

But in all of his endeavors he found pleasure to be ultimately meaningless apart from God (e.g., Ecclesiastes 2:1, 12:8). This is what the Book of Ecclesiastes is all about — realizing hedonism is not the chief goal, but rather to "fear God and keep His commandments, for this is man's all" (Ecclesiastes 12:13).

Even so, cultures around the world dive into hedonism, often failing to realize it. They pursue pleasure and personal happiness at the detriment of others, and this often comes without concern (James 5:4–6).

Pleasure is not of itself a bad thing — it is a gift from God. Pleasure is bad when people engage in the love of wicked pleasure (evil things) or place the pleasure above God instead of recognizing its rightful place (2 Timothy 3:2–7).

There are variations among modern hedonism such as Normative, Prudential, Utilitarianism Hedonic Calculus, and Motivational. Without getting lost in terminology, just understand that much of this is based on the focus of pleasure such as external/physical pleasure versus internal/mental pleasure regarding levels and types of pain; future happiness versus happiness now, and so on.

However, few who might currently be described as hedonists have contemplated their underlying philosophy for pursuing their own pleasures. As a big picture, major divisions in hedonism are simply qualitative versus quantitative hedonism. Qualitative is focusing on the quality of pleasurable things (e.g., demanding good wine rather than cheap beer) while quantitative focuses on the quantity of pleasurable things.

Consider it this way. Two hedonists are arguing. One is a qualitative hedonist and the other is quantitative. The qualitative hedonist says his goal is to get a Ferrari (a very nice and expensive car). The quantitative hedonist says that his goal is to have 11 cars that are all much cheaper — one for each aspect of his lifestyle.

There is a t-shirt that has been popular that says, "He who dies with the most toys wins." This is the battle cry of quantitative hedonism. What few understand is that he who dies with the most toys still dies — and will then face judgment. Hebrews 9:27 says:

And as it is appointed for men to die once, but after this the judgment.

Modern Evolutionary Religious Beliefs

Darwin didn't invent the idea of evolution; he just popularized a particular form of it to attempt to explain life without God. When variant forms of Epicureanism began to revive in the late 1700s and early 1800s with men such as Mr. Erasmus Darwin (Charles Darwin's grandfather) and Professor Jean-Baptiste Lamarck, evolutionists needed a way to explain how new features arise in organisms over time.

Evolutionists today basically adhere to this same religious mythology that Paul argued against in the first century in Acts 17. But it has changed in its mechanisms. Today, instead of a tiny particle as the Greeks proposed, secularists propose that a cosmic egg or an almost infinitely dense hot particle somehow popped into existence from nothing, to begin the universe in accordance with the big bang. Now we arrive at the various modern views of biological evolution.[10]

Lamarckian Evolution

When Epicureanism was rehashed in the late 1700s and early 1800s, the leading view was called Lamarckian evolution. The view was promoted and popularized by Professor Jean-Baptiste Lamarck in France[11] and Dr. Erasmus Darwin (Charles Darwin's grandfather) in England.[12]

This view is famous for its teaching that the giraffe's neck became longer because it kept reaching for leaves that were higher and higher. Then, supposedly, this feature of a longer, stretched neck was passed onto the next generation of giraffes.

Charles Darwin's grandfather Erasmus even wrote a book on Lamarckian evolution called *Zoonomia*.[13] Most people don't know that Charles Darwin used a form of Lamarck's ideas in his book, to give a supposed explanation

---

10. For an extensive discussion on these views, see Terry Mortenson and Roger Patterson, "Do Evolutionists Believe Darwin's Ideas about Evolution?" in Ken Ham, gen. ed., *The New Answers Book 3* (Green Forest, AR: Master Books, 2010), p. 271–282.
11. For his collective works, see: Jean-Baptiste Lamarck, http://www.lamarck.cnrs.fr/index.php?lang=en.
12. Erasmus Darwin, *Zoonomia; or, the Laws of Organic Life*, Volume I (London, England: J. Johnson Publishers, 1796).
13. Ibid.

for new characteristics appearing in new generations. Modern evolutionists would, of course, reject this idea today — even though they hold Darwin's book *On the Origin of Species* as the "Bible" of the evolution movement.

But anyone can test Lamarck's ideas of acquired inheritance. For instance, growing up as a farmer, I (Hodge) can tell you that if you cut the tail off of a sheep (docking) generation after generation, the baby lambs will still come out with a tail! So the evolutionists still needed a different mechanism to try to make evolution work.

Traditional Darwinism

A Christian named Ed Blyth published a number of papers on variations within the kinds of creatures that God created, discussing how the environment influences why such variations succeed or not. He did this about 25 years before Charles Darwin published his seminal work. Darwin, trained as a theologian, read these papers and thought *maybe this is the mechanism that will lead to evolution.* Darwin called this process "natural selection."

Creationists, by and large, believe in the observable process of natural selection (often referred to as "adaptation" or "variation"). Such a process only operates on the information already contained in the genome of a particular kind. No new information is generated — just different combinations of already existing information. This is why we have variations within the dog kind, for example.

Also, sometimes information is corrupted by mutations (cancer, deformations, or extra copies of something such as extra fingers or toes are examples of mutations). These things (selection and mutations) along with created genetic diversity help explain variations in animals (and the formation of different species within a kind — we have several species of the one dog kind like coyotes, wolves, dingoes, etc.). But Darwin thought this process would lead to evolution in the production of brand new characteristics that weren't previously present.

Of course, Darwin was emphatic about natural selection (and some Lamarckian process, too), being the mechanism for this in the first edition of *Origin of Species.* But by the sixth edition, Darwin had backed off of this significantly in his wording, knowing that it wasn't turning out to be the mechanism he desired.[14]

---

14. R. Hedtke, *Secrets of the Sixth Edition* (Green Forest, AR: Master Books, 2010).

But Darwin had now repopularized naturalistic evolution (one kind changing into a different kind — molecules-to-man evolution), and it had started to become a mainstream idea in the population — even though it still lacked a viable mechanism and had no directly observed evidence. Keep in mind that speciation is not evolution in the molecules-to-man sense.

So basically, traditional Darwinism said that natural selection (with aspects of the Lamarckian process of passing along these newly acquired traits, e.g., Darwin's proposed "gemmules"), plus long periods of time would somehow lead to evolution of new kinds of living things (amoeba-to-man).

Neo-Darwinism

Later evolutionists (called Neo-Darwinists), with an understanding of DNA as the molecule of heredity, postulated that *mutations* were supposedly the mechanism to increase complexity by generating new information in the genome. Neo-Darwinists differ from traditional Darwinists who appeal to natural selection alone as that mechanism. Neo-Darwinists do appeal to natural selection as part of the mechanism, but not the process for originating complexity from existing information. They see natural selection as a process for filtering out organisms to allow a more suited (or "better") one to take its place.

This sentiment is what shows like *X-men*, *Spiderman*, *Heroes*, and so on appeal to as well. So basically, Neo-Darwinism could be described this way:

> Natural selection, plus mutation, plus long periods of time leads to evolution.

Many learned evolutionists and creationists alike recognize what mutations really do — they are generally rather detrimental (though in some cases they are nearly neutral or do not affect function too much).[15] But they simply do not result in brand new complex information being generated and added into the genome — despite evolutionists' false claims to the contrary.[16] So,

---

15. See, for example, John Sanford, *Genetic Entropy and the Mystery of the Genome* (Waterloo, New York: FMS Publications, 2005); Lee Spetner, *Not by Chance* (Brooklyn, New York: Judaica Press, Inc., 1997).

16. The best example to date that I've seen evolutionists propose for new information is the nylon-degrading bacteria. However, this was only based on preprogrammed design changes in the plasmids, which are extrachromosomal segments that are autonomous to the bacterial DNA. So with a proper understanding, it doesn't support evolutionary changes at all. Please see Georgia Purdom and Kevin Anderson, "A Creationists Perspective of Beneficial Mutations in Bacteria," *Answers in Depth*, May 27, 2009, https://answersingenesis.org/genetics/mutations/a-creationist-perspective-of-beneficial-mutations-in-bacteria.

a new mechanism is still required for evolutionists to attempt an explanation for the complexities of life forms they believe diversified from a simple common ancestor.

The reason is that we do not observe mutations (the billions that we should be seeing if evolution were true) moving in a positive direction. Cancers, for example, are the result of mutations. Furthermore, after years of experiments on fruit flies, for instance, bombarding them with radiation to cause mutations, they never improve with brand new characteristics (generated by new information), not previously possible! Dr. Lee Spetner states:

> No mutations have ever been observed that have converted an animal to a markedly different species, say from a fly to a wasp.[17]

Punctuated Equilibrium

The problem of mutations gets worse since we do not find the gradual changing of creatures in the fossil record from one to another as evolutionary scientists, especially Darwin, have predicted. This was particularly troubling to evolutionist Dr. Stephen J. Gould from Harvard University, who became the popular advocate of the Punctuated Equilibrium idea, though not all evolutionists jumped on board his particular evolutionary view.

Essentially, Gould argued that things didn't change much over long periods of time, but rather the change happened in short spurts or bursts of evolution in isolated populations. This hypothesis was proposed to eliminate the problem of no undisputed transitional forms in the fossil record.

The idea was that changes happened so fast that you don't see the results of these in the fossil layers, much like you wouldn't see all of the action of a football game if you just looked at a few pictures taken throughout the game. So basically, the evolutionists were not finding evidence for molecules-to-man evolution in the fossil layers (it was nice Dr. Gould was honest about that). Then the evolutionists proposed that they didn't need any fossil evidence because they could explain this away using the concept of punctuated equilibrium.

So punctuated equilibrium suggests that mutations plus natural selection produce short bursts of evolution over long ages — we just don't have a record of it in the fossils. We've heard creationists explain it this way:

---

17. Spetner, *Not by Chance*, p. 177.

It used to be that the reason for no transitional forms in the fossil record and why we don't see molecules-to-man evolution happening, is because it happens slowly over a long time. Now it is proposed that the reason we don't see evolution happening or find transitional forms is because it happened so fast we missed it!

But in the end, the evolutionist still doesn't have an observable and repeatable process to change one kind of organism, like a relatively simple alga, into a totally different kind, such as a more complex dog. The only mechanisms they propose are natural selection and mutations. But both of these are actually working in the wrong direction for evolution.[18]

Modern Evolution's Shortcomings

What new complexity has mutated on a dog to make, say . . . feathers? We see misplaced copies of information, like extra toes or extra fingers (polydactyl, which are actually detrimental), but we don't see totally new characteristics arising like hair on a fish. We observe the result of genes that turn on and off, but that information was already there, and turning these on and off has nothing to do with molecules-to-man evolution (i.e., turning microbes eventually into turkeys).

If evolution is possible, considering the enormous (really incomprehensible) amount of information in living things, where is just one example of matter producing new information? Where do we observe matter generating the code for a brand new characteristic that was not previously present? The evolutionist accepts these things on blind faith.

Religious Nature of Evolution

Evolutionary religions are subsets of the greater secular humanistic religion. Many try to equate evolution as science, but that just gives science a bad name. Science, which simply means knowledge, is observable and repeatable, while molecules-to-man evolution is neither. It is merely a materialistic and naturalistic religion that many have been duped into believing is science. Consider the words of a famous Neo-Darwinist on his religious conviction to evolution:

---

18. We understand that there are variations within these models like neo-Lamarckianism or hopeful monster (an even faster model of punctuated equilibrium), but none offer a viable mechanism for evolution.

> We take the side of science in spite of the patent absurdity of some of its constructs, in spite of its failure to fulfill many of its extravagant promises of health and life, in spite of the tolerance of the scientific community for unsubstantiated just-so stories, because we have a prior commitment, a commitment to materialism. It is not that the methods and institutions of science somehow compel us to accept a material explanation of the phenomenal world, but, on the contrary, that we are forced by our a priori adherence to material causes to create an apparatus of investigation and a set of concepts that produce material explanations, no matter how counter-intuitive, no matter how mystifying to the uninitiated. Moreover, that materialism is an absolute, for we cannot allow a Divine Foot in the door.[19]

Another leading evolutionist writes:

> Christianity has fought, still fights, and will fight science to the desperate end over evolution, because evolution destroys utterly and finally the very reason Jesus' earthly life was supposedly made necessary. Destroy Adam and Eve and the original sin, and in the rubble you will find the sorry remains of the son of god. Take away the meaning of his death. If Jesus was not the redeemer that died for our sins, and this is what evolution means, then Christianity is nothing.[20]

Naturalistic evolutionists even recognize that evolution is an opposing religion to Christianity. It has competing religious claims. For example, you cannot have both special creation by God of an organism and naturalistic evolution of the same organism with no God at the same time. It is logically contradictory. These are two competing religious claims. Biblical Christians recognize this, and naturalistic evolutionists recognize this — the only ones who seem to fail to realize this are the compromised Christians who try to synchronize these very different religions in the oddest of ways.

19. Richard Lewontin, "Billions and Billions of Demons," *The New York Review*, January 9, 1997, p. 31.
20. G. Richard Bozarth, "The Meaning of Evolution," *American Atheist*, September 20, 1979, p. 30.

Refutations

Besides Paul's refutations, there are many more to choose from. For example, the Epicureans and other evolutionists are materialists, which means logic cannot exist in their worldview since logic is not material. Logic is an abstract, immaterial concept that has no grounding in a materialistic worldview, so it is inconsistent for a materialist to appeal to logic in an argument. So the materialistic evolutionists can't even make a logical argument against Christianity to favor evolution without leaving their religion behind them and borrowing from a biblical worldview!

The evolutionists cannot consistently argue that anything is "right" or "wrong" since absolute morality is not material either. The evolutionist cannot logically suggest that biblical creation is wrong without standing on a foundation that evolution (materialistic and naturalistic) is false.

Consider scientific inquiry. Repeatable and observable science is predicated on the concept of God upholding and sustaining the universe in a consistent fashion (e.g., Genesis 8:22; Hebrews 1:3). Christians describe the way God does this and call them the laws of nature. This is what makes repeatable science possible. God upholds laws of nature consistently so we get the same result when we do our experimentation. We have a grounding for our belief in the uniformity of nature that is consistent with our worldview.

Thus, as Bible believers, we know the future will be like the past because an all-knowing God who knows the future has revealed this to man in His Word. This explains why people who generally trusted the Bible developed most fields of science.

But how can the naturalist or materialist, thinking from a worldview without God, know the future? They can't. The consistent evolutionist must admit that the laws of nature could change tomorrow even though they believe in the uniformitarian view of natural processes. In the evolutionary story, at the beginning there were no laws of nature and then there were laws of nature. So if the laws changed in the past, why wouldn't they change in the future?

If the evolutionist argues that they know the laws of nature will remain the same in the future "because they were like that in the recent past," they commit the fallacy of begging the question (a form of a vicious circular argument). They still don't know the future, and knowing the past is irrelevant to knowing the future.

Allow me an illustration to get the point across. What if someone were to state, "Dr. Richard Dawkins, a famous evolutionist, will never die." You might ask, how do you know that this person knows the future — that Dr. Dawkins will never die. And they respond by saying, "The future is like the past and Dr. Dawkins has never died in the past, so therefore he will not die in the future." Do you see the fallacy? The same can be said for the uniformitarian view of history.

Conclusion

Evolution is a fundamental tenet of many religious philosophies. It is also a religious origins account borrowed by many humanistic religions (simply because evolution is one of the few religious models that tries to offer an explanation of origins apart from God or gods). Many have bought into evolutionary ideas so deeply that we might think of them as holding to the religion of evolutionism — looking to evolutionary ideas to account for the origin of the universe and the meaning of existence.

We must acknowledge that evolution fails both theologically and scientifically and cannot account for logic, morality, or uniformity in nature. It is a failed system and *false* religion.

Chapter 10

Dualism and the Types of Religions

Bodie Hodge

> Stop regarding man in whose nostrils is breath, for of what account is he? (Isaiah 2:22; ESV).

> For the ways of man are before the eyes of the LORD, And He ponders all his paths. His own iniquities entrap the wicked man, and he is caught in the cords of his sin. He shall die for lack of instruction, and in the greatness of his folly he shall go astray (Proverbs 5:21–23).

Preliminary Comments about Approaching Dualism

I think we could all agree there are a lot of strange beliefs in the world. So many that all cannot be dealt with in this book series on world religions, cults, and philosophical systems. To deal with dualism, it is appropriate to understand the three major forms of non-Christian religions from another angle.

So how do we deal with all these other religious systems? In the introductory comments of this book series we pointed out there were several ways to lump or group religions. We selected one method for the book series and continued with that scheme throughout the volumes.

But this chapter utilizes a different way of grouping religions that would typically be used to categorize philosophically religious systems. So it is a complementary look from a different angle. This will give us an overview of most religious models and categorize them in a way that we could take these belief systems and place them neatly into one of three categories (the remaining would fall under Christian religious appeals/openly Christian-based religious, four total).[1]

As you read this, there will likely be some new terminology that I will try to briefly define, but don't let this set you back. You should still be able to gather the main points without needing to memorize the technical lingo.

Categories of Religious Belief Systems

In this system, the three major categories are:

1. Spiritual Monism: all things are spiritual/nonmaterial; that is, all things really consist of nonmaterial aspects like a concept world or ultimate reality or ultimate being (e.g., Hinduism, Taoism, or New Age).
2. Materialistic Monism/Atomism: all things are material and there is no immaterial or spiritual realm (e.g., atheism, secular humanism, and materialism).
3. Philosophical/Non-religious/Secular Dualism: there are two (hence *dual*) opposing principles or substances that exist and cannot be broken down any further: *mind/conceptual* (non-material or *ideal* realm) and *matter* (e.g., modern dualism or Platonism).

In brief, these three non-Christian positions are (1) only non-material/spiritual exists, (2) only material exists, and (3) non-material/spiritual (secularistic or no god(s) involved) *and* material exists (in opposition to each other). When you understand the first two it will be much easier to understand secular dualism.

I'd like to add a caveat here. When discussing the dualistic viewpoint, we are not discussing the immaterial or spiritual realm as understood in a Christian sense. We are looking at a secular form of it, as dualism holds to a secular view that rejects any concept of a god. Although there are various forms of dualism, dualists typically still maintain that their immaterial

---

1. These are Bible-based religions or those that borrow heavily from the Bible but then deviate. Volume 1 of the *World Religions and Cults* dealt extensively with these counterfeits of Christianity, showing biblical Christianity as the only viable option.

conceptual realm is not the same as that of most religions, even though it is often denoted as "spiritual."

This is why religions that do entertain a true spiritual sense are dealt with extensively in their own chapters in this book series and not confined to this section. This would be that fourth section — *religious* (like what you see in the first volume of this book series on the Counterfeits of Christianity).

Another caveat also needs to be discussed. There is "religious dualism" which counterfeits Christianity, but this is a polytheistic religion with at least two equal and opposing "gods" where one is good and the other is evil. Not that secular dualism is itself unreligious — it is very religious — but it tries to do so in a *secular* sense without god(s). But the primary and leading form of dualism is Platonism (Idealism) developed by Plato, so that is what will be discussed here. So even though there are various forms of secular dualism, the king of dualism, Plato, will be our focus here.

1. *Spiritual Monism*

Spiritual Monism is united in proclaiming that "everything is one" or "all is one." In other words, the spiritual monist claims that all things are part of one spiritual entity, whether they appear to be physical or not. For example, *all of nature* or *all of the universe* and *all of the conceptual realm* or *realm of the mind* would be understood as merely being a part of one spiritual reality or one ultimate concept of being.

I know what you are thinking — "But we have physical, material things right in front of us!" But this view maintains that what we think and envision as the material world is actually a part of the spiritual realm. In other words, the material realm really doesn't exist in this view; people are merely mistaken to think it does — it is really an illusion (e.g., this concept is called *maya* in Hinduism). Most Eastern religions (Hinduism, Jainism, New Age, Taoism, etc.) are simply variations of this religion outlook.

The argument put forth by spiritual monists is that there is no distinction between the material and immaterial/spiritual realm. They would further argue that "everything is one" and there is really no distinction between anything since "all is one."

As the spiritual monist teaches, humanity's problem is that we misperceive reality by making distinctions when, in reality, there are no distinctions (we fail to properly understand). The goal of humanity is to work to understand how distinctions are not really there, bringing us closer to the "infinite sea of being" or a "state of nirvana" where we are again united with this ultimate state of spiritual reality or being.

Some popular forms of Spiritual Monism are Hinduism and its religious sisters, New Age, and Taoism, although others could be lumped under this religious system. Any philosophical system that is pantheistic (which in a general sense is: "all is God" or "everything together consists of God" or "all is part of God" or "the universe/cosmos is God") is spiritually monistic.

An Arbitrary Worldview?

To evaluate this worldview, we can ask a simple question — How do you know that all is one? The only way to know that all is one is to know all things! And yet, there is no authority within Spiritual Monism except the fallible and limited opinions of man, which are arbitrary. Arbitrariness, like an opinion, carries no weight in a debate. The entire religious set is predicated on the alleged human sages who developed the concept that all is one. And yet, one can't really know all is one outside of an arbitrary assertion!

Building a worldview on arbitrary claims is not a great foundation. If someone proclaimed 2+5=3 and you asked them how they know that 2+5=3, would you believe them if they just said they believed it was so? Not at all! Appealing to ideas of fallible man as an absolute truth shows that the argument has been refuted.

An Inconsistent Worldview?

Consider that the ultimate reality, ultimate spirituality, or ultimate nature is not personal (as taught in Taoism, New Age, Hinduism, etc.). It has never been personal, nor then is it capable of providing personal revelation to assert that truth. That is, if the ultimate spiritual being (all is one) was some form of absolute truth in the first place (after all, *truth* and *error* are one and the same in this view)! Being that it is not personal, how then could personal beings have any revealed knowledge of this ultimate reality or ultimate spiritual state? Such a contradiction provides a devastating argument against this worldview.

Furthermore, if there are no distinctions and our path is supposed to be understanding that there are no distinctions, then this introduces a grand inconsistency. That very claim is a distinction! In other words, it is contradictory at its very premise by saying, there are no distinctions in reality and then claiming we have failed to understand that distinction!

A Necessary Foundation for Logic and Truth?

If all is one, then absolute truth and absolute falsity are also one — therefore truth cannot really exist! If knowledge and lack of knowledge are one, then knowledge breaks down to be meaningless. Spiritual Monism (and the many religions that would be categorized under it) is utterly refuted as a coherent worldview by the fact that it has *no basis* for truth, knowledge, and the like.

Consider the actions of spiritual monists in light of their beliefs. If all is one and there is no distinction, then why do they buy a house for their possessions when there is no distinction between their house and possessions and someone else's house and possessions? Why would they kiss their children and wife (and not someone else's) as if they were special and unique? After all, there would be no distinction between their family and a pile of nuclear waste.

Why not have the monists give you their purse or wallet if there is no distinction between you and them? The religions grounded in Spiritual Monism break down into meaninglessness, arbitrariness, and inconsistency by their own perspective. They do not behave in the world in a way that is consistent with the fundamental beliefs of their worldview.

If one were to respond, "Well, that is the beauty of Spiritual Monism, we don't have to go use that Christian logic in our view, so you can't refute our view using logical arguments." Then we can respond by saying, "Yes, you do believe in logic because you just attempted to make a logical argument to prove me wrong. Thus, you have refuted your own position."

Since contradictions are allowed in their philosophical system, then simply contradict their view — what are they going to do? Are they going to appeal to the logic that they just gave up? The Spiritual Monistic view is easily refuted as an incoherent worldview.

2. Materialistic Monism

In exact opposition to Spiritual Monism, Materialistic Monism maintains that everything is material. In this view, there is no spiritual aspect of reality whatsoever. Everything is seen as material, and there is no spirit or non-material in existence. Everything in reality is an expression of matter and energy interacting. Hence, there is no God or gods whatsoever in this view.

Arbitrariness, Inconsistency, and Foundational Problems

Of course, holding to a strict materialistic concept causes problems because concepts cannot exist since concepts are not material (i.e., immaterial). Nor can logic, truth, knowledge, love, dignity, dreams, conclusions, mind, caring, and so on, because they are not material. These things have no mass and are abstract in their nature. So none of these really exist in the materialistic framework.

What does this mean for the materialistic worldview? It means they cannot even debate the subject without giving up their view and borrowing from a Christian worldview! In other words, to discuss the subject using abstract concepts and logic means that the atheistic position is wrong!

So many materialists, when they become aware of their own limitations, tend to be materialistic by profession but act like dualists to say reason, logic, and so on exist — but they just don't want God involved. But then they have to deal with the arbitrariness, inconsistencies, and other issues that we discussed in the Spiritual Monism section above. But strict materialism is self-refuting (inconsistent) since it cannot account for logic and reasoning in the first place.

3. Philosophical Dualism (Idealism)

As mentioned previously, this is not to be confused with *moral* or *religious dualism*, which is the view that there are two opposites (gods) that govern existence and oppose each other: good and evil. They merely share the same name (dualism).

Though the dualistic nature of religious dualism is related to Idealism, they are different subjects. In light of the pervasiveness of the religious dualistic view in our culture, there is the faulty idea floating around that God and Satan are equal and opposites, but this is not the case (i.e., two opposing eternal gods of good and evil, respectively).

However, Satan was created by God and has no power next to the infinite God of Scripture. The Bible teaches that Satan was once created perfect (Ezekiel 28:15; Deuteronomy 32:4; Colossians 1:16) and very good (Nehemiah 9:6; Genesis 1:31), but fell into sin. One day, God will cast Satan into hell (eternal punishment). Thus, there is no possibility of Satan being any form of co-equal, yet opposite, with God. Hence, Christianity doesn't fall under the *religious dualism* aspect, which is really polytheism (two opposing equal gods).

Returning to the subject at hand — Philosophical Dualism (Idealism) understands that everything is not material, but also recognizes that everything is not spiritual. Platonic dualism (the leading form that goes back to Plato) realized there are absolutes (e.g., logic, truth, concept forms) that do not change alongside our material universe that does change. So he held to a dualistic view of reality.

Plato believed that there is an ideal or immaterial realm of absolute forms or ideas, which he viewed as the first realm since it is unchanging. For example, logic doesn't change and absolute truths do not change, so they must be a part of the ideal realm. And then, there is our material world, which he viewed as a secondary realm because it undergoes constant change.

Plato held that things have *a form* in the first realm that does not change like a "class concept," whereas the world in which we live is subject to that first realm because things here do change but represent an unchanging ideal. What do I mean by class concepts? It means things like letters or numbers or things we can classify.

Consider this example. I can write a "B" on a piece of paper, and you would recognize it as a "B." If I were to erase this "B" and now there is no longer a material "B" on my paper, does that mean that "B-ness" no longer exists in the universe? Not at all. The *concept* of "B" is not dependent on *that material* "B" that I had written with pencil on the paper. There is a class concept of "B" that is not dependent on material — and yet we often use a material "B" to represent this immaterial concept. The same ideal can be represented in different materials as pixels on a digital screen, ink on this page, or carving it into the sand. The ideal form is constant, though its material expression can change.

As another example, I've seen big dogs, hairy dogs, black dogs, hairless dogs, plush-toy dogs, photographs of dogs, stick-figure dogs, shadows of dogs, and we can easily recognize that *concept* of dog. If a new image of some form of dog is found, we can easily classify it as a dog, even though we have not seen every single possible expression of a dog ideal. We recognize the concept of "dog" or "dogness." It was not dependent on the material of a single picture or drawing of a dog or a single living dog.

There is "dogness," "B-ness," truth, logic, absolute morality, and other *concepts* according to Plato that don't change. We see changes here in the material world (e.g., dogs die and return to dust as new dogs are born), yet the forms, ideas, class concepts, logic, and so on do not change. We don't have half logic or half "B-ness."

So Plato and other dualists postulate there is an unchanging, abstract realm of perfect ideas or forms (ideal realm) that they say exists that is not bound to the material universe. But they also assert that the material universe is subjected to this ideal realm so that "dogness," "B-ness," and the law of non-contradiction can exist in the material realm.

Today, we see many people following the basic tenets of Platonism, even if they don't realize they are dualists! Believe it or not, many professing atheists are actually dualists and don't realize it. They argue for materialism, but then agree that truth, love, conclusions, absolute morality, reason, concepts, theoretical mathematics, logic, and other abstract, immaterial concepts exist.

For example, I speak to a lot of atheists who say our existence is purely material, and then they go on to argue for absolute morality (e.g., murder is never acceptable). Or they agree that logic exists even though they say our reality is strictly material. These atheists are acting like dualists when they do this. Now I could go on, but this should explain that dualists hold there are both material and immaterial concepts in their view of the world that are separated in two realms — the realm we are in and an "ideal" realm of perfect ideas/concepts.

With all this in mind, remember that dualism has no God or gods involved — there is no being who governs or created both realms.

Arbitrariness and Inconsistency

Plato's brightest student, Aristotle, proposed a devastating argument that ultimately led to strife between the two. Aristotle basically posed to Plato, *"How do these two realms interact or inform each other?"*

You see, the universe in which we live is still subject to logic. The universe in which we live has "B-ness" in it and has recognizable "dogness" in it. So how does this first realm or ideal realm affect this world (secondary realm)? To which Plato, who was no doubt a brilliant mind, could not answer without telling a myth!

Plato knew he had no answer (see his book *Parmenides*) and realized that any answer he would give was a *mere opinion* (fallacious assertion).[2] It is arbitrary to assume in your own opinion that there is an abstract realm

---

2. Aristotle further elaborates this devastating case as the "Third Man argument" as a refutation.

that informs or interacts with our world. So all Plato could do was appeal to himself for this explanation, which is merely arbitrary and refuted. And even today, this devastating refutation still persists among professing dualists. So the dualistic viewpoint ultimately breaks down into arbitrariness.

Preconditions Problem

It would be inconsistent for dualists to use logic based on an arbitrary realm. The fact that Plato and other dualists use logic would be resting on arbitrariness as well. So why do they try to inconsistently use it to arrive at their positions?

Absolute and invariant logic does exist, after all. But not because it is confined to another realm as they arbitrarily proposed, but it exists as a tool because a logical God created all things and we are made in His image to use that tool! The universe obeys logic because God upholds the universe. The point is that logic exists because of God, and these dualists must borrow logic from God to make sense of anything.

In fact, nothing has meaning without God who gives meaning to things as His creations. Communication exists because we are made in the image of a communicating God. Absolute morality exists because God, an absolutely holy being, sets morality for all. Class concepts belong to God as they reflect His creations. Being made in His image, we can classify things too. So "B-ness" and "dogness" exist because of a God who gives rational meaning to things. And we as image bearers reflect this rational nature.

So immaterial things like logic, concepts, and morality exist not because of some proposed alternative realm, but because of the existence of the God of the Bible. The dualist has no God to connect absolutes to the material world and is left in the desolated rubble of arbitrariness and meaninglessness. When you delete the God of the Bible, things become meaningless.

> The fear of the LORD is the beginning of wisdom, and the knowledge of the Holy One is understanding (Proverbs 9:10).

Conclusion

These three forms — Spiritual Monism, Materialistic Monism, and Philosophical Dualism (Idealism) — all fall short logically and have inconsistencies within their own story. They are arbitrary and cannot make sense of the world in which we live.

The answer to truly understanding the world we live in lies in biblical Christianity, the king of the *religions*. It is not arbitrary, but stands on the authority of the absolute authority, who, by His very nature, is not arbitrary. Biblical Christianity is not inconsistent, as it rests on the consistent and logical all-knowing God who consistently upholds the universe just as He promised by His ultimate power. God is predicated for all knowledge and reasoning to exist.

The answer is clear.

> Where is the wise? Where is the scribe? Where is the disputer of this age? Has not God made foolish the wisdom of this world? (1 Corinthians 1:20).

Chapter 11

Christian Syncretism with Evolution and Other Belief Systems (Compromise)

Bodie Hodge

We live in strange times — I probably don't have to convince you of that.[1] Perhaps all one needs is to read the news over the course of about one week to get a small grip on the complexities of our era.

An example of a strange occurrence is found when we looked at Latin American Syncretism in Volume 2 of the World Religions and Cult series. We, in the Western world, can easily spot where Roman Catholicism had *blended* with paganism, and the adherents couldn't easily see it. We see compromise all around us where two opposing viewpoints are meshed into one strange concoction (brought "in sync" with each other, or when applied to religions, syncretized).

The Israelites were prone to do this from Moses' day (Numbers 25:1–9) through Solomon's day (1 Kings 11:1–4) and made complete in the day of our Lord (when the Israelites joined with Caesar over Christ as their ultimate authority — John 19:15).

One would think it a crazy notion to believe that solid churches that paved the road for Christianity in many parts of the world would have now become intertwined with false religions. But, with sadness, it is true.

---

1. There is nothing new under the sun (Ecclesiastes 1:9).

As citizens of once dominant Christian countries, we Christians in the USA, UK, Germany, etc. never expected such compromise to fill our own backyard. We expect to see this elsewhere, but not in our own pews ... right? How wrong we are if we think such a thing. Does the Church in many parts of the Western world realize they have done the same thing as the pagans and other syncretists?

As an example, a Christian from Latin America can come to the USA or the UK and easily spot where Christians, leaders and laymen, have mixed our Christianity with the religion of evolution. So often, our compromised Christian brethren do not believe they have done the same thing that the Israelites did when they mixed their godly worship with Baal worship — they are just using the modern religion of the day, which is a secular view of evolution.

It is time to step back and have a look at our Christianity. Is it purely biblical or is it blended into a strange concoction with the evolutionary religion of our culture — or other religions like those in the East (New Age, Hinduism, Mysticism, etc.)?

The Four Aspects of Evolution

What is evolution? In its broadest sense, evolution is the naturalistic explanation of the origin and function of the universe, the "*general theory of evolution (GTE)*" or, in laymen's terms, "molecules-to-man," "electron-to-engineer," or "goo-to-you." But within this concept there are really four types of evolution, which are intrinsically connected to make up the whole naturalistic worldview explaining the universe without the need for a divine being. Evolution is a key tenet of the religion of Secular Humanism.

Cosmological/Astronomical Evolution: The big bang (everything came from nothing) created the universe and gradually formed into elements, stars, galaxies, and planetary systems.

Geological Evolution: Millions of years of slow, gradual accumulations of rock layers, including fossils.

Chemical Evolution: Life came from non-living matter, otherwise called abiogenesis.

Biological Evolution: A single, simple life form gave rise to all other life forms down through the ages.

Within the church, there are those who try to fit astronomical evolution, geological evolution, chemical evolution, or biological evolution into the Bible. Some Christians accept one, some, or all of these in their attempts to accommodate the secular beliefs with God's Word. This acceptance undermines the authority of the Word of God. This is ultimately undermining the gospel as it undercuts the Word of God from which the message of the gospel comes.

Let me explain this further, as it is quite important to grasp. The concept of millions of years (geological evolution) is a vital foundation for an evolutionary worldview. Without millions of years, there is no possibility of evolution — even evolutionists concede this (i.e., we don't have evolutionists arguing that all things evolved over the course of about 6,000 years from a single-celled organism). They *must* have millions of years.

Since God said He created all things in six days and rested on the seventh, how do syncretistic Christians deal with the millions of years? Virtually all Christians who have bought into an old earth (i.e., millions and billions of years or long ages) place the millions of years *prior* to Adam.

We have genealogical lists that connect Adam to Christ (e.g., Luke 3). For the compromising Christians, it would be blatantly absurd to try to insert millions and billions of years into these genealogies and say that Adam and Eve were made at the beginning of creation.[2]

Instead, old-earth creationists (as they are often denoted[3]) take these long ages and insert them somewhere prior to Adam; hence creation week has been a divisive point in Christianity ever since the idea of long ages became popular in the 1800s.

Biblically, How Old Is the Earth?

The primary sides are:

- Young-earth proponents (biblical age of the earth and universe of about 6,000 years)[4]
- Old-earth proponents (secular age of the earth of about 4.5 billion years and a universe about 14 billion years old)[5]

---

2. In Mark 10:6, Jesus says, "But from the beginning of the creation, God 'made them male and female.' "

3. In many other cases, those Christians who adhere to long ages are called "compromised Christians" since they are compromising by mixing these two religions' origins accounts (Secular Humanism and Christianity).

4. Not all young-earth creationists agree on this age, though the number is typically thousands, not millions.

5. Some of these old-earth proponents accept molecules-to-man biological evolution and so are called theistic evolutionists. Others reject neo-Darwinian evolution but accept the evolutionary timescale for astronomical and geological evolution, and hence agree with the evolutionary order of events in history.

The difference is immense! Let's give a little history of where the *biblical calculation* came from. We will discuss the old-earth development in the subsequent chapter on philosophical naturalism.

Where Did a Young-Earth Worldview Come From?

Simply put, it came from the Bible. Of course, the Bible doesn't say explicitly anywhere, "The earth is 6,000 years old." And it's a good thing it doesn't; otherwise it would be out of date the following year. But we wouldn't expect an all-knowing God to make that kind of a mistake.

God gave us something better. In essence, He gave us a "birth certificate." For example, using a personal birth certificate, a person can calculate how old he is at any point. It is similar with the earth. Genesis 1 says that the earth was created on the first day of creation (Genesis 1:1–5). From there, we can begin to calculate the age of the earth.

Let's do a rough calculation to show how this works. The age of the earth can be estimated by taking the first five days of creation (from earth's creation to Adam), then following the genealogies from Adam to Abraham in Genesis 5 and 11, then adding in the time from Abraham to today.

Adam was created on day 6, so there were five days before him. If we add up the dates from Adam to Abraham, we get about 2,000 years, using the Masoretic Hebrew text of Genesis 5 and 11.[6] Whether Christian or secular, most scholars would agree that Abraham lived about 2000 B.C. (4,000 years ago). So a simple calculation is:

> 5 days (creation to Adam)
> + ~2,000 years (Adam to Abraham)
> + ~4,000 years (Abraham to present)
> _____
>
> ~6,000 years

At this point, the first five days are negligible. Quite a few people have done this calculation using the Masoretic text (which is what most English translations are based on) and, with careful attention to the biblical details, have arrived at the same age of about 6,000 years, or about 4000 B.C. Two of the

---

6. Bodie Hodge, "Ancient Patriarchs in Genesis," Answers in Genesis, https://answersingenesis.org/bible-characters/ancient-patriarchs-in-genesis/.

Table 1: Jones and Ussher

Name	Age calculated	Reference and date
James Ussher	4004 B.C.	*The Annals of the World*, A.D. 1658
Floyd Nolen Jones	4004 B.C.	*The Chronology of the Old Testament*, A.D. 1993

most popular, and perhaps best, are a recent work by Floyd Jones[7] and a much earlier book by James Ussher[8] (1581–1656). See table 1.

The misconception exists that Ussher and Jones were the only ones to arrive at a date of 4000 B.C.; however, this is not the case at all. Jones[9] lists several chronologists who have undertaken the task of calculating the age of the earth based on the Bible, and their calculations range from 5501 to 3836 B.C. A few are listed in table 2 with a couple of newer ones and their reference.

As you will likely note from table 2, the dates are not all exact, even though the majority lie between 3950 and 4050 B.C. — hovering on each side of 4000 B.C. There are two primary reasons chronologists have different dates.[10]

Some used the Septuagint, or another early translation, instead of the Hebrew Masoretic text. The Septuagint is a Greek translation of the Hebrew Old Testament, completed around 250 B.C. by about 70 Jewish scholars (hence it is often cited as the LXX, 70 in roman numerals). It is good in most places, but appears to have a number of inaccuracies. For example, one relates to the Genesis chronologies where the LXX indicates that Methuselah would have lived past the Flood without being on the ark!

Several points in the biblical timeline are not straightforward to calculate. They require very careful study of more than one passage. These include exactly how long the Israelites were in Egypt and what Terah's age was when Abraham was born. (See Jones and Ussher for a detailed discussion of these difficulties.)

---

7. Floyd Nolen Jones, *Chronology of the Old Testament* (Green Forest, AR: Master Books, 2005).
8. James Ussher, *The Annals of the World* (Green Forest, AR: Master Books, 2003), translated by Larry and Marion Pierce.
9. Jones, *Chronology of the Old Testament*, p. 26.
10. Others would include gaps in the chronology based on the presences of an extra Cainan in Luke 3:36. But there are good reasons this variant is a transcription error and not part of the original text.

Table 2: Chronologists' Calculations

Age of the Earth (range B.C.)	Chronologist
3800–3850	A. Helwigius (c. 1630)
3850–3900	N/A
3900–3950	M. Beroaldus (c. 1675), J. Scaliger (d. 1609)
3950–4000	A. Salmeron (d. 1585), J. Haynlinus, P. Melanchthon (c. 1550), C. Longomontanus (c. 1600), J. Claverius, E. Reusnerus, W. Dolen (2003), Krentzeim, Becke, Frank Klassen (1975), D. Petavius (c. 1627)
4000–4050	James Ussher (c. 1656), Floyd Nolan Jones (1993), E. Faulstich (1986), E. Greswell (1830), J. Cappellus (c. 1600), E. Reinholt, W. Lange, Martin Anstey (1913),
4050–4100	H. Spondanus (1600), Jacob Salianus (c. 1600), J. Ricciolus, M. Michael Maestlinus (c. 1600),
4100–4150	Thomas Lydiat (c. 1600)
4150–4200	Jim Liles (2013),* L. Condomanus, Marianus Scotus (c. 1070)
4200–4950	N/A
4950–5550**	John Jackson, Julius Africanus, Dr. William Hales, George Syncellus, Eusebius, Dr. Benjamin Shaw***

* Jim Liles, *Earth's Sacred Calendar* (Tarzana, CA: Bible Timeline, 2013).

** Utilizing the LXX (Septuagint).

*** Benjamin Shaw, "The Genealogies of Genesis 5 and 11 and Their Significance for Chronology," BJU, December, 2004. Dr. Shaw states the date as "about 5000 B.C." in appendix I, but the specific date is derived from adding 1,656 years (the time from creation to the Flood) to his date of the Flood, which is stated as 3298 B.C. on p. 222.

The first four in table 2 (bolded) are calculated from the Septuagint (others give certain favoritism to the LXX too), which gives ages for the patriarchs' firstborn much higher than the Masoretic text or the Samaritan Pentateuch (a version of the Old Testament from the Jews in Samaria just before Christ). Because of this, the Septuagint adds in extra time. Though the Samaritan and Masoretic texts are much closer, they still have a few differences (see table 3).

Table 3: Septuagint, Masoretic, and Samaritan Early Patriarchal Ages at the Birth of the Following Son

Name of Father	Masoretic	Samaritan Pentateuch	Septuagint (LXX)
Adam	130	130	230
Seth	105	105	205
Enosh	90	90	190
Cainan	70	70	170
Mahalalel	65	65	165
Jared	162	62	162
Enoch	65	65	165
Methuselah	187	67	167
Lamech	182	53	188
Noah	500	500	500

Using data from table 2 (excluding the Septuagint calculations and including Jones and Ussher), the average date of the creation of the earth is 4045 B.C. This still yields an average of about 6,000 years for the age of the earth.

Extra-biblical Calculations for the Age of the Earth

Cultures throughout the world have kept track of history as well. From a biblical perspective, we would expect these dates given for creation of the earth to align much closer to the biblical date than billions of years.

This is expected, since everyone was descended from Noah and scattered from the Tower of Babel. Another expectation is that there should be some discrepancies about the age of the earth among people as they scattered throughout the world, taking their uninspired records or oral history to different parts of the globe.

Under the entry "creation," *Young's Analytical Concordance of the Bible*[11] lists William Hales' accumulation of dates of creation from many cultures. In most cases, Hales says which authority gave the date (see table 4).

---

11. Robert Young, *Young's Analytical Concordance to the Bible* (Peabody, MA: Hendrickson, 1996), referring to William Hales, *A New Analysis of Chronology and Geography, History and Prophecy*, Vol. 1 (1830), p. 210.

Table 4: Selected Dates for the Age of the Earth by Various Cultures

Culture	Age, B.C.	Authority listed by Hales
Spain by Alfonso X	6984	Muller
Spain by Alfonso X	6484	Strauchius
India	6204	Gentil
India	6174	Arab Records
Babylon	6158	Bailly
Chinese	6157	Bailly
Greece by Diogenes Laertius	6138	Playfair
Egypt	6081	Bailly
Persia	5507	Bailly
Israel/Judea by Josephus	5555	Playfair
Israel/Judea by Josephus	5481	Jackson
Israel/Judea by Josephus	5402	Hales
Israel/Judea by Josephus	4698	University History
India	5369	Megasthenes
Babylon (Talmud)	5344	Petrus Alliacens
Vatican (Catholic using the Septuagint)	5270	N/A
Samaria	4427	Scaliger
German, Holy Roman Empire by Johannes Kepler*	3993	Playfair
German, reformer by Martin Luther	3961	N/A
Israel/Judea by computation	3760	Strauchius
Israel/Judea by Rabbi Lipman	3616	University History

* Luther, Kepler, Lipman, and the Jewish computation likely used biblical texts to determine the date.

Historian Bill Cooper's research in *After the Flood* provides dates from several ancient cultures.[12] The first is that of the Anglo-Saxons, whose history has 5,200 years from creation to Christ, according to the Laud and Parker Chronicles. Cooper's research also indicated that Nennius' record of

12. Bill Cooper, *After the Flood* (UK: New Wine Press, 1995), p. 122–129.

the ancient British history has 5,228 years from creation to Christ. The Irish chronology has a date of about 4000 B.C. for creation, which is surprisingly close to Ussher and Jones! Even the Mayans had a date for the Flood of 3113 B.C. (the biblical date being 2349 B.C.).

The meticulous work of many historians should not be ignored. Their dates of only thousands of years are good support for the biblical date somewhere in the neighborhood of about 6,000 years, but not for millions or billions of years.

Origin of Geological Evolution

Prior to the late 1700s, precious few believed in an old earth. The approximate 6,000-year age for the earth was challenged only rather recently, beginning in the late 18th century. These opponents of the biblical chronology essentially left God out of the picture.

Old-earth advocates included Comte de Buffon, who thought the earth was at least 75,000 years old; Pièrre-Simon Laplace imagined an indefinite but very long history; and Jean-Baptiste Lamarck also proposed long ages.[13]

However, the idea of millions of years really took hold in geology when men like Abraham Werner, James Hutton, William Smith, Georges Cuvier, and Charles Lyell used their interpretations of geology as the standard, rather than the Bible. Werner estimated the age of the earth at about one million years. Smith and Cuvier believed untold ages were needed for the formation of rock layers. Hutton said he could see no geological evidence of a beginning of the earth; and building on Hutton's thinking, Lyell advocated "millions of years."

From these men and others came the secular consensus view that the geologic layers were laid down slowly over long periods of time based on the rates at which we see them accumulating today. This view is known as uniformitarianism since it proposes steady geologic processes over long periods of time. Hutton said:

> The past history of our globe must be explained by what can be seen to be happening now. . . . No powers are to be employed that are not natural to the globe, no action to be admitted except those of which we know the principle.[14]

13. Terry Mortenson, "The Origin of Old-earth Geology and Its Ramifications for Life in the 21st Century," TJ 18, no. 1 (2004): 22–26, online at www.answersingenesis.org/tj/v18/i1/oldearth.asp.
14. James Hutton, *Theory of the Earth* (trans. of Roy. Soc. of Edinburgh, 1785), quoted in A. Holmes, *Principles of Physical Geology* (UK: Thomas Nelson & Sons Ltd., 1965), p. 43–44.

Though some, such as Cuvier and Smith, believed in multiple catastrophes separated by long periods of time, the uniformitarian concept became the ruling dogma in geology.

Thinking biblically, we can see that the global Flood of Genesis 6–8 would wipe away the concept of millions of years, for this Flood would explain massive amounts of fossil layers. Most Christians fail to realize that a global Flood could rip up many of the previous rock layers and redeposit them elsewhere, destroying the previous fragile contents. This would destroy any evidence of alleged millions of years anyway. So the rock layers can theoretically represent the evidence of either millions of years or a global Flood, but not both. Sadly, by about 1840 even most of the church elite had accepted the dogmatic claims of the secular geologists and rejected the global Flood[15] and the biblical age of the earth.

After Lyell, in 1899 Lord Kelvin (William Thomson) calculated the age of the earth based on the cooling rate of a molten sphere instead of water (Genesis 1:2).[16] He calculated it to be a maximum of about 20–40 million years (this was revised from his earlier calculation of 100 million years in 1862).[17]

With the development of radiometric dating in the early 20th century, the age of the earth expanded radically. In 1913, Arthur Holmes' book, *The Age of the Earth,* gave an age of 1.6 billion years.[18] Since then, the supposed age of the earth has expanded to its present estimate of about 4.5 billion years (and about 14 billion years for the universe). But there is growing scientific evidence that radiometric dating methods are completely unreliable.[19]

15. Some still accepted a global Flood, but considered it geologically insignificant. This position is often called the Tranquil Flood theory. But when the devastating effects of even a local flood are observed, a tranquil global Flood becomes an absurdity.
16. The earth was without form, and void; and darkness was on the face of the deep. And the Spirit of God was hovering over the face of the waters.
17. Mark McCartney, "William Thompson: King of Victorian Physics," *Physics World*, December 2002, physicsworld.com/cws/article/print/16484.
18. Terry Mortenson, "The History of the Development of the Geological Column," in *The Geologic Column*, eds. Michael Oard and John Reed (Chino Valley, AZ: Creation Research Society, 2006).
19. For articles at the layman's level, see www.answersingenesis.org/home/area/faq/dating.asp. For a technical discussion, see Larry Vardiman, Andrew Snelling, and Eugene Chaffin, eds., *Radioisotopes and the Age of the Earth*, Vol. 1 and 2 (El Cajon, CA: Institute for Creation Research; Chino Valley, Arizona: Creation Research Society, 2000 and 2005). See also "Half-Life Heresy," *New Scientist*, October 21 2006, p. 36–39, abstract online at www.newscientist.com/channel/fundamentals/mg19225741.100-halflife-heresy-accelerating-radioactive-decay.html.

Table 5: Summary of the Old-Earth Proponents of Long Ages

Who?	Age of the earth	Date
Comte de Buffon	78 thousand years	1779
Abraham Werner	1 million years	1786
James Hutton	Perhaps eternal, long ages	1795
Pièrre LaPlace	Long ages	1796
Jean-Baptiste Lamarck	Long ages	1809
William Smith	Long ages	1835
Georges Cuvier	Long ages	1812
Charles Lyell	Millions of years	1830–1833
Lord Kelvin	20–100 million years	1862–1899
Arthur Holmes	1.6 billion years	1913
Clair Patterson	4.5 billion years	1956

Christians who have felt compelled to accept the millions of years as fact and try to fit them into the Bible need to become aware of this evidence. Today, secular geologists will allow some catastrophic events into their thinking as an explanation for what they see in the rocks. But uniformitarian thinking is still widespread, and secular geologists will seemingly never entertain the idea of the global catastrophic Flood of Noah's day.

The age of the earth debate ultimately comes down to this foundational question: Are we trusting man's imperfect and changing ideas and assumptions about the past, or are we trusting God's perfectly accurate eyewitness account of the past, including the creation of the world, Noah's global Flood, and the age of the earth?

When we start our thinking with God's Word, we see that the world is about 6,000 years old. Ancient cultures around the world give an age of the earth that confirms what the Bible teaches. The age of the earth ultimately comes down to a matter of trust — it's a religious issue. Will you trust what an all-knowing God says on the subject or will you trust imperfect man's assumptions and imaginations about the past that change regularly?

Sadly, many theologians in the 1800s began mixing geological evolution (millions of years) with the Bible — even before Darwin had published his work on biological evolution. This opened the door to accepting other forms of evolution as well. Let's take a look at these positions that theologians developed to accommodate evolutionary ideas.

Christian Syncretistic Positions

Here are some of the differing positions within the church — but all having one common factor — endeavoring to somehow fit geological evolution into the Bible.

Gap Theories

In general, these theories accommodate geological and astronomical evolution by placing vast ages in a "gap" in the first few verses of Genesis.

Pre-time Gap: This view adds long ages prior to God creating in Genesis 1:1.[20] The pre-time gap falls short for a number of reasons such as death before sin, allowance of man's ideas about millions of years to supersede God's Word, and the like. As another example, how can one have millions of years of time prior to the creation of time? It is quite illogical.

Ruin-reconstruction Gap: This is the most popular gap theory, which adds long ages between Genesis 1:1[21] and Genesis 1:2.[22] Scottish pastor Thomas Chalmers popularized it in the early 1800s. This idea is promoted in the Scofield and Dake Study Bibles and is often associated with a Luciferian fall and flood — but that would make Lucifer (Satan) in his sinful state very good and perfect since God said everything He made was "very good" after Adam had been created (Deuteronomy 32:4[23]; Genesis 1:31).[24]

Modified Gap/Precreation Chaos Gap: This view adds long ages between Genesis 1:2[25] and 1:3,[26] and it is primarily addressed in the International Conference on Creation article listed in this reference.[27]

---

20. In the beginning God created the heavens and the earth.
21. Ibid.
22. The earth was without form, and void; and darkness was on the face of the deep. And the Spirit of God was hovering over the face of the waters.
23. He is the Rock, His work is perfect; for all His ways are justice, a God of truth and without injustice; righteous and upright is He.
24. Ken Ham, "What About the Gap & Ruin-Reconstruction Theories?" in *The New Answers Book*, Ken Ham, Gen. Ed. (Green Forest, AR: Master Books, 2006); for a technical response see also, W. Fields, *Unformed and Unfilled*, (Burgener Enterprises, 1997).
25. The earth was without form, and void; and darkness was on the face of the deep. And the Spirit of God was hovering over the face of the waters.
26. Then God said, "Let there be light"; and there was light.
27. One refutation of this view is in the Proceedings of the Sixth International Conference on Creationism, 2008, by John Zoschke, *A Critique of the Precreation Chaos Gap Theory*, ed., Andrew Snelling.

Soft Gap: This also includes a gap between Genesis 1:2[28] and 1:3,[29] but unlike previous views, it has no catastrophic events or destruction of a previous state. Furthermore, it merely proposes that God created the world this way and left it for long periods of time in an effort to get starlight here. In essence, this view has a young earth and an old universe. The problem is that stars were created after the proposed gap (day 4), and it is unnecessary to make accommodations for long ages to solve the so-called starlight problem.

Late Gap: This view has a gap between chapters 2 and 3 of Genesis. In other words, some believe that Adam and Eve lived in the Garden for long ages before sin. This view has problems too. For example, Adam and Eve were told by God to be "fruitful and multiply" in Genesis 1:28,[30] and waiting long ages to do so would have been disobeying God's Word. This doesn't make sense. In addition, there is the problem of Adam only living 930 years as recorded in Genesis (Genesis 5:5[31]).[32]

When someone tries to put a large gap of time in the Scriptures when it is not warranted by the text, this should throw up a red flag to any Christian.

Day-Age Models

Each of these views adheres to some form of astronomical and geologic evolution, but most would reject chemical and biological evolution (or at least Darwinian evolution). The name comes from equating each of the days of Genesis 1 to a long period of time.

Day-Age: This idea was popularized by Hugh Miller in the early 1800s after walking away from Chalmers' idea of the gap theory. This model basically stretched the days of creation out to be millions of years long. Some would accept biological evolution (to varying degrees), but most would believe in the special creation of humans even if they allow for other living things to evolve. Of course, lengthening the days in Genesis to accommodate

---

28. The earth was without form, and void; and darkness was on the face of the deep. And the Spirit of God was hovering over the face of the waters.
29. Then God said, "Let there be light"; and there was light.
30. Then God blessed them, and God said to them, "Be fruitful and multiply; fill the earth and subdue it; have dominion over the fish of the sea, over the birds of the air, and over every living thing that moves on the earth."
31. So all the days that Adam lived were nine hundred and thirty years; and he died.
32. Bodie Hodge, *The Fall of Satan* (Green Forest, AR: Master Books, 2011), p. 23–26, https://answersingenesis.org/bible-characters/adam-and-eve/when-did-adam-and-eve-rebel/.

the secular evolutionist view of history simply doesn't match up with what is stated in Genesis 1.[33]

Progressive Creation: This is a modified form of the Day-Age idea (really in many ways it's similar to Theistic Evolution) led by Dr. Hugh Ross, head of an organization called Reasons to Believe. He appeals to nature (actually the secular interpretations of nature) as the supposed 67th book of the Bible, and then uses these interpretations to supersede what the Bible says, thus reinterpreting Genesis to force these ideas into Scripture. Dr. John Ankerberg is also a leading supporter of this viewpoint.[34] This view proposes that living creatures go extinct repeatedly over millions of years, but God, from time to time, makes new kinds and new species all fitting with a (geologically and cosmologically/astronomically) evolutionary timeframe of history.[35]

Theistic Evolutionary Models (each basically adhere to geological, astronomical, and biological evolution)

Theistic Evolution (Evolutionary Creation): Basically, the straightforward reading of Genesis 1–11 is thrown out or heavily reinterpreted to allow for evolutionary ideas to supersede the Scriptures. This view is heavily promoted by a group called BioLogos. They accept the prevailing evolutionist history, including the big bang, and then add God to it, giving Him credit for setting the laws of nature in place to bring about mankind. BioLogos writers have different ways of wildly reinterpreting Genesis to fit evolution into Scripture. Many would say that Genesis 1–11 has nothing to do with how God created, only to offer the Israelites a creation myth like the surrounding nations had.

Framework Hypothesis: Dr. Meredith Kline (1922–2007), who accepted some evolutionary ideas, popularized this view in America.[36] Today,

---

33. Terry Mortenson, "Evolution vs. Creation: The Order of Events Matters!" Answers in Genesis, April 4, 2006, https://answersingenesis.org/why-does-creation-matter/evolution-vs-creation-the-order-of-events-matters/.

34. J. Seegert, "Responding to the Compromise Views of John Ankerberg," Answers in Genesis, March 2, 2005, https://answersingenesis.org/reviews/tv/responding-to-the-compromise-views-of-john-ankerberg/.

35. Ken Ham and Terry Mortenson, "What's Wrong with Progressive Creation?" in Ken Ham, Gen. Ed., *The New Answers Book 2* (Green Forest, AR: Master Book, 2008), p. 123–134.

36. It was originally developed in 1924 by Professor Arnie Noordtzij in Europe, which was a couple of decades before Dr. Kline jumped on board with Framework Hypothesis.

Bruce Waltke holds it in esteem. It is very common in many seminaries today. Those who hold this view treat Genesis 1 as poetry or semi-poetic, with the first three days paralleling the last three days of creation. These days are not seen as 24-hour days, but are taken as metaphorical or allegorical to allow for ideas like evolution/millions of years to be entertained. Hence, Genesis 1 is treated as merely being a literary device to teach that God created everything.[37] However, Genesis 1 is not written as poetry, but as literal history.[38]

Cosmic Temple/Functionality View: Dr. John Walton agrees the language of Genesis 1 means ordinary days, but since he believes in evolution he had to do something to reconcile the biblical text to this belief. Walton proposes that Genesis 1 has nothing to do with material origins, but instead is referring to what he calls "God's Cosmic Temple." By disconnecting Genesis 1 from material origins of earth, he is free to believe in evolution and millions of years.

Other attempts to include evolutionary ideas into Genesis include Revelatory Day View by J.P. Wiseman, Analogical (Anthropomorphic) Day View by C. John Collins, and the Promised Land View (a modified gap theory) by John Sailhamer. In each case, the Bible's plain reading is demoted to allow for evolutionary ideas.

Problems with Evolutionary Syncretism

Global or Local Flood?

> The flood was indeed a river flood. . . . The language of Genesis allows for a regional flood. . . . The parts of modern Iraq which were occupied by the ancient Sumerians are extremely

---

37. Tim Chaffey and Robert McCabe, "What Is Wrong with the Framework Hypothesis?" Answers in Genesis, June 11, 2011, https://answersingenesis.org/creationism/old-earth/whats-wrong-with-the-framework-hypothesis/.

38. Hebrew expert Dr. Steven Boyd writes: "For Genesis 1:1–2:3, this probability is between 0.999942 and 0.999987 at a 99.5% confidence level. Thus, we conclude with statistical certainty that this text is narrative, not poetry. It is therefore statistically indefensible to argue that it is poetry. The hermeneutical implication of this finding is that this text should be read as other historical narratives. . . ." Dr. Steven Boyd, Associate Professor of Bible, The Master's College, *Radioisotopes and the Age of the Earth*, Volume II, Editors Larry Vardiman, Andrew Snelling, and Eugene Chaffin, ICR and CRS, 2005, p. 632. I would go one step further than Dr. Boyd, who left open the slim possibility of Genesis not being historical narrative, and say it is historical narrative and all doctrines of theology, directly or indirectly, are founded in the early pages of Genesis — though I appreciated Dr. Boyd's research.

flat. The floodplain, surrounding the Tigris and the Euphrates rivers, covers over 50,000 square miles which slope toward the gulf at less than one foot per mile. . . . Drainage is extremely poor and flooding is quite common, even without large rainstorms during the summer river-level peak (when Noah's flood happened).[39]

A Christian who believes that Noah's Flood was local and did not cover the entire globe penned these words. In fact, the idea of a small regional flood in Noah's day is often promoted by Christians who mix the Bible's clear teaching with "millions of years" of supposed naturalistic history!

As a reminder, you need to understand that the idea of millions of years comes from the belief that rock layers all over the world were laid down slowly over long ages without any major catastrophes. In other words, the idea of millions of years is predicated on the idea that there could NOT have been a global Flood. Otherwise, a global Flood would disrupt rock layers that exist and rearrange the sediment and lay down new rock layers!

What Does the Bible Say?

Did Noah experience a local flood, which left only a few sediment layers as floods do today? God's record is clear: the water covered the entire globe and killed all the land-dwelling animals on earth not aboard the ark. Such unique conditions are the only consistent way to explain worldwide fossil-bearing layers thousands of feet deep.

Scripture is clear about the historic reality of a global Flood in Noah's day. Genesis 7:17–23 specifically says:

> Now the flood was on the earth forty days. The waters increased and lifted up the ark, and it rose high above the earth. The waters prevailed and greatly increased on the earth, and the ark moved about on the surface of the waters. And the waters prevailed exceedingly on the earth, and all the high hills under the whole heaven were covered. The waters prevailed fifteen cubits upward, and the mountains were covered. And all flesh died that moved on the earth: birds and cattle and beasts and

---

39. Don Stoner, "The Historical Context for the Book of Genesis," Revision 2011-06-06, Part 3: Identifying Noah and the Great Flood, http://www.dstoner.net/Genesis_Context/Context.html#part3.

every creeping thing that creeps on the earth, and every man. All in whose nostrils was the breath of the spirit of life, all that was on the dry land, died. So He destroyed all living things which were on the face of the ground: both man and cattle, creeping thing and bird of the air. They were destroyed from the earth. Only Noah and those who were with him in the ark remained alive.

The Scripture is clear that "all the high hills under the whole heaven were covered" as "the waters prevailed fifteen cubits [that is about ~26 feet,[40] or ~8 m.] upward." All air-breathing land animals and people who were outside the ark who lived on the earth also died (Genesis 7:22–23).

Today, many people, including Christians, unfortunately do not accept the biblical account of a worldwide flood because they have been taught that most rocks and fossils were deposited over millions of years (and therefore not by a global Flood). Until the 1800s, most people from the Middle East to the Western world believed what the Bible records about creation and the global Flood. The secular idea of millions of years did not gain extensive popularity until the 1830s, under the influence of a man named Charles Lyell — who opposed a global Flood!

Based on how slowly some rock layers seem to form today (assuming no catastrophes), Lyell rejected the Bible's claims and declared that the earth's many rock layers must have been laid down slowly over millions of years. But he never witnessed the actual formation of the earlier rocks to see whether a unique, one-time global Flood unlike anything we observe today could lay the majority of the rock layers with fossils.

Lyell's claim was based on his own preconceptions and belief in the religion of naturalism, not his observations. Lyell's idea took hold in Western universities and spread throughout the Western world.

As a response, many Christians simply tried to add this idea of long ages to the Bible. What these Christians should have done was stand on the authority of the Bible and defend the global Flood, which can easily account for the bulk of fossil-bearing rock layers we find all over the world. Naturally, we have had some rock layers since the time of the Flood with local catastrophes such as volcanoes or local floods. But the bulk of the rock layers with fossils came from the Flood of Noah's day.

---

40. Using the long cubit of about 20.4 inches.

Some Christians have tried to put millions of years of rock formation before the global Flood to explain the bulk of the rock layers that contain fossils. But the problem is that the floodwaters would have ripped up a number of these old rock layers and laid down new ones! So this compromise not only fails to explain the rock layers, but also dishonors the clear claims of Scripture. The global Flood makes perfect sense, and it is foolish to stray from God's Word just because some men disagree that it happened.

Although there is tremendous physical evidence of a global flood, ultimately it is a matter of trust in a perfect God who created everything (Genesis 1:1),[41] knows everything (Colossians 2:3),[42] has always been there (Revelation 22:13),[43] and cannot lie (Titus 1:2).[44] The only alternative is to trust imperfect, fallible human beings who can only speculate on the past (see Romans 3:4).[45]

Local Flood Problems

Additionally, there are many problems with the claim that Noah's Flood was local. For instance:

- Why did God tell Noah to build an ark? If the Flood had been only local, Noah and his family could have just moved to higher ground or over a local mountain range or hills to avoid the floodwaters.
- The wicked people that the Flood was intended to destroy could have escaped God's judgment in the same manner. They could have used small boats or floating debris to swim to the edge of the flooded region and survive.
- Why would Noah have to put birds on the ark when they could have flown over the hills to safe ground?
- Why would animals be required to be on the ark to keep their kinds alive on the earth (Genesis 7:2–3)[46] if representatives

---

41. In the beginning God created the heavens and the earth.
42. In whom [Christ] are hidden all the treasures of wisdom and knowledge.
43. I am the Alpha and the Omega, the Beginning and the End, the First and the Last.
44. In hope of eternal life which God, who cannot lie, promised before time began.
45. Certainly not! Indeed, let God be true but every man a liar. As it is written: "That You may be justified in Your words, and may overcome when You are judged."
46. You shall take with you seven each of every clean animal, a male and his female; two each of animals that are unclean, a male and his female; also seven each of birds of the air, male and female, to keep the species alive on the face of all the earth.

of their kinds existed all over the earth outside of the alleged local Flood area?

- Did God fail at His stated task where He said that He would destroy all land animals on the earth since the Flood was *local* (Genesis 6:17)?[47]
- Why would a flood occur over the course of about a year if it were local?
- Why did Noah remain on the ark for about seven months after coming to rest after a little river flood? Does a local flood really have about five months of rising and five months of falling in a river valley? Such a flood would merely carve out a deep valley and wash Noah downstream to the ocean!
- How could the ark have landed in the mountains of Ararat far upstream (and up in the mountains above) from the alleged river valley when all flow is going to take the ark in the opposite direction toward the Persian Gulf?
- The Flood occurred about 1,656 years after creation. If all people outside the ark were judged and drowned in this little local river Flood (e.g., Genesis 7:23;[48] Matthew 24:39[49]) then they were all still living in this one little region on earth. Why didn't the Lord previously confuse their languages and scatter them for disobeying his command in Genesis 1 to be fruitful and multiply (Genesis 1:28)?[50] It only took about 100 years or so after the Flood for God to judge mankind for not scattering at Babel.[51]

The proposal of a local Flood for Genesis 6–8 simply doesn't make sense in the context.

---

47. And behold, I Myself am bringing floodwaters on the earth, to destroy from under heaven all flesh in which is the breath of life; everything that is on the earth shall die.
48. So He destroyed all living things which were on the face of the ground: both man and cattle, creeping thing and bird of the air. They were destroyed from the earth. Only Noah and those who were with him in the ark remained alive.
49. And did not know until the flood came and took them all away, so also will the coming of the Son of Man be.
50. Then God blessed them, and God said to them, "Be fruitful and multiply; fill the earth and subdue it; have dominion over the fish of the sea, over the birds of the air, and over every living thing that moves on the earth."
51. Bodie Hodge, *Tower of Babel* (Green Forest, AR: Master Books, 2013), p. 37–42.

Rainbow Promise

Another problem presents itself. If the Flood were local, then God would be a liar. God promised in Genesis 9:11[52] never to send a Flood like the one He just did to destroy the earth again. Yet the world has seen many local floods. Why the rainbow promise? The Bible says:

> Thus I establish My covenant with you: Never again shall all flesh be cut off by the waters of the flood; never again shall there be a flood to destroy the earth." And God said: "This is the sign of the covenant which I make between Me and you, and every living creature that is with you, for perpetual generations: I set My rainbow in the cloud, and it shall be for the sign of the covenant between Me and the earth. It shall be, when I bring a cloud over the earth, that the rainbow shall be seen in the cloud; and I will remember My covenant which is between Me and you and every living creature of all flesh; the waters shall never again become a flood to destroy all flesh. The rainbow shall be in the cloud, and I will look on it to remember the everlasting covenant between God and every living creature of all flesh that is on the earth." And God said to Noah, "This is the sign of the covenant which I have established between Me and all flesh that is on the earth" (Genesis 9:11–17).

This rules out the idea of a local flood. Some have commented that they think rainbows didn't exist until this point in Genesis 9. However, the Bible doesn't say this. Like bread and wine used in communion, so a rainbow now takes on the meaning as designated by God.

Each old-earth Christian worldview has no choice but to demote a global Flood to a local flood in order to accommodate the alleged millions of years (geological evolution) of rock layers (a global Flood would have destroyed these layers and laid down new ones).[53]

---

52. Thus I establish My covenant with you: Never again shall all flesh be cut off by the waters of the flood; never again shall there be a flood to destroy the earth.
53. Jason Lisle and Tim Chaffey, "Defense — A Local Flood?" in *Old Earth Creation on Trial* (Green Forest, AR: Master Books, 2008), p. 93–106, https://answersingenesis.org/the-flood/global/defensea-local-flood.

Big Bang

Also, the compromise views that accept the big-bang model of the origin of the universe have accepted a view that contradicts Scripture. They have adopted a model to explain the universe without God. So if God is added to the big bang idea, then really . . . . God didn't do anything because the big-bang model dictates that the universe really created itself.[54]

Death before Sin

Each view also has an insurmountable problem in regard to the issue of death before sin that undermines both the authority of God's Word and the gospel.[55] The idea of millions of years came out of naturalism — the belief that the fossil-bearing rock layers were laid down slowly and gradually over millions of years before man.

This idea was meant to do away with the belief that Noah's Flood was responsible for most of the fossil-bearing sedimentary layers. Now in the fossil remains in these rock layers there is evidence of death, suffering, thorns, carnivory, cancer, and other diseases like arthritis.

So *all* old-earth worldviews have to then accept death, suffering, bloodshed, thorns, carnivory, and diseases like cancer before Adam's sin. Now, after God created Adam, He said everything He made was "very good" (Genesis 1:31).[56] This is confirmed as a *perfect* creation by the God of life in Deuteronomy 32:4[57] since every work of God is perfect.

But if one has accepted the millions-of-years idea to explain the fossil record, then millions of years of death, bloodshed, disease, thorns, suffering, and carnivory existed before man. But as the Bible makes clear, it was Adam's sin that caused death (Genesis 2:16–17,[58] 3:19[59]), suffering (e.g., Genesis

54. J. Lisle, "Does the Big Bang Fit with the Bible?" in K. Ham, Gen. Ed., *The New Answers Book 2* (Green Forest, AR: Master Books, 2008), p. 103–110, https://answersingenesis.org/big-bang/does-the-big-bang-fit-with-the-bible.
55. Hodge, *The Fall of Satan*, p. 68–76.
56. Then God saw everything that He had made, and indeed it was very good. So the evening and the morning were the sixth day.
57. He is the Rock, His work is perfect; For all His ways are justice, A God of truth and without injustice; Righteous and upright is He.
58. And the LORD God commanded the man, saying, "Of every tree of the garden you may freely eat; "but of the tree of the knowledge of good and evil you shall not eat, for in the day that you eat of it you shall surely die."
59. In the sweat of your face you shall eat bread till you return to the ground, for out of it you were taken; For dust you are, and to dust you shall return.

3:16–17),[60] thorns, (Genesis 3:18)[61] and the whole reason why we need a new heavens and a new earth (e.g., Isaiah 66:22;[62] 2 Peter 3:13;[63] Revelation 21:1[64]) — because what we have now is cursed and broken (Romans 8:22).[65]

Also, originally, the Bible makes it clear in Genesis 1:29–30[66] that man and animals were vegetarian — however, the fossil record has many evidences of animals eating animals. Genesis 1:30 is verified as a strictly vegetarian diet since man was not permitted to eat meat until after the Flood as recorded in Genesis 9:3.[67] This new provision only makes sense in contrast to the command in Genesis 1:29.[68]

To accept millions of years also means God called diseases like cancer (of which there is evidence in the fossil record) "very good." And because "without shedding of blood there is no remission" (Hebrews 9:22),[69] then allowing the shedding of blood millions of years before sin would *undermine* the atonement. Really, believing in millions of years blames God for death and disease instead of blaming our sin, from which Christ came to rescue us.

Some compromised Christians have objected, saying, *"But that just means the death of humans entered (Romans 5:12),[70] but animals could have*

---

60. To the woman He said: "I will *greatly multiply your sorrow* and your conception; *In pain* you shall bring forth children; your desire shall be for your husband, and he shall rule over you." Then to Adam He said, "Because you have heeded the voice of your wife, and have eaten from the tree of which I commanded you, saying, 'You shall not eat of it': "*Cursed is the ground* for your sake; *in toil* you shall eat of it all the days of your life" [emphasis added].
61. Both thorns and thistles it shall bring forth for you, and you shall eat the herb of the field.
62. "For just as the new heavens and the new earth which I make will endure before Me," declares the Lord, "so your offspring and your name will endure" (NASB).
63. Nevertheless, we, according to His promise, look for new heavens and a new earth, in which righteousness dwells.
64. Then I saw a new heaven and a new earth; for the first heaven and the first earth passed away. Also there was no more sea.
65. For we know that the whole creation groans and labors with birth pangs together until now.
66. And God said, "See, I have given you every herb that yields seed which is on the face of all the earth, and every tree whose fruit yields seed; to you it shall be for food. Also, to every beast of the earth, to every bird of the air, and to everything that creeps on the earth, in which there is life, I have given every green herb for food"; and it was so.
67. Every moving thing that lives shall be food for you. I have given you all things, even as the green herbs.
68. And God said, "See, I have given you every herb that yields seed which is on the face of all the earth, and every tree whose fruit yields seed; to you it shall be for food."
69. And according to the law almost all things are purified with blood, and without shedding of blood there is no remission.
70. Therefore, just as through one man sin entered the world, and death through sin, and thus death spread to all men, because all sinned.

died for billions of years." But this neglects that the first recorded death of animals (to replace fig leaf clothing with animal skins — the first blood sacrifice) in the Bible came as a direct result of human sin in the Garden of Eden (Genesis 3:21).[71]

One cannot deny biblically that there is a relationship between human sin and animal death. Just briefly look at the sacrifices of animals required for human sin throughout the Old Testament. This sacrifice began in the Garden of Eden (the first blood sacrifice as a covering for their sin, a picture of what was to come in the Lamb of God who takes away the sin of the world), that points to Jesus Christ, the ultimate and final sacrifice: . . . for this He did once for all when He offered up Himself (Hebrews 7:27).

Jesus Devastates an Old-Earth View

Allow me to relate this refutation with a discussion I had with a syncretistic Christian. I was attending a Christian conference and staffing an Answers in Genesis booth. As I walked around to look at the other booths at the beginning of this conference, a man quickly came up to me (from his booth), even though there was a crowd waiting to speak with him. He evidently felt the need to confront me (in front of the crowd at his booth) because he saw that I was wearing an Answers in Genesis conference badge.

In a hostile tone, the first thing out of his mouth was something akin to, "Is Answers in Genesis here at the conference? Well, I guess I am going to have to find your booth and set you straight about the age of the earth!" Clearly, I was dealing with a syncretistic (compromised) Christian.

Perhaps you are thinking, "I'm glad I wasn't in that situation." Well, I don't like those situations either! But for some reason, I tend to be in the middle of debates way too often. What ran through my head was, "How did I get myself into *this* situation? I was only walking through the conference halls!" But I realized there was a crowd of people staring as this man began his diatribe, so there I was, blindsided and thrust into a debate.

Needless to say, 2 Timothy 2:24–25 and 1 Peter 3:15 say to always be prepared to give an answer and be ready in season and out of season to rebuke and correct with gentleness and patience. I realized this "out of season" debate was going to occur, but I still needed to do it with gentleness, while being bold.

---

71. Also for Adam and his wife the Lord God made tunics of skin, and clothed them.

I asked this man, "In the context of the first marriage between Adam and Eve, do you think Jesus was wrong in Mark 10:6 when He said that God made them male and female at the *beginning of creation*? Or do you believe that the creation has been around for 13 billions years and marriage first came about near the *end of creation* a few thousand years ago with Adam and Eve?"[72]

Allow me to explain why I asked the question this way. If you start with the Bible, Adam and Eve were created on the sixth day of creation. So Adam and Eve were created about five days after the initial creation event on day 1. Then if you add up the genealogies from Adam to Jesus, you get a few thousand years (about 4,000 years) as discussed above. Most chronologists agree on this point.

But all Christians who have bought into an old earth have much more than 4,000 years between creation and Christ. They insert about 13–15 billion years, to be more precise, between the creation event that they call the big bang and marriage between the first human male and female. They further state that Adam and Eve only showed up a matter of thousands of years ago. So all old-earth scenarios have marriage (between human male and female, which first began with Adam and Eve) about 13–15 billion years after creation, which is the *end of creation*, nowhere near the *beginning of creation*.

Returning to the questioner, it was apparent that he was not ready for that question. What I did was contrast his stated position against what Christ clearly said. And this man knew it right off the bat. So did the crowd watching. They wanted to hear his answer, and so did I.

Realizing he was trapped in a "catch-22," this man immediately changed the subject to talk about what secular scientists believe about the age of the earth. Notice how he shifted from the authority of God's Word to the alleged authority of man regarding evolutionary ideas. I wasn't going to let him do that. He needed to address what Jesus said.

So I again kindly asked, "Was Jesus wrong in your view?" This man who had been so confident and aggressive began to squirm right where he stood. He responded, "I don't want to deal with that."

---

72. In *any* long-age scenario, mankind only showed up on the scene a matter of thousand years ago; so, in a long-age scenario, it would be impossible for marriage between a man and woman to be any earlier than the *very end* of creation about 13 billion years later. The Bible also affirms that we are at the end (Acts 2:17; Hebrews 1:2; 1 Peter 4:7).

At this point, I concluded our conversation by saying, "That is the crux of the issue: either you trust God's Word, or you don't." Hopefully, it was apparent to the crowd that this man was not standing on what Christ said in His Word, but was clinging to outside influences and did not want to address what Christ had said. Frankly, I was nervous, but I was being bold and seeking to be kind and gracious.

Why Is Mark 10:6 So Powerful?

Jesus said the following in the context of marriage and divorce:

> But from the beginning of the creation, God "made them male and female" (Mark 10:6).

> And He answered and said to them, "Have you not read that He who made them at the beginning 'made them male and female' " (Matthew 19:4).

If one believes Christ is Lord and is dedicated to following the words of Jesus, then accepting millions of years becomes an enormous problem. According to any old-earth or old-universe scenario, the creation began many billions of years ago, with man arriving on the scene a matter of thousands of years ago. How could any professing Christ-follower think that Jesus was in error and that marriage between that first man and a woman (whom Jesus clearly believed were Adam and Eve because in the context of Mark 10:6 he quotes from Genesis 1 and 2) only happened at the tail end of 13 or so billion years?

Jesus, the Creator, makes it clear that the first marriage between man and woman (Adam and Eve) came at the *beginning* of creation. From the chronological information given in Genesis 5 and 11 and in other biblical passages, Jesus was speaking about 4,000 years after this creation (an act He was responsible for).

Since the days in Genesis are regular 24-hour days and Jesus was speaking about 4,000 years later,[73] then the first marriage on day 6 was at the beginning of creation, speaking in non-technical language as Jesus was. If the earth is indeed billions of years old, then the first male and female came

---

73. Ken Ham, *The New Answers Book 1* (Green Forest, AR: Master Books 2006), p. 88–112, http://www.answersingenesis.org/articles/nab/could-god-have-created-in-six-days; Bodie Hodge, *The New Answers Book 2* (Green Forest, AR: Master Books, 2008), p. 41–52, http://www.answersingenesis.org/articles/2007/05/30/how-old-is-earth.

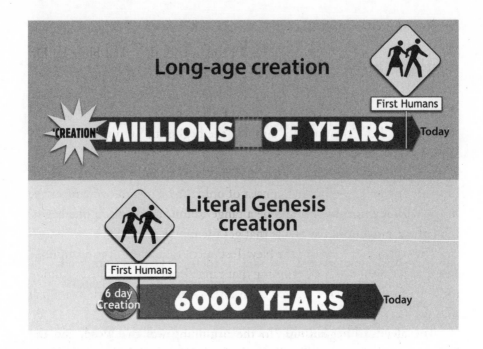

nowhere near the beginning of creation, but at the tail end of creation. This is a major theological problem because it calls into question the truthfulness of Christ in any old-earth/old-universe scenario.

Possible Responses to Mark 10:6

Those who religiously and unquestionably believe in the evolutionary time scale over God's Word (when they syncretize the two religions), yet profess Christ as Lord, have tried to respond. It is because they understand this is a devastating argument from Christ Himself against a "billions-of-years-ago" creation. Of course, the man at the conference did not want to give an answer, but others have tried. There are three common responses that need to be examined.

Some say biblical creationists have the same problem by appealing to Mark 10:6 because Adam and Eve were created on day 6, not day 1 of creation, which they claim *is* the "beginning of creation."

Some insert words into Mark 10:6 to change the meaning to "beginning of the creation *of marriage*."

Some suggest that *beginning* is referring to an entire figurative "six-day" creation period or creation week, regardless of its length.

Looking at Response 1

This popular response by some theologians was dealt a fatal blow by Dr. Terry Mortenson.[74] But let's consider it briefly here. The argument incorrectly makes the assumption that the "beginning of creation" means the "first day of creation." The Bible doesn't say day 1 of creation; it says the "beginning of the creation" (or simply, "the beginning" in the parallel passage of Matthew 19:4).

If you were to watch a movie and then tell a friend about the beginning of the movie, would that consist of only the first word or frame of the movie? Absolutely not; it would be a range of time surrounding the beginning of the movie and the events that get the movie going.

There are other places in the New Testament that affirm "the beginning" was *near* the events of the beginning that range from the absolute beginning to the events that even occurred soon after creation week, such as the fall into sin. Let's look at some of these.

The absolute beginning: "In the beginning was the Word, and the Word was with God, and the Word was God. He was in the beginning with God" (John 1:1–2).

Upon the creation of Adam and Eve (the first marriage): "He said to them, 'Moses, because of the hardness of your hearts, permitted you to divorce your wives, but from the beginning it was not so'" (Matthew 19:8).

After the "very good" creation was completed (Genesis 1:31) but prior to Adam's sin: "He who sins is of the devil, for the devil has sinned from the beginning. For this purpose the Son of God was manifested, that He might destroy the works of the devil" (1 John 3:8).

After sin entered the world so that tribulation can be possible: "For in those days there will be tribulation, such as has not been since the beginning of the creation which God created until this time, nor ever shall be" (Mark 13:19).

If an old-earth proponent uses response 1, then he is conceding that Jesus was wrong. But can Jesus err? No. But for the sake of argument, if Jesus erred on this point, then perhaps Jesus erred in passages concerning salvation. If this were the case, then it would undermine the gospel, which

---

74. Terry Mortenson, "But from the Beginning of . . . the Institution of Marriage?" Answers in Genesis, November, 1, 2004, http://www.answersingenesis.org/articles/2004/11/01/from-the-beginning-of-marriage.

a professing Christian claims to believe. The point is that the entire Bible stands or falls on Christ's truthfulness.

Looking at Response 2

Who is fallible, sinful mankind that he should try to add to Scripture to change the meaning of that Scripture in order to "correct" God's Word to fit with man's fallible ideas about the past? Years ago, when I seriously contemplated the idea of millions of years and the big bang, this was the conclusion at which I finally arrived.

I realized that when I try to add millions of years into Genesis, that I would be required to reinterpret God to "correct" Him. Then it hit me. God is always right, and if we have to "reinterpret" God's Word over and over again to mean something other than what it plainly says, then we, as fallible people, are the ones in error (Exodus 20:11; Matthew 19:4–5; Mark 10:6; and so on)!

Allow me to give a glaring instance of something like this as a preface to responding to this second response on Mark 10:6. When I hear someone add to Scripture in order to make it align with views not clearly expressed in Scripture, I think of the treatment of John 1 by Jehovah's Witnesses.[75]

What Do the "Witnesses" Do?

Jehovah's Witnesses view Jesus as a created archangel named Michael. So John 1 becomes a major problem for Jehovah's Witnesses because Jesus, the Word, is the Creator of all things that has been created. They change the Scriptures in their New World Translation (NWT) to align more closely with their religion:

> In the beginning was the Word, and the Word was with God, and the Word was God (John 1:1).

> Jehovah's Witness change: In [the] beginning the Word was, and the Word was with God, and the Word was a god (John 1:1; NWT).

Notice the change to the Word was "a god" as opposed to "God." Sadly, this is done to change the Bible to conform to Jehovah's Witnesses' fallible,

---

75. See Bodie Hodge, Appendix 2, *World Religions and Cults*, Volume 1 (Green Forest, AR: Master Books, 2015), p 409–424.

unitarian theology, even though the NWT really argues for polytheism (more than one God) in this instance. But the point was to try to demote Christ from being God.[76]

This obvious example causes problems for Jehovah's Witnesses because a created Christ (in their view) really cannot endure and satisfy the infinite wrath of God for sin. The only person who could do that is Christ, *who is God*, as the infinite Son who could satisfy the wrath of an infinite God to truly pay the debt in full. The Jehovah's Witnesses have a false, created Christ who cannot save them, since that created Christ could never take the punishment we deserve any more than we could.

Should We Be Doing the Same Thing as the "Witnesses"?

In a familiar but different fashion, old-earth creationists (syncretists) that utilize response 2 do something quite similar. They essentially insert "of marriage," which changes the meaning. Unlike Jehovah's Witnesses, they do not add this to a new translation, nor does it affect the character of Christ, so I wouldn't dare call my old-earth brethren cultic, but I must admit that this tactic is identical to what many cultists do. I do not want my brothers in Christ to go down that path — as I once traveled down that path myself!

But in common, both Jehovah's Witnesses and old-earth creationists have taken outside ideas and imposed them on the Bible, making it mean something other than what *the text says*. It is essentially either mixing with Unitarian religious beliefs or, in this instance, mixing with secular humanistic religious beliefs (e.g., millions of years).

When people try to interpret Mark 10:6 in a way that makes it compatible with the idea of millions of years, then what is the difference between that and what cultists do with the text? Don't mistake what I'm saying here; old-earth proponents can still be saved as long as they trust in Jesus Christ, the Creator, alone for their salvation. They, unlike those who hold Unitarian views of a created Jesus, still believe in the Jesus of the Bible who is God. But their handling of Scripture, like that of cultists, undermines the truth and authority of the Bible.

Let's now turn our attention to why adding "of marriage" to Mark 10:6 is not a viable interpretation of the text. In refuting Drs. John Ankerberg and Norman Geisler, Dr. Terry Mortenson states the following:

---

76. Bodie Hodge, "Is Jesus the Creator God?" *Answers in Depth*, December 12, 2007, http://www.answersingenesis.org/articles/aid/v2/n1/jesus-the-creator.

They argue that *ktisis* (which is actually the noun "creation" not the verb "create," as [Ankerberg/Geisler] say) in Mark 10:6 should be translated as "institution" so that Jesus should be understood to be talking about the beginning of the institution of marriage, not the beginning of creation. They base this interpretation on the fact that in 1 Peter 2:13 *ktisis* is translated in the NIV as "to every authority instituted among men" or in the NASB as "to every human institution." But they have not paid careful attention to the presence of "among men" (NIV) and "human" (NASB) in this verse.

The Greek text is clear. The phrase under question is *pasē anthrōpinē ktisei,* where the whole phrase is in the dative case (so literally "to every human creation") and the adjective *anthrōpinē* ("human") modifies *ktisei* ("creation"). An institutional authority (such as kings, governors and slave masters, which Peter discusses in the context) is indeed a "human creation." But this is a very different contextual use of *ktisis* than we find in Mark 10:6, where no adjective is used to modify "creation." Furthermore, in Mark 10:6, Jesus could have easily said "from the first marriage" or "from the beginning of marriage" or "since God created man" or "since God created Adam," if that is what He meant.

Finally, if we give *ktisis* in Mark 10:6 the meaning "authority" or "institution," it makes no sense. What does from the beginning of authority or beginning of institution mean? To make it meaningful, Ankerberg and Geisler would have to add a word to the text, which would have no contextual justification.[77]

Furthermore, the Jews and pre-"millions-of-years" commentator Dr. John Gill also affirm this was the beginning of the creation, meaning the creation "of the world." Dr. Gill writes the following:

> Of the world, or of man . . . "from the beginning of the creation of the world," is a way of speaking often used by the Jews [Bereshit Rabba, sect. 3. fol. 2. 3. & sect. 4. fol. 4. 1].[78]

> This may be read in #Ge 1:27 and from thence this sense of things collected; that God, who in the beginning of time, or of the creation, as Mark expresses it, made all things, the heavens,

77. Mortenson, "But from the Beginning of. . . ."
78. J. Gill, Commentary notes on Mark 10:6.

and the earth, and all that is therein, and particularly "man," as the Vulgate Latin, and Munster's Hebrew Gospel supply it here, made the first parents of mankind, male and female.[79]

When it comes down to it, contrary to Christian syncretists' intentions, advocates of this second response are indirectly doing something that the cults also do — they are adding words to Scripture not to make it consistent with some other religious writings, but with the majority view in the scientific community rather than a cult.

Looking at Response 3

If one concludes that "from the beginning of creation" (and likewise "from the beginning" in Matthew 19:4) means "all of the creative period, regardless of its length," then this is saying that there are 13 billion years of time in the "creative period," which is the beginning, *middle,* and even encompasses the bulk of the *end* of the creation by the time Jesus made this statement (see also Acts 2:17; Hebrews 1:2; 1 Peter 4:7)!

It is strange that one would think that 13 billion years or so have passed and that all of it is the beginning of creation — and now suddenly we are at the end after a few measly thousand years. Going back to our movie illustration, this would be like telling someone that the end was the last second of a movie and that the other two hours of it were only the beginning.

So here, old-earth advocates are changing the definitions of the words *middle* and *end* to also mean "beginning." So they are changing the meanings of words to make them align with their old-earth/old-universe view. Such a redefinition of terms is unwarranted.

Conclusion of the Matter

Jesus' statement in Mark 10:6 is reasonable and accurate in the young-earth view, and *any* view of an old earth fails when trying to deal with marriage of man and woman being at the *beginning of creation*. In short, Jesus's words here devastate the concept of an old earth or old universe. Thus, from the perspective of a perfect Christ, there is no reason to mix millions of years and the evolutionary religion with Christianity.

So it makes sense why this man at the conference didn't want to address my question about Mark 10:6. In fact, in retrospect, his response was better

---

79. John Gill, Commentary notes on Matthew 19:4.

than most. At least he realized there was a problem and opted to remain silent and not reinterpret Christ's words. So for that, I commend him.

Sadly, many others are more than willing to try to reinterpret Christ's plain meaning in Mark 10 because of their absolute adherence to millions and billions of years. Mixing these religions undermines the authority of the Bible, and in many cases it directly undermines the gospel itself.

Conclusion

My hope is that Christians who have bought into belief in an old earth and syncretized the evolutionary beliefs with their Christianity will repent and return to the plain teachings in the Bible and stop mixing God's Word with secular beliefs that clearly contradict God's revelation and undermine the gospel by blaming God for death instead of our sin. I do not say this lightly; for once in my past I did very similar things.

Another point to make regarding syncretism is the issue of salvation. Some have asked, can a syncretist get saved? If they repent and believe in the Jesus Christ of Scripture, that He died, and resurrected on the third day, then of course they can be saved.

As a result, some have remarked that mixing these religions is not a big deal. But this is not true. It *is* a big deal. It is an issue of the authority of God vs. the authority of man. If someone compromises by opening the door to mix their Christianity with another religion, then their witness and testimony to others is that they can do that too!

Why would the next generation stop there and not open the door entirely and give up the whole Bible? Based on statistics, the next generation does push the door open and walks away from the Bible and Christianity.[80] So mixing the religions is not an acceptable avenue but needs to be warned against.

---

80. See the statistics in *Already Gone* and *Ready to Return* by Ken Ham et al. (Green Forest, AR: Master Books).

Chapter 12

The Religion of Naturalism

Dr. Terry Mortenson

Naturalism, or philosophical naturalism, is one of the most popular religions in the world today, although most people don't recognize it as such because it has no *obvious* worship centers, clergy, liturgy, or holy book. It has adherents in every country and dominates many countries, especially among the intellectual elites in the culture. It is therefore important to understand this major religion and how it became so popular. But sadly, it has also had a very significant and largely unrecognized influence on the worldview of many Christians, which is an even greater reason for Christians to understand it.

Naturalism is known by other names: atheism, scientific materialism, and secular humanism. Atheists, secular humanists, and other advocates of naturalism will protest that their view is a religion, but would say it is the opposite of religion. So we need to begin by defining "religion." According to the 11th edition of *Merriam-Webster's Collegiate Dictionary*, one definition of religion is "the service and worship of God or the supernatural." That obviously doesn't apply to atheism. But another given by that dictionary certainly does apply: "a cause, principle, or system of beliefs held to with ardor and faith." Many people who hold to naturalism are just as passionate about their belief as the most convinced Christians, Muslims, Hindus, or adherents of any other religion.[1]

---

1. For a good example of this firm belief, see Tim Chaffey, "Feedback: Is Atheism a Religion?" Answers in Genesis, accessed 9/19/2016, https://answersingenesis.org/world-religions/atheism/feedback-is-atheism-a-religion/.

Defining Naturalism

So what are the beliefs of naturalism? The most fundamental belief from which all others flow is that nature or matter is all that exists. It has always existed or it came into existence from nothing. There is nothing outside or before nature, i.e., the material universe that is studied by modern science. There is no God and no supernatural. Although nature has not always existed in its present form, what we see today is the result of time and chance and the laws of nature working on matter. Miracles are not possible, because they would be a violation of the laws of nature. Non-material things such as hopes, plans, behaviors, languages, logical inferences, etc., exist, but they are the result of and determined by material causes.

As Christian philosopher and theologian Ronald Nash summarizes:

> Nature is a self-explanatory system. Any and every thing that happens within the natural order must, at least in principle, be explainable in terms of other elements of the natural order. It is never necessary to seek the explanation for any event within nature in something beyond the natural order.[2]

With this belief in place, other beliefs follow. So, there is no purpose or meaning to life — we are simply the product of time and chance and the laws of nature; there are no moral absolutes that apply to all people in all times; moral values are simply personal beliefs or opinions, which themselves are the result of chemical and physical processes controlling matter. Likewise, there is no life after death, for the laws of nature still apply and our bodies simply decay over time and are mixed in with other non-living matter in the earth.

The late William Provine, atheist and evolutionary professor of history of biology at Cornell University, put his naturalistic view this way:

> Let me summarize my views on what modern evolutionary biology tells us loud and clear — and these are basically Darwin's views. There are no gods, no purposes, no goal-directed forces of any kind. There is no life after death. When I die, I am absolutely certain that I am going to be dead. That's the end for me.

---

2. Ronald H. Nash, *Worldviews in Conflict* (Grand Rapids, MI: Zondervan, 1992), p. 120.

There is no ultimate foundation for ethics, no ultimate meaning to life, and no free will for humans, either.[3]

The world's most famous atheist, Richard Dawkins, similarly said, "The universe we observe has precisely the properties we should expect if there is at bottom no design, no purpose, no evil and no good. Nothing but blind, pitiless indifference. DNA neither knows nor cares. DNA just is, and we dance to its music."[4] The first *Humanist Manifesto* was published in 1933. The first two articles of that document state, "FIRST, religious humanists regard the universe as self-existing and not created" and "SECOND, humanism believes that man is a part of nature and that he has emerged as a result of a continuous process." Flowing out of those two starting points, the fifth states, "FIFTH, humanism asserts that the nature of the universe depicted by modern science makes unacceptable any supernatural or cosmic guarantees of human values. . . . Religion must formulate its hopes and plans in the light of the scientific spirit and method."[5]

It will readily be clear to any thoughtful non-naturalist that this worldview is self-refuting. If nature is all that exists and everything is the result of time and chance and the laws of nature, then the naturalist or atheist can have no trust that his thoughts are telling him the truth for they are the result of chemical and physical processes operating in his brain. In fact, in his religion or worldview, objective absolute truth does not exist. Of course, if everything is the result of material causes, then the naturalist has no valid explanation for the origin or truth of the laws of nature that he relies on to understand the world. And if there is no absolute right and wrong, then the atheist cannot object to what Hitler did to the Jews or to what Muslim suicide bombers do to innocent civilians in a shopping mall. Nor could he object if someone entered his home, robbing him of all his valuables and murdering his family. Hitler, the suicide bomber, and the robber/murderer are just doing what they think is right, but their thoughts are dictated by their own DNA, which is produced by purposeless, directionless chemical and physical processes. Of course, neither Provine, nor Dawkins, nor anyone else can really live according to this religion of naturalism. In fact,

3. William Provine, "Darwinism: Science or Naturalistic Philosophy?" *Origins Research,* vol. 16:1/2 (1994): 9.

4. Richard Dawkins, *River Out of Eden* (New York, NY: Basic Books, 1995), p. 133.

5. "Humanist Manifesto I," American Humanist Association, accessed September 19, 2016, http://americanhumanist.org/humanism/humanist_manifesto_i.

to live, the naturalist must steal from the Christian worldview to argue that there is some truth (including the laws of nature) and some things that are absolutely right or wrong.

How Naturalism Became a Dominant Religion

Today, the religion of naturalism/atheism culturally dominates the Western world and the communist world and is widespread among the cultural elites in many other countries dominated by other religions. In addition, many people who profess to believe another religion are significantly influenced by naturalism in their thinking, and outside of their attendance at religious services at their house of worship they actually live like a naturalist/atheist. How did naturalism become such a widespread belief?

The roots of this modern dominance of the naturalistic religion or worldview can be found in the Enlightenment, an intellectual movement of the late 17th and 18th centuries in Europe that elevated human reason to the place of supreme authority for determining truth and understanding ultimate reality. As a result, such thinkers rejected the authority of the Christian church and the Bible. From this philosophical starting point, both deism and atheism became popular in those same centuries.

Deism is a halfway house on the way to atheism and holds that there is a God who created the universe and endowed it with the laws of nature and then left it to operate and develop according to those laws. So God is distant and has not been involved in the creation since the beginning. Apart from the deists' belief in a rather vaguely defined Creator God and a supernatural beginning to the creation, they were indistinguishable from atheists in their views of Scripture and physical reality.[6] In deism, as in atheism, the Bible is merely a human book, containing errors, and not the inspired Word of God, and the history and function of the creation can be totally explained by the properties of matter and the "inviolable laws of nature" in operation over a long period of time.

Deists and atheists often disguised their true views, especially in England and America where they were not culturally acceptable. Many of them gained influential positions in the scientific establishment of Europe and America, where they subtly and effectively promoted naturalistic thinking.

---

6. A good brief discussion of deism is found in James W. Sire, *The Universe Next Door* (Downers Grove, IL: InterVarsity Press, 2009, 5th ed.), p. 47–65.

Brooke, noted historian of science, comments on the subtle influence of deistic forms of naturalism when he writes:

> Without additional clarification, it is not always clear to the historian (and was not always clear to contemporaries) whether proponents of design were arguing a Christian or deistic thesis. The ambiguity itself could be useful. By cloaking potentially subversive discoveries in the language of natural theology, scientists could appear more orthodox than they were, but without the discomfort of duplicity if their inclinations were more in line with deism.[7]

But the effects of deistic and atheistic philosophy on biblical studies and Christian theology also became widespread on the European continent in the late 18th century and in Britain and America by the middle of the 19th century. As Reventlow concluded in his massive study:

> We cannot overestimate the influence exercised by Deistic thought, and by the principles of the Humanist world-view which the Deists made the criterion of their biblical criticism, on the historical-critical exegesis of the nineteenth century; the consequences extend right down to the present. At that time a series of almost unshakeable presuppositions were decisively shifted in a different direction.[8]

Historians of science agree that modern science was born in the womb of the Christian worldview. The Bible teaches that the Creator is a God of order who created an orderly world to reveal His glory (Psalm 19:1–6). Also, man was created in the image of God with a rational mind, and from the beginning man was commanded to rule over the creation (Genesis 1:27–28). Therefore, man could and should study the creation to discover that order and learn how to use the creation for the good of mankind and the glory of God.

So the biblical worldview, which had dominated the Western nations for centuries, was rapidly being replaced by a naturalistic worldview. Science

---

7. John H. Brooke, *Science and Religion* (Cambridge, UK: Cambridge University Press, 1991), p. 194.
8. Henning G. Reventlow, *The Authority of the Bible and the Rise of the Modern World*, John Bowden, transl. (London: SCM Press, 1984), p. 412.

became the main instrument for producing this transformation. Scientists became the priests of that religion, and through them many others were won to that faith. To understand how this happened, we need to distinguish between two broad categories of science. I like to call them operation science and origin science.

Operation science (also called experimental science or observational science) is what most people have in mind when they hear the word "science." I define it this way:

> The use of observable, repeatable experiments in a controlled environment (usually in a laboratory) to understand how things operate or function in the present physical universe to find cures for disease, produce new technology, put a man on the moon, etc.

Most of biology, chemistry, physics, medical research, and engineering research are in the realm of operation science. Scientists in these fields are studying how things in the natural world operate or function so they can manipulate, copy, utilize, or destroy (harmful) things for the improvement of human life or the environment. This kind of science works on the assumption that the laws of nature are constant and apply everywhere in the universe. Without this assumption scientists would not be able to discover cures for disease or develop new technologies. So this kind of science is essentially naturalistic in methodology: God and miracles are not considered or invoked as an explanation of how things operate.

Bible-believing creation scientists engage in operation science the same way other scientists do, for Scripture indicates that what we call today the laws of nature are simply descriptive of how God normally upholds His creation by His sovereign providence and care (e.g., Genesis 8:22; Jeremiah 31:35–36; Colossians 1:17; Hebrews 1:3). But the laws of nature are not absolute and unchangeable (so that not even God can "violate" them). He altered or suspended some of those laws at the Fall when He cursed His "very good" original creation (Genesis 1:31) because of man's sin (Genesis 3:14–19; Romans 8:19–23) and at the Flood (Genesis 8:21) and in other localized events when He performed miracles, such as the parting of the Red Sea (Exodus 14:19–31), the crossing of the Jordan River (Joshua 3:14–17), and in connection to the ministries of Old Testament prophets, New Testament

Apostles, and Jesus. Bible-believing scientists also cannot categorically rule out the possibility of God doing a miracle today (e.g., in a supernatural physical healing), although Scripture would lead them to believe that these would be on a personal level and extremely rare.

But while operation science is a source of new technology and cure for diseases, it cannot answer the question of how the Grand Canyon formed, for example. How did those horizontal layers of limestone, sandstone, and shale form? They are tens or hundreds of feet thick and cover thousands or tens of thousands of square miles. How were they deposited? In an ocean? In a desert? How long did it take for each layer to form and how much time passed between the layers and how long ago did it all happen? And how did the canyon form? It is 280 miles long (including Marble Canyon at the northeast end), 4–18 miles wide, and a mile deep. Was it carved by a little water eroding hard rock over a long period of time? The work of the Colorado River? Or was it caused by a lot of water eroding wet sediments or relatively soft rock in a short period of time?

Or how did stars and galaxies and the solar system come into existence? How did the first apple trees or rabbits or butterflies or people come into existence and how long ago? How did human language come about? These are historical questions. We can't create any of these things in the laboratory. We can't repeat these events and observe them occurring in the present. We want to know what happened in the unobserved past to produce what we observe in the present. Operation science can't answer these questions because it is studying observable, repeatable processes in the present. At best, we can observe, say, erosion and sedimentation events today and *by analogy* suggest the cause or causes in the past that produced the Grand Canyon and the layers we see exposed. But we can't re-create the Grand Canyon in the lab, and it dwarfs any canyons and sedimentary layers we see forming in recent times.

For historical questions we need what I like to call origin science (or historical science). I define it this way:

> The use of reliable, eyewitness testimony (if any is available) and presently observable evidence to determine the past, unobservable, unrepeatable event or events which produced the observable evidence we see in the present.

Origin or historical sciences include historical geology, paleontology, archeology, and cosmology. They study things in the present to attempt to reconstruct the past. As Martin Rudwick, the leading historian of geology, explains:

> Even at the opening of its "heroic age," geology was recognized as belonging to an altogether new kind of science, which posed problems of a kind that had never arisen before. It was the first science to be concerned with the reconstruction of the past development of the natural world, rather than the description and analysis of its present condition. The tools of the other sciences were therefore inadequate. The processes that shaped the world in the past were beyond either experiment or simple observation. Observation revealed only their end-products; experimental results could only be applied to them analogically. Somehow the past had to be interpreted in terms of the present. The main conceptual tool in that task was, and is, the principle of uniformity.[9]

The success of operation science in producing technology, curing diseases, and raising the general standard of living caused people to trust science as the path to truth about the world. This trust was passed on to the new science of geology and then further to other areas of origin or historical science. So today, many people consider scientists or the scientific consensus to be the authority for determining truth.

As seen in the statements above by Provine and Dawkins, Darwinian evolution is a naturalistic reconstruction of the past to try to explain the origin of living organisms: microbes, plants, animals, and people. However, naturalism's control of origin science did not begin with Darwin's theory of evolution, but over 50 years earlier with the idea of millions of years in geology. In the late 18th and early 19th centuries, deist and atheist scientists attempted to explain the origin of the world and unravel the history of the rocks and fossils. They did so by rejecting the truth of Genesis 1–11 and using the assumptions of naturalism, that nature is all there is and everything must be explained by time, chance, and the laws of nature.

---

9. Martin J.S. Rudwick, "The Principle of Uniformity," *History of Science*, Vol. I (Chicago, IL: University of Chicago Press, 1962), p. 82.

Three prominent French scientists were very influential in this regard. In his *Epochs of Nature* (1778), Georges-Louis Comte de Buffon (1708–88) postulated that the earth was the result of a collision between a comet and the sun and had gradually cooled from a molten lava state over at least 75,000 years (a figure based on his study of cooling metals), though his unpublished writings indicate that he actually believed that the sedimentary rocks probably took at least three million years to form.[10] Buffon was probably a deist or possibly a secret atheist.[11] Pierre Laplace (1749–1827), an open atheist, published his nebular hypothesis in *Exposition of the System of the Universe* (1796).[12] He imagined that the solar system had naturally and gradually condensed from a gas cloud during a very long period of time. In his *Philosophy of Zoology* (1809), Jean Lamarck (1744–1829), who straddled the fence between deism and atheism,[13] proposed a theory of biological evolution over long ages, with a mechanism known as the inheritance of acquired characteristics.

New theories in geology were also being advocated at the turn of the 19th century as geology began to develop into a disciplined field of scientific study. Abraham Werner (1749–1817) was a German mineralogist and a deist[14] or possibly an atheist.[15] Although he published very little, his impact on geology was enormous, because many of the 19th century's greatest geologists were his students. He theorized that the strata of the earth had been precipitated chemically and mechanically from a slowly receding universal ocean. According to Werner's unpublished writings, he believed the earth was at least one million years old.[16] His elegantly simple oceanic theory was quickly rejected (because it just did not fit the facts), but the idea of an old earth remained with his students.

James Hutton (1726–1797) in Scotland was trained in medicine but turned to farming for many years before eventually devoting his time to

10. Buffon's fear of contemporary reaction to this great date led him to put 75,000 years in the published book. See "Buffon, Georges-Louis LeClerc, Comte de," in Charles C. Gillispie, ed., *Dictionary of Scientific Biography* [hereafter DSB], 16 vol. (New York, NY: Scribner, 1970–1990), p. 579.
11. "Buffon, Georges-Louis LeClerc, Comte de," *DSB*, vol. 2, p. 577–78.
12. Pierre Laplace, *Exposition of the System of the Universe*, 2 vol. (Paris: Cercle Social, 1796).
13. Brooke, *Science and Religion*, p. 243.
14. Leroy E. Page, "Diluvialism and Its Critics in Great Britain in the Early Nineteenth Century," in Cecil J. Schneer, ed., *Toward a History of Geology* (Cambridge: MIT, 1969), p. 257.
15. A. Hallam, *Great Geological Controversies* (Oxford: Oxford University Press, 1992), p. 23.
16. Alexander Ospovat, "Werner, Abraham Gottlob," *DSB*, vol. 14, p. 260.

geology. In his *Theory of the Earth* (1795), he proposed that the continents were gradually and continually being eroded into the ocean basins. These sediments were then gradually hardened and raised by the internal heat of the earth to form new continents, which would be eroded into the ocean again. With this slow cyclical process in mind, Hutton could see no evidence of a beginning to the earth, a view that precipitated the charge of atheism by many of his contemporaries, though he was possibly a deist.[17]

Hutton is considered by many to be the father of modern geology. He laid down this rule for reconstructing the past history of the earth: "The past history of our globe must be explained by what can be seen to be happening now. . . . No powers are to be employed that are not natural to the globe, no action to be admitted except those of which we know the principle."[18] By insisting on this rule of geological reasoning, he rejected the biblical accounts of creation and the Flood before he ever looked at the geological evidence. Neither creation nor the Flood were happening when he wrote those words, and according to the Bible, creation week was a series of supernatural, divine acts, and the Flood was initiated and attended by supernatural acts of God.

Elsewhere Hutton wrote, "But, surely, general deluges [i.e., global floods] form no part of the theory of the earth; for, the purpose of this earth is evidently to maintain vegetable and animal life, and not to destroy them."[19] He rejected the global Flood because he insisted on a principle of absolute uniformity and was reasoning that the present is the key to the past. He assumed that the processes of nature have always operated in the past in the same way that we observe today. This was a fundamental error, for the totally trustworthy eyewitness testimony of the Creator in His Word is the key to the past and the present. But Hutton rejected that testimony because of his deistic or atheistic religious views.

Charles Lyell (1797–1875), an Oxford-trained lawyer who became a geologist, was probably a deist (or Unitarian, which is essentially the same).[20] Building on Hutton's uniformitarian ideas in his three-volume *Principles*

17. Dennis R. Dean, "James Hutton on Religion and Geology: The Unpublished Preface to his *Theory of the Earth* (1788)," *Annals of Science*, 32 (1975), pp. 187–93.
18. Quoted in A. Holmes, *Principles of Physical Geology*, 2nd ed. (Edinburgh, Scotland: Thomas Nelson and Sons Ltd., 1965), p. 43–44.
19. James Hutton, *Theory of the Earth* (Edinburgh, Scotland: William Creech, 1795), vol. 1, p. 273.
20. Colin A. Russell, *Cross-currents: Interactions Between Science & Faith* (Leicester, UK: Inter-Varsity Press, 1985), p. 136.

of Geology (1830–1833), Lyell insisted that the geological features of the earth can, and indeed must, be explained by slow, gradual processes of erosion, sedimentation, earthquakes, volcanism, etc., operating at essentially the same average rate, frequency, and power as we observe today. He also insisted,

> I have always been strongly impressed with the weight of an observation of an excellent writer and skillful geologist who said that "for the sake of revelation as well as of science — of truth in every form — the physical part of Geological inquiry ought to be conducted as if the Scriptures were not in existence."[21]

This feigned concern for the Bible was actually an attack on the Bible. It would not be a problem to do geology as if the Scriptures were not in existence, if the Bible said nothing about any globally significant geological events. But it describes two: the third day of creation when dry land appeared (presumably as God raised part of the earth's crust above sea level, which would have been a great erosion and sedimentation event), and Noah's Flood, which was intended to destroy the surface of the earth and would have caused an enormous amount of erosion and sedimentation and buried many plants and animals that would become fossils. To a fellow uniformitarian geologist, Lyell wrote in a private letter that he wanted to "free the science [of geology] from Moses."[22] In other words, he wanted to silence God's eyewitness testimony about the supernatural origin of a fully functioning universe of stars, planets, plants, animals, and people and His testimony about the global Flood of Noah that disrupted the normal course of nature as God initiated some processes and accelerated others to bring about His judgment of the world. Creation and the Flood were rejected for philosophical/religious reasons, not because of anything Lyell and Hutton saw in the rocks and fossils. By the 1840s, Lyell's view became the ruling paradigm in geology.

One more fact needs to be mentioned about geology at this time. The world's first scientific society devoted exclusively to geology was the London Geological Society (LGS), founded in 1807. From its inception, which was at

---

21. Charles Lyell, Lecture II at King's College London on May 4, 1832, quoted in Martin J.S. Rudwick, "Charles Lyell Speaks in the Lecture Theatre," *The British Journal for the History of Science*, vol. IX, pt. 2, no. 32 (July 1976): 150.
22. Charles Lyell, quoted in Katherine Lyell, *Life, Letters and Journals of Sir Charles Lyell, Bart* (London: John Murray, 1881), Vol. 1, p. 268.

a time when very little was known about the geological formations of the earth and the fossils in them, the LGS was controlled by the assumption that earth history is much older than and different from that presented in Genesis. Not only was very little known about the geological features of the earth, but at this time there were no university degrees in geology and no professional geologists. Neither was seen until the 1830s and 1840s, which was long after the naturalistic idea of an old earth was firmly entrenched in the minds of those who controlled the geological societies, journals, and university geology departments.

In *Origin of Species*, Charles Darwin reveals how important Lyell's thinking was for his own theory of evolution: "He who can read Sir Charles Lyell's grand work on the *Principles of Geology*, which the future historian will recognize as having produced a revolution in natural science, yet does not admit how incomprehensibly vast have been the past periods of time, may at once close this volume."[23] In private correspondence he added:

> I always feel as if my books came half out of Lyell's brains and that I never acknowledge this sufficiently, nor do I know how I can, without saying so in so many words — for I have always thought that the great merit of the *Principles* [*of Geology*], was that it altered the whole tone of one's mind & therefore that when seeing a thing never seen by Lyell, one yet saw it partially through his eyes.[24]

So naturalism took control of geology, then spread to biology through Darwin, and astronomers have applied the same assumptions in their hypotheses about the evolution of stars, galaxies, and the solar system. Science has been controlled by an anti-biblical naturalistic philosophical/ religious worldview for over 150 years. In the widely seen 2014 documentary television series, "Cosmos: A Spacetime Odyssey," which has now been developed into a curriculum to teach public school children to believe in cosmological, geological, biological, and anthropological evolution,[25] the

23. Charles Darwin, *The Origin of Species* (London: Penguin Books, 1985, reprint of 1859 first edition), p. 293.
24. Charles Darwin, *The Correspondence of Charles Darwin*, Vol. 3 (Cambridge, UK: Cambridge Univ. Press, 1987), p. 55.
25. For a critique of each episode of this 8-part TV series promoting cosmological, geological, and biological evolution, see the series of web articles by Elizabeth Mitchell at https://answersingenesis.org/countering-the-culture/cosmos-a-spacetime-odyssey/. The articles have also been published as a study guide, *Questioning Cosmos*.

well-known atheist astrophysicist Neil deGrasse Tyson expresses this naturalistic religion memorably:

> Our ancestors worshipped the sun. They were far from foolish. It makes good sense to revere the sun and stars because we are their children. The silicon in the rocks, the oxygen in the air, the carbon in our DNA, the iron in our skyscrapers, the silver in our jewelry — were all made in stars billions of years ago. Our planet, our society, and we ourselves are stardust.[26]

Early 19th-Century Christian Compromise with Naturalism

During the early 19th century, many Christians made various attempts to harmonize these old-earth geological theories with the Bible, not realizing that they were compromising with naturalism. In 1804, the gap theory began to be propounded by the 24-year-old pastor Thomas Chalmers (1780–1847), who after his conversion to evangelicalism in 1811 became one of the leading Scottish evangelicals.[27] Chalmers began advocating this gap theory before the world's first geological society was formed (in London in 1807), and over two decades before Lyell's theory was promoted (beginning in 1830). In part because of Chalmers' powerful preaching and writing skills, the gap theory quickly became the most popular reinterpretation of Genesis among Christians for about the next half-century. However, the respected Anglican clergyman, George Stanley Faber (1773–1854), began advocating the day-age theory in 1823.[28] This was not widely accepted by Christians, especially geologists, because of the obvious discord between the order of events in Genesis 1 and the order according to old-earth theory. The day-age view began to be more popular after Hugh Miller (1802–56), the prominent Scottish geologist and evangelical friend of Chalmers, embraced and promoted it in the 1850s after abandoning the gap theory.[29]

26. Episode 8 ("Sisters of the Sun"). The show was a follow-up to the 1980 television series "Cosmos: A Personal Voyage," which was presented by the atheist Carl Sagan.
27. William Hanna, *Memoirs of the Life and Writings of Thomas Chalmers* (Edinburgh, 1849-52), Vol. 1, p. 80–81; Thomas Chalmers, "Remarks on Curvier's Theory of the Earth," *The Christian Instructor* (1814), reprinted in *The Works of Thomas Chalmers* (Glasgow, Scotland, 1836–42), Vol. 12, p. 347–72.
28. George S. Faber, *Treatise on the Genius and Object of the Patriarchal, the Levitical, and the Christian Dispensations* (London, 1823), Vol. 1, p. 111–166.
29. Hugh Miller, *The Two Records: Mosaic and the Geological* (London, 1854) and *Testimony of the Rocks* (Edinburgh: W.P. Nimmo, Hay & Mitchell, 1856), p. 107–74.

Also in the 1820s the evangelical Scottish zoologist, Rev. John Fleming (1785–1857), began arguing for a tranquil Noachian deluge[30] (a view which Lyell also advocated, under Fleming's influence). In the late 1830s the prominent Congregationalist theologian, John Pye Smith (1774–1851), advocated that Genesis 1–11 was describing a local creation and a local flood, both of which supposedly occurred in Mesopotamia.[31] Then, as German liberal theology was beginning to spread in Britain in the 1830s, the view that Genesis is a myth, which conveys only theological and moral truths, started to become popular.

Not all Christians went along with these old-earth ideas in geology in the early 19th century. A number of theologians and scientists, who collectively became known as the scriptural geologists and some of whom were very knowledgeable in geology, raised biblical, geological, and philosophical arguments against the old-earth geological theories and the various old-earth reinterpretations of Genesis. Their Christian opponents largely ignored their arguments. But many Christians still held to the literal view of Genesis because it was exegetically the soundest interpretation. In fact, up until about 1845, the majority of Bible commentaries on Genesis taught a recent six-day creation and a global catastrophic Flood.[32]

The Continuing Christian Compromise with Old-Earth Naturalism

Phillip Johnson was a long-time professor of law at University of California–Berkeley and the driving force behind the modern Intelligent Design movement. His first book on the subject of origins was *Darwin on Trial* (1991), in which he persuasively showed that the scientific evidence did not support the theory of evolution. He avoided discussion of Genesis and the age of the earth but made it clear that he was not a young-earth creationist. Elsewhere he wrote about the origins debate:

> To avoid endless confusion and distraction and to keep attention focused on the most important point, I have firmly put aside all questions of biblical interpretation and religious

---

30. John Fleming, "The Geological Deluge as Interpreted by Baron Cuvier and Buckland Inconsistent with Moses and Nature," *Edinburgh Philosophical Journal*, 14 (1826): 205–39.

31. John Pye Smith, *Relation Between the Holy Scriptures and Some Parts of Geological Science* (London: Jackson & Walford, 1839).

32. For more on these historical developments, see Terry Mortenson, *The Great Turning Point: the Church's Catastrophic Mistake on Geology — Before Darwin* (Green Forest, AR: Master Books, 2004).

authority, in order to concentrate my energies on one theme. My theme is that, in Fr. Seraphim's words, "evolution is not 'scientific fact' at all, but philosophy." The philosophy in question is naturalism.[33]

Johnson and the other old-earth advocates in the Intelligent Design movement (led by the Discovery Institute in Seattle) apparently have not gone back far enough in their historical studies. He appears to think that naturalism only took control of science after Darwin, or maybe even at the time of the 100th anniversary of Darwin's book. Speaking of the famous international celebration of about 2,000 scientists in Chicago in 1959, Johnson writes:

> What happened in that great triumphal celebration of 1959 is that science embraced a religious dogma called naturalism or materialism. Science declared that nature is all there is and that matter created everything that exists. The scientific community had a common interest in believing this creed because it affirmed that in principle there is nothing beyond the understanding and control of science. What went wrong in the wake of the Darwinian triumph was that the authority of science was captured by an ideology, and the evolutionary scientists thereafter believed what they wanted to believe rather than what the fossil data, the genetic data, the embryological data and the molecular data were showing them.[34]

Nancy Pearcey likewise seems historically shortsighted. In her excellent discussion of the victory of Darwin's theory, she speaks of the Christians who tried to make peace with Darwinian evolution. She states, "Those who reformulated Darwin to accommodate design were hoping to prevent the takeover of the idea of evolution by philosophical naturalism. They sought to extract the scientific theory from the philosophy in which it was imbedded."[35] But those Christians and many before them had for over 50 years

33. See Johnson's introduction to Fr. Seraphim Rose, *Genesis, Creation and Early Man* (Platina, CA: St. Herman of Alaska Brotherhood, 2000), p. 50.

34. Phillip Johnson, "Afterword: How to Sink a Battleship," in William Dembski, ed., *Mere Creation: Science, Faith and Intelligent Design* (Downers Grove, IL: InterVarsity Press, 1998), p. 448–49.

35. Nancy Pearcey, "You Guys Lost," in Dembski, ed., *Mere Creation*, p. 84.

allowed and even advocated (albeit unknowingly) the takeover of geology by naturalism and then advocated the day-age theory or gap theory and local Flood theory to save the old-earth theory. I attended the ID movement conference in 1996 where Pearcey originally presented her paper on this subject. When in the comment period after the presentation I remarked about philosophical naturalism taking control of science decades before Darwin through old-earth geology, and referred to my just-completed Ph.D. work on this matter, I got no response from anyone, either publicly or privately. It seemed that the old-earthers did not want to know about naturalism's involvement in the development of the idea of millions and billions of years of history.

William Dembski has been a prominent voice in the ID movement. He clearly sees naturalism's control of biology when he writes:

> Why does Darwinism, despite being so inadequately supported as a scientific theory, continue to garner full support of the academic establishment? . . . Why must science explain solely by recourse to undirected natural processes? We are dealing here with something more than a straightforward determination of scientific facts or confirmation of scientific theories. Rather we are dealing with competing worldviews and incompatible metaphysical systems. In the creation-evolution controversy we are dealing with a naturalistic metaphysic that shapes and controls what theories of biological origins are permitted on the playing field in advance of any discussion or weighing of evidence. This metaphysic is so pervasive and powerful that it not only rules alternative views out of court, but it cannot even permit itself to be criticized. The fallibleness and tentativeness that are supposed to be part of science find no place in the naturalistic metaphysic that undergirds Darwinism. It is this metaphysic that constitutes the main target of the design theorists' critique of Darwinism.[36]

But what Dembski should have said is:

> In the creation-evolution controversy *and the age-of-the-creation controversy* we are dealing with a naturalistic metaphysic

---

36. William A. Dembski, *Intelligent Design: The Bridge Between Science and Theology* (Downers Grove, IL: InterVarsity Press, 1999), p. 114.

that shapes and controls what theories of biological, *and geological and cosmological* origins are permitted on the playing field in advance of any discussion or weighing of evidence.

Naturalism controls all of science and all three aspects of evolution: biological, geological, and cosmological. But Dembski apparently doesn't see this control in geology and astrophysics, for elsewhere he has said:

> I myself would adopt [young-earth creation] in a heartbeat except that nature seems to present such strong evidence against it. . . . In our current mental environment, informed as it is by modern astrophysics and geology, the scientific community as a whole regards young-earth creationism as untenable.[37]

However, it is not *nature* that presents strong evidence against believing what Genesis 1–11 so clearly teaches. It is the *naturalistic interpretations* of the geological and astrophysical evidence that is against young-earth creation. And the scientific community as a whole regards as equally untenable Dembski's and others' rejection of biological evolution and advocacy of intelligent design. Rejecting biological evolution while at the same time accepting millions of years reveals a serious failure to recognize or admit the role of anti-biblical naturalistic assumptions controlling the interpretation of the scientific evidence.

Even a few young-earth creationists do not seem to see naturalism's control of all of science. Nelson and Reynolds state in their "debate" with old-earth proponents, "Our advice, therefore, is to leave the issues of biblical chronology and history to a saner period. Christians should unite in rooting out the tedious and unfruitful grip of naturalism, methodological and otherwise, on learning."[38] But there never will be a saner period, because the problem here is not intellectual, but spiritual. Sin will continue to darken the minds of people who do not want to submit to their Creator and His Word, causing them to suppress the truth (Romans 1:18–20 and Ephesians 4:17–18). Nelson and Reynolds are also mistaken when they say that "the key thing is to oppose any sort of attempt to accommodate theism

---

37. William A. Dembski, *The End of Christianity: Finding a Good God in an Evil World* (Nashville, TN: B&H Publishing, 2009), p. 55.
38. Paul Nelson and Mark John Reynolds, "Young-Earth Creationism: Conclusion," in J.P. Moreland and John Mark Reynolds, eds., *Three Views of Creation and Evolution* (Grand Rapids, MI: Zondervan, 1999), p. 100.

and naturalism."[39] No, the key is to oppose the accommodation of biblical revelation with naturalistic interpretations of the creation, which is what all old-earth reinterpretations of Genesis are attempting to do. The issue is not a vaguely defined *theism's* marriage with naturalism but rather the adulterous union of *biblical teaching* and naturalism.

Thus, fighting naturalism *only* in biology will not work. Ignoring the Bible, especially Genesis, and its testimony to the cosmic impact of sin and God's judgments at the Fall, the Flood, and the Tower of Babel, even while arguing for design in living things (and even *God's* designing activity), will not lead people to the true and living God, but rather away from Him and His holy Word. Nor will fighting naturalism only in biology, while tolerating or even promoting naturalism in geology and astronomy, break the stranglehold of naturalism on science.

In his book about his "wedge strategy," Johnson explains how Christians should proceed in what he thinks is the coming public dialogue between religion and science. He says, "The place to begin is with the Biblical passage that is most relevant to the evolution controversy. It is not in Genesis; rather, it is the opening of the Gospel of John."[40] He then quotes and discusses John 1:1–3 and then Rom 1:18–20. While those passages are certainly relevant, they do not directly address the creation-evolution and age-of-the-earth debates, as Genesis does. Furthermore, John and Paul clearly believed Genesis was literal history and based their teaching on Genesis, as Jesus did.[41] The following year, in an interview in 2001, Johnson also stated:

> I think that one of the secondary issues [in the creation-evolution debate] concerns the details of the chronology in Genesis. . . . So I say, in terms of biblical importance, that we should move from the Genesis chronology to the most important fact about creation, which is John 1:1. . . . It's important not to be side-tracked into questions of biblical detail, where you just wind up in a morass of shifting issues.[42]

39. Ibid.
40. Phillip Johnson, *The Wedge of Truth: Splitting the Foundations of Naturalism* (Downers Grove, IL: InterVarsity Press, 2000), p. 151.
41. See Terry Mortenson and Thane H. Ury, eds., *Coming to Grips with Genesis: Biblical Authority and the Age of the Earth* (Green Forest, AR: Master Books, 2008), chapters 12–13.
42. Peter Hastie, "Designer Genes: Phillip E. Johnson Talks to Peter Hastie," *Australian Presbyterian*, no. 531 (Oct. 2001) 4–8, http://members.iinet.net.au/~sejones/pjaustpr.html (web article pages 5–6), accessed Oct. 15, 2009.

On what basis does Johnson make the assertion that the most important fact about creation is John 1:1? He has never provided a theological or biblical argument to defend this assertion. It is difficult to see how Johnson's comments indicate anything but a very low view of and indifference to the inspired inerrant text of Genesis 1–11. I suggest that Johnson's failure to see (or to explain to his listeners, if he does see) that the idea of billions of years of geological and cosmic history is nothing but philosophical naturalism masquerading as scientific fact is the reason that he avoids the text of Genesis.

So the "wedge" of the ID movement does not appear to me to be a wedge at all. It is simply a nail, which will not split the foundations of naturalism, as Johnson hopes. It will not lead the scientific establishment to abandon the naturalistic worldview and embrace the biblical view of creation, nor will it lead most people to the true God, the Creator who has spoken in only one book, the Bible.

This failure to see the full extent of the influence of naturalism in science, even by a person warning about the danger of naturalism, is further illustrated in a paper by one of America's greatest evangelical philosophers, Norman Geisler. In 1998, Geisler was the president of the Evangelical Theological Society. As such he gave the presidential address at the November annual meeting of the ETS.[43] In it he warned of a number of dangerous philosophies that are assaulting the Church and having considerable influence. The first one he discussed is naturalism, which he said has been one of the most destructive philosophies. Therefore, he devoted more space to it than any of the other dangerous philosophies that he discussed. As far as his remarks went, it is a very helpful warning about the dangers of naturalism. He even said that, "James Hutton (1726–1797) applied [David] Hume's anti-supernaturalism to geology, inaugurating nearly two centuries of naturalism in science."[44]

What is terribly ironic and very disappointing is that Geisler has endorsed the writings of Hugh Ross, who promotes naturalistic assumptions and thinking in the Church by persuading Christians to accept millions of years and the "big bang" as scientific fact. Also, in Geisler's own *Encyclopedia of Christian Apologetics*, published in the year *after* his ETS presidential

---

43. Norman Geisler, "Beware of Philosophy: A Warning to Biblical Scholars," *JETS*, 42:1 (March 1999), p. 3–19.
44. Ibid., p. 5.

address, he tells his readers, "Most scientific evidence sets the age of the world at billions of years."[45] But it is not the *evidence* that sets the age at billions of years, it is rather the naturalistic *interpretation* of the evidence that leads to this conclusion. Because of this confusion of evidence and interpretation of evidence, Geisler rejects the literal-day interpretation of Genesis 1 and believes that the genealogies of Genesis 5 and 11 have gaps of thousands of years, even though he says that "*prima facie* evidence" in Genesis supports literal days and no genealogical gaps in Genesis.[46] After laying out the various old-earth reinterpretations of Genesis (all of which are based on naturalistic interpretations of the scientific evidence, have serious exegetical problems, and have been refuted by young-earth creationists) he mistakenly concludes, "There is no necessary conflict between Genesis and the belief that the universe is millions or even billions of years old."[47]

But Geisler is not the only evangelical philosopher who is highly trained to spot philosophical naturalism and yet has missed it in this issue of the age of the earth. I am not aware of any leading evangelical philosopher who is a convinced young-earth creationist. Paul Copan, who favors the day-age view and whose book *That's Just Your Interpretation* is enthusiastically endorsed by Ravi Zacharias and J.P. Moreland, says:

> Second, the ultimate issue here is not young-earth versus old-earth creationism or even creationism versus evolutionism (although I myself do not find biological evolution compelling). Rather, the crux is naturalism (all reality can be explained by and operates according to natural laws and processes) versus supernaturalism (a reality exists *beyond* and is not reducible to nature — God, miracles, and so on). What is most critical is *that* God created; *how* he created is a secondary matter. [48]

Herein we see the bewitching influence of naturalism imbedded in old-earth thinking that causes men to ignore or reject God's clear Word. The crux is naturalism versus biblical teaching. Genesis just as clearly teaches *when* and *how* God created as it teaches *that* He created.

---

45. Norman L. Geisler, *Encyclopedia of Christian Apologetics* (Grand Rapids, MI: Baker, 1999), p. 272.
46. Ibid., p. 270 (on the creation days) and 267 (on the genealogies).
47. Ibid., p. 272.
48. Paul Copan, *That's Just Your Interpretation* (Grand Rapids, MI: Baker, 2001), p. 146.

Conclusion

Naturalism is a religion, a worldview, and a philosophy. It dominates science and the thinking of most of the cultural elites in the world. This study shows the error of the statement of C. John Collins in his highly endorsed book on science and faith. Collins is an old-earth proponent and respected Old Testament scholar. He states at the end of his book's section on geology, "I conclude, then that I have no reason to disbelieve the standard theories of the geologists, including their estimate for the age of the earth. They may be wrong, for all I know; but if they are wrong, it's not because they have improperly smuggled philosophical assumptions into their work."[49] He could not be further from the truth on this subject. Without the uniformitarian assumptions of philosophical naturalism controlling geology, there is no evidence for millions of years.

So the age of the earth matters enormously, if we truly want to fight naturalism's control of science and if we want to be faithful to the inspired, inerrant Word of the Creator of heaven and earth, who was there at the beginning of creation and at the Flood and has faithfully and clearly told us what happened.

The evidence is abundant and clear. The enemy has invaded the holy citadel. Naturalistic (atheistic) ways of thinking have captured the minds of millions of people around the world and increasingly polluted the church over the last 200 years through millions-of-years, evolutionary "scientific" theories and through liberal theology. Will we take up the sword of the Spirit (Eph 6:17), especially Genesis 1–11, and help expel the enemy of naturalism? The only alternative is to ignore the invasion and pollution and further abet it by compromise with the evolutionary belief in millions of years.

---

49. C. John Collins, *Science and Faith: Friends or Foes?* (Wheaton, IL: Crossways, 2003), p. 250.

Chapter 13

Materialism

Dr. Tommy Mitchell

The term *materialism* conjures in the minds of most an image of people who pursue a life devoted to the acquisition of material possessions. Materialistic people value comfort and wealth more than spiritual pursuits. They often gauge their success based on having more wealth and possessions than others.

However, there is another type of materialism.

Materialism is a worldview based on the belief that physical matter is all that exists. In essence, to the materialist, matter is all that matters because nothing else is real. In the materialistic worldview, all that exists is material.

Those who adhere to this philosophical outlook maintain that the origin of the world and all the complex things it contains is explainable in material terms. That is, everything that exists is the result of matter and its interactions.

Matter and energy, we observe scientifically, act and react based on so-called "laws of matter" or "physical laws." These physical laws describe how the measureable things in nature — matter, energy, gravity, and time, for instance — behave and interact. The laws of motion, the laws of gases, the laws of thermodynamics, and, as we have learned in more recent decades, the laws of quantum mechanics — these scientific laws set the stage and provide the limits and boundaries for our understanding of matter and energy.

The laws of matter are observable, testable, and consistent. The materialistic philosophy goes beyond these observable laws of science, however, declaring that nothing immaterial even exists.

At one level this does seem to have at least some merit. After all, a bat hits a ball. A glass hits the floor. Fingers hit a keyboard. A plane flies through the air. A frog hops into a pond. Just matter interacting with matter, right? Well, up to a point, perhaps. But let's take a closer look at matter.

Matter

If a materialistic worldview contends that everything we see is the result of matter and its interactions, it would be helpful to know just what matter is.

Matter is the stuff around us. And it is the stuff we are made of. The stuff we can see, feel, touch, and hold. Even the air we breathe, though invisible, is matter. Matter is the physical stuff that exists in our universe. It takes up space and it has mass. You know, stuff.

The nature of matter has been considered and explored for centuries. The ancient Greeks were the first to postulate that there was a fundamental unit of matter. This unit was called an atom. Of course, in those days there was no way this could be scientifically tested or analyzed. Although this concept proved useful to philosophers of that day as they sought to understand the world around them, the idea of the atom was then more of a philosophical construct than a concept subject to scientific scrutiny. The idea that the atom was the fundamental unit of matter did, however, at least to a certain degree, turn out to be correct.

As the centuries passed, man's understanding of the physical world increased. The work of such scientists as Newton and Kepler aided in our knowledge of matter and motion and time. Apples fell from trees, and man's understanding of gravity grew. Planets moved through space, and keen observers discovered that their movements could be analyzed mathematically and accurately predicted. These ideas led many to view the universe as something that worked like a vast clock or some gigantic machine whose movements or outcomes could be precisely determined if all the initial condition were known. Ah, if only life were that simple. . . .

Scientific advances in our day have revolutionized our understanding of matter and motion and time and energy and gravity. While the atom is the basic building block of an element, we once incorrectly thought the atom was the smallest indivisible unit of matter. But now we know the atom consists of subatomic particles whose interactions determine how an atom behaves. We also now know that mass and energy are interchangeable and can be converted one to another. Time once seemed constant, but we now know that time changes with velocity and gravity.

Physics in the modern era is now not so much about atoms and particles, but more about energy and fields, quantum states and probability, space-time and gravity, dark matter and black holes. These are the things that now captivate us. And rightly so, for the more we understand about these things, the more we are awed by just how incredible the world around us really is.

Is That All There Is to It?

As science has advanced, we have learned much, much more about matter. What it is. What it isn't. How it behaves. How it changes. How it interacts with other matter.

But is that all that there is to reality? Actually, no. And does discovering how matter behaves reveal where it came from? Again, no.

We do indeed understand more about matter than ever before. This understanding comes from our observations and experimentation in the PRESENT. That is, we understand how matter acts NOW. We can see and test and evaluate now. We praise God for our ability to examine and evaluate our world in such minute detail.

But . . . does our understanding of matter allow us to conclude that everything that exists is merely the result of matter and its interactions? The materialist would reply that it does indeed provide us the means to conclude that, in fact, matter is all that matters. Many philosophers and scientists have for centuries argued just that, and many still do.

This materialist philosophy, or one of its variations, to one degree or another underlies many modern worldviews. Most prominently, evolution (in the molecules-to-man sense) is dependent on this materialist worldview. The foundation of evolution is the concept that over millions (and billions) of years, living things became gradually more complex. From the simplest one-celled creature until man arrived on the scene, matter interacting with matter caused it all.

Wanting something to be true does not make it true, however, no matter how earnestly the materialist wishes it to be so. The evolutionary materialist will wax endlessly philosophic about how matter rearranged itself to form living things. After all, the very existence of life is proof it MUST HAVE HAPPENED, because materialists can accept no creator other than matter itself.[1] Materialists argue this because they cannot (or will not) accept that there is a God who created.

> For the wrath of God is revealed from heaven against all ungodliness and unrighteousness of men, who suppress the truth in unrighteousness (Romans 1:18).

> . . . who exchanged the truth of God for the lie, and worshiped and served the creature rather than the Creator, who is blessed forever. Amen (Romans 1:25).

Materialism, like molecules-to-man evolution, is merely a way to try and explain how things got here without God. It fails in so many ways.

What's the Matter with Materialism? (See What I Did There?)

As stated, materialism and its variations have been the foundation of many worldviews and philosophies throughout the ages. This fact is staggering given that materialism fails on so many fronts. Here we will consider only a few.

First and foremost, if one holds to materialism as the foundation for understanding the world and how it works, it seems quite reasonable that the materialist should answer the question, "Where did matter come from?" Seems a simple starting place, right?

As it turns out, for the materialist this is not so simple and far from straightforward. The usual response to this question revolves around something called the big bang, which is the most widely accepted secular view of the origin of the universe. It is said by adherents to the big-bang account of history that thirteen and a half billion years ago (give or take a few hundred million years), the universe sprang into existence in a great fireball. From nothing, or so it was once taught.

More recently, many secular scientists have rejected the idea that the universe came from nothing. Their view of this "origin" event has evolved. Now many say that something WAS there in the beginning. Views differ about just what was there.

Big-bang supporters agree that all of space and energy was originally contained in a point called a "singularity" which then rapidly expanded.

---

1. This is the fallacy of begging the question — assuming materialism to prove materialism.

One school of thought argues that it is pointless to talk about how the singularity got there or what came before it because this singularity marks the beginning of time itself. There can be no "before the beginning." There is a certain logic to this, but it does not account for the existence of the singularity. The universe does have a beginning in time, and things that have a beginning require a cause. Yet, this view denies any sufficient cause to create the singularity or to cause it to expand. Indeed, there can be no cause for the singularity if nothing beyond physical material exists, since all material was supposedly contained in the singularity.

Another group of scientists postulates that in this "beginning" there existed some type of gravitational force and that gravity created matter. Although this position is self-defeating, as time (i.e., space-time) and gravity are connected to the material creation, so they really haven't answered the question.

Neither of these scenarios can be documented to have happened using the scientific method. Nevertheless, they are considered to be reasonable scientific explanations for how the universe began. Scientists know this sort of origin event happened, not because they have proven it scientifically but only because matter exists, and no non-materialistic explanation is acceptable to them.

But the same scientists who hold to the big-bang origins theory actually violate scientific laws by their belief. For instance, there is the first law of thermodynamics. A scientific law like this is known to be true because scientific observations never disobey it. The first law of thermodynamics tells us that matter and energy can neither be created nor destroyed. They can only be changed from one form to another, or transferred from one place to another.

Simply put, scientific observations always confirm that you can't get something from nothing. There are no exceptions. Except in the beginning, it seems!

You see, the materialist has to presume that an unobservable exception to the laws of thermodynamics happened in the beginning in order for this universe — a universe in which everything obeys the laws of thermodynamics — to come into being. Thus, the very foundation of the materialistic worldview is shaky at best, being in complete violation of the very laws it supposedly created through random natural processes. It is inconsistent for the universe to come into existence by means of neglecting the very laws that supposedly come from it.

So does physics rescue the materialist? Richard Vitzthum, an expert in philosophical materialism, writes that it has not:

> Yet there should be no confusion on one crucial point. Modern physics is not materialism, and materialism is not modern physics. Materialism makes metascientific assumptions about reality that are irrelevant to the aims of working physicists. In the first place, it assumes as axiomatic that the continuity and interconnectedness of things never ends. The universe did not pop out of nothing, either through supernatural fiat or through vacuum quantum fluctuation. If, as seems increasingly likely, some fifteen billion years ago our cosmos flashed into being in a fireball of inconceivable heat, energy, and violence, it did so from some kind of background state or dimensionality linked to it by processes as consistent and natural as those that link the earth to that first fireball. We don't yet understand the laws and processes that govern whatever kind of material reality lies outside the space-time-mass-energy manifold of our cosmos, hidden as they are beyond or within the so-called singularities, like black holes or the Big Bang, where the physical laws we can define no longer appear to hold. Maybe we never will.[2]

Taking this a step further, some big-bang supporters argue that our universe sprang from another — that the singularity was caused by a quantum fluctuation in another universe. In this view, our universe is just one of many, one part of a cosmic "multiverse." Aside from the fact that this speculation is entirely untestable, it merely pushes the problem back. If our universe came from another, then where did that other universe come from? Some might speculate that the multiverse is itself eternal, and therefore needs no first cause. But where is the evidence that such a multiverse even exists?

As philosopher Thomas Nagel explains, "Well, there is the hypothesis that this universe is not unique, but that all possible universes exist, and we find ourselves, not surprisingly, in one that contains life. But that is a cop-out, which dispenses with the attempt to explain anything."[3]

---

2. Richard C. Vitzthum, *Materialism* (New York: Prometheus Books, 1995), p. 179–180.
3. Thomas Nagel, *Mind and Cosmos* (New York: Oxford University Press, 2012), p. 95.

In other words, the idea of the "multiverse" takes an origins problem that physics cannot solve and multiplies it into an infinite number of origins problems that physics cannot solve. Materialism is a worldview that demands a materialistic beginning for the universe but fails to explain scientifically how that could happen.

The Origin of Life

Just as the materialist cannot easily deal with the problem of the origin of matter, the process by which inert matter combines to form living things is equally challenging. For life to arise spontaneously, the law of biogenesis must be violated.

Simply put, the law of biogenesis states that life comes from life. Period. Living things do not originate from nonliving matter. This is not a matter of speculation or assumption. It is a matter of pure observational science. Throughout history, based on things that have been observed, life has only arisen from life. Without exception. A law with a 100 percent track record is a very reliable law, right?

For the materialist, finding an exception to this law would be a fundamental step in supporting his worldview. No exception has ever been found. Not one. Frankly, materialism fails on this issue alone.

The Mind and Thought

Even if there were one single exception to the law of biogenesis and life did arise spontaneously long ago, there are still a vast number of things to account for. Let's just take one issue to make the case against materialism even stronger: the mind. How did the mind develop? How do our thoughts occur? What defines human consciousness?

Again, for the materialist, this is not an insignificant issue. How does matter give rise to consciousness and thought? Or even logic, reason, truth, knowledge, morality, conclusions, or any concept? These things are clearly immaterial. How can atoms and molecules, randomly interacting, give rise to something as amazing and complex as human thought?

Consider the artistry of Michelangelo, the genius of Albert Einstein, and the humor of Will Rogers. Are these things just the result of matter acting on matter, chemicals bumping around in their brains and in the brains of those who marvel at their genius? For the consistent materialist, the answer must be that creative and scientific genius are material. That is, people's choices, actions, consciousness, awareness — even their very identity — are merely the results of chemicals acting in the brain.

Even Charles Darwin considered this: " 'Even human thoughts,' Darwin provocatively wrote in his notebook, 'were little more than secretions from the brain, no more wonderful than inert matter being subject to gravitation. "Oh, you materialist!" he spluttered gleefully in conclusion.' "[4]

One might argue that in Darwin's time there was not as much under-stood about the brain. In our day and age, this is still a stumbling block for the materialist, as Thomas Nagel admits:

> Consciousness is the most conspicuous obstacle to a com-prehensive naturalism that relies only on the resources of phys-ical science. The existence of consciousness seems to imply that the physical description of the universe, in spite of its richness and explanatory power, is only part of the truth, and that the natural order is far less austere than it would be if physics and chemistry accounted for everything. If we take this problem seri-ously, and follow out its implications, it threatens to unravel the entire naturalistic world picture. Yet it is very difficult to imagine viable alternatives.[5]

Materialism comes up short once again.

Where Does All That Information Come From?

In a materialist worldview, at some time in the distant past, atoms randomly bumping together formed complex molecules, and these complex molecules randomly bumping together formed the first living cell. And so on. As we have seen, this scenario violates the law of biogenesis and therefore could not have ever happened. Even if it did (for the sake of argument), the materialist runs headlong into another problem. The problem is called information.

For a single-celled organism to evolve into a more complex creature, a vast amount of information must be added to the genetic material to code for this increase in complexity. Clearly, a horse is much more complex than an amoeba. So where does all this information to make hair and eyes and legs come from? An excellent question, it seems, as the materialist has no

4. Janet Browne, *Charles Darwin, Voyaging* (Princeton, NJ: Princeton University, 1995), p. 383.

5. Nagel, *Mind and Cosmos*, p. 35.

answer. You see, information is not material. It is not made of matter. It exists, but its origins elude the materialist.

What observational science reveals is that information does not arise spontaneously. Information never pops into existence from nowhere. As Werner Gitt, information technology expert and long-time professor at the prestigious German Federal Institute of Physics and Technology, explains:

> There is no known law of nature, no known process and no known sequence of events which can cause information to originate by itself in matter.[6]

Information always comes from a higher source of information. That source of information is merely a speculation for the materialist. For the Christian, this poses no difficulty whatsoever.

The Laws of Nature

In a materialist universe, how does one account for the fact that the universe itself operates consistently according to many so-called "laws"? From the earliest years in school, children are taught about how the universe works. We understand the motion of planets, the properties of gases, and the manner in which certain atoms interact. We can calculate the instant that a space probe will land on a distant planet or the precise point at which a hardened steel beam will break under pressure. These things are possible only because the universe functions consistently and logically according to physical laws that we have been discovering and describing in detail using science over the past few hundred years.

Just how did these "laws" come into existence? They are not material. Far from it. The laws of chemistry and physics apply to how matter functions and interacts, but they themselves are not material. Mathematics exists. Without it we could not hope to understand the material world, but mathematics itself is immaterial. The laws (or principles) of logic also exist, and neither are they material.

Some materialists have attempted to argue that these laws and principles are merely of human invention. This viewpoint is woefully insufficient, for it ignores the question entirely. It is true that the laws of the universe have been extensively studied and understood by man. Again, we praise

---

6. Werner Gitt, *In the Beginning Was Information* (Green Forest, AR: Master Books, 2006), p. 106.

God for giving us the ability to examine the manner in which the universe works and define the consistent patterns we find. But describing these things is not the same as inventing these things. Man uses logic. Man did not invent logic. The same can be said for the laws of physics or the principles of mathematics.

These laws and principles do not randomly change. There is uniformity in the operation of our world. If these laws did not operate in the past just as they operate in the present, then the materialist is bound to explain why.

For the Christian, understanding the origin of an orderly universe is simple. After all, the Christian serves the Creator God who by His nature is orderly, consistent, and logical. God put into operation an orderly universe that is bound by consistent laws and principles. It is not arbitrary or random. In Jeremiah 33:25 we read about "the ordinances of heaven and earth" which God put into place to govern the operation of the physical world.

How do you explain the immaterial in a materialist worldview? You cannot. Here, again, we see the problem.

Why Then . . .

If this worldview is so inconsistent, so unsupportable, then why do people believe it, support it, and promote it? As with so many worldviews, the materialist is trying to explain the nature of our world without acknowledging God as Creator.

If God is who He claims to be, and frankly all one needs to do is look at the world around us to understand that He is, then we are accountable to Him. You cannot explain or logically understand the universe without acknowledging God as the One who made all things (e.g., Proverbs 1:7, 9:10). The origin of matter, the origin of life, the consistency and orderliness of the universe — all these pose no problem whatsoever for the Christian.

But there are those who deny God. People who look to themselves as the authority. Those who yearn to be as gods, making their own rules and answering only to themselves. They must deny the One who created. To do that they must then be able to explain how everything got here without a Creator.

Every attempt to do so has failed. Materialism is but one example.

Still, man keeps trying, determined to talk around the possibility that God the Creator even exists. Harvard evolutionary biologist and geneticist Richard Lewontin admitted as much in a book review he wrote in 1997:

> Our willingness to accept scientific claims that are against common sense is the key to an understanding of the real struggle between science and the supernatural. We take the side of science in spite of the patent absurdity of some of its constructs, in spite of its failure to fulfill many of its extravagant promises of health and life, in spite of the tolerance of the scientific community for unsubstantiated just-so stories, because we have a prior commitment, a commitment to materialism.
>
> It is not that the methods and institutions of science somehow compel us to accept a material explanation of the phenomenal world, but, on the contrary, that we are forced by our a priori adherence to material causes to create an apparatus of investigation and a set of concepts that produce material explanations, no matter how mystifying to the uninitiated. Moreover, that materialism is absolute, for we cannot allow a Divine Foot in the door.[7]

It is fitting that we conclude this chapter on the highly intellectual subject of materialism by giving the eternal God — who created all that is material and all that is not — the final word on this subject:

> Professing to be wise, they became fools (Romans 1:22).

---

7. Richard Lewontin, "Billions and Billions of Demons," *The New York Review of Books,* Jan. 9, 1997, 31.

Chapter 14

Empiricism

Bryan Osborne

"Don't you believe in flying saucers?" they ask me. "Don't you believe in telepathy? — In ancient astronauts? — In the Bermuda triangle? — In life after death?"

"No," I reply. "No, no, no, no, and again no."

One person recently, goaded into desperation by the litany of unrelieved negation, burst out, "Don't you believe in anything?"

"Yes," I said. "I believe in evidence. I believe in observation, measurement, and reasoning, confirmed by independent observers. I'll believe anything, no matter how wild and ridiculous, if there is evidence for it. The wilder and more ridiculous something is, however, the firmer and more solid the evidence will have to be."[1]

There it is, empiricism in a nutshell. Colorfully illustrated by famed professor, science fiction author, and humanist Isaac Asimov. The general (less vibrant) definition for empiricism is as follows, "the doctrine that all knowledge is derived from sense experience."[2] Empiricism is a worldview that essentially believes all knowledge is gained from observations of what you can see, smell, taste, touch, and hear (even through the use of various

---

1. Isaac Asimov, *The Roving Mind* (Prometheus Books, 1983), p. 43.
2. Dictionary.com, s.v. "empiricism," http://dictionary.reference.com/browse/empiricism.

instruments). Actually, the disciple Thomas unintentionally gives a pretty good summary of empiricism in John 20:25:

> The other disciples therefore said to him, "We have seen the Lord." So he said to them, "Unless I see in His hands the print of the nails, and put my finger into the print of the nails, and put my hand into His side, I will not believe."

Although Thomas relegated himself to empiricism on this point at this time in his life, he was not an empiricist. But there appears to be a growing number of people who are empiricists in this day and age. This makes sense because we are seeing an increase in the religion of humanism in the Western world, and empiricism is a specific outworking of humanism.

According to a study published by Pew Research in 2012, roughly one in six people around the world (1.1 billion, or 16%) claim no "religious affiliation."[3] Ironically, this makes the "Religiously Unaffiliated" the third-largest religious group in the world. Of course, not everyone in this group is an empiricist, but it's probably safe to say that a decent percentage hold to some form of empiricism.

This should get our attention because, as we'll see in more detail later, empiricism is totally antithetical to the biblical worldview. With that in mind it should be noted that the majority of secular scientists and a large portion of higher education academics seemingly embrace some form of empiricism. And many of these same professors believe it is their job, even their "calling," to shape the worldview of their students into their own image. This should put us on alert because, as Adolf Hitler famously said, "He alone, who owns the youth, gains the future."[4]

Take Bill Savage for example, a self-identified political liberal, teacher of English, and college adviser at Northwestern University in Evanston, Illinois. Check his response to data that showed conservative "red" states are producing more children than liberal "blue" states and why he's not worried about it:

> The children of red states will seek a higher education, and that education will very often happen in blue states or blue islands in red states. For the foreseeable future, loyal dittoheads will continue to drop off their children at the dorms. After a

3. "The Global Religious Landscape," Dec. 18, 2012, http://www.pewforum. org/2012/12/18/global-religious-landscape-exec/.
4. http://www.brainyquote.com/quotes/quotes/a/adolfhitle378177.html.

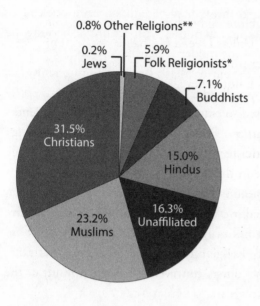

Size of Major Religious Groups, 2010
Percentage of the global population

0.8% Other Religions**

0.2% Jews

5.9% Folk Religionists*

7.1% Buddhists

31.5% Christians

15.0% Hindus

16.3% Unaffiliated

23.2% Muslims

* Includes followers of African traditional religions, Chinese folk religions, Native American religions, and Australian aboriginal religions.

** Includes Baha'is, Jains, Sikhs, Shintoists, Taoists, followers of Tenrikyo, Wiccans, Zoroastrians, and many other faiths.

Percentages may not add to 100 due to rounding.

Pew Research Center's Forum on Religion & Public Life • Global Religious Landscape, December 2012

teary-eyed hug, Mom and Dad will drive their SUV off toward the nearest gas station, leaving their beloved progeny behind. *And then they are all mine* (emphasis added).[5]

That's right, Mom and Dad, you spend all your love, time, energy, and money raising your kids for 18 years and then in four years he'll transform their worldview into the "right" one — his. Children from Christian homes, for example, will be trained to be humanists and empiricists. And this even happens much earlier than college age — as early as middle school and high school![6]

History

The general premise of empiricism is surely as old as human history. The idea was initially articulated in philosophical terms around the third century B.C. in the Greek schools of Stoicism and Epicureanism. Different elements of empiricism flutter within various minds throughout history until Sir Francis Bacon, a creationist nonetheless, gathered them together to a more permanent philosophical home in the 16th century.

5. Bill Savage, "Lessons Learned," *The Stranger*, June 9–15, 2005.
6. Ken Ham, Britt Beemer, and Todd Hillard, *Already Gone* (Green Forest, Arkansas: Master Books, 2009).

For Bacon, the knowledge of primary importance to man was to be found empirically in the natural world. Truth required evidence from the real world and should be pursued through systematic observation, collection, and arrangement of data. As a result of these convictions he became the first to formulate the principles of the modern scientific method.

But it wasn't until the late 17th century that a British philosopher by the name of John Locke explicitly formulated the doctrine of Empiricism. Locke contended that the mind is a *tabula rasa* ("clean slate") on which experiences leave their imprint and shape an individual's thinking.[7] He concluded, for the most part, that humans do not have innate ideas, and knowledge is only possible through experience.

In the early 18th century, Bishop George Berkeley, an Irish philosopher, argued for a radical form of Empiricism eventually to be called Subjective Idealism.[8] In this variation, things only exist because an entity perceives them or by the action of being perceived. He essentially believed that existence was tied to experience, and things continue to exist as a result of the perception of God.

The final "founding father" of modern Empiricism was the Scottish philosopher and atheist David Hume. In many ways, his views on Empiricism were a fusion of the ideas of Locke and Berkeley and are probably best summarized by his quote "the science of man is the only solid foundation for the other sciences."[9] In other words, human experience is the closest thing we are going to get to truth, and the foundation for any logical argument is observation and experience. Hume was a rigid Empiricist who moved the philosophy to a new level of skepticism. His work proved extremely influential on subsequent Western philosophy by impacting many well-known names, including philosopher Immanuel Kant.

These four individuals laid the groundwork for the many variations of Empiricism that would arise over time. Some of these variants include:

- Phenomenalism
- Pragmatism
- Radical Empiricism
- Logical Positivism
- the list could go on

7. John Locke, *An Essay Concerning Human Understanding*, 1690.
8. Bishop George Berkeley, *Treatise Concerning the Principles of Human Knowledge*, 1710.
9. David Hume, *A Treatise of Human Nature*, 1738.

Each one brandishes its own specialized nuances, but all agree to the same core principles. The situation is summarized well in this quote.

> All empiricists hold that experience rather than reason is the source of knowledge. This very general thesis has received very different emphases and refinements, and as such lead to very different kinds of empiricism. Nevertheless, empiricists are united in the claim that knowledge ultimately depends on our senses, and what we discover by them.[10]

It is this "united claim" and general definition that we will consider. Time does not permit us to address each branch of this philosophical tree, so we will direct our attention to the trunk.

Authority

At first glance, it would appear the empiricist appeals to "science" and "nature" as their ultimate authority. For the most part, they see themselves as unbiased witnesses who astutely listen and record what these "forces" have to "say" through observation. Phrases like "The rocks and fossils tell us," "The evidence speaks for itself," "Science says the earth is billions of years old," or "Nature teaches us that evolution is true" are uttered without a second thought. The echoing sentiment in the shadow of these statements is, "These are the facts and they are not to be trifled with — deal with it."

Of course, the inherent problem here is nature, science, evidence, rocks, radioisotopes, etc. do not think or speak. This is the logical fallacy of reification, "attributing a concrete characteristic to something that is abstract,"[11] or personification, attributing a human characteristic to something non-human. These evidences are handled, observed, utilized, and ultimately interpreted by a person who does think and speak. Herein lies the key — every person comes to the evidence with a worldview, a set of basic assumptions presupposed to be true about reality, which is used to form their observations. Ultimately, it is a person's worldview that is used to interpret the evidence. And at the foundational level, there are only two worldviews to choose from — either you start with God's Word as the authority or you trust man's word. Either the revealed Word of God is the foundation on which we stand to

---

10. Norman Geisler and Paul Feinberg. *Introduction to Philosophy- A Christian Perspective.* 10th ed. (Grand Rapids MI: Baker, 1999), p. 113.
11. https://answersingenesis.org/logic/the-fallacy-of-reification/.

understand all of reality, past, present, and future, or it is false, and man, by default, becomes the measure of all things. Empiricism, by its very nature, rejects the idea of supernatural revelation and is thus left with man and his interpretations of reality as its sole authority.

Foundational Beliefs

Evolutionary, Atheistic, or Agnostic Empiricism

In regards to origins, the typical empiricist is going to fully embrace all that naturalistic evolutionary dogma has to offer. With God out of the way and man left as sole authority, evolutionary ideology becomes man's best attempt to explain life in the vacuum of God's absence. So the empiricist readily accepts the major cosmological, geological, and biological evolutionary components. Big bang, billions of years, and molecules-to-man evolution are all confidently asserted as factual history. These things must be true, because in the worldview of empiricism "the facts speak for themselves."

Now to be fair, empiricists do not have to be atheists, they can just as easily be staunchly agnostic. Whereas the atheist says definitively that there is no God, the agnostic says it is impossible to know if a god exists. To the agnostic, God is unknown and unknowable and this makes the idea of an agnostic Christian an oxymoron.

Deistic Empiricism

The God of the Bible has revealed Himself not only in His creation, but also more importantly in Christ and through His Word. At best, an agnostic empiricist can be a deist. A deist concedes that an unknown god started the universe and then let go. God wound the watch, so to speak, and then disappeared without a supernatural trace. All man can know about this god is through observation of the universe; there are no supernatural writings, incarnations, or revelations of any sort. Thus, you can see how the empiricist can feel right at home within this perspective.

With those cards on the table, let's do a quick, though far from exhaustive, comparison between the biblical God and empiricism's possible deistic god. The God of the Bible is omnipotent, omniscient, and omnipresent. He is the Alpha and Omega, Creator and sustainer of all things visible and invisible. His initial creation was perfect, and man has the distinct privilege of being made in His image. Upon man's choice to rebel and violate the

God-given command not to eat of a certain tree, perfect fellowship with God was broken, and death and the Curse entered this world.

From this point onward, the biblical narrative is focused on the Messiah who will come as the ultimate ransom for sin's debt, the Redeemer of mankind and restorer of all things. The Old Testament points to His coming, the New Testament records His coming, and Revelation anticipates His Second Coming, demonstrating His perfect will, sovereignty, and love for us! How do we know all this? Quite simply: the Bible tells us so as God has revealed Himself in Jesus Christ and through His Word, displaying His love and character for all to see.

The deistic god, on the other hand, is quite a different entity. Since he has declined to reveal himself, we can only infer things about him from what we observe (often referred to as natural law). But even then, that cannot really be known. It's fair to say that since he is not intimately involved with his creation he is a bit of an introvert. Does he love us? I guess we can't know for sure, but if he did, don't you think he would want to be with us? If he cared for us, don't you think he would want us to know it and would want to tell us how to live lives that have true meaning, purpose, and direction? It would hardly be groundbreaking to suggest that any child that has been abandoned by one or both parents could testify that is not love.

Also, look at the mess of his creation! Yes, there's beauty, but it's also full of death, suffering, pain, diseases, catastrophes, evil, violence, injustice, malice, etc. And he made it this way! Evidently this is how a deistic god wants things to be with no end in sight. If this is all that is to be known about the deistic god, I'm not sure he is somebody worth meeting.

Afterlife and Salvation in Empiricism?

What happens after death? Well, the biblical God has told us that we all spend eternity somewhere. The question is location, location, location!? In empiricism, whether of the atheist or deistic persuasion, the afterlife is unobservable and therefore unknown and unknowable.

As one might expect, empiricism's view of Jesus Christ is polar opposite of Christianity's. Christianity reveals that Jesus is Immanuel — God with us, God become flesh, 100 percent God and 100 percent man. This hypostatic union is critical to the gospel and Christian doctrine. Empiricism at its best would concede that Jesus was maybe a good teacher, but nothing more, and certainly not God — man is the ultimate authority in Empiricism.

246 — World Religions and Cults • Volume 3

And what about salvation? Biblical teaching says that salvation comes by grace through faith alone in Christ alone. In Empiricism, what do you need saving from? Either god does not exist or he hasn't revealed himself to man. Either way, no standard has been revealed and no instructions for salvation given. Thus, each person decides the parameters of their own salvation — but it has nothing to do with biblical salvation.

Arbitrariness, Inconsistencies, and Refutations

Arbitrariness

As mentioned earlier, empiricism suggests that truth is unveiled through man's senses, observations, and interpretations. Thus, in the empiricist worldview, man is the ultimate authority. But this view is inherently arbitrary. If man is the authority, then which man?

Whose senses, observations, and interpretations rise above all others to be standard-bearer? How can any person's observations and conclusions be trusted as "truth" when so many conclusions of the past have been shown to be egregiously mistaken?

Some might argue that a consensus of a majority can determine "truth," but one needs to look no further than Nazi Germany to realize that is fallacious. Using man as the ultimate authority for your worldview is like trying to nail gelatin to a wall. No matter how many times you try or different strategies you employ, it just won't stick!

Also, empiricism assumes from the start that either God doesn't exist or hasn't revealed Himself. Both of these ideas arbitrarily assume their conclusions. If one chooses to assume a god does not exist, can that person prove it scientifically? Think about it. To prove a god does not exist through empirical means, you would have to know everything. You would have to exist in all places at all times to make sure a god wasn't hiding somewhere. And you would have to be all-powerful to do those things. So in order to prove there is no god, you would have to be god; god would therefore exist, and it's a self-defeating argument.

In like manner, the agnostic empiricist also assumes what they cannot know. They assume that an unknown god does not reveal himself supernaturally. But how do they know that? Did they find this truth by empirical means? No. Did god supernaturally reveal to them that he does not reveal himself supernaturally? How can one simultaneously claim that god is not knowable but know how he chooses to operate? Again, it's a self-refuting argument.

What about the empiricist's view that Jesus was just a good man? Of course, this idea is not restricted to empiricism; it's safe to say the majority of worldviews outside of Christianity hold this view of Christ. But by what standard can they even measure good? What senses did they use to converse with Christ? Off the cuff, this idea may seem rational, but a quick look at the Word of God reveals the impossibility of such a view. Why? Because Jesus Himself plainly states numerous times that He is God. This sentiment reverberates throughout the Bible from cover to cover. Therefore, since Jesus claims to be God, it is impossible for Him to be "just a good man." To para-phrase what C.S. Lewis famously said in his book *Mere Christianity*, Jesus is either a liar, lunatic, or Lord. Either He is who He claims to be — the very Son of God — or He is a madman or the devil in disguise. These are the only options Jesus left us, and each person directly or indirectly chooses one of these three.[12]

Inconsistencies

As noted time and again throughout this book series, the ultimate confir-mation of the biblical worldview is that it alone provides the preconditions necessary to make knowledge and life possible. Only the biblical worldview does this while remaining self-consistent.

Every other worldview, including Empiricism, is ultimately suicidal; it blows itself up by its own assumptions. This highlights Empiricism's most egregious inconsistency: it cannot be proved by its own standard! According to Empiricism, all knowledge is gained through observation.

Now it should be noted that it's perfectly consistent with Scripture to conclude that *some* knowledge can be gained by observation. This makes sense within the biblical worldview that tells us God made everything, He holds it together by the power of His Word, and He made our senses to be able to study the universe He created.

The problem with Empiricism is that it claims *all* knowledge is acquired by observation. Here's the key question; how does the empiricist know that all knowledge is attained by observation? Is this something he observed? Since knowledge itself cannot be "seen," obviously not. But if that's the case, how can Empiricism be verified if indeed all things are known by observation?

12. Later writers have added the option of "legend" to Lewis's trilemma.

If Empiricism is substantiated by something other than observation, it disproves itself. The conclusion is, if Empiricism were true, it would be impossible for the empiricist to actually know it or prove it. Empiricism refutes itself.

This problem is exponential when you realize that many people's observations are not trustworthy. Consider the observations of a person under the influence of drugs; to the empiricist, are their observations truth?

If things weren't already bad enough for the empiricist, their worldview also forces them to practice behavioral inconsistencies. This is the basic principle that "actions speak louder than words." Things like morality, justice, and love are not actually observable, but the empiricist unwittingly acknowledges their truth by his actions.

In essence, the empiricist proclaims one worldview but lives by another. Consider the empiricist who dogmatically claims evolution must be true — that life in all its splendor is merely a series of cosmic accidents such that origin and meaning are reduced to time plus chance and matter. But when he gets home from work he pets his dog with fondness and embraces his family with hugs and kisses, as if they are much more than chemical accidents. And how would he respond if a child of his was brutally murdered?

Would he say, "Oh well, it's a random chance universe and that event was just one chemical accident reacting with another chemical accident. You know, like when baking soda reacts with vinegar. No big deal." Of course not! He would be shocked, broken-hearted, outraged, and in desperate need of justice!

In both scenarios, the actions of the empiricist are quite contrary to his beliefs. He may profess empiricism, but he's actually living according to a different worldview. This shows that in his heart of hearts he knows that his worldview is insufficient to explain the realities of life. Things like freedom, morality, love, and justice are truths easily taken for granted, but only the biblical worldview can adequately account for them. It is only the biblical worldview that makes sense of the totality of reality, both physical and immaterial.

Refutations

So if empiricism, like every other non-biblical worldview, cannot account for the totality of reality, how does the empiricist function in the everyday world? He borrows from the biblical worldview, whether he realizes it or not. A few examples: the uniformity of nature, laws of logic, and absolute morality only make sense within a biblical worldview.

How does the empiricist account for these things within his own worldview? He boldly declares that all truth is discovered by one's senses, but you cannot see a law of logic, trip over a law of nature, or smell absolute morality. All of these things are unobservable and immaterial, yet absolutely true and necessary for life and knowledge.

Only the Bible reveals the omniscient, omnipotent, omnipresent God who created time, space, and matter and is not limited by them. The Creator God, who made all things both visible and invisible, holds them together by the power of His Word and has revealed Himself through His creation and the Scriptures. Outside of this, there is no accounting for the immaterial truths that flood our reality.

So what is the empiricist to do? He trespasses! He stands on biblical principles, probably unaware, and assumes all of these truths with no foundation for them in his proclaimed worldview. Ironically, the empiricist, like every other non-believer, is standing on the biblical worldview to try and argue against the biblical worldview.

The empiricist may contend that this is not the case; that he has morality and uses laws of logic just fine without believing in God. But you do not have to *confess* a belief in God to use the laws and principles He has put in place. The questions in play here are not "Are they true and do you use them?" but rather, "Where did they come from and why are they true?" Ultimately, the empiricist has no answer for these questions. Can he use these laws? Absolutely. Can he explain them within his own worldview? Absolutely not. Therefore, he lives in a fundamentally inconsistent way from his declared worldview.

Conclusion

So why accept a lacking and faulty worldview? In Romans 1:18 we are told that the unbeliever suppresses the truth in unrighteousness. Sinful man does not like the idea of being held accountable to a holy and just God, so he is willing to believe a lie as opposed to facing the truth. The truth is that "all have sinned and fall short of the glory of God" (Romans 3:23) and that "the wages of sin is death" (Romans 6:23). If you are reading this and are not sure that you have fallen short of God's glory, take a look at Exodus 20, the Ten Commandments, God's basic moral code for mankind.

Realize that since God is perfect and perfectly holy, He requires absolute perfection and flawless righteousness to be in His presence. Therefore, to attain entrance into heaven you must have kept His law perfectly, never breaking any of His standards, not even once.

> For whoever shall keep the whole law, and yet stumble in
> one point, he is guilty of all (James 2:10).

Not only that, God is omniscient (all knowing), knowing our thoughts, attitudes, and motives, which also must be completely pure and holy in His sight (see Matthew 5:21–30). One adulterous thought, vindictive motive, or malicious word makes a person a lawbreaker, guilty and fallen short of the glory of God.

You might be thinking to yourself that this kind of standard is impossible — no one can do this! You're right, and that's the point! We are all sinners by nature and by choice because we are all descendants of that first man Adam, who passed on his heritage of sin to all of us. We are incapable of saving ourselves and indeed this is the worst kind of news. But that is what makes the "Good News" so good — the good news that God became flesh, the Last Adam, Jesus Christ, lived a perfect life and died as a flawless sacrifice to pay a debt we never could!

> But God demonstrates His own love toward us, in that while
> we were still sinners, Christ died for us (Romans 5:8).

But that's not the end! Then He rose from the dead, defeating death, so that all who put their faith in Him have their sins forgiven, are clothed in the perfect righteousness of Christ, and have eternal life with Him!

That if you confess with your mouth the Lord Jesus and believe in your heart that God has raised Him from the dead, you will be saved (Romans 10:9).

Christianity provides the ultimate hope for the present and eternity, while Empiricism is an impotent religion of hopelessness that's unable to make sense of the senses or eternity.

That's a truth that resonates with all the senses.

Chapter 15

Afterlife: "What Must I Do to Be Saved?"

Eric Hovind

If you are like me, you skipped to the end of this book to read the conclusion. Seriously, no cheating. Go back and read what you skipped!

Whether this is the first chapter or the last chapter for you, you are still reading this book, which means either you are searching for answers for yourself, or seeking to educate yourself for a defense for what you already believe. Throughout these pages, we discovered that *all religions are not the same* and that tolerance of every religion is not the same as "accepting every religion as true." Even the claim by some that *all religions point to the same goal turns out to be a myth.*

You may describe yourself as an atheist, a skeptic, an agnostic, a seeker, a mystic, or a believer. Regardless of your title, are you certain about your eternal future? Are you unsure of which religion represents truth? Man, am I ever glad you asked that question!

I have some good news and some bad news to share. I'm the kind of guy that wants the bad news first, so that is where I am going to start.

Bad News First

The bad news? Statistics show that ten out of ten people die! I'm going to die one day. Of course I am going to make that the last thing I ever do, but it is going to happen. You too are going to die one day, and the question I have is "Why?"

Have you ever stopped to consider why people (and other things) die? Consider this, if you had a car that repaired itself every time it was damaged, it would last forever. Well, your body has the ability to heal itself and theoretically SHOULD be able to last forever. But it doesn't. Why? In an evolutionary worldview where life just came from matter and figured out how to repair itself, why didn't it figure out how to live forever? Or as a Hindu where nothing is ultimately real, why does death happen to everything? Or in Islam, why would it be the "will of Allah" to make life that simply . . . dies?

The truth is, death was not a part of God's original creation. He had created all of the animals and humans as vegetarians. There was no disease, no suffering, and no death. Death entered the world through the act of sin, which is any thought, word, or deed that breaks God's Law.

When the first man, Adam, and his wife, Eve, sinned, they were sentenced to death (Genesis 3:19). They had been warned, and it was true, death is the punishment for sin. In Adam, and individually, we have all sinned, so we are all sentenced to death. Remember that statistic? Ten out of ten people die. Sin really is the reason for death. When Adam sinned in the Garden of Eden, everything under his dominion fell into decay and death. This included the animals who were under Adam as his dominion (Genesis 1:26–28). When a spiritual being like Satan fell into sin, he was sentenced to death as well — not physical, but eternal hell, or the "lake of fire" (what is called the "second death" in Revelation 20:14).

Physical death is not the end of man, but God revealed that the man who sins will also endure the eternal punishment of the second death as well (Revelation 21:8). Why is it *eternal*? Because we have been made in the image of an *eternal* God. Our soul will continue after death for eternity. So the question of eternity in heaven or hell is arguably one of the most important questions of your life.

This is the reason you think about death and the afterlife. It is why you keep asking the question, "What happens after I die?"

I've heard people say that regardless of which religious organization you identify with, that basically when you die, good people go to heaven and bad people go hell.[1] The Bible teaches this. It says that the unrighteous, or

---

1. There is a misconception about hell in today's culture that Satan rules in hell. But this deception has gone on long enough. Even Satan is a captive there. The description of a fire is quite apt for hell, for all victims are being tormented forever without rest and none are "ruling," not even Satan.

"bad people," will not inherit the kingdom of God (1 Corinthians 6:9). All we need to know now is the definition of righteous and unrighteous. You probably have some of your own standards that you have developed as you have gone through life. Most of us have developed a personal standard of what is good and bad, and most of us feel that our good outweighs our bad. Based on this, many are satisfied that they have a pretty good chance of going to heaven (or a type of paradise in the afterlife) on the merit of their good works. *In fact, every world religion at which we have looked bases any hope of eternal bliss on our good works.*

Since individuals and religions have different ways of determining right and wrong, who is truly responsible for setting "the standard," for determining good and bad? The Bible says that God is the just judge of all of His creation. Do you think the God of the Bible considers you to be a good person? Let's find out.

How many lies have you told in your life? Too many to count, right! What do you call someone who tells a lie? A liar. Lying is not wrong simply because God says so. This standard of righteousness is because God is not a liar, and you have been made in the image of God.

How many times have you taken something that doesn't belong to you? Don't lie about this! What do we call someone who takes things that don't belong to them? A thief. Here again, we see the standard based on God's righteousness. It is wrong to steal because God does not steal.

God is perfectly faithful. His standard of righteousness says that we are to be perfectly faithful. That is why it is wrong to commit adultery. Then Jesus, who was God in human form, said that even looking with lust causes us to commit adultery in our hearts. Who can say that they have never looked with lust? Once again, we fall short of God's standard of righteousness.

Because God is perfect, He says that the use of His name is to be perfect. That's why He says, "Thou shalt not take the name of the Lord thy God in vain." Have you ever taken God's name and used it to swear? That is called blasphemy and it is a very serious sin.

The Bible sets the benchmark for "good" very high. *God's standard of a good person is "perfection!"* (Romans 5:8). Yet, nobody's perfect! Everyone has sinned! The word "sin" is an old archery term that means to "miss the mark." You and I have missed the mark of God's perfection, and not just by a little bit either!

Now, knowing God's standard, do you still consider yourself to be a good person? Do you think a just and holy God should let liars, thieves, adulterers, and blasphemers into heaven, a perfect place where people who miss the mark of God's perfection are not allowed to be?

The reason: If a perfect God allowed imperfect sinners into a His perfect heaven, it would no longer be perfect! Heaven would be no better than the sin-cursed and broken world we live in now. You wouldn't want that forever, and I wouldn't either.

Of course, God can't allow sinners into heaven. He tells us that all adulterers, the sexually immoral, liars, murderers, and so on will not inherit the kingdom of God (1 Corinthians 6:9; Revelation 22:15). He says that He will not hold them guiltless who take His name in vain (Exodus 20:7). Liars and thieves will have their part in the lake of fire (Revelation 21:8). Isaiah 59 says that your sins have cut you off from God. Romans 3:23 says "All have sinned and come short of the glory of God."

Working for Righteousness

Yes, the bad news is that you have missed the mark of perfection. Big revelation, I am sure, but it gets worse. *You can't do enough good works to outweigh the bad works.* In other words, Christianity, unlike every other religion in the world, focuses on trying to fix the problem of sin instead of ignoring it in hopes of good works outweighing the bad.

The Bible even says that all of our "good works" are as filthy rags to God (Isaiah 64:6). He is telling us that there is no way for us to get out of this situation on our own. We are trapped and doomed without someone to rescue us and save us from the destruction we deserve from our past sinful actions. We need someone to save us.

There is more bad news. When we break man's law, we pay man's penalty. When we break God's law, we pay God's penalty. Remember what the Bible says the penalty for sin is? "The wages of sin is death" (Romans 3:23). That is why ten out of ten people die and it has been like this since the first sinners (Adam and Eve).

We are born as sinners into a sin-cursed world (Psalm 51:5) and we all personally choose to sin (Ecclesiastes 7:20; 1 John 1:8), and that sin separates us from God and carries a death penalty that must be paid.

Many in our world fully embrace a sinful, humanistic lifestyle and justify our sinful actions. This humanistic worldview teaches "the end of all being is the happiness of man." In other words, this life is all about making yourself happy. But this statement could mean anything to anybody — one person's happiness could be another's misery. And, that worldview is a dead end! People have tried all kinds of things to obtain fulfillment and purpose, but money, power, and popularity never lead to true, lasting happiness.

That's the bad news. Now let me give you the good news!

Good News

Although we are sinners, God still loves us. God, Himself, even wrote out the plan for our redemption in the Bible so that we could be sure of the path to freedom, forgiveness, and hope. We were created for the purpose of enjoying a relationship with our Creator. We are made in His image after all. There is a path to discover true happiness. True joy is discovered when we realize that the end of all being is not the happiness of man, but the glory of God!

Did you notice something from the other religions addressed in this book? All the major religions of the world claim to POINT to truth. The Hindu scriptures, such as the Vedas, say truth is elusive and hard to find. At the end of his life, Buddha said, "I'm still searching for the truth." Muhammad wrote, "I point to the truth." Jesus Christ never claimed to point to truth. He said, "I am the way, the truth and the life. No one comes to the Father except through Me" (John 14:6).

I have talked to many that would assert the Christian belief that Christ is the only way to heaven is intolerant, dogmatic, and even uneducated in light of the many world religions. By now, if you really read the previous chapters like you were suppose to, you should be able to see through that assertion. We have seen that in reality, there are only two world religions: those that espouse God's Word as truth and those that do not.

Those that reject the Bible are actually the ones being intolerant — intolerant of the ultimate authority, choosing rather to determine truth for themselves. The path to redemption is made plain in Acts 4:12, "Nor is there salvation in any other, for there is no other name under heaven given among men by which we must be saved."

The good news about Jesus Christ being *the* way, *the* truth, *the* life is called the gospel. It is good news because God made a way for us to be saved, to be redeemed from the penalty of sin. God the Son, Jesus Christ, came and lived among men. He lived a perfect life. He never sinned one time. Then

He laid down His life and allowed Himself to be the sacrifice, the payment for our sin. We miss the mark of God's standard of perfection, but God the Son didn't (John 10:15).

Jesus Christ was crucified on a Cross, taking upon Himself the sins of the world — past, present, and future. Three days later, He literally rose from the dead, giving Him victory over death and sin. He paid the debt that we deserved to pay and proclaimed that anyone who believes, who accepts His payment, putting their faith and trust in what He did on the Cross, can be saved from paying that eternal death penalty themselves.

How much does this sin debt cost? In 1978, I was given physical life. It didn't cost me a thing, but it cost someone else a lot. In 2001, I was given spiritual life. My spiritual birth didn't cost me a thing, but it cost Christ everything. Romans 6:23 says, "the *gift* of God is eternal life through Jesus Christ our Lord." It's a gift! You can't earn it. You can't buy it. It is a gift received by faith alone (Ephesians 2:8–10; Titus 3:3–7).

Let us consider this debt further with regards to sin. One sin is worthy of . . . an *infinite* punishment. God is infinite (Psalm 147:5; Isaiah 40:28; Romans 1:20), so naturally the punishment for offending Him would also be infinite. The punishment from an infinite God upon sin, *our sin,* would also be infinite! There is no escape in and of yourself, because you cannot undo your offenses against a holy God.

In fact, the only one in a position to take that punishment for you is God Himself. Which is what He did in the person of Jesus Christ. The infinite Son of God took the punishment for sin upon Himself, and the infinite Father delivered that punishment, so the debt is paid in full.[2]

And God is so powerful that the person of Jesus Christ delivered the proof of everlasting life in the Resurrection (John 10:17). Not only did Christ die the punishment we deserve, but He also came back to life afterward! All that is required of you is faith — involving repentance of your sin and belief in the death, burial, and Resurrection of Jesus Christ alone.

What Is Faith?

Faith sometimes gets a bad rap, being described as something only needed by the weak-minded. The truth is, everyone practices faith! You have faith in

---

2. The Father and Son are not two different "gods," but are one God. The Father, the Son, and the Holy Spirit are the three persons of the one triune God. See the Appendix on the Triune God in volume one for further elaboration.

the food you eat and the air you breathe. You even put faith in drivers that you have never met, trusting that they will not cross those strips of yellow paint on the road as you fly past each other only a few feet apart. Faith is a part of our everyday lives. The most important faith questions we need to ask are, in what or in whom do we place our faith for our eternal destiny and how much faith do we need?

I could put lots and lots of faith in a rickety old chair to hold me; however, my faith won't determine whether the rickety old chair will hold me. I could put very little faith in a rock-solid chair to hold my weight, but my little faith won't change the fact that the sturdy chair has no problem holding me up. You see, it is not the amount of faith, it is the *object* of our faith that matters.

In what are you placing your faith? Good works? Religion? Science? A church? A pastor? A spouse? The Bible teaches us that there is only one thing in which we can put our trust to have salvation — the death, burial, and Resurrection of the Lord Jesus Christ. If you are putting your trust in anything other than Jesus Christ, then you need to repent. That word means "to change your mind." You need to change your mind about what you place your trust in for salvation. Your faith must be in *Christ alone*.

If you have never put your trust in Jesus Christ, forsaking your sin and turning to the one who died on the Cross and rose again to provide the way of salvation for you, then I invite you to do that today. My friends Matt and Sherry wrote a poem as a prayer for people who desire a relationship with God. While there are no magic words to communicate your heart to God that you are sorry for your sin and are seeking His forgiveness, you could make this poem your simple prayer for salvation.

> Jesus, You died upon the Cross and rose again to save the lost.
> Forgive me now of all my sin; come be my Savior, Lord, and friend.
> Take my life and make it new, and help me, Lord, to live for you.

The Bible says in Romans 10:13 that "whoever calls on the name of the LORD shall be saved." That's a promise from the Creator of the universe. His promise is not based on our emotions or feelings, our good works or bad. Salvation is based on the object of our faith, the perfect, infinite, and eternal Jesus Christ.

The God of the universe loves you and desires to have a relationship with you. He wants to give your life true purpose and joy. The gospel really is simple.

Admit that you are a sinner who has come short of the glory of God, and because of your sin, you deserve to be punished.

Believe that Jesus Christ died, was buried, and rose triumphantly over death and sin, paying the punishment for you on the Cross.

Call upon the Lord Jesus. Repent of your sin and of trusting anything but Christ alone for salvation and you can be saved from eternal destruction and be assured of a home in heaven forever.

Our Authority Is the Bible — God's Word

No other world religion has a book of such miraculous power. No other book offers you a loving relationship with a God who loves you enough to let His only Son die for you. No other world religion has a resurrected Savior who came back from death to prove He alone knows what happens after death. Trust Jesus Christ and begin your God-quest journey with your Creator today!

Appendix A

The Bible versus Other Alleged Holy Books

Bodie Hodge

But how do you know the Bible is the right one to pick when there are so many holy books like the Upanishads, Confucius's writings, Book of Mormon, Vedas, Studies in the Scriptures (Charles Russell), and the Qur'an?

It sounds like a buffet where you pick what you want, doesn't it? Many mistakenly think that people just line the holy books up and make their best guess. In other words, you pick based on what *you* think is the truth. But this is not the case at all.

If YOU are the authority on the truthfulness of a religious book, then God (or a god or a set of gods) CANNOT be. Let me state this differently. If one argues that God is the absolute authority by appealing to their own opinions as the ultimate authority, then that person refutes himself or herself. It sounds complicated, but either man is the authority or God is.

So let's look at this issue in more detail.

What Is the Bible Really Up Against?

Some "Holy Books" Do Not Claim to Be the Word of God

This might surprise you, but many "holy books" aren't holy, and they admit it! In other words, they do not claim to be the Word of God. They are like any other writing.

For instance, take the writings by ancient Hindus. The Vedas, Upanishads, or even the Bhagavad Gita are not the revealed word of their god, Brahman (other gods in Hinduism are considered manifestations of Brahman). Brahman is not a personal god, so revelation (i.e., communication) from Brahman would not be a possibility since communication is a personal attribute.

These alleged holy writings are merely various opinions of their ancient sages on the subject. The alleged holy books of Hinduism are nothing more than errant books of man, nothing that should be confused as the inerrant (without error) Word of God, like the Bible. Any writing of an alleged *impersonal* god (e.g., New Age, Scientology, Taoism, etc.) is in the same camp.

Obviously, any book about religions that have no god (e.g., secular religions or many moralistic religions) cannot be a book that could be confused as the Word of God either. So there goes any Buddhist, Confucianist, Epicurean, Stoic, and atheistic writing. Believe it or not, this eliminates Satanism's writings, too (LaVey's *The Satanic Bible* and *The Devil's Notebook* for example). LaVey was actually an atheist arguing for atheism in the books!

Multi-god systems like Germanic or Greek mythologies, Shinto, and so forth are little more than ancestor worship where people were elevated to a god-like status. Oden and Thor are listed in ancient genealogies and were real people who later had god-like attributes attached to them.[1] Again, it would merely be the arbitrary and fallible opinions of man anyway you look at them.

Pagan religions like witchcraft, voodoo, and animism do not have a supreme god who reveals his or her will. This explains why there are such varied beliefs among pagans. It comes down to the mind of mankind anyway. There are no unified, absolute scriptures for paganism.

A deistic god generally remains distant from his creation, so there is no need for this alleged god to communicate with beings within his creation. So by the story of most deists, there should be no Word of God!

Other "Holy Books" Agree the Bible Is True!

Other alleged holy books or prophets often agree the Bible is true. More often than not, they want to add to the Bible.

---

1. Woden/Oden and Thor/Tror are even in my own genealogy that extends back to Noah and Adam.

Jehovah's Witnesses and Charles Taze Russell (their founder and supposed prophet) affirmed that the Bible is true. Russell just opted to *add* his works to it. The Watch Tower Bible and Tract Society (Jehovah's Witnesses) has continued in the same trend as Russell.

Alleged prophet Joseph Smith (founder of the Mormons) and subsequent Mormon leadership also agree that the Bible is true (insofar as it is accurately translated), although, Smith attempted to *add* the Book of Mormon, the Pearl of Great Price, and the Doctrines and Covenants as Scripture. Alleged prophetess Ellen White agreed the Bible is true though her writings were seen by many early Seventh Day Adventists (SDA) as inerrant — an *addition* to Scripture. Encouragingly, we see many SDA today who no longer hold Ellen White in such high esteem and now see the Bible as the *sole* source of doctrine.

Even Muhammad, the prophet of Islam, agreed the Bible is true, and this appears several times in the Qur'an (e.g., Surah 2:40–42, 126, 136, 285; 3:3, 71, 93; 4:47, 136; 5:47–51, 69, 71–72; 6:91; 10:37, 94; 21:7; 29:45–46; 35:31; 46:11–12). But the Qur'an was seen as the true revelation.

Within Roman Catholicism, they agree the Bible is true, but then try to *add* the Apocryphal books (and Papal/Ecumenical authority, which is a response called an "infallible pronouncement" on faith and moral issues if they are called into question). The Jews agreed on much of the Scripture (Old Testament) but then *add* the Talmud, Mishna, etc. (oral traditions put to writing beginning about A.D. 200) while rejecting the New Testament.

This list could continue, but the point is that many who have professed additional writings from God still agree that the Bible is true. So the issue with them is not the Bible. It is their alleged additions that need to be judged and tested by the Bible (previous Scripture). There is little dispute on the Bible.

There is no reason to be exhaustive here. The point is that the Bible has very little competition when you actually look at the issue. It is by no means a buffet line from which to pick and choose. The questions are, "Does the competition even come close?" and "Is the Bible true?" Let's begin with the latter question.

The Authority of Scripture

The God of the Bible is absolute by His very nature. He is the ultimate authority on all things — by extension, His Word is the ultimate authority on all things.

	Bible is true?	But wants to add . . .
Mormons	Yes	Book of Mormon, the Pearl of Great Price, and the Doctrines and Covenants
Jehovah's Witnesses	Yes	Studies in the Scripture, *Watchtower*, and *Awake*
Islam	Yes	Qur'an and Hadith
Seventh Day Adventist	Yes	Ellen White's writings
Roman Catholicism	Yes	Apocrypha and Papal authority
Judaism	Most (OT)	Talmud (Traditions)
Orthodoxy	Yes	Some Apocrypha and Patriarchal authority
Syncretism	Yes	Humanistic Origins (various degrees of evolution)
Bah'ai	Yes	Qur'an and Bahaullah's writings and his sons, modern prophets and the House of Justice
Biblical Christianity	Yes	**Nothing**

God, being the ultimate and final authority, can only reveal Himself by final and absolute authority. In other words, there is no other authority to "prove" God and His Word, as all other authorities are *lesser* than God.

This is why *I, a mere man,* am not in a position to prove God and His Word. If I appealed to my arbitrary opinions on God or His Word, I would be a lesser authority than God — being a fallible and imperfect man.

Can I use *logic* to try to prove God? Even logic is dependent upon God and His being as the ultimate authority. Logic and reasoning are tools that we use to "think God's thoughts after Him." But even logic is a lesser authority than God. All things (man, logic, angels, governments, etc.) are lesser than God, and thus lesser in authority than God and His Word. So only God is left in the position to prove Himself and His Word.[2] God alone is in

---

2. Some might object and appeal to logic that this is a circular argument, thus fallacious. However, circular arguments are *valid* logically. What makes a circular argument fallacious is when it is an *arbitrary* circle. God, being absolute and final, is non-arbitrary. Thus it is valid and sound, so one cannot appeal to this being a fallacious argument.

the spot to reveal to us His absolute existence and His absolute Word. And He did it with the first few words of Genesis.

> In the beginning God . . . (Genesis 1:1).

This initial phrase is the foundation of the rest of Genesis 1:1. Genesis 1:1 is the foundation for the rest of Genesis 1. Genesis 1 is the foundation for the rest of the Book of Genesis, and Genesis is foundational to the rest of the Bible.

The Bible, from start to finish, is equal in authority and is our absolute starting point for all matters.[3] The Bible, the 66 books of Scripture, is the authority in all things — even the existence of God. Any objector would be a lesser authority and, therefore, not in a position to usurp the authority of God.

Man vs. God?

Secularists (humanists) like atheists, agnostics, Epicureans, Nazis, communists, and post-modernists merely appeal to their own authority. Mankind is seen as the absolute authority in their religious convictions. They have no God to which they can appeal. So whether people appeal to Darwin, Hitler, Stalin, or the like, it is always a person or group of people.

People do not have absolute authority. They are arbitrary and lesser authorities. Any argument they try to present to attack God and His Word is flawed from the onset because they are not a sufficient authority on the issue.

"But the Bible Was Written by Mere Men!"

Secularists and others who hold to a "no god" position want to demote God's Word to be like their arbitrary writings. They want to argue that God was not involved in the Bible (since they suppress His existence) and that it is merely a human document. They present a case that the Bible is no different from Darwin's book *The Descent of Man* or Plato's book *Critias*. They rebut, "The Bible was just written by men!"

When it comes to the authorship of the Bible, of course men were involved — Christians would be the first to point this out. Paul wrote letters to early churches and these became Scripture. David wrote many of

---

3. This is called the Transcendental Argument for the Existence of God (TAG). It is not an argument per se, but is the foundation that makes all argumentation possible.

the psalms, Moses wrote the Pentateuch (the first five books of the Bible), and so on. In fact, it is estimated that over 40 different human authors were involved.[4]

But this is not the real issue. The real issue is whether God had any involvement in the authorship of the Bible.

Let's think about this for a moment. When someone claims that the Bible was written by men, they really mean to say it was written by men *without God's involvement.*

This is an absolute statement that reveals something extraordinary. It reveals that the person saying this is claiming to be . . . transcendent. For a person to validate the claim that God did not inspire the human authors of the Bible means he must be omniscient, omnipresent, and omnipotent to know this is the case!

1. *Omniscient:* This person is claiming to be an all-knowing authority on the subject of God's inspiration in order to refute God's claim that Scripture was inspired by Him (2 Timothy 3:16).
2. *Omnipresent:* This person is claiming that he was present, both spiritually and physically, to observe that God had no part in aiding any of the biblical authors as they penned Scripture.
3. *Omnipotent:* This person is claiming that, had God tried to inspire the biblical authors, they had the power to stop such an action.

So the person making the claim that the Bible was merely written by men alone is claiming to be God since these three attributes belong to God alone. This is a religious issue of humanism versus Christianity. People who make such claims (perhaps unwittingly) are claiming that *they* are the ultimate authority over God and are trying to convince others that God is *subservient* to them.

When responding, I prefer to address this claim with a question that reveals the real issue — and there are several ways to do this. For example, referring to omnipresence, I can ask, "Do you really believe that you are omnipresent? The only way for you to make your point that God had no involvement would be if you were omnipresent." Then I can point out that

---

4. Josh McDowell, *A Ready Defense* (Nashville, TN: Thomas Nelson Publishers, 1993), p. 27.

this person is claiming to be God when he or she makes the statement that God had no involvement in the Bible.

Or, in regard to omnipotence, perhaps I can ask, "How is it that you are powerful enough to stop God from inspiring the authors?" Or I could direct the question to the rest of the listeners by simply asking, "Since the only way to refute the fact that God inspired the Bible is to use attributes of God such as omnipresence, omnipotence, and omniscience, do the rest of you think this person is God?" Naturally, I may have to explain it further from this point so the listeners will better understand.

I could also ask, "How do you know that God was not involved?" Other responses include undercutting the entire position by pointing out that any type of reasoning apart from the Bible is merely arbitrary. So the person trying to make a logical argument against the claims of the Bible (i.e., that God inspired the authors) is doing so only because he or she is assuming (though unintentionally) the Bible is true and that logic and truth exist! It is good to point out these types of presuppositions and inconsistencies.[5]

Someone may respond and say, "What if I claim that Shakespeare was inspired by God — then you would have to be omniscient, omnipresent, and omnipotent to refute it."

Actually, it is irrelevant *for me* to be omniscient, omnipresent, and omnipotent to refute such a claim. God, who is omniscient, omnipresent, and omnipotent, refutes this claim from what He has already stated in the Bible. Nowhere has God authenticated Shakespeare's writings as Scripture, unlike Christ the Creator God's (John 1; Colossians 1; Hebrews 1) approval of the Old Testament prophetic works and the New Testament apostolic works — the cap of the canon is already sealed.[6]

A Presuppositional Authority

God exists and His Word, the Bible, is the truth. This is the starting point.

God simply opens the Bible with a statement of His existence and says His Word is flawless (Genesis 1:1; Proverbs 30:5). The Bible bluntly claims to be the truth (Psalm 119:160), and Christ repeated this claim (John 17:17).

---

5. Jason Lisle, "Put the Bible Down," Answers in Genesis, December 5, 2008, www.answersingenesis.org/articles/2008/12/05/feedback-put-the-bible-down.
6. Bodie Hodge, "A Look at the Canon" Answers in Genesis, January 23, 2008, www.answersingenesis.org/articles/aid/v3/n1/look-at-the-canon.

In fact, if God had tried to prove that He existed or that His Word was flawless by any other means (i.e., a lesser means), then any evidence or proof would be greater than God and His Word — which would be contradictory to God's nature. However, all other things are lesser than God.

God knows that nothing is greater than He (e.g., Hebrews 6:13) and by extension, His Word, and therefore He doesn't stoop to our carnal desires for such proofs — instead God offers proof by the impossibility of the contrary (more on this in a moment).

The Bible also teaches us to have faith that God exists and that having faith pleases Him (Hebrews 11:6). Accordingly, we are on the right track if we start with God's Word. God's Word is presupposed as the truth and our starting point, and this is what makes all knowledge, all logic, all argumentation, all intellectual endeavors, etc. possible.

How Do We Know the Bible Is True?

Allow me to dive in a little deeper here by starting with God and His Word as the absolute authority. The Bible is true because any alternative would make knowledge, logic, and truth impossible. The Bible is the only book that has the preconditions for knowledge/logic/truth (i.e., intelligibility). Stated otherwise, the Bible must be predicated as true to make reasoning, truth, and intelligence a possibility.

All other worldviews must borrow from the Bible for the world to make sense. Science, morality, and logic all stem from the Bible being true. If the Bible were not true, then knowledge would be impossible. In other words, if the Bible were not true, nothing would make sense — good or bad . . . everything would be meaningless and pointless.

This doesn't mean someone has to *believe* the Bible to be true, but that the Bible is true regardless. Consider someone who says he doesn't believe air exists. He makes convincing verbal arguments and openly says he doesn't believe in air . . . all the while using air to breathe and speak his argument. It is like this with the critics of the Bible. They argue the Bible is not true and that they have knowledge to say so, all the while borrowing from the Bible, which accounts for truth and knowledge.

Think of it this way: Unless the Bible is true, which accounts for (1) knowledge and (2) truth existing and (3) that we are made in the image of an all-knowing, logical, God of truth (so we can seek to understand the answer), then no one and no worldview can even proceed to answer the question "How do we know the Bible is true?" unless they borrow these attributes from God's Word.

This is called the "impossibility of the contrary" that proves the Bible to be true by God's own Word. By starting with God and His Word as the absolute authority, no other possibility can exist to make knowledge possible.

Additional or Competitive "Holy Books"?

Scripture (God's Word) comes from God, and God cannot contradict Himself. If God were to contradict Himself, then nothing can be trustworthy or known. All knowledge would be arbitrary and nothing could ever really be known. Thus, when God reveals Himself, it will not be in contradiction.

Previous Scripture Is the Judge of Latter Scripture

Furthermore, when God revealed more about Himself in subsequent Scripture, it was consistent with the previous revelation. New revelation builds on previous Scripture as the *previous* judges the latter (newer Scripture). The Holy Spirit revealed this through Moses (e.g., Deuteronomy 13; Acts 1:16).

This is why the New Testament is built on a defense using the Old Testament to prove the New Testament (e.g., Acts 17:10–11). We saw Jesus, the Apostles, and others in the New Testament using the Old Testament witness as their proof of Jesus as the Messiah, for example. The Old Testament judged the New Testament. The New Testament was not contradictory to the Old Testament, but instead fulfilled what the Old Testament was looking toward and built upon its foundation.

A red flag should go up when you hear someone say that previous Scripture (e.g., the Old or New Testament) should be judged based on their alleged "new scripture." They have it backward. In fact, it would be too convenient if the new were to judge the old instead of the old judging the new because anyone could make that claim and put themself into a position of authority greater than God! And many have tried to do just that.

It is all too convenient when the new revelation is seen as authoritative and then the Bible is demoted. Yet this is a trademark for those who pay lip service to the Bible. For example, Mormons say the Book of Mormon and other Mormon writings are the authority and the Bible is secondary based on the interpretation and translation of the Bible according to Mormon teaching. They place the latter Mormon writings in a superior position to the previous (Bible).

The Jehovah's Witnesses do the same thing. The Bible is secondary to their writings and subject to the Watchtower Organization and Charles Russell's view of the Scripture. They have the latter in a superior position to the previous. Islam fairs the same with the Qur'an in a higher position than the Bible. Again, this is back to front.

The same worn-out case is found with Ellen White's writings. Her writings take the forefront and the Bible takes a secondary role, being interpreted based upon her view of the Bible. At the very least, if these alleged prophets viewed their works to be equal to the Bible, then they should have held to the position that their works were equal to but not greater than the previous! Instead, like clockwork, they elevate their own alleged revelations to supersede the Bible. That should be a red flag to anyone.

Sadly, this method of taking the new as authoritative and neglecting the old in light of it is nothing new. Did you realize Jesus had to deal with this? The Jews had been walking away from the Old Testament. They had held to the traditions of the elders (later written down and called the Talmud) as superior to Moses and the Old Testament prophets. They reinterpreted meanings in the Old Testament that destroyed the meanings of passages all for the traditions of man and made useless the commands of God.

The New Testament did not do that. The New Testament Apostles consistently argued their case, *based* upon the Old Testament and gave equal authority to their New Testament Scripture as a fulfillment to the Old Testament. The New Testament books were not seen as superior documents to the Old Testament that now need reinterpreting.

The same occurred throughout the Old Testament. When Old Testament prophets came forth with the Word of God, they did not say their books were superior and that Moses now needs to be seen as secondary or reinterpreted based on their new book. By no means. Their prophetic works were seen as building on the foundation of Moses.

Previous Scripture is to be used to judge latter Scripture. When an alleged new prophet claims the opposite, they stand in contradiction to the Bible and thus are false prophets.

God Will Not Contradict Himself

Another way to know that other religious writings are not from God has to do with contradictions. They contradict God's already stated Word, the Bible.

In the Bible we read that God cannot lie (Titus 1:2; Hebrews 6:18). This is significant because it means that God's Word will never contradict itself. Though skeptics have alleged that there are contradictions in the Bible, every such claim has been refuted.[7] This is what we would expect if God's Word were perfect.[8]

Yet the world is filled with other "religious writings" that claim divine origin or that have been treated as equal to or higher than the Bible on matters of truth or guidelines for living. In other words, these writings are treated as a final authority over the Bible.

Any religious writing that claims divine inspiration or authority equal to the Bible can't be from God if it has any contradictions: contradictions with the Bible, contradictions within itself, or contradictions with reality.

Examples of Contradictions in Religious Writings

A religious writing can be tested by comparing what it says to the Bible (1 Thessalonians 5:21). God will never disagree with Himself because God cannot lie (Hebrews 6:18). When the Bible was being written and Paul was preaching to the Bereans (Acts 17:11), he commended them for checking his words against the Scriptures that were already written. If someone claims that a book is of divine origin, then we need to be like the Bereans and test it to confirm whether it agrees with the 66 books of the Bible. Paul's writings, of course, were Scripture (2 Peter 3:16).

Religious books, such as Islam's Koran (Qur'an), Mormonism's Book of Mormon, and Hinduism's Vedas, contradict the Bible, so they cannot be Scripture. For example, the Koran in two chapters (Surah 4:171 and 23:91) says God had no son, but the Bible is clear that Jesus is the only begotten Son of God (Matthew 26:63–64).

The Book of Mormon says in Moroni 8:8 that children are not sinners, but the Bible teaches that children are sinful, even from birth (Psalm 51:5). The Book of Mormon, prior to the 1981 change, says that Native Americans will turn white when they convert to Mormonism (2 Nephi 30:6).

---

7. There are websites and books dedicated to this subject. To get started, I suggest *Demolishing Supposed Bible Contradictions*, Volume 1 and 2, (Green Forest, AR: Master Books, 2010 and 2012).

8. Keep in mind a crucial point here. *If* the Bible were not true and not from God, then contradictions are acceptable! It is from a biblical perspective that contradictions are a bad thing. If a secular worldview were correct (no God and no Word of God), why not contradict yourself?

Few would dispute that the Vedas and other writings in Hinduism are starkly different (thus contradictory) from the Bible as previously discussed.

Also, such religious writings contain contradictions within themselves that are unanswerable without gymnastics of logic. In the Koran, one passage says Jesus will be with God in paradise (Surah 3:45) and another states that He will be in hell for being worshiped by Christians (Surah 21:98).

None of the apocryphal books of Romanism or Orthodoxy claim inspiration from God. One apocryphal book, Maccabees (1 Maccabees 9:27, 4:46, and 14:41) points out that no prophets were in the land and hadn't been for some time. Since prophets were the mouthpieces of God, how can these books, written during this time that prophets weren't present in Israel, be the Word of God?

The Talmud, which is "the traditions of the elders, tradition of the fathers," "law of the fathers," or "tradition of men," was strictly opposed by Jesus and the New Testament (e.g. Matthew 15:2–6; Mark 7:3–13; Acts 22:3; Galatians 1:13–14; 1 Peter 1:17–19). They are obviously incompatible with the Bible.

If these writings were truly from God, such discrepancies couldn't exist.

False Prophecy

False prophecy is an obvious hallmark of false prophets. A prophet is one who claims to speak for God, often foretelling events. The Holy Spirit, speaking through Moses, writes,

> But the prophet who presumes to speak a word in My name, which I have not commanded him to speak, or who speaks in the name of other gods, that prophet shall die. And if you say in your heart, "How shall we know the word which the LORD has not spoken?" — when a prophet speaks in the name of the LORD, if the thing does not happen or come to pass, that is the thing which the LORD has not spoken; the prophet has spoken it presumptuously; you shall not be afraid of him (Deuteronomy 18:20–22).

Matthew 7:15–20 reiterates a warning against false prophets. How have the alleged prophets since the Bible fared?

Islam

In the Hadith tradition of Sunan Abu Dawud, Book 37 Number 4281–4283, Muhammad claimed that the Antichrist (*Dajjal*) was supposed to

Contradictions with Some Popular Alleged New Scriptures and the Bible

	Bible	New Scripture Claims
Koran (Qur'an)	Jesus is God who became a man as well (Colossians 2:9)	Jesus is not God (Surah 5:17, 5:75)
Koran (Qur'an)	Jesus was crucified (1 Peter 2:24)	Jesus was not crucified (Surah 4:157)
Koran Qur'an)	The Holy Spirit is God (Acts 5:3-4; 2 Corinthians 3:15-17)	The Holy Spirit is the created angel Gabriel (Surah 2:97, 16:102)
Book of Mormon	Salvation is by faith through grace apart from works (Ephesians 2:8–9)	Salvation is by grace and works (2 Nephi 25:23)
Book of Mormon	One God exists (Deuteronomy 6:4; 1 Chronicles 17:20; 1 Timothy 2:5)	Multiple gods exist (Doctrine and Covenants, Section 121:32, 132:18–20)
Jehovah's Witnesses	Jesus is the Creator God (John 1:1–3; Hebrews 1:1–9; Colossians 1:15–19, and distinguished from angels (Hebrews 1:4–8)	Jesus is the created angel, Michael*
Jehovah's Witnesses	Hell is a place of eternal torment for those who do not receive Christ (e.g., Daniel 12:2; John 5:28–29; Matthew 25:41–46; Mark 9:43–48; John 3:36; 2 Thessalonians 1:9; Revelation 14:9–11)	Hell is not a place of eternal torment**
Jehovah's Witnesses	God created in 6, 24-hour days as defined by an evening and a morning in Genesis 1 and rested on the seventh day (Genesis 1:1–2:3; Exodus 20:11; Exodus 31:15–17)	God created in 49,000 years with each day being 7,000 years in duration (Charles Russell, *Studies in the Scripture*, Volume 6, p. 19)

* "Who Is Michael the Archangel," JW.org, accessed August 30, 2016, https://www.jw.org/en/publications/books/bible-teach/who-is-michael-the-archangel-jesus/.

** "What Is Hell? Is It a Place of Eternal Torment?" JW.org, accessed August 30, 2016, https://www.jw.org/en/bible-teachings/questions/what-is-hell/.

come forth six months after the conquest of Constantinople by the Muslims. At the same time, Medina (Yathrib) would be left in ruins.

The Muslim conquest was much later than Muhammad's day, finally occurring in May of A.D. 1453. But no Antichrist ascended in November of 1453 and Medina was not left in ruins.

Mormons (Church of Jesus Christ of Latter-day Saints)

The Mormons have not fared any better.

> Yea, the word of the Lord concerning his church, established in the last days for the restoration of his people, as he has spoken by the mouth of his prophets, and for the gathering of his saints to stand upon Mount Zion, in which shall be the city of New Jerusalem. Which city shall be built, beginning at the temple lot, which is appointed by the finger of the Lord, in the western boundaries of the State of Missouri, and dedicated by the hand of Joseph Smith, Jun., and others with whom the Lord was well pleased. Verily this is the word of the Lord, that the city New Jerusalem shall be built by the gathering of the saints, beginning at this place, even the place of the temple, which temple shall be reared in this generation. For verily this generation shall not all pass away until an house shall be built unto the Lord, and a cloud shall rest upon it, which cloud shall be even the glory of the Lord, which shall fill the house. (Doctrine and Covenants 84:2–5)

> Therefore, as I said concerning the sons of Moses for the sons of Moses and also the sons of Aaron shall offer an acceptable offering and sacrifice in the house of the Lord, which house shall be built unto the Lord in this generation, upon the consecrated spot as I have appointed. (Doctrine and Covenants 84:31)

The Mormon's New Jerusalem and temple was not built in Missouri and definitely not in that generation, which came and went many years ago.

The Mormons have an extensive seven-volume set of the *History of the Church* which was originally *History of Joseph Smith*. It includes Smith's writings and subsequent comments by Smith's secretaries and scribes (those close to him). Then it picks up with Mormon historians once Joseph Smith died. In volume 2, we read:

President Smith then stated that the meeting had been called, because God had commanded it; and it was made known to him by vision and by the Holy Spirit. He then gave a relation of some of the circumstances attending us while journeying to Zion — our trials, sufferings; and said God had not designed all this for nothing, but He had it in remembrance yet; and it was the will of God that those who went to Zion, with a determination to lay down their lives, if necessary, should be ordained to the ministry, and go forth to prune the vineyard for the last time, for the coming of the Lord, which was nigh — even fifty-six years should wind up the scene.[9]

So Smith marked the date of being no later than 56 years for the Second Coming of Christ Jesus. By the context it should be over well before that. This was stated in 1835, before his death in 1844, but 1891, 56 years later, came and went.

Jehovah's Witnesses

The Watchtower Society or Jehovah's Witnesses, who have claimed Charles Taze Russell as the continuous prophet, have had the most failed prophecies in modern times.

1889 True, it is expecting great things to claim, as we do, that within the coming twenty-six years, all present governments will be overthrown and dissolved.[10]

1889 Remember that the *forty years'* Jewish Harvest ended October, A.D. 69, and was followed by the complete overthrow of that nation; and that likewise the forty years of the Gospel age harvest will end October, 1914, and that likewise the overthrow of "Christendom," so-called, must be expected to immediately follow.[11]

For just one sample of the Watchtower Society's failed prophecies surrounding the year 1925, consider:

---

9. Joseph Smith, *History of the Church*, Vol. 2 (Salt Lake City, UT: Deseret News, 1902), p. 182.
10. Charles Russell, *Studies in the Scriptures*, Vol. 2 (Pittsburgh, PA: Watchtower Bible and Tract Society,1889), p. 98–99.
11. Ibid., p. 245.

- In 1918, they wrote, ". . . and since other Scriptures definitely fix the fact that there will be a resurrection of Abraham, Isaac, Jacob and other faithful ones of old, and that these will have the first favor, we may expect 1925 to witness the return of these faithful men of Israel from the condition of death, being resurrected and fully restored to perfect humanity and made the visible, legal representatives of the new order of things on earth. . . . Therefore we may confidently expect that 1925 will mark the return of Abraham, Isaac, Jacob and the faithful prophets of old, particularly those named by the Apostle in Hebrews chapter 11, to the condition of human perfection."[12]

- In 1923 they wrote, "Our thought is, that 1925 is definitely settled by the Scriptures."[13]

Jehovah's Witnesses have failed to predict the end of the world on many occasions including 1908, 1914, 1918, 1925, 1941, and 1975. Their prophecies continue to fail.

Other False Prophets

In the previous section we have focused on three major groups in our culture, but there are plenty of other false prophets. Some are specific and wrong.[14] Others, like Nostradamus, are so vague that they become meaningless. Here are just a few in our modern times (including some secular predictions):

- Harold Camping falsely prophesied that the end of the age would be in 1994 in his book *1994?* That didn't happen. Then Camping revised his date and said it would occur on May 21, 2011. The date came and went. He changed it to October of the same year. That came and went.

- Charles Darwin predicted the Caucasians would exterminate all other races within the not very distant future (measured by

---

12. J.F. Rutherford, *Millions Now Living Will Never Die* (Brooklyn, NY: International Bible Students Association, 1920), p. 88.
13. *Watchtower*, April 1, 1923, p. 106.
14. E.g., (1) Herbert Armstrong (too many to list), (2) Ellen White (claimed to have a vision of heaven in *Early Writings of Ellen G. White,* 1882 (Washington, DC: Review and Herald Publishing Association, 1945), p. 32, http://www.gilead.net/egw/books2/earlywritings/ewindex.html, where she saw the Temple in the Holy City, but the Bible says there is no Temple in heaven in Revelation 21:22), and (3) Jim Jones (who murdered his flock).

centuries at the most).[15] Now we know there is only one race — the human race. This is known from the Bible all along and now confirmed by DNA. This prediction by Darwin never happened and, based on his warped understanding of the human family, never will.

- Clarence Larkin believed the Second Coming would commence no later than A.D. 2000 with a rapture occurring (7 years before).[16]

- Edgar Whisenant's book *88 Reasons Why the Rapture Will Be in 1988* also failed.

- Pat Robertson falsely predicted that Mitt Romney would be elected the president of the United States in 2012, have two terms, and the economy would turn around under his presidency. He attributed this directly to the Lord. Instead, Romney, a Mormon, lost the election.

- William Miller (father of Millerites and Adventism), predicted that Christ would return on March 21, 1844, and then later said October 22, 1844. Clearly, this didn't transpire.

- Al Gore (evolutionist) predicted in January of 2006 that the global warming point of no return for a true planetary emergency would occur in just 10 years. It came and went.[17] This is a failed prophecy.

- Stephen Hawking, Richard Dawkins, Neil deGrasse Tyson, and others have predicted we will find aliens. I'll let you ponder these prophecies!

- Nigel Barber claimed the world would be won as atheism is predicted to defeat religion by the year 2038.[18] Of course,

15. Charles Darwin, *The Descent of Man* (New York: A.L. Burt, 1874, 2nd ed.), p. 178.
16. Clarence Larkin, *Dispensational Truth* (Philadelphia, PA: Rev. Clarence Larkin Est. Publisher, 1918), p. 16.
17. For more false prophecies regarding Al Gore see Larry Tomczak, "10 Ways Al Gore Was Wrong About Global Warming," *Charisma News*, February 16, 2016, http://www.charisman-ews.com/opinion/heres-the-deal/55185-10-ways-al-gore-was-wrong-about-global-warming.
18. Nigel Barber, "Atheism to Defeat Religion by 2038," *Huffington Post Science*, June 5, 2012, http://www.huffingtonpost.com/nigel-barber/atheism-to-defeat-religion-by-2038_b_1565108.html.

atheism *is* a religion so that would be impossible. But I hope readers will take note of this and test it when the time comes.

This is but a taste of the false prophets who have been. Even in the New Testament they dealt with false prophets (e.g., Bar-Jesus in Acts 13:6). We've seen false prophets; the early church had to deal with false prophets (e.g., Marcionism),[19] and it has continued right up to the current times.

The point of this exercise is that if you can't trust alleged prophet or prophecies from someone when they speak, why trust their other proclamations? Jesus wisely said to Nicodemus:

> If I have told you earthly things and you do not believe, how will you believe if I tell you heavenly things? (John 3:12).

Conclusion

Since such alleged holy books and prophets are not from the perfect God, who are they from? They are from deceived, imperfect mankind. They may also be based on deceiving spirits and demons as the Bible reveals:

> Now the Spirit expressly says that in latter times some will depart from the faith, giving heed to deceiving spirits and doctrines of demons, speaking lies in hypocrisy, having their own conscience seared with a hot iron, forbidding to marry,[20] and commanding to abstain from foods[21] which God created to be received with thanksgiving by those who believe and know the truth (1 Timothy 4:1–3).

Even the doctrines of demons come through the mind of man in their manifestations. Mankind's fallible reason is not the absolute authority. God and

---

19. A cult in the second century that taught the heretic Marcion of Sinope should be trusted. Essentially, Marcion wanted the Old Testament to be thrown out as Scripture. He also threw out most of the New Testament with the exception of ten of Paul's letters.

20. Many secularists today forbid and oppose marriage and attack this doctrine. We see these various forms as *perversional* or *adulterous humanism* pervades this culture since the "sexual revolution" that began blooming in the 1960s and is now in full flower.

21. This is the case with alleged prophetess Ellen White. We see this with others too (e.g., Messianic Judaism) which is Peterism. B. Hodge, "Peterism — a False Doctrine that Still Tries to Invade the Church," Biblical Authority Ministries, February 11, 2016, https://biblicalauthorityministries.wordpress.com/2016/02/11/peterism-a-false-doctrine-that-still-tries-to-invade-the-church.

His Word are. Other books may have value, such as historical insight; but they are not the infallible Word of God.

The Bible warns that false philosophies will be used to turn people from the Bible (Colossians 2:8). So people need to stand firm on the Bible and not be swayed (1 Corinthians 15:58; 2 Thessalonians 2:15).

There are two options: place our faith in the perfect, all-knowing God who has always been there, or trust in imperfect, fallible mankind and his philosophies. The Bible, God's Holy Word, is superior to all other alleged holy books. God will never be wrong or contradict Himself. So start with the Bible and build your faith on its teachings so that you please Him.

Is there a need for new revelation after the Bible? Consider the biblical Book of Jude which says:

> Beloved, while I was very diligent to write to you concerning our common salvation, I found it necessary to write to you exhorting you to contend earnestly for the faith *which was once for all delivered to the saints* (Jude 1:3, emphasis added).

Appendix B

What Makes a Christian Martyr Differ from Other Faiths' "Martyrs"?

Troy Lacey

H e was a martyr for a good cause." A person is put to death (often quite brutally) because he refuses to recant his beliefs and teachings when he is demanded to do so by angry opponents. So we have Muslim martyrs, Jewish martyrs, communist martyrs, Christian martyrs, Buddhist martyrs, Hindu martyrs, etc. They are all the same, right? Not really.

What Is a Martyr?

The English word "martyr" is an almost direct transliteration from the New Testament Greek word *martus*, which originally meant a "witness." It was especially used in the early church to signify those who were witnesses of Jesus Christ's death, burial, and Resurrection (e.g., Acts 1:22). Consequently, many of those Apostles died giving testimony of their Lord. In current usage it usually means one who is killed for refusing to renounce their religious faith, practices, and beliefs.[1]

The unspoken assumption is that if the person would renounce his beliefs then he would not be put to death, avoiding martyrdom. History is replete with tales of martyrs, from Old Testament believers, to the Apostles, to the

---

11. *American Heritage Dictionary of the English Language*, s.v. "martyr" (Boston, MA: Houghton Mifflin Company, 1980).

early Church Fathers, and down to our time, especially in areas like Sudan, the Middle East, the Philippines, Indonesia, and parts of South America. For the most part, these have been either Jewish or Christian martyrs, and the logical question to ask would be "Why?" Why not Buddhists or Taoists or Hindu martyrs to the same extent? We will consider that question in due course.

A martyr is someone who believes so strongly in his religion that he is unwilling to compromise when faced with external pressures to convert to another religion. He would rather face death than dishonor himself and his god (either a false god or the true and Living God of the Bible). He does not deem it right (even in those situations where the threat of death is imminent) to even outwardly conform to a "religious conversion," even if he knows he would internally keep his original belief system. This would be construed as failing his god, lying to himself, and giving a poor testimony to the world about his god and religion. Shadrach, Meshach, and Abednego are perfect examples of this type of mindset, although they were divinely spared from becoming martyrs (Daniel 3).

Radical Muslims who blow themselves up in a suicide bombing to kill others are occasionally called martyrs by some, but this is a misnomer. The suicide bomber is not a martyr, but one who has chosen his (or her) own death and is actively pursuing it. He is not dying because he refuses to convert to Christianity (or Buddhism or Hinduism), but rather because of a choice to be an offensive weapon of terror.

For most polytheistic religions, martyrdom is usually not much of a concern, since another belief system can be incorporated into the pantheon of deities and beliefs already present. For example, this is why in India today we can see Jesus Christ being added by Hindu worshipers to the religious festivals and even the pantheon of deities. They will even venerate Jesus as a god without recognizing that He is actually *the Creator God* (John 1; Hebrews 1; Colossians 1).

This is not to say that Buddhist or Hindu adherents never become martyrs. The Tibetan Buddhists have, for many years, been persecuted and martyred by the Chinese government for their refusal to convert to atheistic communism. And Muslims have killed Hindus for their refusal to convert to their version of monotheism as well.

As in all cases of conflict, however, one must remember that religion may not be the only factor in persecution. In the case of the Hindu/Muslim conflict, much of the conflict lies in nationalistic animosity between Pakistanis and Indians. In the case of the Tibetan Buddhists vs. Communist Chinese government, it is as much a conflict about self-government and independence versus centralized government as it is about religion. Therefore, deaths on either side may be the result of skirmishing as opposed to actual cases of direct religious persecution leading to martyrdom.

Why Christian Martyrs Are Often Different

Nevertheless, we do know that such persecution and martyrdom does take place. So what makes the Buddhist or Hindu martyr different from the Christian martyr? How does a Christian missionary to Indonesia who is martyred differ from the Tibetan monk who is martyred?

It basically boils down to two things. First, what was the person who was martyred engaged in doing? What was his lifestyle and business that caused him to be a target? Second, what was the martyr killed for? In the above-mentioned cases of Hindu and Buddhist martyrs, some are engaged in violent or revolutionary activities against another government and so are not true martyrs because they are killed as "enemy combatants."

But many people in this situation are innocent bystanders living in areas viewed as hostile to the government in question. They may be killed inadvertently (or deliberately) because of nationalistic reasons. These deaths would actually be war casualties or genocide, not martyrdom in the religious sense. Others are killed mainly for religious reasons, but without a direct threat to convert or die. These killings are still mostly nationalistic in intent, not true martyrdom. The killing of non-Christians simply because of their religious beliefs and their subsequent refusal to convert to another religion is rare (although not unheard of).

The killing of Christians simply because of their belief and their refusal to deny Christ and convert to a different religion has been recorded countless times since the martyrdom of Stephen in Acts 7 (ca. A.D. 32–35) up to the present time. In fact, it has been said that more Christians are suffering martyrdom today than ever before — up to 100 thousand per year.[2]

There is often additional persecution to Christian populations that causes loss of property, forced displacement from their homeland, or even

---

2. Todd Johnson, "The Case for Higher Numbers of Christian Martyrs," Gordon-Conwell Theological Seminary, accessed January 15, 2016, http://www.gordonconwell.edu/ockenga/research/documents/csgc_Christian_martyrs.pdf.

ends in forced labor camps.[3] According to David Barrett, the "persecution of Christians is more common in our generation than ever in history. The oft-quoted statistic is that more people died for their Christian faith in the last century than in all the other centuries of recorded history combined."[4]

The Christian organization, *Voice of the Martyrs,* lists 52 countries that are currently persecuting Christians.[5] This persecution includes verbal assault, property confiscation, physical assault, unlawful imprisonment, threatenings, torture, psychological intimidation, kidnappings, and murder. In Sudan alone it is estimated that hundreds of thousands of Christians have been martyred and up to 2 million forced to flee their homes, simply for refusing to renounce their Christian faith.[6]

The Romans, Huns, Goths, Vikings, Muslims, Hindus, and other religious groups (including atheism and humanism) have perpetrated martyrdom of Christians since the time of the Apostles, mainly because of their Christian faith. The vast majority of these Christian martyrs were not revolutionaries or dissidents, but ordinary citizens trying to live peaceably among their neighbors. According to principles laid down in Scripture, they paid their taxes, honored the king and governors, loved their neighbors, and gave no cause for offense (Romans 13:1–8; 1 Peter 2:13–17).

Why Christians Are Targets

How then can we account for this vitriol directed at Christianity in excess of other inter-faith conflicts? The answer lies in the exclusivity of the Christian faith and the means of salvation. True Christianity does not teach a multiplicity of ways to "come to God." It does not teach that humans are basically good (Genesis 8:21; Jeremiah 17:9) and just need a divine nudge to get on the right track. It does not teach that man can earn merit with God (e.g., Galatians 2:16). True Christianity teaches what Jesus Christ taught, that He alone is "the Way, the Truth and the Life: no man comes to the Father except through Me" (John 14:6).

Christianity is intricately tied to the authority of the Bible, which details mankind's separation from God due to sin, the remedy that God provided

---

3. "Worldwide Persecution of Christians," Seeking Truth, accessed January 15, 2016, http://www.seekingtruth.co.uk/persecution.htm.
4. David Barrett, *International Bulletin of Missionary Research*, January 2007.
5. Voice of the Martyrs. *Foxe 33 A.D. to Today*, (China: Codra Enterprises, 2007), p. 341–473.
6. Ibid., p. 459–462.

through the death and Resurrection of Christ, how God wants to be worshiped, and how we are to conduct ourselves as ambassadors for Christ. Ephesians 2:1 says that we are all dead in sins until Christ makes us alive; and in verses 8–9 Paul tells us that we are saved (from God's judgment) by the grace of God through faith in Jesus Christ, not by our own good works or merit.

Romans 3:10–18 teaches that we are not righteous in our natural state and that we do not seek after God. Then we read in 1 John 4:10 that God demonstrated His love for us by sending His Son to be the propitiation (substitutionary sacrifice) for our sins. Just as by one man (Adam) judgment came upon all men to condemnation, so by the righteousness of one man (Jesus Christ), the free gift of salvation comes (Romans 5:15–18) through faith if they believe (Romans 3:22).

Therefore, Christians preach a gospel that teaches that all men are sinners, that we all need a Savior, and that Jesus Christ took our sins upon Himself on the Cross to pay for our transgressions. We are told to repent of our sins, believe on the Lord Jesus Christ, and make confession with our mouth (Acts 17:30–31; Romans 10:9–19). Christians understand that God has given us the insight to comprehend His Word. In our natural state we are at war with God and could never understand or please God (Romans 8:7–8). Consequently, we recognize that salvation is of the Lord (Psalm 3:8).

It is this teaching, that we cannot in and of ourselves please or earn merit with God, nor can we work toward our own salvation, that makes Christianity different from all other religions. It is not by works of righteousness, which *we* have done, but according to His mercy that He saves us (Titus 3:5). People do not like to hear that they are sinners, and that they can never please God by their own works or righteousness (Galatians 2:16). Nor do sinners like to hear that God will one day judge every man according to his works (Revelation 20:11–15) and that those works will be deemed at best "filthy rags" in the sight of God (Isaiah. 64:6).

It is for this gospel that Christians are persecuted, some to the point of martyrdom, even today. Jesus Himself told us to expect persecution because they persecuted Him. Therefore, others would persecute His followers (John 15:20). The Apostle Peter wrote that we are not to think it strange that we Christians should suffer persecution (1 Peter 4:12–13). And Paul told Timothy that "all who desire to live godly in Christ Jesus will suffer persecution" (2 Timothy 3:12). It is for this reason that the world hates us. As Jesus said in John 15:18–19, "If the world hates you, you know that it hated Me before it hated you. If you were of the world, the world would love its own. Yet because you are not of the world, but I chose you out of the world, therefore the world hates you."

The Apostle James wrote much about persecution, suffering, and endurance. He wrote that we are "to count it all joy when [we] fall into various trials, knowing that the testing of [our] faith produces patience. But let patience have its perfect work, that [we] may be perfect and complete, lacking nothing" (James 1:2–4). James understood that Christians would suffer persecution, but urged them to continue to spread the gospel, using the example of the Old Testament prophets' proclamation of the Word of the Lord even in times when that message was reviled.

> Therefore, be patient, brethren, until the coming of the Lord. See how the farmer waits for the precious fruit of the earth, waiting patiently for it until it receives the early and latter rain. You also be patient. Establish your hearts, for the coming of the Lord is at hand. Do not grumble against one another, brethren, lest you be condemned. Behold, the Judge is standing at the door! My brethren, take the prophets, who spoke in the name of the Lord, as an example of suffering and patience. Indeed we count them blessed who endure. You have heard of the perseverance of Job and seen the end intended by the Lord — that the Lord is very compassionate and merciful (James 5:7–11).

Christians in America and other Western nations have been blessed to live in lands that legislated religious freedom (a biblical principle, by the way, e.g., Joshua 24:15). Sadly, America is one of just a handful of countries that has such liberty. Most of our Christian brothers and sisters around the world suffer for their faith in one form or another — either at the hands of their government or at the hands of angry mobs bent on silencing their witness for Christ. We are enjoined by our Lord to "weep with those who weep" (Romans 12:15), for we know that we are all of one body in Christ (Romans 12:5). Therefore, we should pray for our brothers and sisters in Christ and also help provide for their needs (Romans 12:13).

Thankfully, we serve a God who providentially works all things in our lives for our good. Nothing ever catches Him by surprise. He will then use even the most trying circumstances to make us more like His Son, Jesus Christ.

> And we know that all things work together for good to those who love God, to those who are the called according to His purpose. For whom He foreknew, He also predestined to be conformed to the image of His Son, that He might be the firstborn among many brethren (Romans 8:28–29).

Some Martyrs and Concluding Remarks

Lastly, let's look at the reaction of some Christian martyrs as they faced their own death. First, we should remember the words of our Lord as He hung on the cross, "Father, forgive them, for they know not what they do" (Luke 23:34).

Next we have recorded in Scripture, the words of Stephen as he was being stoned to death, "Lord, do not charge them with this sin" (Acts 7:60). We read of eyewitness testimony of Polycarp, a disciple of John.

> While being burned to death on a pyre he remarked "I bless You that You have considered me worthy of this day and hour, to receive a part in the number of the martyrs in the cup of Your Christ."[7]

In each of these cases, and many more examples (e.g., *Foxe's Book of Martyrs*), the Christian martyr did not rail against his persecutors, nor curse them. Rather, either they prayed for their persecutors, or they thanked God for allowing the Christian to be a witness unto death for Him.

Many modern-day examples are happening right before our eyes, with Christians (as well as Muslims) being martyred by Boko Haram in Nigeria, Chad, Cameroon, and Niger,[8] and by ISIS/ISIL in Syria, Afghanistan, Iraq, Ethiopia, and other parts of the Middle East.[9] While some of these attacks

7. Ibid., p. 52.
8. "Nigeria: Abducted Women and Girls Forced to Join Boko Haram Attacks," Amnesty International, accessed August 23, 2016, https://www.amnesty.org/en/latest/news/2015/04/nigeria-abducted-women-and-girls-forced-to-join-boko-haram-attacks.
9. Greg Bothelo, "Faith Turns Christians into Terrorist Targets," CNN, accessed August 23, 2016, http://www.cnn.com/2015/04/24/world/terrorists-attacks-on-christianity.

are indiscriminate terrorist attacks that simply target areas with large concentrations of civilians, many are directly aimed at Christians, with the aim to make converts to Islam or kill those who will not convert.

As we look to God's revealed Word as our absolute authority and live lives that reflect its truths, we as Christians should be both salt and light. That light will stand out in a dark world (Matthew 5:14–16) exposing the darkness of sin (Ephesians 5:11). It will also mark Christians as different from the rest of the world and again make them targets for hatred, just as Christ was hated (John 15:18).

As Christians striving to live godly lives, we are to expect persecution (2 Timothy 3:12; Hebrews 12:1–4), whether it be in the form of mockery, being called foolish and scientifically illiterate, having our rights impinged on or denied, or, as we see in many countries around the world, physical persecution and even martyrdom. But we can be exhorted with the words of Christ on this matter: "And you will be hated by all for My name's sake. But he who endures to the end shall be saved" (Mark 13:13) and the promise that Jesus will never leave us nor forsake us (Hebrews 13:5).

Appendix C

Do Secularists Have a Foundation for Morality?

Ken Ham and Avery Foley

Secularists and atheists frequently accuse Christians of behaving "immorally" and religion of being "evil." But such objections to religion bring up an interesting question: how does the secular humanist or atheist define evil and morality and by what authority do they make such statements?

Nothing but Subjective Opinion

For the atheist or secular humanist, there is no foundation for morality besides his or her own subjective opinion.[1] These individuals often throw around words such as *evil, immoral, moral,* or *ethical,* often in the context of Christian religion or Christian individuals. They will say things such as "religion is evil"[2] or that teaching creation to children is "child abuse," but what do they mean by these phrases?

In their worldview, what makes anything immoral or wrong? Really it boils down to nothing more than their opinion.[3] They *believe* that something is wrong and therefore it *must* be. But who is to say that their opinion

---

1. Opinions are arbitrary, and thus fallacious.
2. Clearly, they mean Christianity. They do not argue that their religion of atheism or humanism is evil.
3. Opinions are pointless, as they are not a measure of truth in the least. Consider if someone was of the opinion that 2+2=-9. Such an opinion is worthless.

is the right one? After all, there are many different opinions on what is right and wrong. Who decides which one is right and which one is wrong?

The argument that atheism and secular humanism cannot provide a foundation for morality is a strong argument. Here are a few responses that you may hear if you bring up this objection.

Society Decides Morality

Some atheists will argue that morality is simply decided by the society. For example, here in America our society has decided that murdering an innocent human being is wrong, and therefore that action is morally wrong. But this kind of thinking simply does not hold up to scrutiny.

Society often changes its opinion. One clear example of this is in regard to gay "marriage." What was considered morally wrong by most of society is now legal, applauded, and celebrated by some groups. In this view, homosexual behavior went from being morally wrong to being morally acceptable. What if our society decides that murder is acceptable, as it did in the case of *Roe v. Wade* when America legalized the killing of unborn children? Does murder suddenly become morally acceptable too? What about adultery, stealing, lying, or any other manner of morally reprehensible actions? Would the atheist or humanist accept a society that decides that that society can kill all atheists and humanists? If society is the moral compass, then the compass never points north but rather jumps all over the place and changes with every generation.

Also, if society determines morality, how can one society tell another society what is right or wrong? Most people would agree that the abhorrent actions of the Nazi death camps were morally wrong. But why? Nazi Germany decided as a society that these actions were morally acceptable. What right does our society have to judge their society if morality is simply a societal preference?

Or what about certain Muslim groups? Few would agree that blowing up innocent civilians, slaughtering hundreds of people from other religious groups, kidnapping and enslaving young women, or using children as suicide bombers is morally acceptable. Yet if morality is simply a societal preference, what right does our society have to tell their society that their actions are wrong and must be stopped?

The consistent atheist or humanist can say nothing if that is the ethic a society has decided is right. In this view, the atheist, based on his arbitrary opinion, might not agree with their ethic, but they have no rationale to say anything or try to put a stop to it. If morality is simply decided by societal preference, it fails to make any sense and becomes arbitrary, subject to change by time and culture.

Human Reason

The problem only gets worse when you break it down to a personal level. Some secularists will argue that morality is an individual decision and no one has the right to tell another person what to do (this is called "autonomous human reason"). Of course, the irony of such a statement should be evident. By saying that no one should tell someone else what to do, they have just told someone else what to do!

If the secularists really believed this, then they couldn't say, "religion is evil" in the first place, since it is not their place to say.

If this view of morality is true, then our justice system cannot exist. After all, why should one judge, legislative assembly, or government body impose their view of morality on another individual? If stealing, killing, raping, or abusing is right for one individual, what gives another individual the right to say that view of morality is wrong?

Now this personal morality or human reasoning view stems from the idea that people are basically good and that, left on our own, humans tend to do right and not wrong (again, who defines right and wrong?). But humans aren't basically good! Human experience shows that throughout history humans have committed atrocities, even in our supposedly enlightened Western world. The Bible describes the fallen human heart this way:

> The heart is deceitful above all things, and desperately wicked; who can know it? (Jeremiah 17:9).

> And the LORD smelled a soothing aroma. Then the LORD said in His heart, "I will never again curse the ground for man's sake, although the imagination of man's heart is evil from his youth; nor will I again destroy every living thing as I have done" (Genesis 8:21).

> To the pure all things are pure, but to those who are defiled and unbelieving nothing is pure; but even their mind and conscience are defiled (Titus 1:15).

Autonomous human reason simply does not provide a sufficient foundation for morality.

Did Morality Evolve?

From human experience, we seem to naturally and intuitively know that actions such as murder, stealing, and child abandonment are wrong for all people everywhere. But where does this intuitive sense come from?

Evolutionists, by necessity, believe that morality (along with everything else) is simply the result of evolution. Somehow, after billions of years of death, struggle, atrocities, disease, and suffering, man realized that we should strive to do the opposite! Man should oppose survival of the fittest and try to be moral. In their worldview, we are nothing more than highly evolved animals, and our brains are nothing more than chemical reactions.[4] We are simply the product of our DNA.

This view raises the question of how the strictly naturalistic process of evolution leads to the development of an immaterial, absolute moral conscience that somehow applies to all people everywhere? And what happens if this conscience evolves? Does morality change again?

Furthermore, if we are simply animals, why are we held morally accountable? After all, we certainly don't hold animals accountable for their actions. No lion court exists to punish lions that maul gazelles to death and then eat them. No one jails a female cuckoo for abandoning her babies or forces male rabbits to pay child support. These are simply the things animals in this cursed world do, and no one faults them for doing it. If we are just animals, what makes humans so different?

The problem gets even worse if you argue that our brains are nothing more than random chemical reactions and that we are at the mercy of our DNA. If we are just programmed DNA, then how can we be held accountable for any of our decisions? There is no free will in a view such as this; therefore, there is no accountability for decisions or actions.

Morality simply cannot be the result of naturalistic processes over millions of years. This view does not hold up to close examination, and really is the opposite of what we know to be true from human experience and the Bible's teachings.

---

4. Recall that in the atheistic or humanistic worldview, all things are *natural* and *material*. Nothing immaterial really exists. So the mind cannot exist. But neither can logic, truth, knowledge, *morality*, and so on.

Moral Atheists?

When faced with their worldview's inability to provide a foundation for morality, many atheists respond by claiming that you don't have to be religious to be moral. It's true that plenty of atheists are moral citizens. But those who argue this way have missed the point.

Atheists certainly can be moral. Actually, starting with a biblical worldview, this is to be expected. God has put His law in all our hearts (Romans 2:15) so even atheists, who claim that they don't believe in the Creator God, can adhere to this law and be moral. But the point is that they have no foundation for this morality in their own worldview. They have no basis for saying something is right or wrong, moral or immoral.

The Bible Provides a Foundation for Morality

Secular humanism and atheism cannot account for the existence of morality in their worldview. But what about the biblical view?

According to God's Word, humans were specially created in the image of God (Genesis 1:27). We are not animals nor are our brains simply chemical reactions. As He has from the very beginning, our Creator holds us accountable for our actions (Genesis 2:17) and expects us to be able to choose and distinguish between right and wrong.

As Creator, only God has the authority to tell us what is right and what is wrong. And this standard is not arbitrary. It is based on the unchanging character of the righteous, holy, and perfect Judge of the universe. For example, all murder is wrong because God has created us in His own image and forbids the taking of a human life (e.g., Genesis 9:6; Exodus 20:13; Romans 13:9).

God, the Creator, has given us the Bible — His revealed Word,[5] which clearly lays out what is morally acceptable and what is not. It provides a firm foundation from the very Creator on which we can base our morality.

What is more, God has placed His law in all of our hearts (Romans 2:15). We know right from wrong because of the conscience that God has given all of humanity, and we are held accountable to Him for our actions and decisions (Romans 2:1–16) based on this knowledge of Him that we have.

It should be obvious to anyone who has lived in this world that no one fully obeys God's law. We all fall short of God's perfect standard, as Scripture

---

5. His Word is absolute and not arbitrary, like the opinions of man.

makes abundantly clear (Romans 3:23). We even fall far short of imperfect human standards! Why is this? Genesis gives us the answer.

The first two people, Adam and Eve, were created morally perfect, but they chose to rebel against their Creator (Genesis 3). No longer were they morally perfect; now they had a sin nature, which they passed on to each of their children (Romans 5:12–21). All of their descendants — every person on earth — is now a slave to sin (John 8:34) and in rebellion against God.

The Bible provides a firm foundation for morality and provides the answer for why all people have a moral conscience and why we cannot live up to this knowledge of morality. But there's more.

The Answer Is the Gospel

Not only does the Bible explain why there is a universal moral code, why everyone knows it, and why no one can consistently live up to it, but the Bible also provides the solution to our shortcoming. When Adam and Eve sinned, they received the penalty that their rebellion deserved — death (Genesis 2:17). We all sinned and continue to sin in Adam, so we all deserve the penalty of death (Romans 5:12). No matter how hard we try, we can never live up to God's perfect moral standard (Romans 3:23). We certainly are in a dire position, deserving nothing but condemnation and death.

But because of His great love for us and according to His mercy (Ephesians 2:4), the Creator came to earth as the God-man, a descendant of Adam just like us (1 Corinthians 15:45). But unlike us, He perfectly kept God's law (Romans 10:4). He then chose to *become* sin for us (2 Corinthians 5:21), taking the sins of the whole world upon Himself when He died on the Cross (1 John 2:2).

He took the penalty that we all deserve — death — for us (Romans 4:25, 5:8). But He didn't stay dead. He rose victoriously from the grave, defeating death (2 Timothy 1:10; Hebrews 2:14). He now offers forgiveness and eternal life to all who will repent (Acts 3:19), believe (John 3:18), and trust in Him (Romans 10:9).

Only the Bible provides a consistent foundation for morality that applies to all people everywhere. And only the Bible provides the hope that we need through the person of Jesus Christ, our Creator, Savior, and Lord.

Appendix D

Intelligent Design Movement

Dr. Georgia Purdom

The Intelligent Design Movement (IDM) entered the modern origins debate in 1991 with the publication of Phillip Johnson's book *Darwin on Trial*. Johnson was a lawyer who essentially "tried" Darwinism in a court of law. He found the evidence for Darwinism so lacking that he decided it could not "win" the case as a viable explanation for the origin of living things. Since that time, the IDM has gained increasing recognition and publicity for challenging Darwinism.

What Is Intelligent Design?

The Discovery Institute's Center for Science and Culture is the flagship organization of the IDM. On their website they state, "The theory of intelligent design holds that certain features of the universe and living things are best explained by an intelligent cause, not an undirected process such as natural selection."[1] The ID theory does not name the intelligent cause, and it does not claim that everything is designed. Many proponents of the theory still hold to certain aspects of evolution (e.g., common ancestry of apes and humans) and believe the earth and universe are billions of years old.

The modern IDM has its historical roots in the natural theology movement of the 18th and 19th centuries. Christian philosopher William Paley

---

1. "Frequently Asked Questions," Discovery Institute, accessed September 19, 2016, http://www.discovery.org/id/faqs/.

(1743–1805) reasoned that if one walked across a field and came upon a watch, the assumption would be that there had to be a watchmaker — the complexity and purpose of the watch points to the fact that it is not the result of undirected, unintelligent causes, but the product of a designer.

Natural theology sought to support the existence of God through nature (general revelation) apart from the Bible (special revelation), since the Bible was facing much criticism at that time. The scientific knowledge of the complexity of living things was grossly deficient, leading some to believe that natural causes were sufficient to bring everything into existence. Natural theology was an affront to that line of thinking, much like the ID theory is to Darwinism in modern times.

In the last 100 years or so, there has been an explosion of knowledge about the complexity of cells, DNA, and microorganisms. Thus, the need for a designer has become even greater. The current IDM has more than just philosophical arguments for a designer; it uses scientific evidence drawn from biology, chemistry, and physics.

Irreducible Complexity = Design

The Discovery Institute lists three areas in which they think the evidence for design is apparent.

1. Evidence for design in physics and cosmology — these evidences focus on the laws of the universe necessary for life on earth.
2. Evidence for design in the origin of life — these evidences focus on the "complex and specified information" (CSI) necessary for the origin of life.
3. Evidence for design in the development of biological complexity — these evidences focus on the CSI necessary for living things.[2]

I will focus on the evidence for design in biological complexity since this is the area for which the IDM is most well known.

The ID theory purports that the hallmark of designed living things is *irreducible complexity*. Dr. Michael Behe, ID proponent and author of *Darwin's Black Box*, defines irreducible complexity as:

---

2. "What Is the Science Behind Intelligent Design?" Discovery Institute, May 1, 2009, http://www.discovery.org/a/9761.

> A single system composed of several well-matched, inter-
> acting parts that contribute to the basic function, wherein the
> removal of any one of the parts causes the system to effectively
> cease functioning.[3]

Some examples are the biochemistry of vision, the mammalian blood-clotting pathway, and the bacterial flagellum. These biological pathways and structures consist of many factors, and *all* the factors and parts are necessary for the pathway or structure to function properly.

Behe further explains that the gradual process of Darwinian evolution cannot form these irreducibly complex systems:

> An irreducibly complex system cannot be produced directly
> (that is, by continuously improving the initial function, which
> continues to work by the same mechanism) by slight, successive
> modifications of a precursor system, because any precursor to an
> irreducibly complex system that is missing a part is by definition
> nonfunctional.[4]

Evolution works via the mechanism of small, gradual steps of random chance mutation that "keeps" only that which is immediately helpful. The changes must confer a survival advantage to an organism that allows it to survive better than others of its kind. Better survival means the organism is more likely to reproduce and pass on the changes to the next generation and increase the number of organisms carrying the changes. The mechanism by which evolution works actually prevents organisms from evolving complex biological pathways and structures.

For example, if only three of the many proteins involved in vision were formed in an organism (at one time by random chance), the organism could not see. There would be no survival advantage and so that organism would not necessarily survive better than others to pass on those changes to the next generation. Evolutionary processes do not allow the organism with the changes to preferentially survive and reproduce in the hopes that in a future generation the rest of the vision proteins will form.

Evolution is goalless and purposeless; it does not have a mind and cannot see or plan for the future. The information in the DNA for the vision

---

3. Michael Behe, *Darwin's Black Box* (New York, NY: Simon and Schuster, 1996), p. 39.
4. Ibid.

proteins is likely to be lost in future generations since it serves no immediate purpose that confers a survival advantage. Since evolution cannot accumulate the vision proteins in a step-wise fashion, it would have to start at square one again in each organism to develop the proteins (by random chance mutations) necessary for vision. It's improbable that all the necessary vision proteins would evolve by random chance in a single organism; thus, evolution does not have a mechanism to develop these complex biological pathways and structures.

How Is Irreducible Complexity Detected?

The question of whether a feature of a living organism displays design can be answered by using what is called an explanatory filter. The filter has three levels of explanation:

1. Necessity or Law — did it have to happen?
2. Chance — did it happen by accident?
3. Design — did an intelligent agent cause it to happen?[5]

This is a logical, common sense approach used by individuals every day to deduce cause and effect. For example, consider the scenario of a woman falling:

1. Did she have to fall? If the answer is no, then we have to ask the next two questions.
2. Was it an accident?
3. Or was she pushed?

Crime scene investigators use this explanatory filter every time they examine a crime scene. They need to decide if what happened was an accident or if a crime was committed by a "designer."

If we apply this explanatory filter to living organisms, a feature must be designed if the first two questions are answered no. Let's evaluate the vision pathway that results in sight with respect to these questions:

1. The vision pathway is compatible with, but not required by, the natural laws of biology and chemistry. It is not a necessity specified by natural phenomena.
2. It is complex because the vision pathway is composed of many proteins so it could not have happened by chance. Complex

---

5. William Dembski, "Signs of Intelligence," in: William Dembski and James Kushiner, eds., *Signs of Intelligence* (Grand Rapids, MI: Brazos Press, 2001), p. 171.

structures fall into two categories: ordered complexity and specified complexity. A snowflake is structurally complex, but does not contain information (specified complexity) so it represents a form of ordered complexity. It is the direct result of natural phenomena rather than a product of intelligent design.[6] DNA, on the other hand, does contain information and is an example of specified complexity that does require an intelligent designer.

3. The vision pathway has specified complexity because it has information that results in sight. All the proteins must be present and interact with each other in a specified manner in order for vision to occur. The vision pathway meets all the requirements for irreducible complexity so it must be the product of intelligent design.

Is the IDM a Religion, Science, or Neither?

ID proponent and theologian William Dembski states:

ID is three things:
a scientific research program that investigates the effects of intelligent causes [science];
an intellectual movement that challenges Darwinism and its naturalistic legacy;
and a way of understanding divine action [religion].[7]

The IDM focuses on what is designed rather than answering the questions of who, when, why, and how. Those within the movement believe this promotes scientific endeavor by looking for function and purpose in those things that are designed, whereas an evolutionary mindset presupposes waste and purposelessness and aborts further scientific thinking.

I would agree that the IDM challenges Darwinism; however, I would not say that it is science or religion, even though it has religious and scientific aspects. It's a worldview that acknowledges a "higher power" which will affect how those who hold it view the natural world and do science. In addition, many ID proponents hold a variety of religious views in regard to the "intelligent designer," making it difficult to define the IDM as a religion.

6. While snowflakes are not the direct result of intelligent design, it was God who designed and created the natural laws by which snowflakes form.
7. William Dembski, "Science and Design," *First Things* 86, October 1, 1998.

Evidential vs. Presuppositional Approaches

Proponents of IDM take an evidential approach when looking at the natural world. For example, the vision pathway (evidence) is irreducibly complex, so it must have been designed. But that is essentially where the ID argument ends. It does not answer who the designer is or when, why, or how the designer designed it.

The reason they do this is to have a "big tent" strategy in which they get as many people as possible (regardless of their religious beliefs about the who, what, where, when, and why of the designer) to oppose Darwinism. The hope is that the more people who oppose it, the more seriously their ideas will be taken and the more progress they can make in scientific and educational realms.

Christians in IDM look at it as a "first step" toward getting people to acknowledge a designer which they hope will result in further conversations that might lead them to know the designer is the God of the Bible.

Biblical creationists tend to take a presuppositional approach and use the framework of the inerrant Word of God when looking at the natural world. We would agree that the vision pathway is designed, but we know that because of the Bible. This also allows us to answer the other questions of who (God), when (approximately 6,000 years ago), why (His will), and how (by His Word). Everything in the natural world has been designed by God (Genesis 1) but corrupted by man's sin (Genesis 3) and impacted by a global Flood (Genesis 6–9). This context is very important because without this understanding the IDM runs into a major problem when it comes to the identity and characteristics of the intelligent designer (discussed later).

It is simply not sufficient to say what is designed without answering the questions that are sure to naturally follow — who, when, why, and how. The IDM is unable and unwilling to answer these questions because their "big tent" strategy means that people in the movement hold to a variety of answers to these questions. Many within the IDM would categorize their evidential approach to science as neutral since they only ask if things in the natural world are designed. However, no approach is neutral because every scientist has certain beliefs or presuppositions when they approach the evidence.

It is ironic that ID proponents refuse to see this about their own approach, considering that they claim the problem with Darwinism is the presupposition that nothing supernatural exists. ID proponents at the very least begin with the presupposition that allows for a supernatural intelligent designer.

The natural theology movement of the 1800s failed because it did not answer the next logical question: if it is designed, then who designed it? Most within this movement claimed that design pointed to the God of the Bible, but by divorcing general revelation (nature) from special revelation (the Bible) they opened the door to other conclusions. Deism (another movement of the same period) took the idea of excluding the Bible to the extreme and said God can only be known through nature and human reason, and that faith and revelation do not exist.

Since IDM proponents do not adhere to a particular theological framework, most have no problems with the universe and earth being billions of years old (i.e., the big bang and no global Flood) and still allow biological evolution (possibly being more guided) to play a role. For example, many in the IDM believe in common descent, (the evolutionary tree of life) including that humans and chimps share a common ancestor.

However, they fail to understand that a belief in long ages for the earth formed the foundation of Darwinism. Without billions of years, evolution doesn't have the time to accomplish the evolution of all living things from a single-celled common ancestor. The IDM thus fails to challenge and even accepts one of the core tenets of Darwinism, rendering it much less effective in providing a viable alternative to origins. The IDM is not opposed to evolution, only a purely naturalistic form of evolution.

IDM Is Not Silent about the Designer

Even with claims of neutrality and just answering the question of "what" is designed, the IDM by default is making certain claims about the intelligent designer. The design says something about its designer. For example, if someone designs a raincoat but it doesn't keep the person wearing it from getting wet, we would say the designer was incompetent. Without the biblical framework, what does the natural world "say" about the designer?

Michael Behe in his book, *The Edge of Evolution*, tries to answer this question in relation to the parasite that causes malaria:

> Malaria was intentionally designed. The molecular machinery with which the parasite invades red blood cells is an exquisitely purposeful arrangement of parts.

What sort of designer is that? What sort of "fine-tuning" leads to untold human misery? To countless mothers mourning countless children? Did a hateful, malign [sic] being make intelligent life in order to torture it? One who relishes cries of pain?

Maybe. Maybe not. A torrent of pain indisputably swirls through the world — not only the world of humans but the world of sentient animal life as well. Yet, just as undeniably, much that is good graces nature. Many children die, yet many others thrive. . . . Does one outweigh the other? If so, which outweighs which? Or are pleasure and pain, good and evil incommensurable? Are viruses and parasites part of some brilliant, as-yet-unappreciated economy of nature, or do they reflect the bungling of an incompetent, fallible designer?

Maybe the designer *isn't* all that beneficent or omnipotent. Science can't answer questions like that.[8]

I agree that scientists can't answer those questions without a biblical worldview, which is why it's so important to have a biblical framework when doing science! The design says something about its designer and without the proper framework to understand it Behe describes a horrific designer. He believes the designer purposefully designed malaria to infect people, resulting in death for some. He suggests this might be some sort of "population control" by the designer and that maybe the designer is not all that nice and not all-powerful. Although Behe is Roman Catholic, this is certainly not a picture of the Creator God we know from the Bible.[9]

These beliefs of Behe shouldn't be all that surprising — as I have stated previously, many IDM proponents believe in various forms of evolution. If they also believe in the God of the Bible, then they believe He used millions of years of death, disease, and suffering as recorded in the fossil record to bring about mankind and every other living thing. Death is integral to evolution — it's all about survival of the fittest. Rather than death being a punishment for sin (Genesis 2:16–17 and 3:19), death existed for millions of years before mankind existed to sin. What does this say about God?!

Scripture is clear that death is the last enemy (1 Corinthians 15:26) and that death is the punishment for sin (Romans 6:23). Scripture is clear that

---

8. Michael J. Behe, *The Edge of Evolution* (New York, NY: Free Press, 2007), p. 237–238.
9. Many Roman Catholics would disagree with Behe on this point, as well.

originally everything was "very good" (Genesis 1:31), including the organism that in a fallen world causes malaria. Originally, its molecular machinery did something different that did not inflict pain or harm or cause disease. But as a result of sin, all creation is cursed (Romans 8:22) and organisms have changed as a result of mutations and other processes, allowing them to cause much human misery.

How could God use evolution, which is filled with millions of years of death, disease, and suffering, and then call it "very good"? God becomes the author of evil instead of evil being the result of man's actions (Genesis 3:6). Rather than God being loving, patient, kind, good, merciful, etc. as the Scripture describes Him, He is cruel, vicious, and unloving. If ID ideas without a biblical framework are to be a first step in leading someone to know more about God, why would anyone want to take the next step?

And if God is the author of evil, how can He be the solution to evil? Scripture makes it clear that because of the sin of the first Adam we need the death and Resurrection of the Last Adam, Jesus Christ (1 Corinthians 15:21–22, 45). The problem of sin begins in Genesis (Genesis 3), and the solution of sin is found in Jesus Christ (Romans 10:9). If instead, as many Christians within the IDM believe, God used death and suffering to bring about mankind and every other living thing, then death cannot be the punishment for sin. What then is the purpose of Jesus Christ dying a physical death on the Cross if the punishment for sin is not death? What did Christ die to redeem us from if the punishment for sin is not death?

The IDM does not necessarily acknowledge the God of the Bible as Creator or Redeemer, so the "designer" they postulate is not only responsible for the origin of evil but offers no final solution for the evil in this world. And by all appearances, evil will continue to reign supreme. A "god" like this is nothing more than any other false god in this world religions series.

However, when we trust the Bible, we read that evil was brought into this world by man's actions (Genesis 3), Jesus clearly conquered death by His Resurrection (Romans 6:3–10), and one day death will no longer reign (Revelation 21:4).

The Creator Cannot Be Separated from His Creation

Romans 1:20 states that all men know about God through His creation. However, just recognizing that there is a designer is only one part of it —

which is enough to leave a person without excuse. Colossians 1:15–20 and 2 Peter 3:3–6 point to the inexorable link between God's role as Creator *and* Redeemer.

In Colossians, Paul talks about God, in the person of Jesus, as Creator, and moves seamlessly to His role as Redeemer. Paul sees creation as a foundation for redemption. In 1 Peter, Peter states that people started disbelieving in the Second Coming of Christ because they started doubting God's role as Creator. Again, God's role as Creator is foundational to His role as Redeemer.

Recognizing a designer is not enough to be saved; submitting to the Redeemer is also necessary. While some might consider the IDM a noble attempt to counter the evolutionary indoctrination of our culture, it falls far short of a thoroughly biblical response and even embraces much evolutionary thinking.

We must not separate the creation from its Creator — knowledge of God must come through both general revelation (nature) and special revelation (the Bible). The theologian Louis Berkhof said, "Since the entrance of sin into the world, man can gather true knowledge about God from His general revelation only if he studies it in the light of Scripture."[10] It is only then that the *entire* truth about God and what is seen around us can be fully understood and used to help people understand the bad news in Genesis and the good news of Jesus Christ.

---

10. Louis Berkhof, *Introductory Volume to Systematic Theology* (Grand Rapids, MI: Eerdmans Publishing Co., 1938), p. 60.

Appendix E

Is Evolutionary Humanism the Most Blood-stained Religion Ever?

Bodie Hodge

Introduction: Man's Authority or God's Authority ... Two Religions

If God and His Word are not the authority . . . then by default . . . who is? Man is. When people reject God and His Word as the ultimate authority, then man is attempting to elevate his or her thoughts (collectively or individually) to a position of authority *over* God and His Word.

People often claim that "Christians are religious, and the enlightened unbelievers who reject God are *not* religious." Don't be deceived by such a statement — for these nonbelievers are indeed religious . . . *very* religious, whether they realize it or not. For they have bought into the religion of humanism.

Humanism is the religion that elevates man to be greater than God. Humanism, in a broad sense, encompasses any thought or worldview that rejects God and the 66 books of His Word in part or in whole; hence, *all* non-biblical religions have humanistic roots. There are also those that *mix* aspects of humanism with the Bible. Many of these religions (e.g., Mormons, Islam, Judaism, etc.) openly borrow from the Bible, but they also have mixed *human* elements into their religion where they take some of man's ideas to supersede many parts of the Bible, perhaps in subtle ways.[1]

---

1. For example: in Islam, Muhammad's words in the Koran are taken as a higher authority than God's Word (the Bible); in Mormonism, they have changed nearly 4,000 verses of

There are many forms of humanism, but secular humanism has become one of the most popular today. Variant forms of secular humanism include atheism, agnosticism, non-theism, Darwinism, and the like. Each shares a belief in an evolutionary worldview, with man as the centered authority over God.

Humanism organizations can also receive a tax-exempt status (the same as a Christian church in the United States and the United Kingdom) and they even have religious documents like the *Humanist Manifesto*. Surprisingly, this religion has free rein in state schools, museums, and media under the guise of neutrality, seeking to fool people into thinking it is not a "religion."[2]

Humanism and "Good"

Christians are often confronted with the claim that a humanistic worldview will help society become "better."[3] Even the first *Humanist Manifesto*, of which belief in evolution is a subset, declared: "The goal of humanism is a free and universal society in which people voluntarily and intelligently co-operate for the common good."

But can such a statement be true? For starters, what do the authors mean by "good"? They have no legitimate foundation for such a concept, since one person's "good" can be another's "evil." To have some objective standard (not a relative standard), they must *borrow* from the absolute and true teachings of God in the Bible.

Beyond that, does evolutionary humanism really teach a future of prosperity and a common good? Since death is the "hero" in an evolutionary framework, then it makes one wonder. What has been the result of evolutionary thinking in the past century (20th century)? Perhaps this could be a test of what is to come.

Let's first look at the death estimates due to aggressive conflicts stemming from leaders with evolutionary worldviews, beginning in the 1900s, to see the hints of what this "next level" looks like. See Table 1.

---

the Bible to conform to Mormon teachings and add the words of Joseph Smith and later prophets as superior to God's Word; in Judaism, they accept a portion of God's Word (the Old Testament) but by human standards, they reject a large portion of God's Word (the New Testament) as well as the ultimate Passover lamb, Jesus Christ.

2. Although the U.S. Supreme Court says that religion is not to be taught in the classroom, this one seems to be allowed.

3. One can always ask the question, by what standard do they mean "better"? God is that standard, so they refute themselves when they speak of things being better or worse. In their own professed worldview it is merely arbitrary for something to be "better" or "worse."

Table 1 Estimated deaths as a result of an evolutionary worldview

Who/What?	Specific event and estimated dead	Total Estimates
Pre-Hitler Germany/ Hitler and the Nazis	WWI: 8,500,000[a] WWII: 70 million[b] [Holocaust: 17,000,000][c]	95,000,000
Leon Trotsky and Vladimir Lenin	Bolshevik revolution and Russian Civil War: 15,000,000[d]	15,000,000
Joseph Stalin	20,000,000[e]	20,000,000
Mao Zedong	14,000,000–20,000,000[f]	Median estimate: 17,000,000
Korean War	2,500,000?[g]	~2,500,000[g]
Vietnam War (1959–1975)	4,000,000–5,000,000 Vietnamese, 1,500,000–2,000,000 Lao and Cambodians[h]	Medians of each and excludes French, Australia, and U.S. losses: 6,250,000
Pol Pot (Saloth Sar)	750,000–1,700,000[i]	Median estimate: 1,225,000
Abortion to children[j]	China estimates from 1971–2006: 300,000,000[k] USSR estimates from 1954–1991: 280,000,000[l] U.S. estimates 1928–2007: 26,000,000[m] France estimates 1936–2006: 5,749,731[n] United Kingdom estimates 1958–2006: 6,090,738[o] Germany estimates 1968–2007: 3,699,624[p] Etc.	621,500,000 and this excludes many other countries
Grand estimate		~778,000,000

a. *The World Book Encyclopedia*, Volume 21, Entry: World War II (Chicago, IL: World Book, Inc.), p. 467; such statistics may have some variance depending on source, as much of this is still in dispute.
b. Ranges from 60 to 80 million, so we are using 70 million.
c. Figures ranged from 7 to 26 million.
d. Russian Civil War, http://en.wikipedia.org/wiki/Russian_Civil_War, October 23, 2008.
e. Joseph Stalin, http://www.moreorless.au.com/killers/stalin.html, October 23, 2008.
f. Mao Tse-Tung, http://www.moreorless.au.com/killers/mao.html, October 23, 2008.
g. This one is tough to pin down and several sources have different estimates, so this is a middle-of-the-road estimate from the sources I found.
h. Vietnam War, http://www.vietnamwar.com/, October 23, 2008.
i. Pol Pot, http://en.wikipedia.org/wiki/Pol_Pot, October 23, 2008.
j. This table only lists estimates for abortion deaths in few countries; so, this total figure is

likely very conservative as well as brief stats of other atrocities.

k. Historical abortion statistics, PR China, compiled by Wm. Robert Johnston, last updated June 4, 2008, http://www.johnstonsarchive.net/policy/abortion/ab-prchina.html.

l. Historical abortion statistics, U.S.S.R., compiled by Wm. Robert Johnston, last updated June 4, 2008, http://www.johnstonsarchive.net/policy/abortion/ab-ussr.html.

m. Historical abortion statistics, United States, compiled by Wm. Robert Johnston, last updated June 4, 2008, http://www.johnstonsarchive.net/policy/abortion/ab-unitedstates.html.

n. Historical abortion statistics, France, compiled by Wm. Robert Johnston, last updated June 4, 2008, http://www.johnstonsarchive.net/policy/abortion/ab-france.html.

o. Historical abortion statistics, United Kingdom, compiled by Wm. Robert Johnston, last updated June 4, 2008, http://www.johnstonsarchive.net/policy/abortion/ab-unitedkingdom.html.

p. Historical abortion statistics, FR Germany, compiled by Wm. Robert Johnston, last updated June 4, 2008, http://www.johnstonsarchive.net/policy/abortion/ab-frgermany.html.

Charles Darwin's view of molecules-to-man evolution was catapulted into societies around the world in the mid-to-late 1800s. Evolutionary teachings influenced Karl Marx, Leon Trotsky, Adolf Hitler, Pol Pot, Mao Zedong, Joseph Stalin, Vladimir Lenin, and many others. Let's take a closer look at some of these people and events and examine the evolutionary influence and repercussions.

World War I and II, Hitler, Nazis, and the Holocaust

Most historians would point to the assassination of Archduke Francis Ferdinand on June 18, 1914, as the event that triggered World War I (WWI). But tensions were already high, considering the state of Europe at the time. Darwinian sentiment was brewing in Germany. Darwin once said:

> At some future period, not very distant as measured by centuries, the civilized races of man will almost certainly exterminate and replace the savage races throughout the world. At the same time the anthropomorphous apes . . . will no doubt be exterminated. The break between man and his nearest allies will then be wider, for it will intervene between man in a more civilized state, as we may hope, even than the Caucasian, and some ape as low as a baboon, instead of as now between the negro or Australian [Aborigine] and the gorilla.[4]

Darwin viewed the "Caucasian" (white-skinned Europeans) as the dominant "race" in his evolutionary worldview. To many evolutionists at the

---

4. Charles Darwin, *The Descent of Man* (New York: A.L. Burt, 1874, 2nd ed.), p. 178.

time, mankind had evolved from ape-like creatures that had more hair, dark skin, dark eyes, etc. Therefore, more "evolved" meant less body hair, blond hair, blue eyes, etc. Later, in Hitler's era, Nazi Germany practiced *Lebensborn*, which was a controversial program, the details of which have not been entirely brought to light. Many claim it was a breeding program that tried to evolve the "master race" further — more on this below.

But the German sentiment prior to WWI was very much bent on conquering for the purpose of expanding their territory and their "race." An encyclopedia entry from 1936 states:

> In discussions of the background of the war much has been said of Pan-Germanism, which was the spirit of national consciousness carried to the extreme limit. The Pan-Germans, who included not only militarists, but historians, scientists, educators and statesmen, conceived the German people, no matter where they located, as permanently retaining their nationality. The most ambitious of this group believed that it was their mission of Germans to extend their kultur (culture) over the world, and to accomplish this by conquest if necessary. In this connection the theory was advanced that the German was a superior being, destined to dominate other peoples, most of whom were thought of as decadent.[5]

Germany had been buying into Darwin's model of evolution and saw themselves as the superior "race," destined to dominate the world, and their actions were the consequence of their worldview. This view set the stage for Hitler and the Nazi party and paved the road to WWII.

Hitler and the Nazis

World War II dwarfed World War I in the total number of people who died. Racist evolutionary attitudes exploded in Germany against people groups such as Jews, Poles, and many others. Darwin's teaching on evolution and humanism heavily influenced Adolf Hitler and the Nazis.

Hitler even tried to force the Protestant church in Germany to change fundamental tenets because of his newfound faith.[6] In 1936, while Hitler was in power, an encyclopedia entry on Hitler stated:

---

5. *The American Educator Encyclopedia* (Chicago, IL: The United Educators, Inc., 1936), p. 3914 under entry "World War."
6. *The American Educator Encyclopedia* (Chicago, IL: The United Educators, Inc., 1936), p. 1702 under entry "Hitler."

. . . a Hitler attempt to modify the Protestant faith failed.[7]

His actions clearly show that he did not hold to the basic fundamentals taught in the 66 books of the Bible. Though some of his writings suggest he did believe in some form of God early on (due to his upbringing within Catholicism), his religious views moved toward atheistic humanism with his acceptance of evolution. Many atheists today try to disavow him, but actions speak louder than words.

The Alpha History site (dedicated to much of the history of Nazi Germany by providing documents, transcribed speeches, and so on) says:

> Contrary to popular opinion, Hitler himself was not an atheist. . . . Hitler drifted away from the church after leaving home, and his religious views in adulthood are in dispute.[8]

So this history site is not sure what his beliefs were, but they seem to be certain that he was not an atheist! If they are not sure what beliefs he held, how can they be certain he was not an atheist?[9] The fact is that many people who walk away from church become atheists (i.e., they were never believers in the first place as 1 John 2:19 indicates). Hitler's actions were diametrically opposed to Christianity . . . but not atheism, where there is no God who sets what is right and wrong.[10]

Regardless, this refutes notions that Hitler was a Christian, as some have falsely claimed. Hitler's disbelief started early. He said:

> The present system of teaching in schools permits the following absurdity: at 10 a.m. the pupils attend a lesson in the catechism, at which the creation of the world is presented to them in accordance with the teachings of the Bible; and at 11 a.m. they attend a lesson in natural science, at which they are taught the theory of evolution. Yet the two doctrines are in complete contradiction. As a child, I suffered from this contradiction, and

7. Ibid., p. 1494 under entry "Germany."
8. Religion in Nazi Germany, http://alphahistory.com/nazigermany/religion-in-nazi-germany/, April 3, 2013.
9. Romans 1 makes it clear that all people believe in God, they just suppress that knowledge, and this is also the case with any professed atheist.
10. For an extensive treatise on Hitler's (and the Nazis') religious viewpoints, see J. Bergman, *Hitler and the Nazi Darwinian Worldview* (Kitchener, Ontario, Canada: Joshua Press Inc., 2012).

ran my head against a wall. . . . Is there a single religion that can exist without a dogma? No, for in that case it would belong to the order of science. . . . But there have been human beings, in the baboon category, for at least three hundred thousand years. There is less distance between the man-ape and the ordinary modern man than there is between the ordinary modern man and a man like Schopenhauer. . . . It is impossible to suppose nowadays that organic life exists only on our planet.[11]

Consider this quote in his unpublished second book:

The types of creatures on the earth are countless, and on an individual level their self-preservation instinct as well as the longing for procreation is always unlimited; however, the space in which this entire life process plays itself out is limited. It is the surface area of a precisely measured sphere on which billions and billions of individual beings struggle for life and succession. In the limitation of this living space lies the compulsion for the struggle for survival, and the struggle for survival, in turn contains the precondition for evolution.[12]

Hitler continues:

The history of the world in the ages when humans did not yet exist was initially a representation of geological occurrences. The clash of natural forces with each other, the formation of a habitable surface on this planet, the separation of water and land, the formation of the mountains, plains, and the seas. That [was] is the history of the world during this time. Later, with the emergence of organic life, human interest focuses on the appearance and disappearance of its thousandfold forms. Man himself finally becomes visible very late, and from that point on he begins to understand the term "world history" as referring to the history of his own development — in other words, the representation of his own evolution. This development

11. Adolf Hitler, 1941, translated by Norman Cameron and R.H. Stevens, *Hitler's Secret Conversations*, 1941–1944 (The New American Library of World Literature, Inc., 1961).
12. Adolf Hitler, edited by Gerald L. Weinberg, translated by Krista Smith, *Hitler's Second Book* (U.K.: Enigma books, 2003), p. 8.

is characterized by the never-ending battle of humans against animals and also against humans themselves.[13]

Hitler fully believed Darwin as well as Darwin's precursors — such as Charles Lyell's geological ages and millions of years of history. In his statements here, there is no reference to God. Instead, he unreservedly flew the banner of naturalism and evolution and only mentioned God in a rare instance to win Christians to his side, just as agnostic Charles Darwin did in his book *On the Origin of Species*.[14]

One part of the Nazi party political platform's 25 points in 1920 says:

> We demand freedom of religion for all religious denominations within the state so long as they do not endanger its existence or oppose the moral senses of the Germanic race. The Party as such advocates the standpoint of a positive Christianity without binding itself confessionally to any one denomination.[15]

Clearly this "positive Christianity" was an appeal to some of Christianity's morality, but not the faith itself. Many atheists today still appeal to a "positive Christian" approach, wanting the morality of Christianity (in many respects), but not Christianity.

Christianity was under heavy attack by Hitler and the Nazis, as documented from original sources prior to the end of WWII by Bruce Walker in *The Swastika against the Cross*.[16] The book clearly reveals the anti-Christian sentiment by Hitler and the Nazis and their persecution of Christianity and their attempt to make Christianity change and be subject to the Nazi state and beliefs.

In 1939–1941, the Bible was rewritten for the German people at Hitler's command, eliminating all references to Jews and made Christ out to be pro-Aryan! The Ten Commandments were replaced with these twelve:[17]

---

13. Hitler, *Hitler's Second Book*, p. 9.
14. In the first edition of *Origin of Species*, God is not mentioned, in the sixth edition, "God" was added several times to draw Christians into this false religion. See Randall Hedtke, *Secrets of the Sixth Edition* (Green Forest, AR: Master Books, 2010).
15. "Nazi Party 25 Points (1920)," http://alphahistory.com/nazigermany/nazi-party-25-points-1920/.
16. B. Walker, *The Swastika against the Cross* (Denver, CO: Outskirts Press, Inc., 2008).
17. "Hitler Rewrote the Bible and Added Two Commandments," Pravda News Site, 8/10/2006, http://english.pravda.ru/world/europe/10-08-2006/83892-hitler-0/; Jewish References Erased in Newly Found Nazi Bible," Daily Mail Online, August 7, 2006, http://www.dailymail.co.uk/news/article-399470/Jewish-references-erased-newly-Nazi-Bible.html.

1. Honor your Fuhrer and master.
2. Keep the blood pure and your honor holy.
3. Honor God and believe in him wholeheartedly.
4. Seek out the peace of God.
5. Avoid all hypocrisy.
6. Holy is your health and life.
7. Holy is your well-being and honor.
8. Holy is your truth and fidelity.
9. Honor your father and mother — your children are your aid and your example.
10. Maintain and multiply the heritage of your forefathers.
11. Be ready to help and forgive.
12. Joyously serve the people with work and sacrifice.

Hitler had *replaced* Christ in Nazi thought; and children were even taught to pray to Hitler instead of God![18] Hitler and the Nazis were not Christian, but instead were humanistic in their outlook, and any semblance of Christianity was cultic. The Nazis determined that their philosophy was the best way to bring about the common good of all humanity.

Interestingly it was Christians alone in Germany who were unconquered by the Nazis and suffered heavily for it. Walker summarizes in his book:

> You would expect to find Christians and Nazis mortal enemies. This is, of course, exactly what happened historically. Christians, alone, proved unconquerable by the Nazis. It can be said that Christians did not succeed in stopping Hitler, but it cannot be said that they did not try, often at great loss and nearly always as true martyrs (people who could have chosen to live, but who chose to die for the sake of goodness.)[19]

Hitler and the Nazi's evolutionary views certainly helped lead Germany into WWII because they viewed the "Caucasian" as more evolved (and more specifically the Aryan peoples of the Caucasians), which to them justified their adoption of the idea that lesser "races" should be murdered in the struggle for survival. Among the first to be targeted were Jews, then Poles, Slavs, and then many others — including Christians regardless of their heritage.

---

18. Walker, p. 20–22.
19. Walker, p. 88.

Trotsky and Lenin

Trotsky and Lenin were both notorious leaders of the USSR — and specifically the Russian revolution. Lenin, taking power in 1917, became a ruthless leader and selected Trotsky as his heir. Lenin and Trotsky held to Marxism, which was built, in part, on Darwinism and evolution applied to a social scheme.

Karl Marx regarded Darwin's book as an "epoch-making book." With regard to Darwin's research on natural origins, Marx claimed, "The latter method is the only materialistic and, therefore, the only scientific one."[20]

Few realize or admit that Marxism, the primary idea underlying communism, is built on Darwinism and materialism (i.e., no God). In 1883, Freidrich Engels, Marx's longtime friend and collaborator, stated at Marx's funeral service that "Just as Darwin discovered the law of evolution in organic nature, so Marx discovered the law of evolution in human history."[21] Both Darwin and Marx built their ideologies on naturalism and materialism (tenants of evolutionary humanism). Trotsky once said of Darwin:

> Darwin stood for me like a mighty doorkeeper at the entrance to the temple of the universe. I was intoxicated with his minute, precise, conscientious and at the same time powerful, thought. I was the more astonished when I read . . . that he had preserved his belief in God. I absolutely declined to understand how a theory of the origin of species by way of natural selection and sexual selection and a belief in God could find room in one and the same head.[22]

Trotsky's high regard for evolution and Darwin were the foundation of his belief system. Like many, Trotsky probably did not realize that the precious few instances of the name "God" did not appear in the first edition of *Origin of Species.* These references were added later, and many suspect that this was done to influence church members to adopt Darwinism. Regardless, Trotsky may not have read much of Darwin's second book, *Descent of Man,* in which Darwin claims that man invented God:

---

20. *Great Books of the Western World*, Volume 50, Capital, Karl Marx (Chicago, IL: William Benton Publishers, 1952), footnotes on p. 166 and p. 181.
21. Gertrude Himmelfarb, *Darwin and the Darwinian Revolution* (London: Chatto & Windus, 1959), p. 348.
22. Max Eastman, *Leon Trotsky: The Portrait of a Youth* (New York: Greenberg, 1925), p. 117–118.

The same high mental faculties which first led man to believe in unseen spiritual agencies, then in fetishism, polytheism, and ultimately in monotheism, would infallibly lead him, as long as his reasoning powers remained poorly developed, to various strange superstitions and customs.[23]

Vladimir Lenin picked up on Darwinism and Marxism and ruled very harshly as an evolutionist. His variant of Marxism has become known as Leninism. Regardless, the evolutionist roots of Marx, Trotsky, and Lenin were the foundation that communism has stood on — and continues to stand on.

Stalin, Mao, and Pol Pot, to Name a Few

Perhaps the most ruthless communist leaders were Joseph Stalin, Mao Zedong, and Pol Pot. Each of these were social Darwinists, ruling three different countries — the Soviet Union, China, and Cambodia, respectively. Their reigns of terror demonstrated the end result of reducing the value of human life to that of mere animals, a Darwinistic teaching.[24] Though I could expand on each of these, you should be getting the point by now. So let's move to another key, but deadly, point in evolutionary thought.

Abortion — The War on Babies

The war on children has been one of the quietest, and yet bloodiest, in the past hundred years. In an evolutionary mindset, the unborn have been treated as though they are going through an "animal phase" and can simply be discarded.

Early evolutionist Ernst Haeckel first popularized the concept that babies in the womb are actually undergoing animal developmental stages, such as a fish stage and so on. This idea has come to be known as *ontogeny recapitulates phylogeny*. Haeckel even faked drawings of various animals' embryos and had them drawn next to human embryos looking virtually identical.[25]

---

23. Charles Darwin, *The Descent of Man and Selection in Relation to Sex,* chapter III ("Mental Powers of Man and the Lower Animals"), 1871, as printed in the *Great Books of the Western World*, Volume 49, Robert Hutchins, ed. (Chicago, IL: Wiliam Benton Publishers, 1952), p. 303.

24. R. Hall, "Darwin's Impact — The Bloodstained Legacy of Evolution," *Creation* Magazine 27(2):46-47, March 2005, http://www.answersingenesis.org/articles/cm/v27/n2/darwin.

25. Lithograph by J.G. Bach of Leipzig after drawings by Haeckel, from *Anthropogenie* published by Engelmann; public Domain, https://commons.wikimedia.org/w/index.php?curid=8007834.

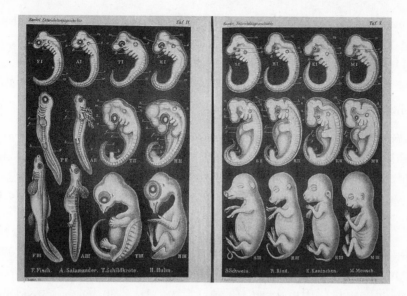

These drawings have been shown to be completely false.[26] Haeckel himself partially confessed as much.[27] However, this discredited idea has been used repeatedly for a hundred years! Textbooks today still use this concept (though not Haeckel's drawings), and museums around the world still teach it. Through this deception, many women have been convinced that the babies they are carrying in their wombs are simply going through an animal phase and can be aborted. Author and general editor of this volume, Ken Ham, states:

> In fact, some abortion clinics in America have taken women aside to explain to them that what is being aborted is just an embryo in the fish stage of evolution, and that the embryo must not be thought of as human. These women are being fed outright lies.[28]

---

26. Michael Richardson et al., *Anatomy and Embryology*, 196(2):91–106, 1997.

27. Haeckel said, "A small portion of my embryo-pictures (possibly 6 or 8 in a hundred) are really (in Dr Brass's [one of his critics] sense of the word) 'falsified' — all those, namely, in which the disclosed material for inspection is so incomplete or insufficient that one is compelled in a restoration of a connected development series to fill up the gaps through hypotheses, and to reconstruct the missing members through comparative syntheses. What difficulties this task encounters, and how easily the draughts — man may blunder in it, the embryologist alone can judge." The Truth about Haeckel's Confession, *The Bible Investigator and Inquirer*, M.L. Hutchinson, Melbourne, March 11, 1911, p. 22–24.

28. Ken Ham, *The Lie: Evolution*, chapter 8, "The Evils of Evolution" (Green Forest, AR: Master Books, 1987), p. 105.

314 — World Religions and Cults • Volume 3

Evolutionary views have decreased the value of human life. Throughout the world the casualties of the war on children is staggering. Though deaths of children and the unborn did exist prior to the "evolution revolution," they have increased exponentially after the promotion of Darwinian teachings.

Conclusion

Is evolution the cause of wars and deaths? Absolutely not — both existed long before Darwin was born. Sin is the ultimate cause.[29] But an evolutionary worldview has done nothing but add fuel to the fire.

In spite of the wars and atrocities caused by those who subscribed to an evolutionary worldview in recent times, there is still hope. We can end the seemingly endless atrocities against the unborn and those deemed less worthy of living, including the old and impaired.

In Egypt, Israelite boys were slaughtered by being thrown into the Nile at the command of Pharaoh (Exodus 1:20). And yet, by the providence of God, Moses survived and led the Israelites to safety, and the Lord later judged the Egyptians.

In Judea, under the Roman Empire, subordinate King Herod the Great commanded the slaughter of all the boys under the age of two in and around Bethlehem. And yet, by the providence of God, Jesus, the Son of God, survived and later laid down His life to bring salvation to mankind as the Prince of Peace. Herod's name, however, went down in history as an evil tyrant and murderer.

In this day and age, governments readily promote and fund the killing of children, both boys and girls, and sometimes command it, through abortion. By providence, however . . . you survived. While we can't change the past, we can learn from it. If we are to stop this continuing bloodshed, we must get back to the Bible and realize the bankrupt religion of evolutionary humanism has led only to death — by the millions. We need to point those who think humanity is the answer, to the Savior who took the sins of humanity on Himself to offer them salvation.

---

29. *The New Answers Book 1*, gen. ed. Ken Ham, chapter 26, "Why Does God's Creation Include Death and Suffering?" (Green Forest, AR: Master Books, 2006), p.325–338, http://www.answersingenesis.org/articles/nab/why-does-creation-include-suffering.

Appendix F

Responding to Atheist Propaganda

Ken Ham

Christians need to understand that many secularists have put together a very effective propaganda machine as a part of their effort to impose their atheistic religion on the Western culture. They intimidate Christians and influence the government to limit freedom of religion (particularly in regard to Christianity).

To help counteract this aggressive effort, Christians — wherever they are in the West — need to be aware of the terms being used in the secularist campaign and what Christians need to be doing to help counter this campaign.

Secularists know the adage that if you "throw enough mud at the wall, some of it will stick." If enough false information and misleading accusations are spread, people will begin to believe them. This is nothing new, as Nazis did this very thing leading up to WWII. In our day and age, this has happened in a number of places.

1. The use of the word *science*

Here is how I discussed the word *science* during my debate with Bill Nye "The Science Guy":

> Public school textbooks are using the same word *science* for observational and historical science. They arbitrarily define *science* as naturalism and outlaw the supernatural. They present

316 — World Religions and Cults • Volume 3

molecules-to-man evolution as fact. They are imposing the religion of naturalism/atheism on generations of students.[1]

I also stated the following during the debate:

> The word *science* has been hijacked by secularists in teaching evolution to force the religion of naturalism on generations of kids. . . . The creation/evolution debate is really a conflict between two philosophical worldviews based on two different accounts of origins or historical science beliefs. The word *science* is defined as "the state of knowing: knowledge as distinguished from ignorance or misunderstanding."[2]

Scientific pursuit needs to be broken into two parts: experimental (observable or operational) science and origins (historical) science. Both creation and evolution involve historical science (belief about the past) and observational science (such as the study of genetics, mixing chemicals in test tubes, or building computers).

Experimental science that builds our modern technology is accomplished through the scientific method. Origins or historical science is the non-repeatable, non-observable science dealing with the past — which enters the realm of beliefs (really, religion).

In almost all of today's government-run educational systems, the religion of secular humanism — with its foundation of naturalistic evolution based on man's word/beliefs about the past (molecules-to-man evolution) — is guised in textbooks, lectures, and secular museums as so-called "science." But the same word, *science*, is used for the experimental science that helps build technology.

Because students aren't taught the difference between historical and observational science, they are brainwashed into thinking that molecules-to-man evolution is the same science as what has built technology — which it is not. It is what we call a "bait-and-switch fallacy" (a fallacy in logic). It's really a conflict between two philosophical worldviews that are based on two different accounts of origins or historical science beliefs.

---

1. Ken Ham and Bodie Hodge, *Inside the Nye-Ham Debate* (Green Forest, AR: Master Books, 2014), p. 33.
2. Merriam-Webster Online Dictionary, s.v. "science," http://www.merriam-webster.com/dictionary/science.

Because of this misuse of wording by the secularists, Christians need to be using the terms *observational science* and *historical science* over and over again! The secularists hate these terms, for they don't want people to know they actually have a religion (a worldview) they are trying to impose on the masses. Their propaganda campaign, which confuses the meaning of the word science and attempts to indoctrinate people in evolutionary ideas, has been very successful.

To help counter their efforts, we need to keep delineating between "observational" and "historical" science as much as we can — much to the consternation of the secularists!

2. The use of the word *religion*

The word *religion* has a variety of definitions, but one of the main definitions (as given by the *Merriam-Webster Dictionary*) is "an interest, a belief, or an activity that is very important to a person or group."[3]

Atheists have effectively propagandized the culture to indoctrinate people to think that if you believe in God as Christians do, then that is religion — however, if you don't believe in God and believe the universe and all life arose by natural processes, then supposedly that is not a religion! But as we constantly point out, atheism and humanism are religions — beliefs meant to explain life by natural processes, without the supernatural involved.

Atheists go ballistic when I say in many articles that they are trying to impose their religion of naturalism on the culture. But the point is, they are!

Just because atheists refuse to acknowledge it does not mean they are not doing it. In fact, due to the atheist propaganda effort, it's one of the reasons we are losing Christian symbols (crosses, Nativity scenes, and so on) across the nation.

Furthermore, in the United States and other Western countries, the government is imposing a religion on millions of children when they insist that schools only teach evolution in science classes and not biblical creation. Officials insist that evolution is deemed to be "science" and creation is "religion." Evolutionists have been indoctrinating people with a false view of the words *science* and *religion*.

I am encouraging Christians, as much as they can, to use the word *religion* to describe secularism. When a secular group like the Freedom from

---

3. Merriam-Webster Online Dictionary, s.v. "religion," http://www.merriam-webster.com/dictionary/religion.

Religion Foundation or Americans United for the Separation of Church and State lodge a lawsuit to get a cross removed from a public place or a statue with someone praying, and so on, then we need to make sure to be vocal about the fact that secularists have imposed their religion of atheism.

Furthermore, why are these same organizations refusing to sue for the removal of symbols of atheism, evolution, and naturalism? It is a double standard.

Some secularists want to deny that humanism and atheism should be considered religions, but even various U.S. courts have ruled and described in their decisions that humanism should be viewed as a religion. In Oregon, an inmate sued, with the assistance of the American Humanist Association, to have a humanist study group recognized as a religious study group along with Bible studies in the prison.

Arguing based on the Establishment Clause of the First Amendment, the inmate won the right as the district judge ordered secular humanism to be viewed as a religion. Even so, humanism had previously been viewed as a non-theistic religion in the rationale for the Supreme Court case of *Torcaso v. Watkins*. This is the first ruling that clearly establishes atheistic secular humanism as a religion whose practice should be protected under the First Amendment.[4]

Additionally, the U.S. military has commissioned humanist chaplains to serve those soldiers who deny God's existence.

3. The word *intolerance*

Intolerance/intolerant is defined in the *Merriam-Webster Dictionary* this way:

> Unwilling to grant equal freedom of expression especially in religious matters; unwilling to grant or share social, political, or professional rights.[5]

Intolerantly, secularists often accuse Christians who, for example, take a stand on marriage being one man for one woman based on the Bible, as being intolerant. But in fact, Christians are the ones who are tolerant of

---

4. The U.S. Supreme Court in *Torcaso v. Watkins*, 81 S.Ct. 1681 (1961), stated the following: "Among religions in this country which do not teach what would generally be considered a belief in the existence of God, are Buddhism, Taoism, Ethical Culture, Secular Humanism, and others."

5. Merriam-Webster Online Dictionary, s.v. "intolerant," http://www.merriam-webster.com/dictionary/intolerant.

others. You see, Christians who stand on God's Word will authoritatively speak against gay marriage, but they should not be intolerant of the people who disagree with them.

I find that those who call Christians "intolerant" are really the ones who are intolerant! So when a fire chief in Atlanta, Georgia, is fired by a city council because his personal beliefs concerning marriage are based on the Bible, Christians need to be vocal about the city council's being intolerant and imposing their humanistic religion on people under their jurisdiction!

4. The word *proselytize*

The *Merriam-Webster Dictionary* has this definition of *proselytize*:

> To try to persuade people to join a religion, cause, or group.[6]

Actually, America's courts have not been able to give an accepted definition of this word. Some people claim that just telling someone about the gospel of Jesus Christ is supposedly trying to force one's belief on someone (their definition of proselytizing). Christians will certainly share their beliefs and the hope of forgiveness of sins with others, but they recognize that they cannot force someone to become a Christian. Only God can change people's hearts.

In reality, it's the secularists who are trying to force their religion on others as they intimidate people to accept the basic tenets of their religion, such as evolutionary naturalism. Many atheists don't necessarily use the word *proselytize*, but they claim that a Christian working in a government institution or a government-funded place cannot bring their Christianity into the workplace.

Yet many professors at government-subsidized universities will openly proclaim their atheism (and even attack the Bible and the Christian faith) in their classes, but if a professor were to admit he was a Christian and make statements about his religious beliefs to the students, he would likely be disciplined or fired.[7]

More and more we see intolerant secularists trying to limit the Christian influence by attempting to intimidate Christians not to bring their

---

6. Merriam-Webster Online Dictionary, s.v. "proselytize," http://www.merriam-webster.com/dictionary/proselytize.

7. For some examples, see Jerry Bergman, *Slaughter of the Dissidents* (Southworth, WA: Leafcutter Press, 2012), https://answersingenesis.org/store/product/slaughter-dissidents/?sku=10-2-345.

Christianity into their workplace — all the while they want the freedom to impose theirs. They ultimately want Christianity eliminated altogether from the public arena. Meanwhile, secularists are free to exercise their religion wherever they want to.

Conclusion

As secularists are successful in getting the governments to teach evolution as fact to millions of students in Western nations and will not allow biblical creation to be taught in science classes, we should be pointing out their deceptive use of terms. Indeed, the secularists continually misuse the word *science* as they indoctrinate people into a false worldview of naturalism so they can impose that religion on young people. At the same time, they exhibit their intolerance of Christianity and Christians in the culture.

The secularists want to express their beliefs throughout society and want Christians to keep their beliefs inside their churches. In reality, governments are sanctioning the religion of naturalism and that it be imposed on millions of children and teens. At the same time, Western nations have supported a growing intolerance of anything Christian and are limiting free speech and the freedom of religion in trying to squelch the free exercise of Christianity.

I challenge Christians, especially Christian leaders, to be more vocal in this battle, boldly proclaiming the gospel to unbelievers and calling Christians back to the authority of the Bible. As we stand firmly and boldly on the truths of Jesus Christ as the Creator and Savior in our apologetic arguments, we must also use correct terms like *historical science, observational science, religion*, and *intolerance* when engaging the secularists in the ongoing war against Christianity in Western nations.

That is why you will find Answers in Genesis using these terms in our articles, billboards, and other outreaches, as we do our best to help undo the work of the atheists' propaganda campaigns and point people to the hope that we have in Jesus Christ, as we give a defense of the Christian faith.

Appendix G

Responding to Skeptics

Roger Patterson

The humanistic thinking that underlies the philosophy of a majority of those in the West has colored every aspect of life. And that makes perfect sense — culture is a reflection of the religious views (cultus) of the people who make up the society. As go the people, so go the schools, the government, entertainment, etc. One of the key areas where this influence is seen is in the government-run schools.

In America and other Western countries, there is a naturalistic bias that permeates the science classrooms and a progressive bias that colors the social studies classes. Science is limited to only anti-God, naturalistic ideas, especially those promoting evolutionary ideas (cosmological, geological, and biological). While there is some latitude in social studies classrooms to discuss various religious ideas, Christianity is certainly demonized in many settings. However, is it really the public school's job to offer religious instruction? Well, if our religious views color everything we do, then there is no separating the sacred from the secular activities of our days.

So how would you respond to someone in a discussion of what should be taught in the public schools? That response is going to depend on a lot of factors, but the following exchange shows how to expose the false beliefs and arbitrary claims of a skeptic while directing them to the truth found in the

Bible and ultimately declare the glorious gospel of Jesus Christ.[1] The original letter appears as block quotes with the responses inserted between.

Can Public Schools Be "Neutral"?

> Insofar as the Humanist Manifesto declares there is no God, public schools must not be humanist. But neither may they endorse any particular creed they must be deity neuter. Public schools, since they are supported by mandatory taxation, must not teach any religious viewpoint (including atheism). Would you like it if your children were taught to reverence Vishnu?
>
> You say you want Creationism taught along with Evolution? Fine, but whose Creation mythos — Aztec, Greek, Norse, Hindu, etc?
>
> Yes, science means knowledge but knowledge is achieved only through observation and reasoning never revelation. Revelation is not repeatable (on demand) and hence not subject to the scientific method. Even Scripture acknowledges that God is unknowable. The basis of scientific study is the presumed constancy of physical laws but since God is an entity and therefore capable of mercy, no analysis can predict His actions.
>
> — L.W., U.S.

I agree that humanism should not be promoted in the public school systems, but the fact remains that it *is* the dominant worldview presented to children. If science in the public schools is restricted to teaching only naturalistic explanations for the origin and history of life on earth, then this is biased against any deistic religion, and therefore is promoting the humanist religion above any other religion that does not hold this philosophy (more on this in a moment).

Humanist groups are accepted as "religious" institutions on college campuses and are granted tax-exempt status by the government in the same way that churches and traditional religious denominations are. If schools must be "deity neutral," then the public school system fails to meet this standard. Man is the measure of all things and becomes the de facto deity in the religion of

---

1. This feedback originally appeared on the Answers in Genesis website in response to an email received concerning an article written by Ken Ham. Roger Patterson, "Can Public Schools Be 'Neutral'?" Answers in Genesis, accessed October 7, 2016, https://answersin-genesis.org/public-school/can-public-schools-be-neutral.

humanism. So, if humanism is promoted in the classrooms, then the class-rooms are not deity neutral.

There are other religious worldviews that do not believe in a distinct deity — Buddhism and Taoism are two examples — but the U.S. Supreme Court has recognized that these worldviews should be considered religions as is evident in the following statement:

> Among religions in this country which do not teach what would generally be considered a belief in the existence of God, are *Buddhism, Taoism,* Ethical Culture, *Secular Humanism* (emphasis added), and others. (*Torcaso vs Watkins*, 81 S.Ct. 1681 (1961))

If we look at the Humanist Manifesto III, we see that three of the major tenets of the religion of humanism are:

1. Knowledge of the world is derived by observation, experimentation, and rational analysis. Humanists find that science is the best method for determining this knowledge as well as for solving problems and developing beneficial technologies. We also recognize the value of new departures in thought, the arts, and inner experience — each subject to analysis by critical intelligence.

2. Humans are an integral part of nature, the result of unguided evolutionary change. Humanists recognize nature as self-existing. We accept our life as all and enough, distinguishing things as they are from things as we might wish or imagine them to be. We welcome the challenges of the future, and are drawn to and undaunted by the yet to be known.

3. Ethical values are derived from human need and interest as tested by experience. Humanists ground values in human welfare shaped by human circumstances, interests, and concerns and extended to the global ecosystem and beyond. We are committed to treating each person as having inherent worth and dignity, and to making informed choices in a context of freedom consonant with responsibility.[2]

2. "Humanism and Its Aspirations, Humanist Manifesto III," American Humanist Association, http://americanhumanist.org/Humanism/Humanist_Manifesto_III.

If science in the public schools is based on the idea that "[k]nowledge is derived by observation, experimentation, and rational [read: "without supernaturalism"] analysis," then, again, it is promoting the humanist religion above any other religion that does not hold this philosophy.

If science teachers in the public schools are only allowed to teach that "humans are an integral part of nature, the result of unguided evolutionary change," then it is promoting the humanist religion above any other religion that does not hold this philosophy.

If the public school system is teaching that "ethical values are derived from human need and interest as tested by experience" (as is evident in the teaching of situational ethics and the absence of any absolute truth), then it is promoting the humanist religion above any other religion that does not hold this philosophy (see a pattern?).

Since all of the above conditions can be shown to be true, then the public school systems are promoting the religion of secular humanism, an atheistic religion, above all other views, cleverly and deceptively worded as "science," while other religions are relegated to "humanities" or "religious studies."

The problem that we face is related to the myth of neutrality — every system of thought must begin with a set of assumptions and is, therefore, not neutral. The public school systems cannot be neutral on the issue of the origin and history of life on earth. They are choosing to teach one view at the exclusion of others, which is not exactly neutral.

> Public schools, since they are supported by mandatory taxation, must not teach any religious viewpoint (including atheism)

But the fact is that they *do* promote atheistic, humanistic philosophies, as I have detailed above!

The irony is that the most outspoken proponents of removing religion from the public schools are those who place their faith in the humanist religion. They claim that they are trying to achieve the "separation of church and state" (a phrase and concept absent from the U.S. Constitution or its amendments), while they are instilling their religious values in the students attending public schools.

> Would you like it if your children were taught to reverence Vishnu?

No, I would not like it if my children were taught that Vishnu, Brahman, autonomous human reasoning, Zeus, or any other false god should be reverenced. There is only one true God who has revealed Himself to mankind in the Bible. To teach my children to reverence any other false god would be to violate the first and second of the Ten Commandments. But if my children were in public schools, they would be taught to reverence autonomous man and human reasoning above God, and that is no different. Children in public schools are still being taught to worship "a god made in man's image" — an idol in the eyes of the one, true living God.

Biblically, I am required to teach my children that some other people worship false gods, and that act of worship goes against the clear teaching of the Bible (Proverbs 22:6; Exodus 20:3–4; Psalm 40:4, 34:11). That is why I homeschool my children and why Ken Ham was encouraging Christian parents to think carefully and biblically about placing their children in a "temple of humanism."

You say you want Creationism taught along with Evolution?

I am not sure where you got this idea, but Answers in Genesis does not promote the mandatory teaching of biblical creation in public schools. However, we do not agree that naturalistic evolution, a tenet of Secular Humanism, should be the only idea taught to explain the history of life on earth, particularly if even naturalistic inconsistencies with this position are also censored.

It would be unwise for a Christian to expect a teacher trained by the humanistic, evolutionary university system to present creation in a respectable fashion anyway. As I was being trained to be a science teacher in two different state universities, I was taught everything from an antibiblical psychological, humanistic, and evolutionary perspective. At that time, I was an atheist myself, and I embraced the philosophies. I believed that human reasoning was the absolute source of truth — and I was trained to teach my students that view. Now that I am a Christian, I rely on the Bible for authority in every area of my life (to the best of my ability), and as I look back, I realize that in an atheistic view, there was no such thing as absolute truth anyway.

The relatively new, purely naturalistic view is not the only view of the history of life on earth. As mentioned in the article you are responding to, there is no valid reason that science should be arbitrarily limited to only naturalistic explanations. If science is to be based solely on those things that can be observed, tested, and verified by repeating the event, then neither the evolutionary origin of life from non-living matter nor any supernatural creation account should be taught in the science classroom. If public school systems are not going to allow views that are not observable and repeatable, then why accept the unscientific humanistic view that has the same problem? The only answer is that there is a bias toward the humanist religion in the "neutral" public school systems.

> Fine, but whose Creation mythos — Aztec, Greek, Norse, Hindu, etc?

As I recall from my public school days, the mythology and religious views of the Babylonians, Greeks, Romans, and Egyptians were taught in great detail. In fact, one of the most memorable social studies units of my youth was a detailed description of the Egyptian culture and religious views. Why can public schools teach these religious ideas openly but may face the threat of lawsuits if the name of Christ is even mentioned with respect to a major religious holiday? But the question still remains: Why does the humanistic evolutionary myth get free reign in the classroom, particularly in the sciences? Religion *is* taught in schools — just not the Christian religion!

> Yes, science means knowledge but knowledge is achieved only through observation and reasoning never revelation.

How can you be so emphatic? To say that a transcendent God cannot communicate with man (revelation) means you are claiming powers of transcendence (an attribute of God). To make this claim you are claiming to know every single thought and conversation, whether in thoughts, dreams, or aloud, of every single person who has ever lived to say God never communicated with them, which is omnipresence and omnipotence (attributes of God). This sort of statement reveals a humanistic reasoning: that people are seen as the final authority — "as gods" themselves.

Furthermore, you may make this claim, as was made in the *Humanist Manifesto III* mentioned above, but on what grounds do you make it? This is an arbitrary definition and is based on the religious beliefs of humanism at this point in history. What does it mean to reason, if your brain is the product of random, unguided interactions of matter and energy? How can you trust such reasoning? If the universe exists as the result of random, unguided processes, then why should we expect to find order in it? Why should natural laws be consistent if they are the result of random processes?

As I view the world from a biblical perspective, I have a reason to believe in reasoning. The God of the Bible is a God of order, and He has created the universe in a logical way. Even the great scientists of the past based their work on this belief. Kepler said that science was an act of "thinking God's thoughts after Him." He obviously believed in a Creator that used logic and order in His creation. It is because God has made the world to operate in an orderly way that we can study the world and expect the natural laws to behave in a consistent way. Science is possible because of God, not in the absence of God.

On what basis do you make the claim that revelation never provides knowledge? With the Bible as my authority, I make the claim that the fear of the Lord is the beginning of wisdom and that we could understand nothing if we had not been created in His image (Job 28:28; Psalm 111:10; Proverbs 1:7, 29, 2:5, 9:10, 15:33, etc.).

> Revelation is not repeatable (on demand) and hence not subject to the scientific method.

Neither is the origin of life from unguided, evolutionary processes, nor rational thought, nor an emotion, nor the existence of logic, nor the origin of information, nor the formation of the first stars, nor Abraham Lincoln's life, nor even your birth!

In order to be consistent in your thinking, you must also claim that none of the items mentioned above are scientific. I think you fail to recognize the difference between operational science and historical science.

> Even Scripture acknowledges that God is unknowable.

Where does the Bible say this? It says in Isaiah 55:8–9 that His *ways* are higher than our ways, but not that God is unknowable. In fact, Jesus, who is the Creator God says:

> "I am the good shepherd; I know my sheep and my sheep know me" (John 10:14; NIV).

"If you really know me, you will know my Father as well. From now on, you do know Him and have seen Him" (John 14:7; NIV).

Romans 1:18–23 also makes it clear that some attributes of the Creator can be known from His creation, so all are without excuse. Science can help us understand how the world works, but only when we look at the world from a biblical perspective. If you want to properly understand a 3-D picture, you have to look at it through the proper, colored lenses. If you want to understand the universe that was created by God, you have to look at it through the lens of Scripture.

> The basis of scientific study is the presumed constancy of physical laws but since God is an entity and therefore capable of mercy, no analysis can predict His actions.

Once again I must ask how naturalistic science can explain the constancy of the laws of nature without using a circular argument. There are many reasons to assume consistency with the God of the Bible. We start with the Bible as our authority, so we have a basis for making our claim.

I am not sure how you conclude that because God is an entity that He must be capable of mercy. There is no logical reason that conclusion is necessary. I do agree with your conclusion, as it is consistent with the Bible, but you may not realize that you are borrowing from the Bible to make such a claim. God is described as a God of mercy, but He is also described as a God of wrath because He is a just God. How could we know mercy if we did not know wrath?

We can predict one future action of God because He has revealed it to us in the Bible. We can be certain that He will one day act as the just judge of everyone. This is because we are all guilty of sinning against our Creator by breaking His commandments — and because God is a just judge, He must punish sin. I know that I am guilty of sinning against a perfectly holy and eternal God and that I deserve to spend an eternity paying that fine. I recognize God's wrath, but I also recognize His mercy — both described in the Bible.

In God's mercy He has made a way that we can have our penalty for sin placed on the account of His Son Jesus Christ. Jesus came to the earth and lived a perfect, sinless life, died on the Cross, was buried, and rose again on the third day. If anyone will receive Jesus Christ as Lord and Savior through repentance and faith, God's wrath will be turned away from them, and they can receive His mercy. If they do not, then God's justice demands their punishment. So, the biggest question is not whether we should teach creation in public schools or if nature follows certain patterns, but where we will spend eternity.

How about you? If God judges you, as the Bible tells us He will, will you have the innocence that only Christ can give you or your own guilt? I would ask that you seriously consider that question above all of the other things mentioned. We can debate the merits of social systems and scientific understanding, but where we will spend eternity is much more important than any of those things.

Appendix H

Evolution (Not Creation) Is a "God of the Gaps"

Prof. Stuart Burgess

When a false god is called upon to solve gaps in knowledge, this is sometimes referred to as "god of the gaps."[1] For example, if someone did not know that ice is formed when water freezes and proposed that there was an "ice god" that occasionally causes ice to spontaneously appear, then they would be guilty of using a "god of the gaps" explanation. Mythologies are known for their various "gods of the gaps."

Biblical Creation Is Not a "God of the Gaps"

Atheists have often accused Christians of invoking God to fill in a gap in scientific knowledge. Even the great scientist Isaac Newton has been accused by atheists of using a "god of the gaps" explanation when he said that the universe reveals evidence of design.[2] But creationists like Newton do not believe in a god of gaps, but a God of absolute necessity. Newton recognized that the universe could not exist without the supernatural creative power of an Almighty Creator.

Newton and most of the other founding fathers of science could see that the universe can only be fully explained with a combination of natural and

---

1. When doing this, it is a form of arbitrariness.
2. Marcelo Gleiser, "What the 'God of the Gaps' Teaches Us About Science," *WPSU*, April 8, 2015, http://radio.wpsu.org/post/what-god-gaps-teaches-us-about-science.

supernatural explanations. Creationists invoke God in origins, based on the revelation of this supreme God, and supernatural action is necessary as it steps beyond the laws of science. For example, according to the conservation of matter and energy (the first law of thermodynamics), it is impossible for a universe to come into existence without the supernatural intervention of an all-powerful being.

The Bible is scientifically correct when it states that divine supernatural power is required to create the universe (Genesis 1:1) and life (Genesis 2:7) and different kinds of creatures (Genesis 1:24). The Bible is also scientifically accurate that divine supernatural power is required to uphold all things (Colossians 1:17) — which include the laws of science. Rather than being accused of superstition, the Bible should be commended for correctly identifying the areas of origins where a supernatural Creator is necessary.[3]

Biblical Creation Is Not Anti-Science

Creationists are sometimes accused of ignoring scientific evidence and being anti-science. But belief in God in no way diminishes zeal for how life works and how the universe operates. The great pioneer scientists of the 17th to 20th centuries were inspired by their belief in God. Likewise, modern-day scientists who are biblical creationists find their belief in a purposeful universe to be helpful in their work.

Biblical creationists are always eager to learn from real scientific discoveries in every area of science. I personally have designed rockets and spacecraft for the European Space Agency and NASA using the latest scientific knowledge in physics and engineering. I have a patent on a special gearbox that was used on the world's largest civilian spacecraft and have been awarded three national prizes for the development of technology for spacecraft.

The only "science" that creationists do not use is the speculative "science" of evolution that has nothing to do with useful operational science (observable and repeatable science). Evolutionary ideas like "apelike creature-to-man charts" that supposedly chart human evolution are based on pure speculation and not useful to science and technology in any way.

---

3. These instances are not arbitrary appeals, but based on the absoluteness of who God is in how He works to create and uphold creation.

Evolution Is Guilty of "God of the Gaps" Explanations

Ironically, it is actually evolutionary believers that are guilty of "god of the gaps" explanations. When secular biology books attempt to explain why creatures or plants have a certain design, the answer is almost always "evolution did it" or "natural selection did it" without any explanation as to how the design feature could evolve by chance.[4]

This is what leading atheist and evolutionist Dr. Richard Dawkins has written about the origin of life:

> We have no evidence about what the first step in making life was, but we do know the *kind* of step it must have been. It must have been whatever it took to get natural selection started . . . by some process as yet unknown.[5]

The above quote is a classic example of evolution being a "god of the gaps" explanation. There is a total gap in what evolution can explain about the origin of life, and Dawkins invokes the god of evolution to fill in the gap and asserts that natural selection "must" have gotten started somehow. But natural selection by itself cannot create anything; it can only "select" or filter things already created.[6]

When my daughters did a two-year advanced biology course at high school in the United Kingdom, the teachers kept saying that "evolution did this" and "natural selection did that" for the origin of features like fins and wings and hearts and lungs. Near the end of the course, one of my daughters challenged the teacher and said, "Miss, you keep saying 'evolution did it,' but you never actually explain how evolution did it." The teacher had to confess that my daughter made a valid criticism, and the rest of the class agreed.

Since evolution has no credible evidence, biology books use examples of adaptation as supposed examples of evolution. Darwin's finches and resistant bacteria are held up as classic examples of evolution even though they are not evolution at all. These adaptations involve no new information, but simply a

---

4. These are reification fallacies.
5. Richard Dawkins, *The Greatest Show on Earth: The Evidence for Evolution* (New York: Free Press, 2009), p. 419 (emphasis Dawkins').
6. This observable process called *natural selection* was described in detail long before Charles Darwin, by a creationist named Ed Blyth.

shuffling of existing genes, which is what is expected with natural selection. Natural selection and adaptation are actually in opposition to onward-and-upward evolution.

Evolution Is Guilty of Being Anti-Science

Ironically, it is evolutionists, not creationists, who are guilty of ignoring scientific evidence.[7] Over the last 70 years there have been many thousands of experiments with sophisticated equipment trying to create life in the laboratory (called "abiogenesis") from dead matter and energy.[8]

However, all of these experiments have clearly demonstrated that life cannot come about by chance. Evolutionists have a choice. Either they accept the laboratory experiments or ignore them and put faith in the god of evolution. They have chosen to ignore the evidence and exercise blind faith in chance.

Evolutionary philosophy holds back scientific progress by seeking false evolutionary explanations of origins. If you refuse to believe that a jumbo jet was designed, it will affect the way you investigate the complexity of the aircraft. If you believe that the aircraft evolved by chance, you will not have your mind open to possibilities of coordinated design.

When the human genome was discovered to have far more information than expected, evolutionists immediately jumped to the conclusion that it was "junk" DNA because evolution predicts bad design not sophisticated design. However, subsequent work showed that the junk DNA was not junk at all, but highly coordinated information with important functions. That example shows how evolutionary assumptions hold back science.

A few years ago, I spoke to a senior professor of microbiology at my university (who is an agnostic) and asked what he thought of the theory of abiogenesis — the theory that life can evolve from dead matter. He said the concept was a type of "superstitious black magic." The biology professor had no Christian bias and had been taught the dogma of evolution for decades, but he could still see that abiogenesis was not real science but so speculative that it could be called black magic.

---

7. Elizabeth Mitchell, "Evolutionary Call to Arms," Answers in Genesis, June 1, 2012, https://answersingenesis.org/creation-vs-evolution/evolutionary-call-to-arms/.

8. Ken Ham, "Challenging Atheists at the Kentucky State Fair," *Around the World with Ken Ham* (blog), September 2, 2014, http://blogs.answersingenesis.org/blogs/ken-ham/2014/09/02/challenging-atheists-at-the-kentucky-state-fair/.

The Missing Link: Yet Another Gap in Evolution's Knowledge

When Darwin published his *Origin of Species* more than 150 years ago, one of the problems with his model was that there was a missing link between man and apes. That missing link is still missing today despite extensive searches for fossil evidence of evolution all over the world.

Based on fossil evidence, humans have always been strikingly different from apes. Humans walk on two legs, whereas apes walk on all four limbs. Humans have an arched foot, whereas apes have a flexible foot like a hand. Fossil evidence shows that no ape-like creature has ever had an arched foot for walking upright. As with every other aspect of the evolutionary religion, the evolutionist ignores the gaps and encourages everyone to put their faith in the god of evolution.

Evolution Is Like a Magic Wand

I recently talked with another senior professor of microbiology at my university (another agnostic), and he made a surprisingly frank admission about evolution being a "god of the gaps." He is not a creationist but like many biologists can see the serious weaknesses in evolution (although he keeps his views discreet for fear of losing his job).

This microbiologist told me that evolution could be described as a "magic wand." He said that he has noticed how even the experts say "evolution did this" and "natural selection did that" without any actual explanation being given and no demonstration in the laboratory. He said that the evolutionist could explain any aspect of origins by simply waving a magic wand and saying "evolution did it."

Paying Homage to the God of Evolution

Evolution makes no useful contribution to scientific and technological advances. However, there is an unwritten rule in the modern secular biology community that after completing a scientific study (on a topic not linked to evolution), evolution is mentioned in the write-up as being the explanation for the origin of features of design.

In the same way that a religious essay is finished by paying homage to a particular god, so in modern secular biology, essays are finished by paying homage to evolution. I have personally worked on biology-related projects where this is exactly what has happened. The end result is that the community blindly believes that the god of evolution must be true.

A Battle of Worldviews

Biblical creation versus evolution is not "faith versus science," but a worldview that includes God versus a worldview that has excluded God. Evolution is not a scientific theory because it has an unjustified assumption that God was not involved in origins. It is wrong for Christians to be accused of having a hidden religious agenda, because biblical creation openly declares its worldview.

Ironically, it is actually evolution that hides its atheistic agenda by pretending to be just science. If Isaac Newton and the other great scientists were here today, they would be astonished and saddened at the atheistic bias in modern secular science.

Giving Credit to the Creator

In modern society, a scientist is not allowed to say, "God did it" for any aspect of creation, whether it is ultimate origins or the origin of any detailed design feature. The phrase "God did it" is seen as anti-scientific. But if God is the author of creation, then He deserves acknowledgment and credit for His work. And if God is the author of creation, then scientific investigation can only be helped by recognizing God as Creator.

If you refused to believe that a jumbo jet had been designed, then that would be dishonoring to the designers. How much more dishonoring it is when secular science and the secular media refuse to acknowledge that creation has a Designer. Thankfully, there are many scientists today who are prepared to acknowledge the Creator despite the risk to their jobs and careers.

Such scientists can have the satisfaction of knowing they stand shoulder to shoulder with the greatest scientists that ever lived such as Newton, Kepler, Pascal, Faraday, Maxwell, Kelvin, and Flemming. And by the way, the last three great scientists in this list knew of Darwin's theory and rejected it — a fact that secular science has never publicized.